D1393611

The Arts Council of Great Britain
and the
Centro Internazionale di Studi di Architettura
Andrea Palladio, Vicenza

Andrea Palladio 1508-1580

The portico and the farmyard

Catalogue by Howard Burns
in collaboration with
Lynda Fairbairn and Bruce Boucher

The Arts Council of Great Britain 1975

Drawings for the models and for the modern plans and
elevations of Palladio's buildings were prepared by Dr
Arch. Andzej Pereswet Soltan and Eua Pereswet Soltan.
Models by Pietro Ballico, Schio (constructed to a scale of 1:33)

Exhibition designed by Alan Stewart
Installation by Beck and Pollitzer Limited
Catalogue designed by Herbert Spencer
and Christine Charlton
Printed by Graphis Press, London

© Howard Burns, Lynda Fairbairn, Bruce Boucher

Soft cover ISBN 0 7287 0063 8
Hard cover ISBN 0 7287 0062 X

Cover:
16th century plan of Vicenza (detail)

731877
600076452

cu

CONTENTS

ACKNOWLEDGEMENTS

In 1973 the Centro Internazionale di Studi di Architettura 'Andrea Palladio' mounted in his great Basilica an exhibition of the work of Palladio. The exhibition aroused international interest and admiration and the Arts Council sought the permission and collaboration of the Centro to bring the architectural models from the exhibition to London.

We greatly appreciate the readiness and enthusiasm with which Signor Giugliemo Cappelletti, President of the Centro, and Professor Renato Cevese, Director, responded to our request, and all the assistance they have given us in arranging this exhibition. Encouraged by Professor Cevese we have expanded the exhibition to include paintings, furniture, objects and documentary material which have been selected by Mr Howard Burns to illustrate a concept which is developed in the catalogue he has written. We are much indebted to Mr Burns for the time and thought he has devoted to the realisation of this ambitious project.

We have received the most generous support from all lenders headed by Her Majesty The Queen, who has graciously consented to the loan of paintings and drawings from the Royal Collection. Special mention must be made of the President and Council of the Royal Institute of British Architects for the loan of more than one hundred Palladio drawings and books. The exhibition has benefited from the restoration of the Palladio drawings, made possible by the generous assistance of the Leche Trust and Mr Angus Ackworth and in the process of being carried out by Miss Catherine Baker.

We are honoured by the support of the Italian Minister of Foreign Affairs, Onorevole Ministro Mariano Rumor and the Minister of Fine Arts, Onorevole Ministro Giovanni Spadolini. We are also grateful for the support and cooperation of the Italian Institute in London, especially Professor Mario Montuori, Signora Beghé and Signora Barzetti.

Special thanks are due to Miss Lynda Fairbairn, who has assisted Mr Burns in the preparation of the exhibition and its catalogue, as well as to Mr Bruce Boucher who has also worked on the catalogue.

We should like most particularly to thank Dr Herbert Spencer and Miss Christine Charlton who have designed the catalogue and Graphis Press Ltd who have printed it in an exceptionally short space of time; also Mr Alan Stewart and Mr Douglas Allsop, who are responsible for the design of the installation.

Robin Campbell
Director of Art

Joanna Drew
Director of Exhibitions

AUTHORS ACKNOWLEDGEMENTS

Howard Burns would like to thank the following for their help in the preparation of the exhibition and its catalogue:
Dr Marzio dell'Acqua, Professor Alessandro Ballarin, Professor Sir Anthony Blunt, Dr Alan Braham, Mrs Jehane Burns, Dr David Chambers, Signor Gian Luigi Corazzo, Dr William Curtis, Mr Charles Eames, Dr Gabriella Ferri Picaluga, Signor G Girardello, Professor John Hale, Dr Deborah Howard, Professor Michael Jaffé, Dr Manfred Leithe-Jasper, Mr Jay Levenson, Miss Jane Low, Professor David MacTavish, Professor Monsignor Giovanni Mantese, Sir Oliver Millar, Signor Giancarlo Pavesi and his associates, Mr Philip Pouncey, Professor Lionello Puppi, Dr Vittor Luigi Braga Rosa, Professor Gunter Schweikhart.

Dr Gaetano Panazza, Pinacoteca Civica 'Tosio Martinengo' Brescia; Professor Herbert Kreutner, Kunsthistorisches Institut, Florence; Dr Anna Forlani Tempesti, Gabinetto di Disegni Florence; Professor Luigi Menegazzi, Museo Civico 'Luigi Bailo' Treviso; the Director and staff of the Archivio di Stato, Venice; Professor Vittore Branca, Secretary-General of the Fondazione Giorgio Cini, Venice; Professor Francesco Valcanover, Soprintendente alle Gallerie e Opere d'Arte Venice; Dr Alessandro Bettagno, Fondazione Giorgio Cini; the Director and staff of the Archivo di Stato Vicenza; Dr Maria Cristofari, Dr Laura Oliver and the staff of the Bertoliana Library Vicenza; Professor Wolfgang Lotz, Director of the Bibliotheca Hertziana Rome, and President of the Academic Committee at the CISA Vicenza; Signora Maria Vittoria Pellizzari, Dr Fernando Rigon, Signorina Valeria Sensati of the CISA Vicenza; Professor Gino Barioli, Director, Dr Andreina Ballarin, Signorina Clara Bassanello, Museo Civico Vicenza; Dr Giorgio Sala, Mayor of Vicenza.

At Chatsworth Mr Peter Day and Mr Thomas Wragg; at the Courtauld Institute of Art, London Miss Catherine Baker, Mrs Constance Hill, Mr Michael Hirst, Mr Rupert Hodge, Mrs Klebinder and staff, Mrs Stella Newton, Mr Stephen Rees-Jones, Mrs A.Ribiero, Professor John Shearman, Mr John Sunderland, Witt Librarian, Mr Philip Troutman (Galleries); at the British Museum Mr Brian Cook, Mr John Gere, Mr Eric Harding, Mr D.Haynes, Mr Kenneth Jenkins, Mr Reginald Williams; at the British Library Mr John Barr, Mrs Anne de Lara, Dr D.Turner and Mr I.Willison; at the Victoria and Albert Museum Dr Charles Avery, Mr John Beckwith, Mr Claude Blair, Mr Robert Charleston, Mr John Hardy, Miss Wendy Hefford, Mr Simon Jarvis, Mr Donald King, Mr John Mallet, Mr Antony Radcliffe, Mr Peter Thornton; at the RIBA, Drawings Collection, Mr John Harris and his staff and at the RIBA Library Mr David Dean and Mr Paul Quarrie; at the Tower of London Mr H.L.Blackmore, Dr Alan Borg, Mr A.R.Dufty, Mr Russell Robinson; at the Ashmolean Museum, Oxford Mr Christopher Lloyd, Mr Hugh MacAndrew; at the Museum of the History of Science, Oxford Mr Francis Maddison; at Worcester College, Oxford Dr Richard Sayce and Miss Leslie Montgomery.

LIST OF LENDERS

United Kingdom

Her Majesty The Queen 136, 186, 225, 234, 359, 487

Barnard, Lord 289
Cambridge, Fitzwilliam Museum 12, 295, 496
Devonshire, The Trustees of the Chatsworth Settlement
  (Devonshire Collection) 34, 49, 60, 78, 79, 159, 160, 184,
  197, 203, 228, 239, 268, 279, 283, 286, 358, 362, 380, 381, 403,
  456, 488, 498
Harewood, The Earl of 282
Hopetoun, The Earl of 297
London,
  The Armouries, H.M. Tower of London 233
  British Library Board 2-4, 8, 10, 14, 15, 18, 139, 145-7, 150,
  167, 169, 177, 179, 190, 191, 205, 210, 230, 241, 265, 266,
  298, 299, 305, 364, 397, 481
  Trustees of the British Museum 123-7, 183, 214-6, 267, 281,
  311, 428, 457-61, 486
  Courtauld Institute of Art, Witt Collection 219, 261
  Trustees of the National Gallery 86, 227, 291, 483
  The Royal Institute of British Architects 35-7, 40, 46, 50-2,
  55, 56, 58, 66-9, 71, 76, 77, 156-8, 163-5, 170, 178, 189,
  193, 194, 200, 201, 207-9, 224, 244, 248, 254, 258-60, 270,
  284, 314, 321, 322, 324-6, 329, 331, 332, 342-4, 347, 348,
  350, 365-8, 387, 389, 393, 402, 407-12, 414-6, 420-3, 426,
  433, 434, 437-52, 469, 471, 473, 480, 482, 484, 489, 491
  Victoria and Albert Museum 82, 84, 87-119, 121, 122,
  128-34, 180-2, 226, 236, 237, 247, 263, 271, 280, 462-4,
  494, 495
Loyd, Mr C.L. 272
The Methuen Collection 302
National Trust, Tatton Park 26
  Upton House (Bearsted Collection) 83

Northumberland, His Grace the Duke of 120
Oxford,
  The Visitors of the Ashmolean Museum 135, 185, 188, 231,
  235, 238, 273, 354, 490, 492, 493
  The Governing Body of Christ Church 187, 388
  Museum of the History of Science 155, 166, 171-5
  The Trustees of the Ruskin School of Drawing 262
  The Provost and Fellows of Worcester College 57, 339, 431
Private collections 85, 249
Rothschild, Mrs. Kate de 242, 288
Weidenfeld, Sir George 218
Weitzner, Julius H. 81
Windsor, Eton College 229
York, City Art Gallery 240

Italy

Brescia, Pinacoteca Tosio Martinengo 427
Florence, Kunsthistorisches Institut in Florenz 141
Mantua, Accademia Polironiana 293
Treviso, Museo Civico 'Luigi Bailo' 277, 363
Venice, Gallerie dell'Accademia 278
Vicenza, Biblioteca Bertoliana 390
  Centro Internazionale d'Architettura Andrea Palladio 199
  Museo Civico di Vicenza 1, 5-7, 285, 374, 375, 465

Netherlands

Amsterdam, Rijksmuseum 176

INTRODUCTION

Harmony

Palladio is the most familiar of Italian architects. His name at once calls to mind great porticoed country houses and façades articulated with classical orders. But the very familiarity of Palladio is an obstacle to seeing him clearly. Palladio's harmonious, but densely wrought compositions, the result of intense study and reflection, tend to merge with much blander later imitations, skilfully adapted without any particular intellectual commitment from the ready-made models provided by Palladian publications. Palladio, and all the effort and achievement of the initial invention, can easily become confused with Palladianism. The valid and interesting parallel between the world of the Veneto villas and that of the English country house can itself mislead: a Vicentine noble, who felt the need to have the threshing floor visible from his villa windows, or who might die in convulsions after being bitten by a hen (Monza, 1888, p.24) is just not the same as an eighteenth-century English duke, and their houses are not the same either, however much they may superficially resemble one another.

When the Centro d'Architettura in Vicenza generously offered the material (above all, the models) prepared for its own great Palladio exhibition in 1973, two courses were open: either to concentrate on Palladio himself or on Palladio and English architecture. We have chosen to concentrate on Palladio himself, as the enormous quantity of material relating to him in this country (itself a testimony to the importance he has had for English architecture) makes this possible, and as memories of the recent Inigo Jones exhibition (1973) are still fresh.

Palladio deserves to be considered in himself. He is one of the greatest and most original of all architects and created a whole new range of effective solutions to the design problems which faced him. The fact that he used the classical orders and studied Vitruvius and ancient Roman buildings should not mislead one into thinking that Palladio was derivative or not an architect in the modern sense. The study of the antique was for him the study of the basic principles of design. What he derived from it differs substantially from what his predecessors and contemporaries derived from their study trips to Rome. His use of the orders and of ancient Roman architectural motifs is motivated not by antiquarian pedantry, but by the desire to create a rational, functional, and visually attractive architectural system. Palladio is radical, clear headed, and innovatory in his approach to design. His aims and procedures are of enduring interest and value.

This exhibition attempts to present Palladio in relation to the world in which he worked. It is a common error to consider architects of the past as unfettered absolute creators of the buildings which they designed. We have tried in some measure to combat this view. Palladio was conditioned by his cultural environment, and his designs were determined by factors of site, patronage, building materials, budget, etc., just as are the designs of an architect today. Palladio himself ruefully acknowledges the fact: 'often it is necessary for the architect to fit in with the views of the people who are spending, rather than with what (i.e., the rules) one should observe' (1570, II, p.3). Instead of following Palladio's career chronologically or considering his building types one by one, we have devoted sections of the exhibition to Vicenza and Venice, the cities in which Palladio chiefly worked, showing something of how they functioned and how Palladio related to their functioning. In the section of villas, we have included paintings recording villa life and have displayed traditional farm instruments. In the section on the Interior we have tried to show something of the furnishing and use of palaces and villas. In dealing with Palladio himself, in the Palladio section, we illustrate aspects of his life, his studies, his contacts and friendships, and in that on his Architectural System we examine his design procedures, as well as his favourite architectural solutions, and how he arrived at them. All the way through we have tried, in so far as our knowledge permitted us, to tell it how it was, to concentrate on the way in which Palladio really worked, to establish the design problems which confronted him, to show literally and metaphorically the relationship between the portico and the farmyard.

The richness of this exhibition could not have been achieved without the solid basis provided by the Vicenza exhibition. An exhibition of this sort, and its catalogue, depends upon an enormous quantity of earlier research, which for reasons of space and time cannot all be directly acknowledged. But some principal sources must be mentioned: the great volumes of Zorzi; Renato Cevese's fundamental catalogue of Vicentine villas; Ackerman's brilliant book of 1966. Much of the historical information on Vicenza derives from Monsignor Giovanni Mantese's learned, humane, and lively books and articles. Lionello Puppi's *Scrittori Vicentini* (1973) has opened new perspectives for the study of Palladio, and his *Andrea Palladio* (1973) constitutes a painstaking and penetrating synthesis, which we have drawn on throughout this catalogue.   H.B.

CATALOGUE NOTE

Paintings are in oil unless otherwise stated. All drawings exhibited are by Andrea Palladio unless otherwise stated. Measurements are in centimetres; the height precedes the width. A complete chronological list of the works cited in abbreviated form in the catalogue will be found at the end. The following abbreviations have been used in this catalogue. Each entry is initialled by its author:

B.B.	Bruce Boucher
H.B.	Howard Burns
R.C.	Renato Cevese
L.F.	Lynda Fairbairn
J.H.	John Harris
M.K.	Martin Kublik
D.M.	David MacTavish
F.M.	Francis Maddison
A.R.	Antony Radcliffe
J.S.	John Shearman
A.T.	Antonio Torre
A.S.F.	Archivio di Stato, Florence
A.S.V.	Archivio di Stato, Venice
A.S.vi.	Archivio di Stato, Vicenza
B.B.V.	Biblioteca Bertoliana, Vicenza
Marc. Ital.	Biblioteca Marciana, Venice, Italian manuscript
Bollettino C.I.S.A.	Bollettino del Centro Internazionale di Studi D'Architettura, Vicenza
BM Add. MS.	British Museum, Additional manuscript
C.I.S.A.	Centro Internazionale di Studi Architettura
D.B.I.	Dizionario biografico degli Italiani
R.I.B.A.	Royal Institute of British Architects
U.A.	Uffizi Architectural drawing

Palladio lived and worked in Vicenza from 1524, till his death in 1580. He gave it much of the character it possesses today. But Vicenza was also of very crucial importance for Palladio, and the particular nature of the city and its ruling class furnished him with an escalator to fame and influence which he might, for all his exceptional talents, not have found in another city.

At first sight, this is a surprising statement. Vicenza was not a capital city, nor even the largest of the cities of the Italian mainland dominions of the Venetian State. In 1548 Vicenza, with about 21,000 inhabitants, was notably smaller than the neighbouring cities of Verona (52,000), Brescia (43,000), Padua (32,000), not to speak of Venice itself (150,000). Yet not even Verona and Padua, where two very able architects were available (Sanmicheli in Verona, Falconetto in Padua), can show such extensive and distinguished architectural activity in the sixteenth century as can Vicenza. The chief reasons for this are the wealth of the local Vicentine nobility, and their culture, energy, and ambition, which, for all their internal feuds, expressed itself in important collective ventures (the Basilica and the Teatro Olimpico) as well as in the construction by individuals of palaces and villas. Important too was the role of one exceptionally cultured and influential member of the local establishment, Gian Giorgio Trissino. It was he who seems to have given Palladio his name (itself probably an element in Palladio's success), he who decided to launch a new architectural style in his native city, and he also who carefully prepared Palladio for his role of putting Vicenza (and thereby its ruling class), by means of architecture, firmly on the map.

Vicenza was rich in the fifteenth century, and by the early 1530s it had largely recovered from the physical and economic devastation brought about by war in the period 1509–15. Contemporaries, above all the Venetian governors (*Rettori*) of the city in their informative official reports, constantly speak of the agricultural wealth of the province of Vicenza, with its abundant production of grain, cattle, wine, and fruit, and they also write of its flourishing silk industry, producing in 1596 140,000 lbs of silk, worth 300,000 ducats, and 13,500 ducats per annum in tax to the Venetian state (Memo, 1569; Mantese, 1971–2, pp.78–9). An indication of this wealth is that the population of the province of Vicenza was greater than that of provinces of Veneto cities with higher populations, and the tax yield from Vicenza which went to Venice (111,297 ducats in 1554, against 120,000 ducats from Padua in the same year), was very high in relation to the population of the city. And this wealth, whether from agriculture, or from the silk industry, was in great part concentrated in the hands of the Vicentine nobility, who constituted the villa and palace building class. And though no systematic survey exists of the distribution of wealth among Vicentine nobles, the vast rural holdings of many of Palladio's patrons, revealed by their tax returns, indicate an inner group within the nobility, owning a very high proportion of land and wealth, as well as dominating the local politics of the city. It is important too, to emphasise that in the provinces of Treviso and Padua, which were closer to Venice, Venetians had by the mid-sixteenth century bought up a considerable portion of the land. In 1554, according to a report of the outgoing *Podestà*, only a quarter of the cultivable land in the province of Padua was in the hands of Paduan citizens, as against one third in the hands of the Venetians, and one third in the hands of the church. But in 1588 Venetians were estimated as owning only three per cent of the land in the Vicentino (Woolf, 1968, p.182). The Vicentines therefore had kept for themselves the land on which the wheat and the vines grew, and the pastures on which Vicentine cattle grew fat. And so far from being economically colonised by the Venetians, many Vicentine nobles themselves owned estates in the provinces of Padua and Verona. They also actively traded in silk. Thus in a document of 1552, Marc'Antonio Thiene, the builder of Palazzo Thiene, and one of the great landowners of the province, appointed a representative to collect from Venetian banks, above all the Dolfin bank, money due to him at the great trade fairs of Lyons and Frankfurt (ASVi, Not.B. Piacentini). And in 1563 it was correspondence hidden in bales of Vicentine silk which betrayed to the Inquisition the Protestant beliefs of Alessandro Trissino and other prominent Vicentines (Olivieri, 1967).

Wealth is only the means to indulge a taste for building in an innovatory style, and although architecture was an accepted and familiar way of expressing wealth and status, fine horses, gold chains, and rich clothes were an equally comprehensible language. But the Vicentines were as conscious of the most effective and up to date ways of cutting a fine figure in the world, as they were sensitive to considerations of prestige. Some observers put the matter more crudely: 'the Vicentine', wrote Trissino of his fellow countrymen 'is overbearing, envious, armed, rapacious', and in his earlier draft he had tried before crossing them out, 'murderous, false and treacherous' (Trissino mss, 8/1, pp.114–5). Bitter feuds between the nobles were a constant worry for the Venetian *Rettori*, and confrontations between opposing groups of nobles accompanied by their armed servants, on occasion gave a Wild West character to the streets and piazze of the city. A stab in the back or a shot from an arquebus was a not infrequent product of these quarrels, and the Vicentine noble Fabio Monza expressed in his diary his uneasiness about possible violent explosions of hostility at public gatherings, whether tournaments in the Piazza, or plays at the Teatro Olimpico.

This aspect of Vicentine life is only the extreme, delinquent expression of a general tendency towards ambition and rivalry, which on the whole took more peaceful forms, like palace building. 'Between the citizens', wrote the Podestà Alvise Muazo in 1539, 'there is a certain discord which . . . comes from no other reason except that each one wants to be greater than the other'. But Vicentine ambitions were clearly not limited to internal rivalries, and the general prestige of the city served the individual interests of its noble citizens, many of whom, from ambition or economic necessity, followed careers in France or at the Imperial court, or at Italian courts, and naturally saw their personal prestige as bound up with their place of origin. The outgoing *Podestà* (the chief Venetian officer) of Vicenza, Andrea Malipiero, wrote in 1555 that 'the citizens of that city are given to business and very industrious, subtle, imaginative (*ingeniosi*), rich magnificent and splendid and the greatness of their spirit leads them to desire . . . your Serenity (the Doge) . . . to fortify that city, as it seems to them that it is a mere village compared with other (fortified) cities'. Vicenza was centrally placed within a day's ride from numbers of cities (Verona, Padua, Mantua, and Venice) and within easy reach of Brescia,

Ferrara, Modena, and Milan. Vicenza observed and was observed by these other cities, and the desire to equal and outdo them certainly lies behind the acceptance of Palladio's costly and magnificent project for the Basilica, the building of the Teatro Olimpico, and the City Council's encouragement of private palace building (53 and 59).

The desire to build splendidly, already reflected in 1525 by Dragoncino's (2) praise of the late Gothic 'Golden House' (the Palazzo da Schio) in Vicenza does not wholly explain the Vicentines enthusiastic adoption of the innovatory architecture which Palladio offered them. He wrote, 'I shall be reckoned very lucky to have found gentlemen of such noble and generous mind, and excellent judgment that they have listened to my arguments, and abandoned that outmoded style of building, without any grace or beauty.' They listened to his arguments partly because of the backing which Trissino (149) had given to the new style, and partly through a quickness to register new architectural developments in Verona (Sanmicheli's gates and palaces), Mantua (Giulio Romano's works), Venice (Serlio's books on architecture and Sansovino's buildings) and Padua (Bembo and Alvise Cornaro, and Falconetto's work), while numbers of Vicentines, in addition to Trissino, would have known something of architectural developments in Rome. All four of the major architectural figures present in Northern Italy (Serlio, Sansovino, Sanmicheli and Giulio Romano) were invited to Vicenza to give their opinion on the Basilica, between 1538 and 1542 (30). In fact, a period of only five years, from 1537 when Trissino's villa was largely finished (148), till 1542, the date of the contract for the construction of Palazzo Thiene (47), saw a rapid and complete updating of the architectural tastes and ambitions of the local establishment, which has its final confirmation in the City Council's decision of 1549 to begin work on Palladio's project for the Basilica.

The Vicentine nobles listened favourably to Palladio's arguments not only because they were 'subtle and imaginative', but because as a class, they were well educated, and had (in every sense) a firm grasp on the culture of their time. If one reads through the lists of the hundred members of successive City Councils, one finds a surprisingly high number of councillors (only nobles could sit on the Council) with doctorates. These *dottori* were usually graduates of the University of Padua, mostly in law, a few in medicine, and often constituted more than 40 per cent of the total. Others, it should be remembered, had attended the University, but had never taken a degree. This high proportion of nobles with degrees struck Andrea Malipiero, who attributes it to the fact that the Vicentine nobility elected judges from their own number, who sat as the city's principal court, under the presidency of the Venetian Podestà. 'There follows', he wrote, 'that many of these nobles have studied letters, so that their College of Lawyers consists of 74 Doctors, the majority of whom are very able and intelligent persons.' Many Vicentines were probably inclined, like Fabio Monza, to stay at home now and again with a good book (Monza, 1888, p.24), and the city supported a flourishing bookshop/lending library (Mantese, 1968) which in 1596 included the architectural books of Serlio, Alberti and Palladio, as well as Cosimo Bartoli's book on surveying (*ibid*, p.47). The library of the Accademia Olimpica (founded in 1556 by a group of nobles, and a few others, including Palladio), from early in its existence contained copies of Alberti, of Vasari's *Lives*, and Barbaro's *Vitruvius* for the use of members (Ziggiotti ms, fol.10 v). This cultural involvement of the Vicentine nobles had two sides to it. In part, it was disinterested, and in the extreme cases of those nobles whose involvement with Protestant ideas forced them to leave Italy, it carried with it consequences potentially damaging to both the class and the individual interests of those involved.

Thus Trissino with considerable perspicacity warns his son Giulio that if the Lutheran ideas with which he is dabbling, despite his position as Archpriest of the Cathedral in Vicenza, make headway among the country people, they will cease to pay the ecclesiastical tithes which the Trissino family enjoys (Morsolin, 1894, 504). Alessandro Trissino, who managed to escape after being arrested for heresy (he ultimately settled in Geneva) accepts, and wants his fellow Vicentine nobles to accept the full consequences of the Protestant sympathies which many of them shared. He urges them rather than reach a tacit compromise with the corrupt church of Rome, to suffer martyrdom, or abandon the whole splendid world which Palladio helped to create for the Vicentine nobility 'the possessions and the palaces which are none else but bonds . . . with which the devil . . . holds you tethered in his realm' (Oliveri, 1967).

On the other hand, as Puppi (1973–II) has suggested the cultural involvement of the Vicentines was a means of ensuring that cultural developments should be in line with the interests of the ruling class. It was therefore not simply that the Vicentines listened to Palladio: they also set up a cultural and social framework controlled by themselves (above all through the Accademia Olimpica) within which Palladio developed and communicated his 'arguments' on good architecture. They listened to him, but he was also their man, serving their ends, enhancing their prestige, through very specialised means, like the construction of theatres and the performance of plays, which both reflected the interests cultivated by Palladio and his patrons, and caused a stir among the less talented, and less well served elites of neighbouring cities. Impressing these neighbours was ultimately not an abstract matter of 'prestige', but meant appointments or influence for Vicentine nobles, at Venice, Mantua or Ferrara, and advantageous marriages for their sons and daughters.

Just as Vicentine culture has two sides to it, so does the relationship existing between Palladio and his noble employers. On the one hand there was certainly an element of condescension and paternalism, which even if not explicit (though it does come across, perhaps with deliberate exaggeration, in the dialect poems which Palladio's friend Maganza addressed to local personages), is in any case implicit in Palladio's very modest earnings. On the other hand deep ties of loyalty and mutual affection developed between Palladio and members of the local establishment. The noble Fabio Monza (not a rich man however) records his going to a Council meeting 'to help Palladio', when it was proposed to suspend work on the Basilica, as well as news from Venice brought back to Vicenza by Palladio, and a simple dinner which he shared with Palladio in Venice, who helped to do the shopping: all this in one year, 1563 (Monza, 1888). Palladio was clearly a trusted intimate of a much richer man, the Protestant Odoardo Thiene, owner with his brother of the villa at Cicogna (see 153 below). With other patrons too, Mario Repeta and Giacomo Angaran, there was the bond not only of cultural interests, and a long and close friendship, but probably also of unorthodox and only privately expressed religious ideas (Puppi, 1973–II, pp.37–41). Generally it should be remembered that though an aristocratic manipulation of culture and what we should call the 'media', which at that time certainly included architecture, did exist in Vicenza, and numbers of leading Vicentines were used to the life of the princely courts, Vicenza, and indeed the whole of the Veneto was free from those extremes of flattery, and even sheer tyranny, which Papal Rome or Grand Ducal Florence could illustrate in abundance. Veneto society was oligarchical, but the oligarchy was a wide one, and though it was dominated by its richest and most prominent members, checks and balances were built into the system, both institutionally, and at the level of automatic social mechanisms. The feuds and the opposing line-ups of the leading Vicentines (16) in fact can be seen as a mechanism of this sort. The system itself had within its general aristocratic character a pluralistic aspect and therefore allowed more space for Palladio to operate, than would have been the case in a princely state. It gave Palladio a multitude of effective patrons, not just one effective princely patron, who would be likely to determine personally what sort of buildings his favourite courtiers were going to put up, probably – in the last analysis – at his expense. This was the normal situation in Rome or Florence. The less oppressively hierarchical world of the Veneto allowed Palladio, in publishing his architectural projects, to cut down on the flattery, to the benefit of a clear presentation of his own achievement and his own ideas about architecture. Palladio wrote: 'in arranging these designs, I have not taken account of the grades or dignities of the gentlemen who shall be named, but I have put them in the order which best suited me, given that they are all very honourable persons. But anyway, let us turn to the buildings themselves . . .' (Palladio, 1570, II, p.4).

Vicenza, then, was a city where wealth was very great in relation to its population. Its ruling class was well educated, involved in professional activities and trade, open to new ideas, whether religious or architectural, and ready to try and make a distinguished career abroad, rather than live modestly at home. The Vicentine nobles were therefore very different from the well-educated but poor nobles of Bergamo who 'would not hear of engaging in trade' (Podestà of Bergamo, 1553) or from the idle and very rich nobility of Brescia, with their splendid silk and velvet clothes, their coaches and fine horses, who were 'soft and devoted to leisure, and do not frequent the public squares, but the greater part of the time stay at home in their ground floor rooms with their doors open, and visit one another, and indulge in gaming' (Podestà of Brescia, 1553). The

Vicentines were competitive among themselves, but collectively united in maintaining their position in the world. Unlike their Paduan neighbours, they owned most of the land in their province, and they had a large say in local administration. Using their City Council they defended their privileges, and increased the prestige of the city through public works (above all the Basilica) and the encouragement of private palace building. Their wealth, culture, intelligence and ambition, and their determination to cut a fine and independent figure in the world, as well as the moral and religious seriousness of certain of them, and their readiness to establish a close relationship with their city's remarkable architect, lie behind Palladio's emergence, and much of his subsequent achievement. H.B.

FRANCESCO MAFFEI C.1620–60

1 San Vincenzo with the standard
Canvas: 135 × 119
Lent by the Museo Civico, Vicenza

This early work of Maffei (Barbieri, 1955 and 1973, pp.31 and 47) follows the usual iconography for San Vincenzo, who holds Vicenza in one hand, and the standard in the other. The saint is shown holding the silver model of the city, offered to the Madonna of Monte Berico (the sanctuary church on the hill overlooking the city) on the occasion of the plague of 1576–7. The model was finished in 1581, and Palladio himself was involved in supervising its execution. It was melted down in the later seventeenth century (Zorzi, 1966, pp.144, 154–6; Barbieri, 1973, pp.30–1). H.B.

GIOVAN BATTISTA DRAGONCINO DA FANO

*2 Nobilta di Vicenza del Dragoncino, stampata nella inclita citta di Vinegia per Francesco di Alessandro Bindoni & Mapheo Pasini, compagni: Nel 1525 di Ottobre
Lent by the British Library Board (11427.a.19)

The frontispiece of this attractive little book, the earliest guide to Vicenza and its province, shows a view of the city from outside the Porta Castello. The monuments which symbolise the city, clocktower, Basilica, Cathedral are all shown (compare Giovanni Bellini's *Pietà* in the Accademia in Venice). The eulogistic verse description of the marvels and splendours of Vicenza has clearly the character of a propaganda exercise, sponsored by certain leading Vicentines. It is dedicated to Francesco Porto, owner of the splendid Palazzo Porto at Thiene, which is described here, and holder of the important position of Collateral (Paymaster General of Cavalry) of the Venetian State (Marzari, 1591, p.168, and oral communication, John Hale). Dragoncino's host and guide was Marc'Antonio Valmarana. The references are the ones which later became familiar: the nobility of the Vicentines, their splendid palaces, the choice wines of the area, the silk industry. The tone is Ariostean and the social ideal presented that of chivalry (Puppi, 1973–II, pp.13–4). H.B.

2

LUCRETIO BECCANUVOLI

3 Tutte le donne Vicentine, maritate, vedove, e dongelle, 1539
Lent by the British Library Board (C.62. b.12)

Beccanuvoli's *All the Vicentine Women, Married, Widows, and Damsels*, is an exhaustive verse catalogue of the noble ladies of Vicenza, each of whom is given a brief description: 'vase of chastity, urn of fidelity'; with a dress never before seen on earth'. The book is addressed to Giovan Battista Maganza, Palladio's friend (000) and Beccanuvoli now and again breaks off his interminable sequence of names and epithets to show that he does not take his task too seriously: 'tired is the mind, tired is the pen, and tired is my hand'. The list leaves no doubt (it gives the maiden and married name) as to the extent to which the leading families were linked by marriage ties: Lucretia Thiene Cheregata, Giulia Porta Cheregata, Leonora Poiana Thiene, Biancamaria Thiene Valmarana, Anna Trissino Thiene, etc. On the lives of these ladies of Vicenza little information is readily available. Some doubtless deceived their husbands (Bandello, 1740, I, pp.113ff.), and some were killed by them 'on account of suspicion' (Monza, 1888, p.44). Wills tend to show fathers as fond of their daughters and their wives, and ready to leave the management of their estates in their widow's hands (provided, of course, that they remain chaste and do not remarry) until their sons come of age. Alessandro Thiene and his wife erected in 1544 a magnificent pyramid monument to their seventeen-year-old daughter, which has been attributed to Sanmicheli (Kahnemann, 1960, p.210) but could equally well be by Giulio Romano, with its echo of Raphael's Chigi tombs (Mantese, 1964-IV, p.261). Fabio Monza ordered a painting by Tintoretto for his daughter Laura when she went into a monastery (Monza, 1888, p.14). Giovan Luigi Valmarana, in his will of 1554, left generous doweries to his daughters (3,500 ducats each) and stipulated that his wife should have complete control of his estate after his death. It was she, in fact, who commissioned the Palazzo Valmarana after her husband's death. Teodoro Thiene, in his will of 1577, wrote of 'Isabella Gonzaga my consort whom I love and have loved ... dearly for her rectitude (*honestà*) and because I know that I was equally loved by her with a reciprocal love'. Women's place and influence was largely within the family. The well known poetess Maddalena Campiglia, who enjoyed a considerable reputation, is an exception (Mantese, 1971) though in addition to the women who had entered monasteries, many Vicentine ladies were involved in charitable and religious activities (for instance, Giovan Luigi Valmarana's daughter Deianira and her friends: Mantese, 1974, pp.532-40).

Beccanuvoli's book is prefaced by a brief description of the theatrical performance, with a set designed by Serlio, held in the courtyard of the Palazzo Colleoni-Porto in 1539 (64). H.B.

GIACOMO MARZARI
4 La Historia di Vicenza
In Venetia appresso Giorgio Angelieri, 1591
Lent by the British Library Board (660.6.21)

Giacomo Marzari was a Vicentine noble who followed a legal career (Monza, 1888, p.24). The first part of his book describes the city, its history, and its institutions. The second part is an invaluable 'Who's Who' of distinguished Vicentines, including Palladio, and many of his patrons. The book ends with woodcuts of the Ponte San Michele and the ruins of the

Teatro Berga in Vicenza. It was republished in 1604, and recently by Forni, Bologna. H.B.

GIROLAMO FORNI C1530–1610 or later
5 Isabella Valmarana Thiene (?)
Canvas: 113 × 96
Lent by the Museo Civico, Vicenza

The generally accepted attribution rests not on a solid knowledge of Forni's style, but simply on his being recorded as one who 'as he was well off as regards fortune's gifts, as a mere pastime, and out of his native and pure generosity' exercised a notable inborn talent for portraiture (Marzari, 1591; Barbieri, 1962, p.212). The usual identification of the sitter with Isabella Thiene Valmarana (not to be confused with Isabella Nogarola Valmarana, builder of the Palazzo Valmarana) appears to be traditional. Ascanio, son of Gio. Alvise Valmarana (6) is recorded as marrying a member of the Thiene family, but he died before 1575 and given the youth of the lady, and the date of her costume (about 1590, oral communication Stella Newton) a more likely explanation is that this lady is Isabella Valmarana Thiene (illegitimate daughter of Ascanio) who married Lodovico Thiene. Leonardo Valmarana was appointed guardian of Isabella, and it is worth noting that Forni was closely connected with him, describing Valmarana as 'his most loving patron' and appointing him executor of his will (Mantese, 1974, pp.6 and 393). The rich dress, belt, jewels and bracelets, the embroidered handkerchief, and the hand on the lute are all signs of the lady's superior status. H.B.

GIROLAMO FORNI C.1530–1610 or later
*6 The Valmarana family
Canvas: 156 × 256
Lent by the Museo Civico, Vicenza
(Donation Paolini Porto Godi)

This painting underwent a substantial restoration in 1973. The attribution to Forni (5) lacks a secure basis, and it is not even established that Forni's activity as a painter had begun by the probable date of this painting (1558 or earlier). The attractive informality of the rendering owes much to group portraits by Licinio (120). The accepted identification of the family as that

6

7

of Giovan Luigi Valmarana (d.1563) is supported by Isabella Valmarana's medal portrait which has features in common with the lady in the portrait, and (if the baby is a boy) by the listing of four sons and five daughters in Giovan Luigi's will of 1559, though by that date the eldest daughter, Dona Margarita, was already a nun (ASVi, Not. Fulvio Mosto; cf. Mantese, 1974, pp.6 and 531–2). The older children hold madrigal books, probably for different voices. Giovan Luigi was closely associated with Palladio, first as a commissioner for the decorations for the entry of Cardinal Ridolfi in 1543 (137) then, as an eloquent exponent of the reasons for adopting Palladio's design for the Basilica, and as one of the first commissioners supervising its construction. He had literary interests and composed a tragedy (Marzari, 1591, p.170) as well as being a leading figure in the exclusive and aristocratic Accademia dei Costanti, the short-lived rival to the Accademia Olimpica. (Puppi, 1973–II, pp.50ff). H.B.

GIOVANNI BATTIST MAGANZA THE ELDER (?) 1513–86

*7 Portrait of Ippolito Porto 1517–72

Canvas: 124 × 102

Lent by the Museo Civico, Vicenza (Donation Paolina Porto Godi)

An attribution to G.B.Maganza the Elder (139) goes back to the deed of gift in 1826 and has therefore some weight of tradition behind it but (especially given the considerable loss of paint surface) neither this attribution, nor a more recent one to G.B.Maganza the Younger have much solid basis. Neither the pose nor the portrayal in rich but casual dress are characteristically Italian, and if the painting is Italian at all, one should ask whether this may not be a copy of a portrait (a miniature perhaps) made when Ippolito was serving in the German wars in the late 1540s. Ippolito, one of the many Vicentine nobles who followed a military career, entered Venetian service in about 1550 and spent most of his time in Vicenza. Fabio Monza gave his trumpeter a New Year tip in 1563 (Monza, 1888, p.22). His deeds are celebrated in a fresco cycle in the Palazzo Trissino-Baston in Vicenza (*Catalogo*, 1972, p.134). He died of fever at Corfu in 1572, during the Turkish wars (Marzari, 1591, p.191; Barbieri. 1962; *Il Gusto*, 1973; Mantese, 1971; and Mantese, 1974, index). H.B.

8 Ius Municipale Vicentinum 1567

Venetiis, Ioan Gryphius excudebat ad instantiam Bartolomaei Contrini, MDLXVII

Lent by the British Library Board (24.e.9)

The statutes of Vicenza set out the laws defining the role of the Podestà and the Capitanio, as well as of the Council, as reformed in 1541. The volume also contains building and fire regulations, regulations relating to the rivers, a list of feast days and processional days, and provisions regarding the annual trade fair. The local sumptuary laws of 1536 and 1564 are given in full (fols. 217ff): coaches should be neither gilded nor carved with figures (this was not observed – Montano Barbaran had a gilded coach in his stable); no one except knights should wear gold chains; no one should wear shirts embroidered elsewhere but at the collar and sleeves (7) and the embroidery should not cost more than two ducats; the number of dishes at banquets, which cause 'the greatest damage to finances, and the body' should be limited.   H.B.

The government of the city and its territory

In 1404 Vicenza became part of the Italian dominions of Venice. From then on the Vicentines paid taxes to Venice, and from the countryside were recruited soldiers and sailors for the Venetian state. The supreme authorities in the city were the Podestà (Governor) and the Capitanio, Venetian nobles appointed for sixteen-month terms of office, and known collectively as the *Rettori* (Rectors). With this term they signed their joint letters, which were sealed with a little seal bearing the symbol of the Venetian state, the winged lion of St Mark. The Podestà supervised the administration of justice, as well as judging in appeal all cases which were not referred to courts in Venice. His residence, the Palazzo del Podestà stood next to the Basilica, on the other side of the clocktower. His colleague the Capitanio was responsible for the administration of taxation and finance, and the organisation of the militia, and other military matters, including the training of gunners, and the state of the fortifications. These officials received frequent instructions from the Venetian government, the more formal ones in the form of Ducal letters (15) and they wrote regularly to Venice (16) as well as making formal reports at the end of their term of

office (11). The chief preoccupations of the Podestà emerge as law and order, both in the city and the territory, and in times of bad harvests and high prices, the acquisition of sufficient grain, hidden and hoarded in the countryside, to keep the urban poor alive, and with them, famished peasants from the province. The successive Capitani were constantly engaged in repressing tax evasion, smuggling to avoid gate taxes, and frauds perpetrated by tax officials. They were also kept busy organising the militia, holding military reviews on the Campo Marzo (Monza, 1888, p.13), and encouraging the local artillery group, whose shooting range is shown clearly on the left of the 1580 view of Vicenza (20). During the war with the Turks, which culminated with the battle of Lepanto, the Capitanio Bernardo, the loggia of whose official residence was reconstructed at this time after a design by Palladio, has nothing to say in his correspondence about the loggia, but a great deal about the difficulties of manufacturing biscuits for the fleet.

The Rettori had their duties and the rules governing their conduct set out for them in their often beautifully bound and illuminated official documents of appointment (10, 12, 14). These rules included stipulations aimed at avoiding excessive familiarity with local families (the Podestà could not act as a godfather, nor accept private hospitality, except in special circumstances). They seem to have carried out their duties with energy, intelligence, and relative humanity, though no *Podestà* of Vicenza goes so far in expressing humane concern as Gabriele Moresini, Podestà of Verona, who in 1558 declared his health to have been ruined by the strain of finding food for the poor, and wrote that 'I have never, through the grace of the lord God, spilt blood, cut off hands, nor put out eyes, nor cut off tongues', as he might well have done on the basis of the existing laws.

The Rettori clearly did their best in difficult circumstances, and though the good of the Venetian state was always their first preoccupation, the common good, and the protection of the poor was seen by them as both good policy and right in itself. They also in general seem to acquire considerable affection for the city, and speak of it in a friendly, often eulogistic tone, as if their personal administrative record would be judged by the virtues or defects of the town they had been sent to govern. They were not, in fact or in law, absolute rulers. The feuds of the nobility, and violence and banditry in the countryside could never be decisively repressed, though the Podestà Andrea Malipiero in 1555 reported good results from the use of a 'flying squad' of thirty cavalrymen. In the administration of justice they were flanked by a bench of local judges, and in day to day administration by the City Council, consisting of one hundred nobles, elected annually by the *Consiglio Maggiore* to which all adult male nobles belonged. The Council of One Hundred in turn elected *Deputati* (aldermen) who served for two month terms, with eight of them in office at a time. The city had its own income, chiefly derived from the rent of shops under the Basilica and round the central square, and usually in excess of 4,000 ducats p.a. (Marzari in 1590 says it was 6,000 duc.). This paid municipal salaries, for the repair of roads, and for the building work on the Basilica, including Palladio's salary. Most of Palladio's Vicentine patrons served regularly as aldermen or Deputati, and some of them served also as building commissioners responsible for administering the work on the Basilica. The Vicentines also exercised authority over a great part of the territory, as they appointed the officials (*Vicari*) who administered justice in the eleven *Vicariati* (administrative districts) into which the province of Vicenza was divided. Four small areas, including Bagnolo, were family jurisdictions, while two Venetian nobles governed the walled towns of Lonigo and Marostica (Mantese, 1964, p.533). This considerable degree of local autonomy served to enhance the independent and self-conscious character of the Vicentine ruling class. H.B.

JACOPO BASSANO C.1515–92

9 The Rettori of Vicenza, Silvano Cappello and Giovanni Moro, 1573
Photograph

This is a detail from the large canvas now in the Museo Civico in Vicenza, and originally painted for the room in the Palazzo del Podestà where the City Council met (Barbieri, 1962, p.20). The Podestà and the Capitanio are shown in their red official dress. H.B.

10 Commission from Doge Andrea Gritti to Nicolo Morosini, as Capitanio of Vicenza, 1531
Vellum: 24.8 × 34.3 (open)
Lent by the British Library Board (Add. MS.15518)

On folio 1, Morosini has written in his own hand 'I Nicholo Morexini, son of the late Messer Zacharia, note how on 15 October 1531 I was appointed Capitanio of Vicenza and made my entry on 6 February. And Messer Lodovicho Michiel my successor made his entry and replaced me 18 May 1533. I note that when I was appointed to the said Capitaniate I was 33 years and 3 months old on which day may God be praised'. The decorated title page has the Morosini arms, the lion of St Mark, two heads of Roman emperors, and Morosini kneeling before the Virgin and Child. The rest of the volume, containing the Capitanio's duties, is neatly written with coloured initial letters, and chapter headings in purple ink. H.B.

11 End of term report of the Captain of Vicenza, Nicolò Morosini, 1533
Photograph

The report (ASV, *Senato, Relazioni dei Rettori*, b.51) consists of nine pages written in Morosini's own hand and gives a scrupulous account of the matters under Morosini's charge (the militia, the gunners, financial matters). On this first page he relates that he had set up a shooting competition with a three ducat prize for the gunners and had held twelve parades of the *archibusieri*. This sort of painstaking encouragement of the formation of trained military men, to which the captains of the mainland cities gave such attention, was of critical importance for the maintenance of the security of the Venetian state, and it reflects the way in which much of its administrative and fiscal policy was determined by war, or the need to be ready for it. H.B.

*12 Commission of the Podestà of Vicenza Pietro Tagliapietra, 1535
Illuminated manuscript page
Lent by the Fitzwilliam Museum, Cambridge

This is the illuminated first page of Tagliapietra's official

NOS ANDREAS
GRITI DEI
GRATIA DVX
VENETIA RETC

COMMITTIMVS
tibi nobili viro dilecto ciui et fideli nostro Petro Dechataiapera &
in Christi nomine vadas a sis De nostro mandato POTESTAS ciuitatis
nostra VINCENTIA per menses XVI et tantum plus quantum
successor tuus illuc venire distulerit

12

document of appointment which has at some stage been removed from the rest of the volume (compare 14 and 10 which are complete). The Tagliapietra arms, identical to those over a portal leading towards the Podestà's palace (13) appear below, St Mark and his lion above, together with Tagliapietra's own saint, Peter, and St Sebastian, for whom he must have had some special devotion, is painted on the right. As David Chambers has pointed out (lecture, Warburg Institute, 1974) the initials $T^o\ V^v$ crudely scratched at the bottom of the page, are not the artist's signature as has been suggested (Zuccolo Padrono, 1971) but an obviously mistaken later attribution to T(izian)o Ve(neto).

The text is the conventional one 'We Andrea Gritti by the Grace of God Doge of Venice etc. commit to you the noble man, beloved citizen and our faithful Pietro of the house of Tagliapietra that you should be by our order Podestà of the city of Vicenza for sixteen months and however much longer your successor should take in coming there'. Tagliapietra was in office from 6 May 1535 until 7 December 1536 (*Il Gusto*, 1973, p.31) and in his end of term report he suggested ways 'to obviate the so many brutal murders which happen day by day' (ASV, *Relazioni*). H.B.

*13 Portal, Domus Comestabilis, Vicenza, 1536
Photograph

The 1973 restoration of the two-sided portal which leads from the upper Logge of the Basilica to the House of the Constable revealed the date 1536, cut in the pediment of the inner side. The exceptional elegance of the mouldings, the harmoniousness of the proportions, and the date all suggest that this is an early work of Palladio, executed at a time when he was working as a member of the workshop at Pedemuro S.Biagio, on the renovation of Trissino's villa at Cricoli. The doorway which is one of the most notable in the whole of Vicentine sixteenth-century architecture, is somewhat higher on the side towards the interior of the Domus, and stands in a close relationship to a design published by Serlio (Serlio, 1619, VII, p.77, fig. A). The two identical shields in the architrave of the inner face bear the arms of the Podestà of Vicenza, Pietro Tagliapietra, who held office from 6 May 1535 to 7 December 1536 (oral communication, H.B.). R.C.

13

14 Commission of Nicolò q(uondam) Giovanni Donà as Podestà of Vicenza, 1574
Vellum: 24.1 × 19
Lent by the British Library Board (BM Add. MS.18066).

The illuminated first page has unfortunately been torn out of this volume, but it is dated 5 August 1574 (f.184) and references in the text (f.2) make it clear that it is a commission to a Podestà of Vicenza. According to the list published by

Bressan and Lampertico (1877), Donà was appointed on 15 April 1574, but one could expect him not to go to Vicenza for some six months, so that the date is consistent with the volume being his. The fine red leather binding, with gold embossed panels, is of a sort often employed for official documents. A similar binding appears on the covers of a volume of decrees of the Council of Ten, on display in the Victoria and Albert Museum, London.   H.B.

15 Letter from Doge Antonio Priuli to the Rettori of Vicenza, 1619
Vellum: 23.5 × 43.8
Lent by the British Library Board (BM Add. MS.15141, item 12)

Official communication from the Venetian government went out under the name of the Doge, and had a distinct form and format, of which this is a typical example. It comes from a volume which contains a whole series of letters addressed to the Rettori of Vicenza, dated from 1610 onwards. After the formal greeting to the Podestà and the Capitanio of Vicenza, the letter continues 'We understand that there is to be found in that city, leading a scandalous life, the wife of the noble Piero Bembo . . . to the ignominy of her aforesaid husband, with whom she has had children, and has lived for the space of many years, and as this is not to be tolerated . . . we charge you, that using all possible discretion . . . you should arrest her . . . and send her to the prisons of the Heads of the Council of Ten'. The letter is minuted at the bottom of the page 'It was replied that she is not to be found in these parts . . .'   H.B.

*16 The feuds of the Vicentine nobles in 1540
ASV, *Capi del Consiglio dei X, Lettere di Rettori*, b.223, no.224
Photograph

Agostino Contarini, Podestà of Vicenza, wrote to the Council of Ten on 22 April 1540 that 'the audacity of the citizens of Vicenza caused by the hatreds and rancours that burn continually among them is growing daily to such a point that indeed I foresee an unheard-of massacre, with the desolation of this city, as they all have taken up arms together with a great number of their servants'. As Contarini points out, they were legally able to carry arms in many cases (for instance, that of the Thiene brothers) as they were registered soldiers. At the end of

his letter he lists the opposing factions which, on the one side, include future patrons of Palladio (Marcantonio and Adriano Thiene, and the Porto family, probably including Iseppo) and on the other, the owner of the Villa Godi (Zavanazzo, 1964-5 Puppi, 1973–II, p.20).   H.B.

17 Inscription recording murders, Corso Palladio 172, Vicenza
Photograph

Only a few doors away from the house of Valerio Belli is a handsome contemporary inscription, which records 'This is th place where there was the house of the very wicked Galeazzo da Roma who with Iseppo Almerico and other accomplices committed atrocious murders in this city on the 3rd of July 1548'. Paolo Almerico, the builder of the Rotunda was almost certainly a relation of Iseppo, and he himself, though finally acquitted, was in prison in Venice from 1546 to 1548 on a murder charge (Mantese, 1964–II).   H.B.

JACOPO VERONESE
18 Dialogo che trata di l'arte di bombardier, 1562
Paper: 31.7 × 45.7 (open)
Lent by the British Library Board (BM Add.MS.10.897)

Jacopo Veronese, as he says in the full title of his manuscript treatise on the gunner's art, 'was head of the gunners' at Orzinuovo, the important Venetian fortress town in the

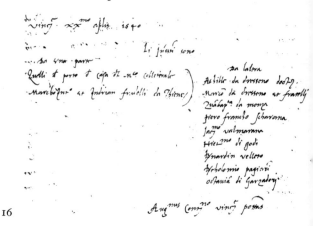

16

province of Brescia. In 1541 the *Sindaci di Terra Ferma* wrote of Orzinuovo: 'the gateway to your most important fortress' which should be 'cared for like the pupil of the eye' (ASV, *Senato, Relazioni*, b.32, fol.159v). In 1557 there were 'five gunners and they have many pupils, who will turn out expert' *Ibid*.b.33). Jacomo's treatise illustrates both the range of specialised treatise writing in the sixteenth century (by no means confined to architectural treatises) and the organisation of 'schools' of gunners recruited from skilled trades in the Venetian mainland cities. The reports of the Capitanio of Vicenza give much space to the gunners (11) and the range where they practised is clearly visible on the 1580 map of Vicenza. H.B.

The topography and functioning of Vicenza

Vicenza, Marzari wrote in 1590, 'has the form of a crab, or of a scorpion'. In the year of Palladio's death a bird's eye view of the city was drawn (20) which gives a detailed impression of the appearance of the town, which in any case has not changed radically. The central area, ringed by walls and water is surrounded on three sides by the inner walled suburbs, the *Borghi*, which project like pincers on either side of the Campo Marzo, which was used as a parade ground, the site of the annual trade fair, and in time of plague, as a temporary isolation area for the infected. The centre of the city is crossed by a street (the *strada maggiore*), now the Corso, lined with substantial houses and palaces, and porticoes. To the north of the Corso run three streets of palaces of leading families, including four palaces by Palladio (Thiene, da Porto, Valmarana, and Barbaran). To the south of the Corso lies the Cathedral and the Bishop's Palace, and nearby the central administrative and market area, dominated by the clocktower and the Basilica. Wood and cattle were sold on the Piazza dell' Isola in front of the Palazzo Chiericati, and at one end of this area stood the entrance to the port, where boats carrying passengers and goods from as far away as Venice could land. Piazza Castello, at the other end of the main street served as a wood market (it was forbidden, 'for the ornament of the city and the convenience of passers by' to encumber the main street with wood stacked for sale). Wood and lime, brought in by the Porta Berga had to be sold immediately inside the gate, to restrict clutter and mess.

The Borghi were much less densely built up than the central part of the city. They contained most of the town's monastic institutions, and had spacious gardens and orchards, many of them used for growing mulberry trees, to feed the silkworms. Particularly interesting is the spacious fourteenth-century 'new town', the Borgo of the Porta Nuova to the north west, laid out on a grid plan, with wide streets (22). To the left of the Porta Castello was the large ornamental garden of the Valmarana family, which still exists, but has lost its formal layout and its centrally placed *tempietto*, which, although it has not been mentioned by writers on Palladio, could well have been designed by him.

Sixteenth-century industry was dependent on water, not only for processes like fulling, tanning, and dying, but also for power. There were three main clusters of mill wheels on the city's two rivers, the Bacchiglione and the Rerone, and these would have powered not only flour mills, but probably also served to operate large furnace bellows, heavy hammers and other machinery in the iron working shops opposite the Isola. In 1554 in Padua, where Palladio's father had been a miller, there were fifty-three mill wheels (ASV, *Senato, Relazioni*, b.32), and Vicenza must have had almost as many. The long frames for drying cloth are clearly visible in the bottom left of the 1580 map.

These topographical features provided the framework for patterns of life. In part these were seasonal: 'up till now', wrote the Podestà of Vicenza on 16 December 1539, 'life has been peaceful and tranquil, but now that the nobles are returned from outside from their villas in the country, one sees nothing but arms'; and on 13 October 1548 the Capitanio of Vicenza wrote 'winter is approaching, when with the long nights many in this city, as is their custom, begin to go about in armed bands . . . for no other purpose, but that of . . . disturbing peaceful and quiet living'. The calendar was a whole series of fixed events. At Carnival time there were usually tournaments in the Piazza; in the autumn was the annual fair, when shops in the city were closed by law, and traders had to set up their wares in temporary shops, laid out in the 'streets' on the Campo Marzo. There were the market days, when the countrypeople came into the town to sell their produce, and the frequent religious festivals, when the law courts in the Basilica were not in session, and the Rettori, the eight Deputati, the Colleges of the Judges and Notaries, and the twenty-four guilds with their standards (80), together with the local clergy, all turned out to go in procession to one of the city's churches. Time was reckoned on a twenty-four-hour system starting at sundown, a system which expressed the way in which life was regulated by the sequence of day and night, their lengths altering throughout the year (171). The hours rang out from the bell of the great tower in the piazza, which could be heard, it was said (Marzari, 1591) ten miles off. The tower was, together with the Basilica and the Cathedral (2), a symbol of the city, and one of the two galleys which the Vicentines fitted out to fight at Lepanto was in fact called *La Torre di Vicenza* (Mantese, 1964–II, p.251). Its chimes marked the hours at which workers in building trades started work, and laid off (more or less from dawn to dusk). They indicated the second hour of the night, after which it was illegal to go about without a lantern; the third hour of the night, which was closing time for the wine shops; the fourth hour of the night after which dyers and tanners could discharge their dyes and dirty waste into certain legally defined tracts of the rivers (*Statuti*, 1567). H.B.

GIACOMO DALL'ABACO and HIERONIMO DALLA TORRE
19 Bird's eye view of the western part of the city, 1563
Photograph, reproduced in colour on the catalogue cover

This is a small detail from a large map of the land to the west of the city (Pen and ink, coloured: 103 × 171.5; ASV, *Beni Inculti*, Vicenza Mazzo 59B). It is signed, and dated 4 September 1563. The detail shows the main road from Verona, the Porta di Castello, an empty space where the Valmarana garden was already in existence by 1580, and the Cathedral and Basilica, with what appears to be an indication of one of the lower bastions towards the Cathedral (Kubelik, 1974). H.B.

BATTISTA PITTONI C.1520–83
*20 Bird's eye view of Vicenza, 1580
Pen and ink and blue wash: 130 × 140
Facsimile of the original in the Biblioteca Angelica, Rome

This detailed record of the appearance of Vicenza in the year of Palladio's death was first published and discussed by Ackerman (1971) who dated it c.1571 on the basis of internal evidence. More recently Barbieri (1973) has shown its close relationship to the view of Vicenza which appears in the Gallery of the Geographical Maps in the Vatican, decorated under the general direction of the cartographer and mathematician, Egnazio Danti (175) between 1580 and the end of 1581. In fact as Barbieri shows, there is little doubt that this is the drawing of Vicenza for which Pittoni was (in his own view) underpaid in the first quarter of 1580, which was despatched to Rome on 22 January 1580. The drawing has a grid of squares over it, to facilitate copying. Pittoni himself was the son of Girolamo Pittoni, the sculptor and witnessed Valerio Belli's will in 1546. Pittoni only gave the final form to the plan and did not execute the survey on which it was based. An oversight in the view, like the omission of the campanile of the church of San Bartolomeo already in existence since 1542, is probably to be explained by the use of earlier surveys of the city: a particularly important one was made in 1526, and perhaps further consideration should be given to the possible role of Girolamo da Ponte (Barbieri, 1973, pp.25–6).
The representation of Vicenza in the Vatican, a recognition not conferred on every city of Vicenza's size (only fourteen Italian cities were included) has much to do with the fact that Pope

21

*21 Houses in Contrà Piancoli, Vicenza
Photograph

This attractive street gives an impression of the mixture of
styles in Vicenza, and the character of the sixteenth-century
architecture in the city which cannot be ascribed to Palladio.
In the foreground is the gothic Casa Scroffa, followed by the
Casa dal Toso (in scale, and even in general scheme, comparable
with Palladio's Casa Cogollo) and the Palazzo Garzadori, for
which the name of Palladio has been suggested, but in general
not accepted (Barbieri, Cevese, Magagnato, 1956,
pp.192ff.). H.B.

22 Street scene in the Borgo di Portanuova
Photograph

This 'new town' fourteenth-century extension to the city
(Mantese, 1958, pp.369ff.), was laid out with wide partly
porticoed streets, which represent a late medieval and
Renaissance ideal of planning, which normally could only be
realised in new developments. H.B.

Gregory XIII's spiritual adviser was the Vicentine theologian
Spirito Pelo Anguissola. But it is also an indication of the
Vicentines' success, to which Palladio had made a notable
contribution, in keeping their city's fame alive: in this context
it is worth recalling Palladio's dedication of his edition of
Caesar's *Commentaries* to Gregory XIII's nephew, Jacopo
Buoncompagno (206). H.B.

The city centre and the Basilica

Vicentine life centered around the building which we call the Basilica (following Palladio's publication of it as a 'Basilica of our times', as opposed to an ancient Basilica) and in Palladio's own time it was known as the *Palazzo della Ragione* (Palace of Justice) or simply as the *Palazzo*. On the ground floor were municipally owned shops (25) and the city's prison. The vast first floor hall was the place, 'where the majority of law cases, and private and public business is discussed and decided, as well as being a resort common to everyone' (Resolution of the Greater Council, 1574, in Zorzi, 1964, p.67). Palladio himself wrote of the similar building in Padua that 'everyday the gentlemen gather in it, and it serves them as a covered piazza' (III, p.42). The Maggior Consiglio met in it, mass was performed there annually to celebrate San Vincenzo's day, and in 1561 and 1562 the Accademia Olimpica put on plays there, in a temporary theatre erected after Palladio's design. Once Palladio's new logge were complete, it served as a grandstand for the privileged to watch spectacles in the Piazza (28).

The shops were those of the wool and silk merchants, and goldsmiths. On the corner toward the Duomo was a shop selling books and paper, where Palladio may well have bought paper for his drawings (Mantese, 1968). The Basilica was surrounded on all four sides by piazze, each with distinct functions, laid down as far as marketing went, in bye-laws. The maps of 1481 and 1580 give a clear picture of the area. The main piazza, the Piazza Maggiore, had a completely official character: down one side of the Palazzo del Podestà, the clocktower, and the Basilica; down the other the residence of the Capitanio, with its loggia, from which the town's herald made all official proclamations, and further on the *Monte di Pietà* (Charity Bank) set up in the late fifteenth century to make loans to the poor on reasonable terms. At the bottom end of the Piazza stood the column surmounted by the lion of St Mark, set up in imitation of the Piazzetta in Venice (two columns had been quarried, but the second was not erected until 1640). A bye-law of 1526 states that 'it should not be permitted for anyone in anyway to occupy the public piazza destined for the use of the nobility'. Dragoncino describes the scene in this 'magnificent, civil, and spacious piazza' in 1525, with each of the nobles intent on his own thing. 'Everywhere there were Doctors, and Knights, . . .

there is he who directs his thoughts to public matters, he w to letters, he who to love, and he who to arms attends, he w dresses soberly, and he who on a charger, in silk and beautif gold is resplendent, and he who liberally maintains courtes When Dragoncino wrote, the social ideal of chivalry had n yet been replaced by that of the cultured gentleman, versed Caesar's military tactics and the architectural rules of Vitruviu However something of the contrast he describes betwee individual nobles appears in that between the sober *pat familias*, Gian Alvise Valmarana, and the dandified soldie Ippoloti da Porto (6 and 7).

Executions were carried out by the column. Bread sellers stoo just beyond the column, grain was sold in a marked-off are towards the East, and on the far side of the church of the Serv was 'the Piazza of Wine'. Fruit and vegetables were sold whe they are still sold today, on the far side of the Basilica (26 Milk, cheese and olive-oil were also sold here, and sellers oranges and lemons stood in the middle of this piazza .In th smaller piazza at the end of the Basilica towards the Duom fish was sold, and the women who came in from the country t sell cherries and pears stood in a line in front of the Basilic (Mantese, 1964, pp.620–1).

Palladio's involvement with the central area of the city was long one. It possibly began with work on the portal of th church of the Servi (1531), and continued with the door of th *Domus Comestabilis*, dated 1536 (13). He presented a design fo the Basilica in 1546, and between 1549 and his death in 158 directed work on the building. Across the Piazza, the new Loggia del Capitaniato was built to Palladio's design in 1571–2 These works, however, were only significant episodes in a lon history of urban improvement in the area, which went back t the mid fifteenth century, when equally important works wer undertaken: the completion of the clocktower, the rebuildin of the Basilica, the erection of the column on the Piazza. In th fifteenth century, too, took place demolitions which enlarge the piazza space beyond the column, and in front of the Servi New shops were constructed under the Basilica in 1530, and i Palladio's own time there were other improvements, wit which Palladio was not involved: the completion, and th decoration with frescoes by Zelotti of the facade of the Mont di Pietà; the demolition of shops which encumbered the win market 'for the ornament and decoration of the city' in 1562, and again in 1567 the demolition of the other shops on the main piazza, in front of the Podestà's palace, as 'the Piazza Maggiore is one of the most important and honourable parts of the city, so that one should with every diligence seek that it should be not only surrounded by noble and honourable buildings, but should be as spacious as possible, so that it should be more beautiful' (A.T., b.130). H.B.

23 Plan of the centre of Vicenza in 1481

Pen and ink: 43 × 61
Facsimile, after the original in the Archivio Torre, Vicenza (n.156, fasc.8)

Ettore Motterle found and published a copy of this plan (Motterle, 1971) and then found the original. He died before he could publish it, but what he had written was edited and seen through the press by Barbieri (Motterle, ed Barbieri, 1973). The drawing despite its childish style and its way of drawing the elevations of the buildings over the area which they occupy in the plan, contains much precise information about the 'Peronio', or city centre immediately before work began on the earlier logge of the Basilica in 1481. The functions of the various market areas are shown, and the future site of Palladio's Loggia del Capitaniato is shown as an open area. H.B.

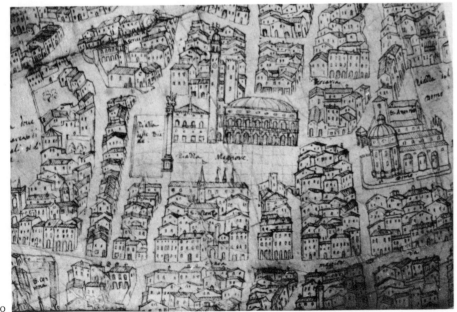

20

Bird's eye view of Vicenza, 1580

25

25

27

CRISTOFORO DELL'ACQUA C.1734–87

24 View of the Piazza Maggiore, Vicenza, 1770–80
Engraving: 31.3 × 45.2
Photograph

*25 Late fifteenth-century shop under the Logge of the Basilica, 1495–6
Photograph

NORTH ITALIAN (BERGAMO?)

26 A fruit seller, c.1650
Canvas: 138 × 92.1
Lent by the National Trust (Tatton Park)

The young peasant woman, in her best clothes, has come to town for market day. She sits on the steps of a public building or palace (note the window mouldings), selling fruit, just as women sold fruit in front of the Basilica in Vicenza. Behind her is a banner showing a priest being shot while he kneels at an altar, an event which has several close parallels in the criminal records of the time (Zanazzo, 1964–5). The fact that a priest was a victim may have led to his assuming a place in popular devotion, celebrated by the smaller banner.   L.F.

26

27 **The side of the Basilica towards Piazza delle Erbe, Vicenza**
Photograph

Fruit and vegetables are still sold here, as they were in the sixteenth century. Giulio Romano suggested raising the level of this piazza, which is considerably below the level of the main Piazza, on the other side of the Basilica.   H.B.

28 **Festivities in the Piazza Maggiore, Vicenza, 1680**
Engraving: 26.5 × 21
Photograph from an original in the Museo Civico, Vicenza

This is a lively early representation of the use of the Piazza as a setting for spectacles and festivities, with the logge of the Basilica used as a grandstand.   H.B.

29 **La Rua** (the Wheel)
a) Engraving, 1680: 45.8 × 16.9 Photograph
b) Photograph, 1914

The destruction of La Rua during the last war brought to an end a Vicentine institution, similar to the 'Explosion of the cart' in Florence or the 'Machine' in Viterbo. This towering pyramidal construction which contained a large wheel (hence its name) was brought out not only at the feast of Corpus Domini, but on any notable occasion: it was displayed in the Piazza to celebrate the entry of Cardinal Ridolfi in 1543 (Zorzi, 1964, p.168) and it was proudly displayed again for the entry of Bishop Matteo Priuli in 1565 (Zorzi, 1964, p.170). It was originally invented by the College of Notaries in 1444 as their contribution to the Corpus Domini festivities, and its unusual form was suggested by the wheel which had the notaries' names inscribed on it, to indicate their turns of duty. In 1585 responsibility for its maintenance passed from the notaries to the city (Mantese, 1964, pp.586–8).   H.B.

30 **The logge of the Basilica, Vicenza**
Photographs

Palladio's contribution to the Basilica did not concern the main structure (built between 1450 and 1460) but only the logge

28

which surround it on three sides. The whole effect of the building depends however on this external feature, which meant, as a Council resolution of 1558 says, that 'there is no doubt whatsoever that this our palace is not outdone in either architecture or beauty by any other public building in Italy' (Zorzi, 1964, p.58).

The original logge, built between 1481 and 1494, collapsed along the side towards the Cathedral in 1496. The city at once consulted the architect in charge of the work on the Ducal Palace in Venice, Antonio Rizzo, but little was done before war and the hard times which followed, made further attention to the problem impracticable. By the later 1530s the situation must have become painful to the prestige-conscious Vicentines, and there followed invitations to Sansovino in 1538, Serlio in 1539, Sanmicheli in 1541 and 1542, and finally Giulio Romano, late in 1542, to give their opinions on the problem. None of these architects' ideas met with approval, and one suspects that Giulio himself, impressive and socially more than acceptable though he was ('no common architect' the Council resolution calls him) both disappointed the Vicentines by proposing a cheap, utilitarian, rebuilding of the logge, and bewildered them by his suggestion that they should totally remodel their central piazze (33). Meanwhile, consciously or unconsciously (probably the former), Trissino and other members of the ruling group had been preparing Palladio, a local man, dependable and on the spot, to make

Vicenza outshine Verona and Brescia architecturally, and go some way towards competing with Venice itself. Even Trissino's taking Palladio to Rome in 1545, and 1546–7 can be seen in this light (Puppi, 1973, p.270). The design which Palladio presented, together with Giovanni da Pedemuro, in 1546 aroused enough interest for a wooden model of one bay to be called for by the Council. Then in 1549 the Council voted by 99 votes to 17 to go ahead with construction on the basis of Palladio's design. By 1564 the lower arcades towards the Piazza and the Duomo were complete, and work began on the upper order. The building, whose speed of construction was dictated by what could be spared out of the city's income, was finished in 1616. The total cost was 60,000 ducats (Zorzi, 1964, pp.43ff; Barbieri, 1968; Puppi, 1973, pp.266ff.).

Palladio's solution satisfied the local desire for a magnificent building, as well as coping with the problem of fitting a grand exterior to a pre-existing structure. A basic need was to arrange the new bay system so that it gave unimpeded access, and was axially aligned with the two broad passageways, which cross the centre of the building, as well as with the two arcades (whose width, tiresomely about 1.5m. narrower than the passageways, could not be altered) across the short ends. A second problem had to be considered. The passageways demanded wide bays, but an arch over a groundfloor bay of this span would rise considerably higher than the floor level of the storey above. Palladio considered (35 and 36) restricting the width of the bays by using very wide piers, with double pilasters applied to them, but this would have had the effect of darkening the arcades and shops under the Basilica, as well as narrowing the entrance to the broad passages across the building.

Palladio brilliantly found a way out of the problem through the use of a fashionable motif, which he had already employed elsewhere (46), the so called *Serliana* (from its frequent appearance in Serlio's books on architecture). Giulio Romano had used it when he modernised the interior of the great Gothic church of San Benedetto Po near Mantua (c.1537–c.1542); Serlio probably had suggested its employment on the upper storeys of the Basilica (Zorzi, 1964, fig.24) and Sansovino, in a rather different way enlivened the upper storey of his Library façade with it. In all these cases the ultimate inspiration was probably the Roman arch at Aquino. The Serliana dealt with all the problems at once. It enabled the bays to correspond to the openings behind, without the arch rising too high. It was a motif which could absorb, without difficulty, the difference in width between the end bays and the others. It let (especially with the lively round openings which Palladio cut through the spandrels) plenty of light into the shops and arcades below, and the salone windows above. And the smaller columns mediated between the scale of the great half columns, and that of passers by, making the building both more magnificent and less austere. In designing the logge Palladio took into consideration the work of modern architects, and his knowledge of ancient buildings (the Theatre of Marcellus, the Portico of Pompey, and the great warehouses round the Trajanic port at Ostia). From this material, as in so many of his works, he created a solution which was functionally and aesthetically extremely satisfying, as well as distinctly personal (Ackerman, 1966, pp.87–92; Barbieri, 1968, pp.59ff; Puppi, 1973, p.271; Cevese, 1973, pp.112–7). H.B.

*31 The Basilica, seen from the Loggia del Capitaniato
Photograph

TIZIANO VECELLIO c.1488/90–1576
*32 Portrait of Giulio Romano, c.1536
Canvas: 108 × 87
Photograph

Giulio Romano was a friend of Titian, and the two artists collaborated on the Gabinetto dei Cesari in the Palazzo Ducale Mantua (c.1536–8). The portrait is close in style to Titian's portraits of Francesco Maria della Rovere, 1536–8 and of Alfonso Davalos, dateable 1536.
Giulio, the most talented of Raphael's assistants, after Raphael's death in 1520, inherited some of the most prestigious commissions in Rome, including the Sala di Costantino and the Villa Lante. Late in 1524 after lengthy negotiations he moved to Mantua and became court artist to the Gonzagas, with control over all aspects of architecture and planning in their territory. His talent, his former connection with Raphael, and his position at the Mantuan court made him the most prestigious architect in Northern Italy (Frommel, 1973, pp.218–21). In 1542 he was called to Vicenza to give his views

31

32

on the Basilica (33), and he possibly provided an outline project for the Palazzo Thiene (47). Giulio is painted holding a plan, and this recalls Vasari's account of his visit to Mantua in 1541, when Giulio showed him his drawings of antique buildings and his own projects for buildings in Rome and Northern Italy. The plan is an unidentified project, which has been associated with a Palatine church for the Gonzagas (Shearman, 1965, pp.174–7).   L.F.

GIULIO ROMANO C.1499–1546

33 **Autograph memorandum on the Basilica, Vicenza, 1542**
Photograph

At the end of November 1542 after mention (by the Thiene?) had been made in the City Council of 'Giulio Romano, not a common architect, and highly celebrated' it was decided to invite him to give his opinion on the Basilica. He was fetched from Mantua in December, stayed in Vicenza for fifteen days, and was paid the handsome sum of 50 gold scudi. The respect in which he was held is also reflected in his writing his report on the Basilica directly in the massive minute book of the City Council (A.T., *Liber Partium*. I, p.145). His design however was ultimately, and massively rejected in 1549 in favour of Palladio's much more radical and magnificent project. Giulio's reputation as an extravagant, bizarre architect is totally misleading. He only provided the bizarre when it was called for. His approach to architectural design is sensible, sober, and highly professional. In his report he assumes (incorrectly as it turned out) that the Vicentines wanted to complete their building cheaply. He thus proposes casing the columns already prepared, to make piers, but basically following the late fifteenth-century scheme. In Albertian fashion he warns against any attempt to alter the Gothic articulation of the core of the building, as this would only weaken the structure disastrously. He makes proposals for rationalising the arrangement of stairs and the passageways across the Basilica. As a long term project, once everything else had been done, he throws out an idea: 'to adorn and complete the Palace it would be necessary to lower the main piazza and raise to the same level the piazza of the fruit market (27). All around the piazze should be equal, so that the Palace should be planted in the middle of a piazza, which should be surrounded by porticos like a cloister, . . .' The parallel with the piazza at Loreto, or the

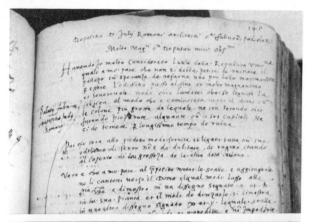

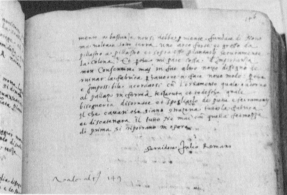

33

34

Piazza and Piazzetta in Venice is clear (Zorzi, 1937, pp.144–7; Puppi, 1973, p.270; Forster, 1973). Palladio's scheme followed Giulio's only in leaving the Gothic ornament under the logge untouched. The Vicentines preferred to wait until 1617 to complete their magnificent palace, rather than have Giulio's sensible, cheap scheme in a much shorter time.   H.B.

MARC'ANTONIO PALLADIO after Sanmicheli
*34 Elevation of the outer facade of the Porta Nuova, Veron
Pen, ink and wash over chalk and incised construction lines:
58.4 × 74.3; the strip projecting on the left: 19.4 × 26.2
Lent by the Trustees of the Chatsworth Settlement

This impressive and hitherto unnoticed drawing can be attributed to Palladio's nephew, on the basis of handwriting, and drawing style. Marc'Antonio is documented as often working with his uncle from 1551 onwards (Zorzi, 1961, pp.307–8). The Porta Nuova was basically constructed between 1533 and 1540, though in 1546 it still lacked the 'cavalier' or gun emplacement on top of the gate structure. A final date is provided by the arms of the Rettori of Verona in office in 1550–1 (Kahnemann, 1960, pp.126–9; Puppi, 1971, p.27).

Though the closeness of the drawing to the Porta Nuova leave little doubt as to identification (the dimensions too are fairly accurate, with eleven feet marked for the central arch, five feet for the side ones) the drawing raises problems. It is not a precise record of the gate. The decorated bands over the side arches and in the imposts are missing, and the smaller arches are too close to the pilasters. No shields or sculptured key stone are shown. It seems likely therefore that Marc'Antonio has copied an earlier project by Sanmicheli, rather than drawn directly from the gate itself. The plan of the cavalier (?) at the top of the sheet, the small sketch added on a strip at the side, and the section of the fortifications (note the tiny human figure) could indicate either an involvement of Marc'Antonio in these works, or simply a record of the existing situation.
The fact that this drawing is by one of Palladio's closest collaborators, and almost certainly belonged to Palladio, is an additional testimony to the relationship between Sanmicheli and Palladio. Sanmicheli, more than Giulio, and much more than Sansovino, was the living architect who most

36

influenced Palladio. His sure sculptural sense in the use of masonry, his skill in extracting dramatic effects from stark, bold treatments (Palazzo Pompei) and from rich detailing, and his way of combining the two, was a fundamental lesson for Palladio. Palladio adopted whole sections of Sanmicheli's vocabulary, including the smooth bands which continue entablatures where they are not supported by an order, and pilasters with entasis.   H.B.

35 Project for the logge of the Basilica
Pen, ink, and wash: 36.7 × 28.3
Lent by the Royal Institute of British Architects (XIII/9)

This project is strongly influenced by Sanmicheli, not only in its paired pilasters and its sober rustication, but even in a small detail like the imposts of the lower arches. Palladio here could even be adapting a suggestion by Sanmicheli for the Basilica: Sanmicheli, after all, was actually a guest in the house of Giovanni da Pedemuro when he was consulted on the Basilica (Zorzi, 1937, p.143; cf. Puppi, 1973, p.22, no.49). The massive piers, almost as wide on the ground floor as the arches themselves, would have darkened the interior. The only real reason for their width is to restrict the width of the openings, and thereby ensure that the arches do not rise above the level of the upper floor. The drawing is certainly before 1549, and probably not later than 1546, the date of the presentation of Palladio's first project.   H.B.

*36 Project for the logge of the Basilica
Pen, ink, and wash: 15.8 × 28.6
Epsilon handwriting
Lent by the Royal Institute of British Architects (XVII/22)

As in the case of no.35 the influence of Sanmicheli is dominant in the lower order. The *serliane* of the upper level are similar to those of projects of the early 1540s (Villa Valmarana etc.), and though they anticipate Palladio's definitive solution, they read as slight, isolated elements, not bound tightly into a unified scheme, as are the serliane in the executed building.   H.B.

37 Study for the upper logge of the Basilica
Pen and ink: 45.7 × 36.9
Lent by the Royal Institute of British Architects (XIII/8)

Work began on the upper order, specifically on the two bays on either side of the corner towards the Cathedral, in 1565. This drawing, which shows a corner bay in plan and elevation antedates the definitive project, as it differs from it in certain details: the frieze, for instance, is not pulvinated. The drawing must be dated before 18 April 1566, as by that date Palladio had decided to add a base to the pedestals below the columns (Zorzi, 1964, p.61). The solution of pedestals without bases, proposed here, appears in the Palazzo Chiericati and Palazzo Thiene.   H.B.

38 The Loggia del Capitaniato, Vicenza, 1571–2
Model and photographs

The loggia in front of the Capitanio's residence was a meeting place (Zorzi, 1964, p.121). It was from there that the city herald read proclamations, and where auctions were held (with the bid falling not rising) for the contract for the annual fair. One such auction is recorded in 1595, with the successful bidder declaring 'It's mine' when the price had fallen to 955 Lire (A.T., no.156, oral communication Gabriella Ferri Picaluga). The financial arrangements for the rebuilding of the unsafe, earlier loggia were established in April 1571, and the Council appointed two of its members as building commissioners. Work went ahead very rapidly on this basically brick structure, so that the 'profiles . . . to be given to the most distinguished Capitanio', consigned by Palladio 1 March 1572, can only have been designs for the final details. The painter Fasolo, who died in August 1572, possibly falling from the scaffolding in the great upper salone, decorated the panels of the wooden ceiling (Zorzi, 1964, p.113).

The Loggia met with instant admiration: 'it will be of such beauty that it will adorn our piazza to the marvel of everyone', the City Council declared. It had no precedent in other public loggee, and was independent of the schemes of ancient triumphal arches, which Palladio had drawn and studied. The design was derived on one hand, from functional requirements and site, and on the other from those drawing board investigations of architectural forms. These had begun with Palladio's studies of ancient buildings, but above all from the 1560s onwards had assumed an autonomous, abstract character, always guided however by strong sense of how architectural Palladio's forms actually look, full-size and in three dimensions. A comparison with the elevation of the cortile project for Palazzo Porto (Palladio, 1570, II, p.10) is therefore pertinent.

One knows that the Council in 1565 resolved to build a new loggia (though nothing was done about it), with the Council Chamber in its upper room, next to the Captain's Loggia (Puppi, 1973, p.377). Although Palladio and the Council in 1571 may have considered an eventual extension of the new Loggia towards the Duomo, the Loggia was almost certainly designed as a unit complete in itself. Excessive discussion of the number of bays by which Palladio may have wanted to extend the Loggia can distract from the building as it was deliberately built. That is, on a site defined by a street on one side and houses on the other, with the function of a public loggia below, and hall of the Captain's residence above. Three bays were almost inevitable, to provide a central emphasis. The choice remained between a clear differentiation on the exterior of the two levels or a more unified scheme. For the main façade, but not the side façade, Palladio opted for a single unifying giant order. The columns could not have been any higher, because they would have then (if a satisfactory width/height ratio was to be maintained) become too wide, and have reduced the width of the bays, as well as contrasted too strongly with the scale of the Basilica. Nor could they have been raised high on pedestals, as this would have created difficulties in inserting the arches. The window frames therefore cut unorthodoxly into the architrave, and were accompanied by a series of other

39

dramatic elements: the massive balconies, the jutting cornices, and the splendidly modelled column bases. The result was one of Palladio's most startling and successful works.   H.B.

*39 The Loggia del Capitaniato and a portion of the Monte di Pietà
Before the demolition of houses to the left of the Loggia
Photograph

*40 A sketch for the balcony of the Loggia del Capitaniato
Pen and ink: 29 × 36.4
Lent by the Royal Institute of British Architects (VII/2)

On this sheet of studies for the reconstruction of the Baths of Agrippa is a tiny sketch which clearly shows in a very summary way the balcony of the Loggia, supported by the two massive blocks. Below is the arch, and to the right, the side of one of the great columns. It is impossible to say whether the sketch was actually an early idea for the Loggia, or a doodled reminiscence of it.   H.B.

*41 Detail of the composite order of the Loggia del Capitaniato
Photograph

42 Project for a loggia
Pen, ink, and wash: 37.5 × 57
Photograph: Museo Civico, Vicenza (VIC.D.19)

This loggia design makes an interesting comparison with the Loggia, and although there are indications that more than three bays were intended for it, the weight of opinion is against this being a project for the Capitaniato (Puppi, 1973, pp.378–9). With the steps projecting on the left, it would have taken up more or less all the available space between the Cathedral end of the Piazza, and the street corner at which the present Loggia terminates. Moreover, the way in which this loggia was raised on steps and the projection into the Piazza of the steps themselves, would have given an alien character to the structure. The problem of the destination of this loggia remains open. H.B.

SEBASTIANO SERLIO 1475–1554
*43 Proposal for modernising an old-fashioned palace
Photograph

This drawing from Serlio's manuscript Book VII in Vienna (it appears reversed in Serlio, VII, 1619, p.137) shows how to turn

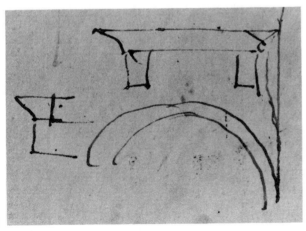

a gothic palace, with its door placed off centre, into a symmetrical modern design. It was a type of conversion which became frequent in the sixteenth century, as out of date palace façades (Palladio, II, p.4) became increasingly embarrassing to their owners (cf. Serlio's moral tale, VII, 1619, p.156). H.B.

*44 View of the Contrà Porti
with the gothic Palazzo Colleoni-Porto and Palladio's Palazzo da Porto-Festa
Photograph

45 Palazzo Civena, Vicenza
Photographs

This was the first town palace by Palladio to be completed: a medal found in the foundations was dated 1540, and the building was finished by 7 April 1542, six months before work started on Palazzo Thiene. Palladio's authorship of the palace has been confirmed by his surviving projects for the building (Puppi, 1973, pp.242–5). The façade followed Trissino's villa at Cricoli (148) in breaking brusquely with traditional forms, and resembled it in details like the window frames and the pedestal and balcony zone. The rusticated lower storey and the paired order above it derived ultimately from Bramante's House of Raphael. The traditional Venetian central first floor loggia was replaced by a Roman system of equal bays, and the salone, as in Palazzo Chiericati, ran across the central portion of the building. The ground plan (originally only seven bays wide) and the use of a *serliana* at the end of the entrance vestibule have much in common with the villa projects of these years. H.B.

40

41

43

44

46 Project for Palazzo Civena

Pen, ink, and wash over brown chalk underdrawing:
32.3 × 23.2
Lent by the Royal Institute of British Architects (XVII/14)

Both plan and elevation correspond closely to the executed
building. The plan simply adds a cross vaulted hall and external
stairs to the area beyond the vestibule, which, as executed,
terminated with the two columns of the *serliana*. The elevation

shows windows with consoles (cf.13), little niches between the
pilasters, and on the ground floor a motif probably suggested
by the inner side of Sanmicheli's Porta Nuova at Verona.   H.B.

47

*47 Palazzo Thiene, Vicenza
Model and photographs

Palladio described merely as a stonemason, was a witness on
10 October 1542 to the contract between Marc'Antonio Thiene
and three builders for 'the building and making of a house' for
the two Thiene brothers. There is little doubt that this refers to
the present palace, especially as piers are mentioned,
presumably those of the cortile (Zorzi, 1964, p.213). Alessandro
Vittoria was engaged in the decoration of the palace between
1552 and 1553, and the dates 1556 and 1558 are inscribed on the
exterior and in the cortile. The building itself is clearly
unfinished, just the corner of a huge scheme for an island site,
with a pedimented central block on Vicenza's main street,
which Palladio published (1570, II, p.13) and has been
translated into a model. The scale and magnificence of the
project is unique among Palladio's palace designs, and it was
only paralleled by contemporary buildings in Rome: the
Cancelleria, Bramante's Tribunali, the Palazzo Farnese.
The square plan, the four roughly blocked out columns of the

vestibule, the rustication of the piers of the cortile, the lower
storey of the exterior, and the first floor windows (49) are all
elements derived from Giulio Romano. This gives a
considerable force to the note which Inigo Jones made in his
copy of the *Quattro Libri* in 1613, against the plate of Palazzo
Thiene: 'Scamozzi and Palermo said that "these designs were
of Giulio Romano, but adjusted by Palladio", and so it seems'
(Jones, ms.). The possibility of Giulio's involvement in the
design has been seriously considered recently (Ackerman, 1966,
p.94; Puppi, 1973, p.254; Forster, 1973) and the continuing
contact of the noble and very rich Thiene family with the
Gonzagas, whose architect was Giulio, gives further weight to
this hypothesis (Puppi, 1973, p.254; Forster, 1973). Teodoro
Thiene (married to Isabella Gonzaga) wrote in his will in 1577
that his son should as part of his education spend some time
'in the courts of Mantua or Rome or similar' (Mantese,
1969–70, pp.96, 139).
Without further documentation, one can only sketch a
conjectural history of the palace: Gian Galeazzo Thiene
maintained close contact with the Gonzaga court in Mantua,
and possibly obtained a project for rebuilding his palace from
Giulio soon after the latter's arrival in Mantua in 1524. Giulio
drew up a project incorporating the window design which
he had just used in Rome in his own house (49). Otherwise he
adapted to the requirements of a large city palace the plan
he had devised for the Palazzo del Te (Puppi, 1973, p.254). If
the design was not made as early as this, Giulio drew on the
same motifs for a design which was ready at the very latest by
1542. The City Council's invitation to Giulio was probably
at the suggestion of the Thiene, and followed his involvement
with their palace. (Burns, 1973–II). Palladio was present when
the contract was drawn up with the builders, either as the
executing architect or more probably (hence his description as
lapicida) as the representative of the stonemason's firm which
was going to execute the stonework. The local tradition,
reported by Inigo Jones, that Palladio himself carved two
capitals for the façade has perhaps some truth behind it.
It should be stressed that the builders undertook to do the
brickwork and the construction, including putting the
stonework into place, but had no responsibility for working
the stones. The ground floor of the palace, including both
façade and vestibule, and cortile, with its uneven rustication,
is more or less completely Giulio's invention. The first floor,

though it preserves Giulio's general scheme (the window tabernacle on the exterior, the tall order reminiscent of Giulio's Palazzo Maccarani cortile) reflects much more strongly Palladio's style as it had developed by the late 1540s. It is not even necessary to hypothesise as Puppi does a delay in construction: the probable rate of building would have ensured that this part was not executed (and hence the designs for details, all of which reveal Palladio's personality) until 1546 or after, that is the year of Giulio's death, and the year in which Palladio returned from an important study trip to Rome. So much for conjecture. The Thiene owned the greater part of three sides of the site shown in the *Quattro Libri*, and the existing palace clearly reveals that some version of this project was originally intended. A tiny sketch (51) probably executed after 1550, shows Palladio, however theoretically considering the relationship of the complete palace scheme to the site. Palladio published the palace in 1570 without the slightest suggestion that it was not all his own work. It is always possible though unlikely, that Palladio independently produced a thoroughly Giuliesque project in 1542, or that Giulio's suggestions may have been only sketches, or even purely verbal: 'Why don't you have a square plan, with columned vestibules, and rusticated ground floor and windows like my Roman house'? By the late 1560s, Palladio found the undiluted Giuliesque elements in the design unacceptable, and toned them down in preparing the plates of the palace for his book (52). Much more than the Palazzo Civena, the Palazzo Thiene established a new model to be emulated by Vicentine palace builders, which entirely abandoned the scheme of the Venetian palace façade. It is no coincidence that the builder of the magnificent Palazzo Porto Festa was married to Marc'Antonio Thiene's sister. Though Palladio rejected many of the palace's main features in his later designs, its four-columned vestibule became one of the central elements in his subsequent palace schemes.   H.B.

ANONYMOUS GERMAN (?) ARTIST C.1530

49 The facade of Giulio Romano's house in Rome
Pen, ink, and wash: 28.1 × 20.1
Lent by the Trustees of the Chatsworth Settlement

Giulio's house in Rome no longer exists, and its appearance can only be reconstructed from a handful of contemporary drawings. It stood near Trajan's column, and was probably built in the period 1523–4 (certainly not later), and was almost certainly a modernisation of an existing structure, rather than a total rebuilding (Frommel, 1973, II, pp.216–23). The Chatsworth drawing has been published, but without a correct identification, or even the information that it was at Chatsworth (Loukomski, 1939). The verso carries a plan of the Villa Madama as executed, and a well-known antique base at San Marco, Rome, and an inscription in German, which appears to be in the same hand as the drawing.

The drawing may not be entirely trustworthy (no window piercing the sarcophagus shaped bench in order to light the cellar is shown) but it does provide some clarifications. An upturned antique capital (from Giulio's collection of antiquities?) stood outside the door, perhaps for use as a mounting block. The portal led to a vestibule, and inside on the right appear steps, then a door. An inscription, not a relief, was inserted beneath the ground floor window. The smaller upper floor window had an unusual window frame, with little panels at top and bottom. Giulio obviously lavished all his inventiveness on the façade of his own house, and his attempt to make the façade of a small house (which was far from being a palace, as its dimensions were only 10.5m × 5.3m) as monumental and impressive as possible is precisely comparable to that of Palladio in the Casa Cogollo (59). For its size, this was an exceedingly influential work. Its rustication was echoed in details of Sanmicheli's Palazzo Canossa. Palladio or Giulio himself used the extraordinary and effective window tabernacle on Palazzo Thiene, and Alessi cited it again on the exterior of Palazzo Marino in Milan.   H.B.

50 Study for the facade of a palace
Pen and ink with chalk: 21.5 × 34.6
Lent by the Royal Institute of British Architects (XVII/7)

This drawing, because of the rustication and the window tabernacles, has usually been associated with the Palazzo Thiene. There is no definite indication that it was a project for that palace, and the scheme (apparently a triumphal arch in the middle of the façade) was not repeated there. It was probably a study for the first floor of a façade, and on the ground floor the paired pilasters would have framed the entrance portal, which would have lead into a four columned vestibule. Even if the

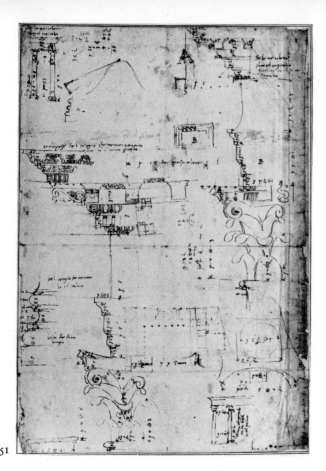

executed and hence was probably made after 1551–2. The round columns shown in the cortile are in fact Palladio's shorthand for piers. The drawing is particularly interesting in that with an oblique line Palladio shows the relationship of the palace and its projecting central block to the main street in Vicenza, and thereby demonstrates how the palace would have dominated the vista up and down the street. H.B.

52 Studies for the Quattro Libri plates of Palazzo Thiene
Pen and ink: 27.8 × 38.2 (before separation)
Lent by the Royal Institute of British Architects

These drawings, which are closely related to the *Quattro Libri* plates, 'emend' the actual building, to bring it into line with Palladio's stylistic preferences of the 1560s. Thus in the drawing of the cortile, on the left, the rusticated piers have been regularised and loose their unpredictable, Giuliesque knobbliness. The pedestals of the order above have had a base element added to them – a change which Palladio about this time also made in his design for the upper order of the Basilica (37). H.B.

53 The Palazzo Chiericati, Vicenza
Model and photographs

The Palazzo Chiericati is an astonishingly original work, and, as much as the Basilica, a measure of how distinct and notable an architectural personality Palladio had developed by 1550. Its design certainly depends on a careful consideration of elements derived from Sanmicheli, Serlio, and the antique, as well as local tradition. But the final result cannot be confused with any of its points of departure.
On 15 November 1550 Girolamo Chiericati, who the year before had spoken eloquently in favour of Palladio's Basilica project, paid Palladio the modest sum of four scudi for making the plan and façade elevation of his house 'during many past months'. Two preliminary studies for the façade have survived (56 and 57), which imply an initial consideration of a central projecting portico, but no one which ran the whole length of the building. A long portico, however, was the best way to make use of the wide, but shallow site, given that the portico was constructed over public ground. Chiericati, on 1 March 1551, in fact asked for the permission to build a portico,

drawing has nothing to do with the Palazzo Thiene, it can fairly safely be dated in the years 1542–50. H.B.

*51 Sketch plan of Palazzo Thiene
Pen and ink: 42.4 × 29.2
Lent by the Royal Institute of British Architects (XIV/4)

On a sheet of lively free hand sketches from the antique (probably sketches based on drawings already made by Palladio), is a small faint plan of Palazzo Thiene, which corresponds closely to the plan in the *Quattro Libri*. It corresponds exactly to the part of the building which was thirteen feet wide, out into the piazza 'for my greater convenience and for the convenience and ornament of the whole city', having been advised to do so, 'by experienced architects and by many honoured citizens'. The request was granted by a Council vote of 96 to 17 (Zorzi, 1964, p.203). The style, but not the idea of such a portico, was new. Palladio had already employed it on a similar site (an open space, overlooking a river) on the Casa Civena (45): compare the late fifteenth-century Palazzo Angaran by the Ponte degli Angeli. Work continued till 1554 and then, apart from the decoration of the interior, seems to have come to a halt, with only the three bays on the left and the first bay of the central portion complete (Barioli, 1963; Puppi, 1973, p.281ff.). The palace was only finished in the late seventeenth century, and the lively and successful pinnacles and statues do not belong to the original project.

The plan (55) of the block behind the portico was probably suggested by that of Sanmicheli's Villa Soranza (Puppi, 1971, p.156). The basic scheme of the elevation, as was noted by Dalla Pozza, was more or less identical to an elevation published by Serlio in 1540 (Dalla Pozza, 1943, p.77), and Zorzi's reasonable objection that in terms of plan Serlio's scheme was quite different from Palladio's (Zorzi, 1964, p.202) no longer holds, given Palladio's conscious reading into elevation drawings of spatial arrangements which they were not originally meant to represent (Burns, 1973–II). The Doric entablature was quoted directly from Sanmicheli, and the elevation of the wall under the portico was lifted straight from Palladio's own drawing of the Temple of Mars Ultor in Rome (Burns, ibid.). The great interest of the project lies in the thoroughly antique solution of superimposed loggie, providing a fine view over the cattle market to the mill wheels on the far side of the river (20 and 54) and the way in which Palladio had looked with a fresh eye, not conditioned by contemporary conventions, at antique architecture Hence the long stretches of straight entablature over columns, the bold (but truly antique) motifs of the fused columns where the central block projects slightly, and of the termination of the portico with an arch, derived from the Portico of Octavia in Rome (Puppi, 1973, p.286). The steps, designed to raise the service rooms under the portico above flood level, were modelled on those of a Roman temple front. The villa-like site of the building called forth these solutions, and they were often repeated by Palladio in his subsequent villa and suburban projects.   H.B.

54 Bird's eye view of the Piazza dell' Isola, Vicenza, 1655
Photograph

This drawing was discovered by Kubelik (ASV, *Rason Vecchie*). It shows the piazza in front of Palazzo Chiericati, and provides a further indication of the appearance of Palladio's palace for Giulio and Giudo Piovene, demolished in 1818 (Puppi, 1973, pp.388ff.). On the far side of the River Bacchiglione there is a group of mills (Kubelik, 1974).   H.B.

MARC'ANTONIO, nephew of Palladio
55 Plan of the Palazzo Chiericati, Vicenza
Pen, ink, and wash: 27.9 × 41
Lent by the Royal Institute of British Architects (XVII/8)

The handwriting is unmistakably that of Marc'Antonio, who is documented as carving 'bulls' heads' and other high quality details for the palace between 1552 and 1554 (Zorzi, 1964, p.203). The plan is divided into two self-contained parts, with separate stairs, which share only the vestibule downstairs and the sala above. Girolamo Chiericati and his distinguished son Valerio seem to have lived without discomfort in the left-hand unit – all that was built in Palladio's time. It is worth asking whether Girolamo's brother Giovanni, whose house was round the corner towards Santa Corona (Zorzi, 1964, p.204), may not in fact have owned part of the right half, and that it was his failure to come into the scheme (which has all the appearance of a two-brother residence) which blocked further building. Marc'Antonio has shown only door-sized openings at the ends of the portico. This is either a mistake, or was actually an earlier intention, before the arch was decided on. Oddly this feature is reproduced in the *Quattro Libri* plan (II, p.6), which seems to be reproduced directly from Marc'Antonio's drawing.   H.B.

56 Project for the facade of the Palazzo Chiericati, Vicenza

Pen, ink, and wash over lead underdrawing: 39.6 × 56.3
Lent by the Royal Institute of British Architects
(Burlington-Devonshire Collection, drawer 8./11)

This drawing has been rightly attributed to Palladio and shows
a scheme, somewhat reminiscent of that for Palazzo Thiene,
for a projecting pedimented central wing (47) (Forssman, 1962,
p.36; Puppi, 1973, p.384). Unlike the executed building, the
portico projects only in front of the central five bays, and these
carry a massive pediment, anticipating two order villa schemes.
A festive character is given to the façade by small festoons,
though for this type of decoration on palaces one need not look
even as far as Raphael's Palazzo dell' Aquila in Rome, but need
only recall the Palazzo Sangiovanni in Vicenza itself (Barbieri,
Cevese, Magagnato, 1956, fig.122) and contemporary modes of
festive decoration. The Doric columns without bases facilitate
access to the portico, as well as being archaeologically justifiable
(Palladio, 1570, I, p.22). H.B.

57 Study for the upper order of the facade of Palazzo Chiericati, Vicenza

Pen and ink: 44.6 × 59
Lent by the Provost and Fellows of Worcester College, Oxford

The scheme is closely connected to the RIBA project with a
projecting central portico (56; Harris, 1971; Puppi, 1973,
p.284). H.B.

58 Facade of the Palazzo Chiericati, Vicenza

Pen, ink, and wash: 28.7 × 39.5
Lent by the Royal Institute of British Architects (XVII/5)

This drawing corresponds in most details except the upper
entablature to the executed building. The style suggests a study
for the plate in the *Quattro Libri*, rather than for the building
itself, and this hypothesis is in some measure supported by the
note in the hand of Palladio's son Orazio at the top of the
page. H.B.

59

*59 The facade of the Casa Cogollo, Vicenza, 1559–62

Photograph

In 1559 the notary Pietro Cogollo was granted Vicentine
citizenship on condition that within three years he should spend
250 ducats in ornamenting the façade of his house (Zorzi, 1964,
p.234). Cogollo was a prominent figure. In 1567 he was in
charge of decoration and improvements to the *Podesta*'s
palace. For years he was the notary employed by Palladio's
patrons and friends Odoardo and Teodoro Thiene to draw up
their legal settlements, which were often witnessed by Palladio
or his son Orazio (Zorzi, 1968, pp.102–4; Mantese, 1969–70).

These contacts go back at least to 1557 (Mantese, *loc. cit.*, p.84) and have a tone of intimate affability: 'To the magnificent Piero Cocollo like an honoured brother . . . From Cicogna 5 August 1560 . . . Odoardo Thiene' (*ibid.*, p.85). Through the Thiene Cogollo must have been in frequent and friendly contact with Palladio.

The remarkable façade of his house has been accepted as a work of Palladio by certain scholars (Dalla Pozza, Zorzi, Puppi) but rejected by others (Cevese, Ackerman: for a summary, Puppi, 1973, pp.331–2). No documentation exists which definitely settles the matter. The façade does not closely resemble any other work by Palladio, but to approach it in terms of simple comparisons with other works is unhelpful. It is necessary to consider what the design problem facing the architect was, and whether the way it was solved is characteristic of Palladio. The façade was small, squeezed between an oratory (now demolished) on one side, and a house on the other. The street was lined with porticos at this point. On the two upper floors the wall facing on to the street, as in so many other small houses, had to contain a fireplace between the two windows. The solution needed to be magnificent (at a guess, the executed façade did cost about 250 ducats) and ideally had to carry visually, as it can be seen from a good portion of the Piazza dell' Isola, and therefore is the closing episode in a vista which, on the left, is dominated by Palazzo Chiericati (Puppi, *loc. cit.*).

Palladio probably recalled the façade of Giulio's house (49) which was audaciously dominated by the monumental combination of rusticated portal and window tabernacle. Unlike Giulio, Palladio was able to place a monumental element centrally, with half columns supporting a jutting entablature, and rectangular openings at the side to give further light and access to the portico. This unit, boldly modelled, is effective from a distance, and when seen in a raking view. With its centrally placed columns and narrow side bays, it is like a simplified version of the Basilica bay, turned inside out. Above the columns, fluted pilasters frame an area of wall, closed because of the fireplace behind, and originally decorated with a fresco by Fasolo. The sequence from high to shallow relief is concluded by the simple treatment of the upper floor. Not only is this an optimum solution, but there is no detail which does not have parallels elsewhere in Palladio's work (as Zorzi noted, the first floor tabernacle resembles the windows for

the palace at Brescia, and the fleshy horizontal moulding at the level of the springing of the arch is highly characteristic of Palladio). The ground floor rectangular openings recall Poiana, and the Villa Forni and the Casa Cogollo lend each other mutual support as works by Palladio. The use of a dominant central element, where columns and pilasters are concentrated, while the walls at the side are tied into the centre by horizontal bands and cornices, is a feature of many of Palladio's villa and palace projects. The project for the palace of Giulio Capra in the same street (Puppi, 1973, p.349), with its very narrow side bays, ending with a razor cut, not a pilaster, and with a moulding right across the façade at the height of the top of the balconies is strikingly close to the Cogollo façade. It should be noted that there is no basis for the traditional identification of the Casa Cogollo as 'the House of Palladio'.   H.B.

FRANCESCO MUTTONI active 1704–60
60 Plan and elevation of Casa Cogollo, Vicenza
Pen, ink, and wash: 292 × 456
Signed, lower right: *Fran.co Muttoni Arch.to*
Lent by the Trustees of the Chatsworth Settlement

This is one of a group of unnoticed drawings by Muttoni at Chatsworth (000), which are similar in character to the group conserved in the Raccolta Cappelletti, in the CISA. Muttoni was the author of a detailed and important study of Palladio (Muttoni, 1740–8, and 1760; Puppi, 1973–III, pp.182–3), and the drawings may well have been connected with its preparation. Muttoni briefly but accurately rendered the elevation and ground plan of the house, which he mistakenly indicated as Palladio's own home. A courtyard with a well divided the house in two parts, and stairs led up from the courtyard to the room over the street, which, like the façade, was decorated by Fasolo.   H.B.

61 Project for the palace of Giulio Capra, for the main street in Vicenza
Photograph from the *Quattro Libri*

Though Palladio (1570, II, p.21) says the building was begun, no trace of it exists, nor even an indication of the date of the project. The elevation has points in common with Casa Cogollo, and Puppi has pointed out the relationship of the plan to that of Palazzo Valmarana (Puppi, 1973, p.350).   H.B.

*62–3 Palazzo da Porto-Breganze, Vicenza
Photographs

Vincenzo Scamozzi first mentioned the Palazzo da Porto-Breganze as among those buildings which he had 'finished' and gave as its owner Alessandro da Porto (1615, III, p.266). Giulio da Porto, the father of this Alessandro, was the nephew of Archdeacon Simone da Porto, whose name has recently been advanced as the commissioner of the building (Mantese, 1966–7, pp.237–8). In the eighteenth century Muttoni and Bertotti-Scamozzi ascribed the design of the palace to Palladio, and their attribution has met with general acceptance (Puppi, 1973, pp.395–6). The executed portion and Bertotti-Scamozzi's reconstruction correspond to Palladio's style in one of his most fertile periods, from the late 1560s to the early 1570s. Begun after the *Quattro Libri*'s publication (1570), the Palazzo da Porto-Breganze was among the last of Palladio's palace designs, but it was as original as any of the works which preceded it. According to the plausible reconstruction by Bertotti-Scamozzi (1776, pp.67–9), there would have been a large order façade of seven bays and a cortile of two orders terminating in a hemicycle. Although solutions with hemicycles appear in several of the villa plans, notably the Villa Sarego, its presence here was unique among the palaces. Like the Loggia del Capitaniato (38), and the drawing of the so-called Venetian palace façade (Puppi, 1973, pp.388–90), the façade of the Palazzo da Porto-Breganze was dominated by a large order of engaged composite columns. Like the Loggia the palace was planned for a large square in which it would be a commanding element. Indeed, there was in the façade a merging of Palladio's monumental and palace styles, manifest in the subordination of all elements to the composite order, the lack of horizontal divisions, and the

absorption of the ground floor into the podium of the columns.   B.B.

64 Teatro Olimpico Vicenza
1580–5
Photographs

The Teatro Olimpico was remarkable both for being a permanent theatre building, based on ideas about the appearance of ancient Roman theatres, and for its elaborate fixed scene, with its illusionistic receding 'streets'. Both elements have their roots in Rome: it was Raphael who planned a permanent (but never executed) outdoor Vitruvian theatre for the Villa Madama, and Raphael and Peruzzi who introduced illusionistic scenes of much greater elaboration

62

than anything seen before (Neiinendam, 1969). Peruzzi's pupil Serlio designed a wooden theatre in the courtyard of the Gothic Palazzo Porto in Vicenza in 1539 (Zorzi, 1968, pp.250–1). The theatre, recorded by him (Serlio, 1619, II, fols.43v–44v) had an auditorium arranged in a semicircle, an orchestra, stage and set. The emphasis in Serlio's text was on the scene, in which, putting his skill in perspective to the best use, he presented a unified setting, with a construction of painted flaps receding diagonally from the single opening in the proscenium to the back wall of the stage. In his book he also published three types of sets based on Vitruvius' descriptions and contemporary practice: the Tragic with sober, classical architecture, obelisks and pyramids; the Comic, which was also architectural, but with the sober architecture of the Tragic scene replaced by everyday buildings, including comic elements like the house of a procuress and an inn; and the Satyric scene, shown as a landscape.

The acclaim which the spectacle, the innovatory set, the costumes, and the clothes of the audience, both noble Vicentines and foreigners, received, prompted the characterisation of the city as a whole by Beccanuvoli (1539) as 'more virtuous than Athens, greater than Milan, and richer than Venice, her mistress' (Zorzi, 1968, p.250). The use of the theatre as a means of bringing acclaim and prestige to the city and its nobles, was exploited by the Accademia Olimpica in their productions of *Amor Costante* by Alessandro Piccolomini in 1561, and *Sofonisba* by Giangiorgio Trissino in 1562. The latter was performed at Carneval in a semi-permanent theatre which was constructed by Palladio in the *salone* of the Basilica (it was dismantled and stored). His design is known through two frescoes in the theatre's vestibule commemorating these events (74).

Palladio's early studies of amphitheatres and the Vitruvian theatre confirm the general scheme presented by Serlio, but the studies of the Teatro Berga in Vicenza, the major source for Palladio's reconstruction of the Vitruvian theatre in Barbaro's book (1556, V, pp.156–7), led to a correction of Serlio's set. The Teatro Berga as reconstructed by Palladio had a solid scene front with three openings and narrow 'streets' leading off them. It was reconstructed in the Barbaro plate, in elevation, as a solid wall with superimposed orders decorated with statues and reliefs, with three openings through which the architectural sets in exaggerated perspective are visible. It was to this type of set which Palladio returned for the Teatro Olimpico.

In 1579, after a long break in its theatrical activity, the Accademia Olimpica decided to produce a pastoral play, and following that decision they resolved to build a permanent theatre, and applied to the Council for a site. In May 1580 they were granted a site belonging to the old prisons by the Ponte degli Angeli (Zorzi, 1968, pp.284–7). It was the shape of the site which suggested the half amphitheatre plan rather than the semicircular plan which Palladio knew from Vitruvius and surviving examples. The theatre was to be paid for by the members, but in 1581, when they were lagging behind in their payments, the project received the sponsorship of the Maggior Consiglio (Zorzi, 1968, p.290; Mantese, 1974, pp.928–34). Palladio's design must have been completed by May 1580. Work continued, hardly interrupted by Palladio's death in August 1580, until 1583. The scene front was now complete but there was no set. A model and drawings are recorded (Zorzi, 1968, pp.288–9; Puppi, 1973, pp.436–7), but only one preparatory study survives. In this design Palladio returned to the plate for Barbaro's *Vitruvius* (1556), where the scene front is a field for a programme of sculptural decoration which dominates the set. The statues with their emblems and inscriptions on the pedestals of the columns and in the pedimented niches, executed between 1581 and 1584 by Agostino Rubini, Ruggero Bascapè, and Domenico Fontana, were paid for by the members of the Academy and represent themselves (Puppi, 1967–II, pp.144–5). The decision for each member to pay for his own statue, taken in 1580 (Zorzi, 1968, p.290), clearly indicates the intention from the first to use the set, ornamented with all'antica portraits and reliefs of scenes of the Hercules myth, as a celebration of the ruling class, as well as a setting for plays whose performance furthered their aims. The set became no more than part of this general context (Puppi, 1973, p.437). This use of an antique scheme to celebrate modern personages is exactly paralleled by the festive architecture which Palladio created for Henry III in 1574 (264). In 1581, the Academy decided to perform a tragedy instead of a pastoral play. The text was chosen and they acquired the land to build the perspective sets. Angelo Ingegneri, the Ferrarese theatrical director was called in to consult on the lighting in 1583. In 1584 Scamozzi was asked to design the set and meet the requirements of the director. Ingegneri in his *Della poesia rappresentativa . . .* (1598) states that tragedies

65

required a realistic setting, in this case Thebes, and that the set
and stage should be used to resolve the technical problems of
lighting, music, entrances and exits, and movement. To
satisfy the requirements of Ingegneri, Scamozzi altered
Palladio's theatre. He enlarged the two side openings in
Palladio's design in order to reveal as fully as possible the deep
perspectives of Thebes, which he designed (79). As well as
changing the scene front, Scamozzi changed the stage. He
extended the two projecting wings, placing behind them two
more street openings for the actors' entrances and exits,
thus producing a box stage. The festoons which he designed
across the front of the stage for the curtain are the point of
departure for the modern proscenium arch. The curtain when
drawn up covered the ceiling of the stage (Puppi, 1971,
p.88ff; ibid., 1973, p.439).

On 3 March 1585 the Teatro Olimpico opened with the
production of Sophocles' *Oedipus Rex* translated by Orsatto
Giustiniani. Palladio's stage and set had been changed for a
single event, but the change has been permanent. Filippo
Pigafetta recorded that 'they arrived early, that is between
sixteen and twenty hours and the play began at one-thirty in
the morning so that some of us including myself were in the
theatre about eleven hours without regret', and that when the
curtain went up, first there was the softest fragrance and the
sound of trumpets and drums, and from the perspectives one
heard the sound of distant music of different instruments and
voices (Puppi, 1971, pp.92–3).   L.F.

***65 The interior of the Teatro Olimpico from behind
the colonnade**
Photograph

The half amphitheatre form is clearly visible. The columns
above the steps derive from Palladio's reconstruction of
ancient theatres (71).

66 Section of the Roman amphitheatre at Verona
Pen and ink over incised construction lines and chalk
underdrawing: 27.8 × 28.5
Epsilon handwriting
Lent by the Royal Institute of British Architects (VIII/19)

The upper part of the amphitheatre is reconstructed.
The use of perspective suggests that it was copied from a
drawing by another artist.

67 Plan and elevation of the Coliseum, Rome
Pen, ink, and wash over incised construction lines: 44.3 × 28.9
Epsilon handwriting
Lent by the Royal Institute of British Architects (VIII/4)

This reconstruction is probably based on other artists'
drawings. An incidental point of some interest is the
diamond-shaped formation in the top right, a reflection of
Palladio's interest (doubtless stimulated by Trissino) in ancient
military formations (cf. Eliano, 1552, f. 16v; Puppi, 1973–II,
fig. 4).   H.B.

68 Reconstruction of the Vitruvian theatre
Pen, ink, and wash over incised construction lines and chalk
underdrawing: 28.7 × 43.9
Epsilon handwriting
Lent by the Royal Institute of British Architects (X/131)

The plan, like the plan of the Teatro Berga in Barbaro's
Vitruvius (1556, p.154), shows how the disposition of the parts
of the Vitruvian theatre could be obtained by drawing a circle
within which are inscribed four equilateral triangles which
touch the circumference at equally spaced points. On the right,
shown in perspective section, is the interior with a colonnade
above the seats, a scheme which Palladio followed in the

Teatro Olimpico. On the right is a section through the auditorium, and the elevation of the column screen of the fixed scene.   L.F.

69 Reconstruction of the Teatro Berga, Vicenza
Pen, ink and wash: 30.3 × 42.2
Epsilon handwriting
Lent by the Royal Institute of British Architects (X/1)

The Roman Teatro Berga of which substantial ruins survived in Palladio's time (Marzari, 1591, illustrations) was one of the sources for Palladio's re-creation of a Roman theatre in the Teatro Olimpico, though it is less close to it than the theatre at Pola (71) with its flat scene.   H.B.

70 Reconstruction of the scene of the Vitruvian theatre, 1556
Photograph

This design, published in Barbaro's Vitruvius (pp.156–7) replaces the superimposed colonnades of Palladio's earlier reconstruction (68) with the closed scene front which Palladio knew from the Teatro Berga (69), which had three openings set into deep niches. The scheme, with its provision for an extensive sculptural programme was Palladio's point of departure in designing the Teatro Olimpico.   L.F.

71 Plan and elevation of the Roman theatre at Pola
Pen, ink and wash over incised construction lines: 27 × 18.7
Lent by the Royal Institute of British Architects (X/3)

This can be identified as a reconstruction of the theatre at Pola on the basis of Serlio's plate (III, 1540, p.51). The seats are topped by a colonnade, the narrow stage with three openings cut in a solid wall recalls the Teatro Olimpico.   L.F.

72 Printed list of the members of the Accademia Olimpica, 1596
42 × 31.5 (maximum dimensions)
Photograph: Accademia Olimpica, Vicenza

This is the earliest of the surviving printed lists of the Accademicians, and contains the names of many of those whose statues adorn the theatre (73), or who had direct connections

with Palladio. Thus the *Principe* (President) of the Accademia is Trissino's grandson. Pompeo Leonardo Valmarana, owner of the Palazzo Valmarana, Palladio's son Silla, and Fabio Monza's son Torquato figure among the members.   H.B.

*73 Statues of the Accademicians
Photograph

This view across the upper order of the scene shows the Accademicians rich enough to pay for statues of themselves (as Palladio's son Silla was not) in antique costume. These are the people who sponsored the theatre and the plays put on in it, the most prestigious and stylistic exponents of a widespread contemporary enthusiasm for the theatre, which, at its other homely extreme is reflected in the play within a play in *A Midsummer Night's Dream.*   H.B.

74 The performance of Sofonisba, 1562
Fresco in the vestibule of the Teatro Olimpico
Photograph

One of a series of frescoes in the Accademicians' salone, now the vestibule of the Teatro Olimpico, documented as being in existence in 1584 (Zorzi, 1968, pp.305–7), and commemorating in its decoration the Accademia's theatrical

73

productions up to 1595. The design of the set of Trissino's *Sofonisba* (145) performed in the wooden theatre in the Basilica in 1562 is known only through the frescoes, but the architecture suggests that it represents Palladio's scheme. The actors performed in front of a scene which recalled a triumphal arch in the arrangement of the large central arch and small side openings, and more particularly the arch of the Sergii at Pola, drawn by Palladio. Another fresco representing the performance of the *Amor Costante* in 1561 (Zorzi, 1968, fig.463) shows the same set.   L.F.

75 The performance of Oedipus Rex, 1585
Fresco in the vestibule of the Teatro Olimpico
Photograph

One of a series of frescoes in the Accademicians' salone in the Teatro Olimpico. The fresco represents the theatre's inaugural production of Sophocles' *Oedipus Rex* in 1585. The actors performed on Scamozzi's enlarged stage in front of the scene, with its deep 'streets' clearly visible, and entered through the side streets.   L.F.

GIOVANNI BATISTA ALBANESI 1576–1630
76 Scene of the Teatro Olimpico, Vicenza
Pen, ink, and wash: 37.6 × 80.5 Signed: *Gio Batta Albanesi F.*
Lent by the Royal Institute of British Architects (XIII/4)

Albanesi is best known for his work as a sculptor, though his architectural activity has recently been surveyed (Puppi, 1969–70; Mantese, 1974, pp.1290–4). This handsome drawing, as Puppi notes, appears simply to be a survey of the existing building, fairly accurate, but tending to play down the contrasts of light and shade. The drawing folds where the two side walls abut the scene at right angles. A Vicentine foot of 35.4 cm is drawn at the bottom of the sheet.   H.B.

MARC'ANTONIO PALLADIO, son of Palladio
*77 Alternative solutions for the Teatro Olimpico
Pen, ink, and wash: 14.7 × 89
Lent by the Royal Institute of British Architects (XIII/5)

This is the only drawing to survive from the planning phase of the Teatro Olimpico and, given the closeness of the right-hand version to the final design, belongs to a late phase in the evolution of the project. Its chief purpose seems to be as a draft of the sculptural programme, and Palladio probably here called on Marc'Antonio because of his capacity (he worked as sculptor) as a figural draughtsman. The drawing style is quite different from Palladio's own, and a comparison with a drawing certainly by Marc'Antonio (78) leaves no doubt that this too is by him.   H.B.

MARC'ANTONIO PALLADIO, son of Palladio
78 Theoretical study of a Doric portal
Pen and ink over brown chalk: 44.7 × 29.8
Lent by the Trustees of the Chatsworth Settlement

A comparison with Marc'Antonio's signed receipts (Zorzi, 1959, fig.326) establishes beyond a doubt that this is a drawing by him. The drafting style is identical to the well known drawing of the Teatro Olimpico (77) whose authorship is hereby established. This hitherto unnoticed study for a Doric portal does not seem to be for a particular commission, but instead to set out, with the text which accompanies it, the rules for designing doric portals.   H.B.

VINCENZO SCAMOZZI 1552–1616
79 Study for the scene of the Teatro Olimpico
Pen, ink, and wash: 29.2 × 40.7
Lent by the Trustees of the Chatsworth Settlement

This study corresponds closely to the left side of the central 'street', and is skillfully contrived to provide a varied succession of receding forms. The architecture is much more ornate than anything one would expect in a real street scene of the time. This is only one of a series of drawings for the scene which Scamozzi made in 1584 (the others are in the Uffizi: Zorzi, 1965). All of them show the perspective diminution of the buildings in order to create the illusion of depth. Scamozzi

77

in his notes below the buildings distinguishes between the
houses of citizens, and the grander ones of nobles.   H.B.

DOMENICO CAMPAGNOLA (?) 1482/4 – after 1562

**80 Design for a processional standard, showing San
Vincenzo**

Pen and ink: 30.4 × 24.7
Photograph: *Gabinetto dei Disegni. Galleria degli Uffizi,*
Florence, 1769 F

Attributed by Fiocco (1939) to Pordenone, this drawing is now
generally considered to be by Campagnola (note on the
mount; oral communication A.Ballarin). It should however be
noted that the composition, and the *putto* type have points in
common with Pordenone, and that there is another drawing in
the Uffizi (1739 F) by Pordenone, which shows San Vincenzo
carrying Vicenza in one hand, and the standard in the other.
This is the normal way of representing San Vincenzo (*Il Gusto,*
1973, p.175) and the question of the purpose of the drawing

arises. The decorative frame almost certainly rules out that this
is an altarpiece design and suggests that it is for a processional
standard, to be carried in the city's frequent religious
processions, commissioned by one of the city's richer civic
bodies, for instance the College of Notaries.   H.B.

THE INTERIOR

layout

Palladio's remarks about the design of palace and villa interiors are short and to the point. He says that cellars, store rooms for firewood, larders, kitchens, servants' dining halls, laundries, bread ovens, and other service rooms should be 'somewhat underground', and out of sight (Palladio, 1570, II, pp.3–4). Similarly latrines should be tucked away where they will be neither seen nor smelt. As for the other rooms, they should be 'large, middling and small', and all conveniently connected with one another. The small rooms will serve as 'studies (*studioli*), libraries, or places to keep riding gear and other things which we need to use each day, and which should not be kept in the rooms (*camere*) where one sleeps, eats, and receives guests'. Palladio here follows contemporary usage: *camere* however richly furnished, were basically bed-sitters, where all three of these activities could take place. The likely presence of beds in all but service rooms, reception halls, and small studies or store rooms is well illustrated by Trissino's project for his town house in Vicenza: even on this ground floor plan many of the rooms have beds, which he indicates with dotted lines (149). The large rooms were called *sale*, they were usually centrally placed over the entrance hall, and unlike the *camere* do not have fireplaces. Palladio writes that they 'are used for festivities, for banquets, for stage sets for the performance of plays, for weddings, and similar amusements'. In ordinary houses and apartments something of the sala/camera/kitchen and service room hierarchy is preserved (60 and 270). But in the one room dwellings of the very poor, all the functions which in a palace were separated by stairs, vestibules, and courtyards were uncomfortably and unhygienically crowded together in a single space; dominated by the bed and the fireplace (257).

Palladio's palace for Montano Barbaran had its contents listed in full in 1592 (ASVi; Mantese, 1971–2, p.43). In addition to the kitchen, the granary above the kitchen, the cellar on the corner, the wardrobe (*salvarobba*), and various storerooms, sixteen living rooms are listed, all on the ground floor or first floor.

The sala, immediately over the vestibule, was sparsely furnished: one long table, two smaller tables, eight benches, nine chairs, four paintings. The other rooms between them contained thirteen bed-steads (*lettiere*), most of them clearly four-posters, six other beds, and a variety of chairs, seven tables, trunks, chests, and boxes. In addition to the four paintings in the sala, there were nine others, some in gilt frames, including, rather oddly deposited in the granary along with a grain measure and a grain shovel, 'a large gilded (i.e. gold framed?) painting of the Madonna'. In the kitchen, alongside the pots and pans, were shovels for taking the bread out of the oven, a pestle and mortar, and three bed-warmers, which would have been similar to those still to be seen today in antique shops. There was only one writing desk (it contained papers), presumably Montano Barbaran's, in a first floor room leading off the loggia. This room also contained two bedsteads and a bed. Smaller items included six pairs of firedogs, of which those described as 'a pair of large bronze fire dogs' may well have been of the same elaborate type as those exhibited here (111). There were sixteen canopies of rich fabrics for the four posters, various tapestries and wall hangings, eight green cloth hangings for door openings, one hundred and twenty tablecloths of various sorts (sixteen of them dirty), and one hundred and fifty sheets. In addition to larger pieces, including eight candlesticks, there were '181 large and small pieces of maiolica . . . which majolica has the Barbaran arms', in the same way as pieces exhibited here carry the arms of the families for whom they were made (99 and 101). Dinner guests of course assessed their host's dinner service as well as his food. Fabio Monza records in his diary 'I dined with the Capitanio (of Vicenza) together with many other nobles and officials; the dinner service was of the most beautiful maiolica, the food not in great quantity, but excellent, with things done in sauce, including tasty little partridges' (Monza, 1888, p.44). Two flutes seem to be the only sign that remained of Montano's musical interests (he had died four years earlier).

The palace's nineteen beds are probably not a guide to the number of people who actually slept in it (in 1546, for example, only twelve people, including servants, lived in the Villa Godi). Instead the large number of beds represents a very necessary capacity to entertain not only friends from other cities, but if need be, distinguished visitors. Marzari (1591) records the

The salone at Palazzo Valmarana

Just as processions and ceremonies, for which public buildi[ng] and public squares provided the setting, were the means [of] expressing the splendour of the state or the city, and the pa[r]ticipation in its life of the various groups which sustained it, [so] private festivities, for which palaces were the setting, were t[he] means for families to celebrate their own solidarity, th[eir] alliances with other families, and display their position with[in] local society. Hence the need for sale which 'should have gr[eat] capacity: so that a great number of people can conveniently [be] there, and see what is happening' (Palladio, 1570, I, p.52). [In] Vicenza the most spectacular (and influential) private entertai[n]ment in Palladio's time was probably the play performed [in] 1539 in a temporary theatre designed by Serlio and erected [in] the cortile of the palazzo Colleoni-Porto (Zorzi, 1969, pp.25[0-] 251). Much more modestly Fabio Monza borrowed som[e] tapestries from a friend to decorate his sala, on the occasion [of] his daughter-in-law's giving birth to a son (Monza, 1888, p.31[).] The most usual form of private celebration was a banquet, oft[en] followed by a ball. Banquets were usually in the sala, with t[he] guests seated at a long table. Veronese's *Marriage at Cana* (249) [is] a somewhat exaggeratedly lavish rendering of a contemporar[y] banquet, though accurate as regards the type of wine glass[es] (97), the multiplicity of dishes on the table, and the presence [of] musicians. According to a highly experienced organiser [of] princely and aristocratic banquets, who had arranged banque[ts] for Ottavio and Giulio Thiene among many others, the lon[g] table should be placed at least six feet from the walls and at lea[st] nine from the sideboards (*credenze*) and wine waiters' table[s] (Rossetti, 1584). He is insistent on what constitutes a banquet. [It] must have five courses: one cold, two hot, one of fruit, then th[e] guests washed their hands, and the upper tablecloth was re[-] moved, revealing another, before the final course of swee[t] meats (*confetture*), a Venetian speciality, was served. Thus at on[e] of the five banquets with which Giulio Thiene, Conte d[i] Scandiano, celebrated his wedding 'once the upper cloth, which[h] was embroidered with flowers had been lifted, and people ha[d] washed their hands, another tablecloth, worked with flower[s] and little birds was revealed' (*ibid*, p.54). Each course consiste[d] of a dozen or more different dishes, so that eggs, salad, sparrow[s] fried with oranges, *salsa verde* with a little garlic, octopus an[d] oysters in sauce, served on bread was only a part of one cours[e] (*ibid*, p.117). Rossetti recommends that retiring rooms, fitte[d] out with 'beds, tables and urinals' should be prepared off th[e]

entertainment by Guido Piovene of the Duke of Savoy in 1566, and 'a few months ago', of the Duke of Mantua and the Marquess of Monferrato, as well as the hospitality offered by Leonardo Valmarana to the Empress in 1581. Both the Palazzo Piovene (54) and the Palazzo Valmarana were designed by Palladio and their grandeur assumes a functional aspect when seen in relation to the entertainment of these royal personages, who were the patrons and employers of the palace owners. The same applies to the rich furnishings. 'What shall I say', writes Maganza of Leonardo Valmarana's palace, 'of so many rooms finely adorned with tapestries, seats, and richly decorated beds? Without counting those banquets which you have given at your own expense, and so abundantly' (Zorzi, 1964, p.251).

The kitchen at the Villa Godi

The Sala at Villa Poiana

dining hall, and advised tight security measures for the silver. He also recommends, in calculating the number of plates needed, a 20 per cent allowance for breakages and mishaps. After dinner the room would be cleared, and as Rossetti puts it 'one danced eternally'. In preparation for such occasions Fabio Monza records that 'the dancing master has been here today to teach dancing for the first time to my daughter Margherita' (Monza, 1888, p.29), and books on dancing were also available (Caroso, 1581). A ball with musicians on a raised platform, is shown in a painting exhibited here (81).

Ordinary meals were obviously much simpler, and were served at the round or square tables which were present in most of the rooms in a palace, and were also used for playing cards and board games (107). Meals in the garden or in the country were common (Rossetti describes how they should be organised) and light tables, like the beautiful one exhibited here (88), would be used on such occasions.

Alongside the banquets and receptions one should not forget the private and everyday events which took place in palaces and villas: a youth of the family standing in the doorway, watching people go by (Bandello, 1740, I, p.113); his lawyer brother coming out of the ground floor room which he used as his office (*ibid*, p.116); the idle Brescian nobles dropping in on one another to play cards and board games; callers banging on the splendid door knockers (112) when the main door was closed; Teodoro Thiene writing out his will in his study at his villa at Cicogna, designed by Palladio (Zorzi, 1968, p.104); Polissena Monza giving birth with difficulty in the middle of the night, without the aid of midwives (Monza, 1888, p.31); Odoardo Thiene, in the presence of his brother Teodoro, his notary Pietro Cogollo, and his most trusted intimates, Palladio and Maganza among them, putting his affairs in order before departing for ever for Protestant lands (Zorzi, 1968, p.104).

Palladio designed villas and palaces. In consultation with his patrons he gave them rooms of useful sizes, conveniently related to one another. He designed internal doorways, and often the fireplaces. He gave rooms different sorts of vaults, or a beam ceiling in place of a vault, and he concerned himself with floor treatments. But he did not, as far as one knows, design their interior decoration, though the painted architectural

scheme at Poiana, for instance, not so different from Palladio 'Corinthian hall' (Palladio, 1570, II, p.40) could well ha been the result of consultation between painters and architect In the famous case of the Veronese frescoes in the Vil Maser, Palladio had probably no part in the choice of th scheme (Wolters, 1968; Puppi, 1973–II, pp.315–6). In this o instance Palladio in describing the building omits his usual bri but eulogistic mention of the artists who worked on the decor tion. But he was not a neo-classical artist, intent on imposing completely uniform style on architecture, decoration an furnishings. The decoration of interiors with stucco and fresco was a specialised matter, which he seems (or probably mo accurately, his patrons seem) to have been content to leave, pe haps after consultation, in the hands of the specialists, with man of whom he had amicable contacts over many years, fo instance with Vittoria (182), the elder Maganza (7), Indi (183), Canera, Brusasorci (184), Fasolo, Zelotti (186), an Veronese (176 and 249). And there are no Palladian candlestick or sideboards, at least before the eighteenth century. Palladio buildings were decorated and furnished in the decorativ language of the time, which is rich, flexible, surprisingl uniform up and down Italy, and applicable to the most divers objects, from door-knockers (112, 113, 114) and bellows (116 to chairs (89), and even the title page of Palladio's own boo on architecture (cf. Shearman, 1967). Palladio probably felt no the slightest inconsistency in the presence (in the right place, tha is not as dominant elements) of contemporary motifs alongsid his own more limited and rigorous architectural vocabulary He incorporates modish cartouches and stucco work on th façades of Palazzo Valmarana, Palazzo Barbaran, and th Loggia del Capitaniato, and any attempt to set up anachron istic oppositions between a 'Palladian' style, and a 'Mannerist decorative style, or to regard these elements as intrusions on th purity of Palladio's concepts, perpetrated by irrepressible stucc artists, can be dispelled by reference to drawings in whic Palladio from the start provides for such decorative episode within the framework of his overall design.   H.B.

LODEWYCK TOEPUT, called POZZOSERRATO C.1550–C.1610

81 A ball in a palace
Canvas: 61.5 × 108.5
Lent by Julius H. Weitzner

Prof. A. Ballarin (orally) has suggested the name of Pozzoserrato, in his early Veneto period, shortly after 1582 the date of his arrival in Treviso, and at the same time as the *Autumn* in the National Gallery of Prague (Ballarin, 1969, pp. 58–63). The ball takes place in what appears to be the central hall of a Venetian palace. There is a beam roof, windows with circular panes (84), and an ornate lantern hangs from the ceiling (82). Men and women sit in different parts of the hall and the orchestra plays on a raised platform. The ornately dressed couple in the foreground could be recently married (balls were held to celebrate weddings), and the dancing couples are shown in attitudes which recall G. Franco's engravings for F. Caroso's *Il ballarino*, a treatise on dancing published in Venice in 1581. L.F.

*82 Lantern
Italian (Venetian) c.1570
Wood: h.213, diam.86.3
Lent by the Victoria and Albert Museum (7225–1860)

The lantern of carved wood is decorated with cartouches, satyrs and cupids in full relief, and painted in flesh tints. It was originally fitted with glass panels and may well have contained an oil lamp. It is said to have come from the Palazzo Gradenigo and it is very similar to the lamp lighting the hall in Pozzoserrato's Ball (81). L.F.

SCHOOL OF JACOPO TINTORETTO 1518–94
*83 The Wise and Foolish Virgins
Canvas: 87 × 98
Lent by the National Trust (Bearsted Collection, Upton House)

The theme is the admonitory parable of the coming of the Kingdom of Heaven (Matthew 25: 1–13). Three versions of this painting are known. Pallucchini (1950, p.110) considered the copy in the Boymans van Beuningen Museum, Rotterdam (cf. *Catalogus*, 1962, p.140, no.2567) as the prototype and the copy in the Johnson Collection, Philadelphia (cf. Sweeny, 1966, p.76, no.211) as a later school product; apparently he was unaware of the Upton house version, which is architecturally the most ambitious of the three and would seem to share a date of 1546–9 with the version in Rotterdam (Pallucchini, *loc. cit.*). One copy of this painting belonged to the Vicentine noble family of Gualdo, whose collection of art was considerable (Puppi, 1972, p.58). The architectural setting closely reflects that of contemporary Venetian or Veneto palaces. The centrally placed sala, with its richly decorated wooden ceiling and large windows with circular panes (84) is located immediately above the entrance vestibule. As at the Palazzo Valmarana a projecting balcony with an iron railing overlooks the cortile. The kitchen is shown here to one side on the ground floor. The palace is lit by torches, lamps, and candles, and the fire risk, especially in the wooden ceilinged upper rooms, needs no comment. B.B., H.B.

*84 Window pane
Italian, Venetian, probably sixteenth century
Spun glass: diam. 14
Lent by the Victoria and Albert Museum (5233–1901)

This is said to have come from a window in the Baptistery of St Mark's, Venice. Venetian windows were made from roundels of this type, called *rui* (81 and 83). L.F.

GIORGIO VASARI 1511–74
*85 An allegory of Faith
Panel: 78.7 × 172.7
Private collection

Faith is baptising a child and holding a cross. This is one of nine panels from a ceiling in the Palazzo Corner Spinelli on the Grand Canal, a palace of the late fifteenth century modernised internally by Sanmicheli. Vasari was in Venice in 1541–2 (though he probably did not meet Palladio until 1566), and in April 1542 was commissioned to decorate the ceiling (Schulz, 1961, pp.507–11). His design follows a North Italian tradition of illusionistic ceiling painting established by Giulio Romano in the Sala di Psiche in the Palazzo Te in Mantua and by Pordenone's ceiling in the Sala dei Pregadi in the Ducal Palace in Venice (1535–8), destroyed by fire in 1577. These ceilings consisted of symmetrically arranged panels around a central

82

83

85

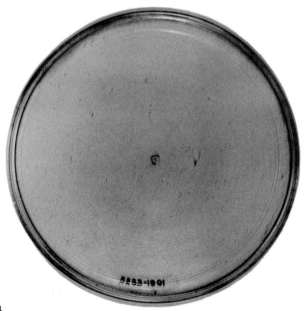

84

87

88

square or lozenge, set into a rich carved ceiling frame. Vasari's figures, shown in foreshortening, fill the picture frame, and the backgrounds are unified. This type of ceiling set the fashion for many other sixteenth-century ceilings in Venice and the Veneto, including, for instance the ceiling of the salone of Palladio's palace for Montano Barbaran and the reconstructed Sala dei Pregadi in the Ducal Palace (280). L.F.

LAMBERT SUSTRIS C.1515–95

86 Solomon and the Queen of Sheba
Canvas: 78 × 185
Lent by the National Gallery

The architecture is the dominant element in the composition, and in this respect the painting belongs to a Venetian tradition, established, on the one hand, by Titian's *Presentation of the Virgin* for the Scuola della Carità and, on the other, by Paris Bordone and Tintoretto on the basis of the Tragic Scene, published in Serlio's Book II (cf. Gould, 1962, and 1975, pp.313–4). Sustris has varied the usual scenographic formula by using a temple portico seen in perspective rather than a street with buildings converging in the distance. The pantheonic porch and stuccoed decoration of the temple reflect a taste close to Palladio's in the Tempietto at Maser. The attribution to Sustris by Berenson (1957, I, p.168) has been reconfirmed by Ballarin, who places the painting in the early 1560s, contemporary with *The Archangel and Tobias* in Vienna and prior to the *Diana and Acteon* at Christ Church, Oxford (1962, p.80, no.33). B.B.

*87 Sideboard
Italian c.1550
Carved walnut: 109 × 190.5 × 63.5
Lent by the Victoria and Albert Museum (1375–1904)

Known as a credenza, there are two drawers above and cupboards with shelves below. L.F.

*88 Folding table
Italian, sixteenth century
Wood inlaid with ivory: 79 × 153·5 × 92
Lent by the Victoria and Albert Museum (236–1869)

This type of table was used for travelling, or card games and picnics. L.F.

89 Chair
Italian c.1550
Walnut: 101 × 51.4 × 42
Prov: Spitzer Collection
Lent by the Victoria and Albert Museum (W.104–1910)

This is a carved sgabello chair with a tapering back. The arms may be those of the Della Rovere family. L.F.

90 Armchair
Italian second half 16th century
Walnut: 123 × 60.4 × 43
Lent by the Victoria and Albert Museum (323–1894)

The armchair has a gilded and embossed leather back and seat, and is trimmed with silk fringe fixed with gilt-headed nails. On the left and right of the back are two embossed figures representing Geometry and Astrology. L.F.

91 Cross-framed folding armchair
Italian 16th century
Carved walnut: 104 × 70
Lent by the Victoria and Albert Museum (7185–1860)

This type of chair was used as a travelling chair, generally for events in gardens or in the country. It appears frequently in paintings of such scenes. L.F.

92 Cassone
Italian 16th century
Wood picked out with gold: 71 × 173 × 56
Lent by the Victoria and Albert Museum (7706–1861)

The chest is carved in high relief with allegorical figures of Spring and Summer. The coat of arms has not been identified. L.F.

93 Cypress chest
Venetian c.1530
Cypress wood: 43 × 104 × 57
Lent by the Victoria and Albert Museum (4886–1858)

This travelling chest is decorated with designs of mythological scenes in inkwork (incised lines are filled with mastic). These ink work chests are typical Venetian products, which were exported all over Europe. L.F.

94 Pair of candelabra
Italian 16th century
Gilded wood: 136 × 46
Lent by the Victoria and Albert Museum (22 & 22a–1821)

95 Damask
Italian 16th century
Red and yellow silk: 95.3 × 101.6
Lent by the Victoria and Albert Museum (474–1884)

The pattern, which is not a full repeat, represents a vase and probably flowers with a crown. It was a popular pattern in the Renaissance, and here it is associated with plant forms in a decorative cartouche. The design is large scale and could be for a wall hanging, though such designs were not uncommon in dress fabrics. L.F.

96 Lampas
Italian 16th century
Red, yellow and white silk: 146.1 × 55.9
Lent by the Victoria and Albert Museum (426–1893)

This is a dress fabric in a renaissance design of flowering plants within an ogival lattice with leaf forms. L.F.

*97 Drinking glass
Venetian second half 16th century
Glass: diam.22.3
Inscribed on the base: S.ALFONS GALARA . . . CAP DE JUSTIA.
Lent by the Victoria and Albert Museum (C215–1936)

97

102

This glass known as a tazza, has traces of gold decoration and a hollow blown lion's mask stem, with the name of its owner (?) on the base. There are glasses of this type in Veronese's *Marriage at Cana* (249). L.F.

98 Goblet
Venetian Second half of 16th century
Glass: h.18.4
Lent by the Victoria and Albert Museum (C214–1936)

The goblet has traces of gilding and has a hollow blown lion's mask stem. L.F.

99 Base of a glass dish
Venetian c.1522
Enamelled glass: diam.8.9
Lent by the Victoria and Albert Museum (C170–1936)

The arms of Doge Antonio Grimani, 1521–3 with the Ducal beretta are enamelled in the centre of the dish. This would have formed part of a service used by the Doge, and follows the standard practice of displaying family arms on tableware. L.F.

100 Standing dish
Italian Venetian early 16th century
Glass: diam.22.3
Lent by the Victoria and Albert Museum (175–1936)

The plate has a border in etched gold dotted with enamel. The arms in the centre have not been identified. L.F.

101 Plate
Italian Faenza c.1530
Mark: the firewheel of the Casa Pirota workshop
Maiolica tin glaze: diam.24.2
Lent by the Victoria and Albert Museum (1800–1855)

The plate is painted in dark blue, yellow, orange, copper green, and white. In the centre are the arms of the Giustiniani, and the rim is decorated with a symmetrical pattern of cherubs, paired dolfins and wings in a foliate scroll (Rackham, 1940, no.283). L.F.

*102 Dish
Italian Padua c.1550
Maiolica tin glaze: diam.27.5
Lent by the Victoria and Albert Museum (1750–1855)

In the centre there are the arms of the Muglia or de Mula family of Venice. The rim is decorated with blue and white plant forms within a narrow border of arabesques. L.F.

103 Dish
Venetian c.1550
Maiolica tin glaze: diam.45.5
Attributed to the workshop of Domenigo da Venezia
Lent by the Victoria and Albert Museum (1768–1855)

The dish is painted with blue, yellow, brown, copper green, manganese purple and opaque white. This beautiful dish is decorated with clusters of fruit surrounding a satyr's mask. On the back there is a sketch in blue of a Venetian lady standing by a tree (Rackham, 1940, no.970). L.F.

104 Dish
Italian Paduan, 1550–60
Maiolica tin glaze: diam.29.2
Lent by the Victoria and Albert Museum (1749–1855)

The dish is painted in blue, yellow, brown, copper green, manganese purple and opaque white. In the middle there is a camel surrounded by flowers on coiled stems (Rackham, 1940, no.993). L.F.

105 Small bowl
Italian c.1500–20
Sgraffito: h.5.5, diam.13
Lent by the Victoria and Albert Museum (C404–1914)

The bowl is painted in copper green, yellow and manganese purple. The inside is decorated to simulate a five-petalled flower with foliage; the outside is left plain (Rackham, 1940, no.1393). L.F.

106 Drug pot
Italian Padua 16th century
Sgraffito: diam.26.7, h.29.2
Lent by the Victoria and Albert Museum (4621–1858)

The design painted in copper green, and in relief represents a wide band of foliage in a scroll pattern (Rackham, 1940, no.1404). L.F.

*107 Games board
Italian Venetian c.1570
Ebony inlaid with lapis lazuli: 48.5 × 28 × 2.5
Lent by the Victoria and Albert Museum (W.9–1972)

One half of a double-sided games board: one side for chess, and the other for backgammon. The missing half would have had the other half of the backgammon board on the inside and a 'Nine Men's Morris' board on the outside. The panels are inlaid with an alternating design in two-colour lapis lazuli (blue white, and dark blue-gold). The gold moresque designs recall the decoration of the damascened drawing set (155). L.F.

108 Candlestick
Venetian late 16th or early 17th century
Bronze: h.22.6
Prov: Jules Soulages, Toulouse
Lent by the Victoria and Albert Museum (560–1865)

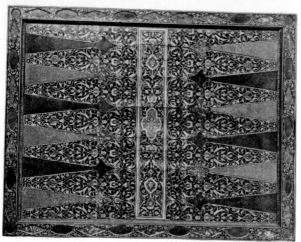

107

An elaborate perfume-burner in the Walker Art Gallery, Liverpool (no.6236), of which the base rests on three harpies and the raised cover is supported on three kneeling boys, decisively connects the candlestick (one of a pair in the Museum) with a more common class of candlestick supported on three harpies. For this latter type, with extensive literature, see Pope-Hennessy (1965, no.486). A pair of the harpy type of candlesticks with sockets identical to that of the present candlestick, acquired together with it from the Soulages Collection, are in the Museum. The harpy candlesticks are commonly assigned to the workshop of Niccolo Roccatagliata (active at Venice 1593–1636), and both they and the rarer kneeling boy type relate directly to his documented work. If it may be assumed that Roccatagliata's shop was geared to the production of such minor artefacts, both types are likely to have been made there. A second pair is in the Ashmolean Museum (Fortnum Collection).   A.R.

109 Candlestick

Paduan or Tridentine mid-16th century
Bronze: h.22.7
Prov: George Salting
Lent by the Victoria and Albert Museum (M691–1910)

The candlestick is of highly unusual design. A variant pair with the same stem, but lacking the relief around the base, were

formerly in the Morgan Collection (Bode, 1910, no.199, pl.CXXXVI, as Venetian, first half of the sixteenth century). The masks and other decorative motifs on the stem are closely related to those which appear on bronze *secchielli* at Trento, one of them with an *impresa* of Bernardo Cles, Bishop of Trento (d.1539), established by Venturi (1907, pp.386–7), Gerola (1934, pp.150–1) and Cessi (1967) as the work of Vincenzo and Gian Girolamo Grandi. The relief of a marine triumph on the base, which recalls those on certain *pastiglia* boxes of the second quarter of the sixteenth century, one of which bears the arms and *imprese* of Cles, is consistent in style with marble reliefs on the *cantoria* in S.Maria Maggiore, Trento, carved by the Grandi in 1532–42. It is likely that the candlestick was made in the shop of the Grandi either at Trento in 1532–42 or at Padua thereafter.   A.R.

STUDIO OF ALESSANDRO VITTORIA 1525–1608

110 Jupiter and Juno

Bronze: h.33 (each)
Lent by the Victoria and Albert Museum (A18, 19–1961)

The figure of Jupiter is one of numerous copies of a Vittoria model, of which the finest copy is that in the Kunsthistorisches Museum, Vienna (Planiscig, 1921, p.475). In pose the Jupiter reflects two of Sansovino's Loggetta figures (Apollo and Mercury), and is similar to the statuette of St Thomas which Vittoria made for Tommaso Rangone about 1566 (Gerola, 1924–5, pp.343–4). Stylistically the Jupiter seems also to belong to the early 1560s.
The Juno appears to be a work of the 1580s, a time in which the sculptor's treatment of drapery and figure was deeply imbued with the style of Parmigianino. Like the Jupiter, the figure of Juno exists in numerous copies, the finest being the one in the Museo Civico, Padua (Planiscig, 1921, pp.492–3). In pose and drapery, the Juno recalls the figure of Faith from the tomb of Domenico Bollani, now in the Museo Civico, Brescia (Cessi, 1962, pl.5) and finished by 1578. It also has strong affinities with the Daniel on one of Vittoria's most important works, the altar of the Mercers in San Giuliano, Venice, which was in its final stages by 1584 (Predelli, 1908, p.193). Both figures were originally intended to decorate firedogs. Dr Manfred Leithe-Jasper has drawn attention to a pair of firedogs in the National Maritime Museum, Greenwich, which still are

surmounted by a Jupiter and Juno modelled after Vittoria's figures (oral communication, 1975). **B.B.**

*III   Pair of andirons (five dogs)
Venetian first quarter of the 17th century
Bronze: h.116 and 117.5
Prov: Jules Soulages, Toulouse
Lent by the Victoria and Albert Museum (8431, 8431a–1863)

The bases bear the arms of Barbaro of Venice. The surmounting statuettes of Adonis (or Meleager) and Venus (or Atalanta) recur as a pair on andiron bases of different design in the Ca' d'Oro, Venice and others sold in Paris in 1965 (Palais Gallièra, Lot 413), and without their bases in the Museo Civico, Padua and the Palazzo Venezia, Rome; these last together with a variant pair with the attributes of Apollo and Diana from a companion set of andirons. Ascriptions by Planiscig to

Girolamo Campagna (d.1625) of the Venus (1919, p.134, no.205; withdrawn, 1921, pp.566–8, in favour of Aspetti) and of the Adonis (1921, p.546) are supported by Santangelo (1954, p.45) and Pope-Hennessy (1961, no.159) and, with reserve, by Rossi (1968, p.46) and Marchiori (1971, pp.39–40, nos.161–4). The Adonis closely resembles Campagna's marble St Lawrence in S. Lorenzo, Venice (1615–8), and the Venus is analogous to an andiron figure of Galatea inscribed I.C. (Palais Gallièra, 1965, Lot 412). Both must derive from late models by Campagna. **A.R.**

112   Doorknocker
Venetian 1595–1605
Bronze: 33 × 27.5
Prov: Dr W.L.Hildburgh
Lent by the Victoria and Albert Museum (M473–1956)

The knocker, which is hitherto unpublished, bears in the central cartouche the arms of Grimani of Venice surmounted by a Doge's cap. Marino Grimani was Doge from 1595 to 1605, and the knocker must therefore have been made between these years. The design does not relate significantly to any other known type of Venetian knocker. **A.R.**

113   Doorknocker
Venetian third quarter of the 16th century
Bronze: 37 × 32.5
Prov: Jules Soulages, Toulouse
Lent by the Victoria and Albert Museum (573–1865)

The design is unusually elaborate. Simpler knockers of closely related design occur, as noted by Fortnum (1876, p.158) in both Emilia and Venice. Two such were recorded by Grevenbroeck in Venice (1758, pls. 33, 44), and examples closely related to these in the Victoria and Albert Museum could well have been made in the same workshop as the present knocker. As noted by Weihrauch (1967, pp.152–4) the design depends from nereid sarcophagi and both this knocker and another of simpler design in the Beit Collection (from a house at Padua, Bode, 1913, no.261: other versions Victoria and Albert Museum, no.555–1877; Bologna, Palazzo del Governo, Marchetti, 1969, p.35; formerly Venice, Palazzo Bragadin, Grevenbroeck, 1758, pl.8) are associable with a drawing in Munich ascribed to

114

115

known knocker of the same design (private collection, Siena) also has a Brescian provenance. That the knocker is, however, likely to be of Venetian, rather than Brescian, origin is suggested by the fact that one of the same design was recorded by Grevenbroeck on a house in Venice (1758, pl.4). The knocker in the British Museum bears the inscribed letters G.C. The general style of the knocker, which is of highly individual design, is consistent with the sculptural work of Girolamo Campagna around the first decade of the seventeenth century, and it is not impossible that it derives from a design by him.   A.R.

*115 Head of a Jubilee hammer
North Italian 1550
Bronze: l.6
Prov: Earl of Cadogan
Lent by the Victoria and Albert Museum (136–1865)

In Jubilee years the sealed door of St Peter's was opened by the Pope with a silver hammer and those of the other three basilicas by specially deputed cardinals with bronze hammers. Very few such hammers survive. One in the Louvre bears the Borgia arms and appears to have been used by Cardinal Giovanni Borgia at the Jubilee of 1500 (Houston, 1966, p.106, no.76). Another of the same basic design, but more elaborate (private collection, New York), bears the arms of Marcello Cervini (Cardinal from 1539; Pope, as Marcellus II, in 1555), and would have been used at the Jubilee of 1550. These two were probably made in Rome. The present example bears the arms of the Venetian Cardinal Andrea Cornaro, Bishop of Brescia, 1543–51, and must also have been made for the Jubilee of 1550. It is of radically different design from the other two, and was probably produced in a North Italian (possibly Venetian) workshop.   A.R.

116 Bellows
Venetian late 16th century
Wood, leather and bronze: 76 × 28
Lent by the Victoria and Albert Museum (7698–1861)

The bellows bear the arms of the Giustiniani and Rossi families of Venice (oral communication, A.R.).

the circle of Sansovino. Weihrauch ascribes the present knocker to Danese Cattaneo (d.1573), and it does seem likely that it was made in Venice in the third quarter of the sixteenth century.   A.R.

114 Doorknocker
Venetian early 17th century
Bronze: 36 × 27.5
Prov: a Martinengo palace in Brescia; John Webb
Lent by the Victoria and Albert Museum (588–1853)

Acquired in Brescia before 1853, the knocker is stated by Fortnum (1876, pp.158–9) to have come from 'one valve of the huge *portone* of the Palazzo Martinengo-dobblo . . .' This house can no longer be identified. In the centre is an escutcheon from which the arms have been erased, perhaps on change of ownership of the palace. The companion knocker from the other valve of the same door, of identical design and with similarly erased arms, is now in the British Museum (Waddesdon Bequest; Read, 1927, p.1, no.4). The only other

120

117 Handbell

Possibly Brescian, second half of the sixteenth century
Bell-metal: h.11
Prov: Sangiorgi, Rome; Alfred William Hearns
Lent by the Victoria and Albert Museum (M28–1923)

The arms have been identified as those of Rossi of Venice, but the bends are sinister instead of dexter, and the identification is not conclusive. The decoration includes a peculiar leaf motif. The same motif occurs on a group of candlesticks and oil-lamps of bell-metal identified by Planiscig (1932) as the work of a founder named Gasparo on the strength of one such candlestick, now in the Museo Poldi-Pezzoli, Milan, signed

'GASPAR' and dated 1551. Several other handbells closely similar in design to the present bell carry the same distinctive leaf motif, and all must be the work of the same founder. One of these, in the Museo del Castello Sforzesco, Milan, is dated 1589, giving the latest known date for this foundry. Gasparo was assumed by Planiscig to have been Venetian, but an inscription on the bell in Milan associates it with Brescia. In view of the eccentric design of these pieces compared with known products of Venetian foundries of the period it may well be that Gasparo worked in Brescia. The tassel is a modern replacement. A bell with a tassel is shown on the table in Raphael's Uffizi *Portrait of Pope Leo X*.   A.R.

18 Handbell

Venetian mid-16th century
Bell-metal: h.9
Prov: Dr W.L.Hildburgh
Lent by the Victoria and Albert Museum (M199–1938)

The bell carries engraved around the top the appropriate inscription 'PVLSV MEO SERVOS VOCO'. In two cartouches on the top surface are twice engraved the letters 'A.M.', presumably the initials of the original owner. The arms, which appear twice on the flanks, have not been identified. Other, apparently Venetian, handbells with the same or a similar inscription cast in relief do not seem to be from the same foundry. Although the decoration of this bell is somewhat unusual, it is of a generally Venetian character.   A.R.

19 Mortar with pestle

Italian first half of the 16th century
Bell-metal: h.13.7
Lent by the Victoria and Albert Museum (M28, 28a–1938)

The mortar is of exceptionally high quality. A poorly cast mortar with major casting flaws with an identical band of vine scroll, clearly from the same foundry, is in the Columbia Museum of Art (Pope-Hennessy, 1965, no.579, fig.603).   A.R.

BERNARDO LICINIO C.1489–C.1560

120 A painter and his pupils

Canvas: 82.5 × 127
Lent by the Duke of Northumberland

The accepted attribution to Licinio derives from the similarity between this painting and *The portrait of a family* in a signed and dated (1537) work by Licinio in the Borghese Gallery, Rome. The young man on the right of the Borghese group holding a statue is the same as the young man in this painting, as is the statue.

It is well known that the drawing of ancient works of art was one of the basic trainings for sixteenth-century artists, but it is sometimes forgotten that much of the material copied and studied, was not in Rome, but actually in the studio. Artists collected antique fragments, casts after ancient sculpture, gems, coins, drawings, engravings of ancient and modern classics, collections of inscriptions and small bronzes, as a source of motifs for use in their own works, and as material which the pupils could draw (Low, 1973). Thus the Vicentine artist Valerio Belli (181) in his will of 1546 (Mantese, 1964, p.639) mentions drawings after the antique, casts, bronzes and ancient and modern sculpture, and Palladio's friend Danese Cattaneo, in his will of 1572, left his pupil Gerolamo Campagna, all his casts and drawings (Rigoni, 1970, p.232).   L.F., H.B.

Medals

Roman coins, above all those of the Roman emperors, systematically collected from the time of Petrarch onwards, provided the model of relief portraits in bronze, but for the Renaissance the medal soon became more than a likeness, conveying something of the character and personal attributes of the subject (Hill, 1912, pp.1–25). As most medals were larger than coins, they allowed scope for the artist's talent while imposing the discipline of a compact medium. From the time of Pisanello to the sixteenth century, medals were cast from a wax mould; struck medals, produced from dies in the same way as coins, began to be favoured from the sixteenth century for their greater facility of production (Babelon, 1927, pp.63–72).

Medals often commemorated events, like the founding of San Francesco della Vigna by Andrea Gritti (130) or the Palazzo Valmarana by Isabella Valmarana, as well as more personal occasions like the eightieth birthday of Doge Hieronimo Priuli (123). Whether exchanged by friends or distributed by princes, medals were a sort of artistic visiting card, capable of almost indefinite reproduction. The sculptor Alessandro Vittoria produced a number of medals, among the best being that of Pietro Aretino (127). Two of his medals exhibited here deserve special mention. The double medal of Vittoria and Bernadino India (125) probably dates from 1552, when both artists worked on the decoration of Palazzo Thiene in Vicenza (Cessi, 1960, pp.62–4). During the same stay in Vicenza, Vittoria also made a set of medals of the children of Marc'Antonio Thiene and that of Caterina Chiericati (126), praised in a letter by Pietro Aretino (Cessi, 1960, pp.50, 94–5).

Also exhibited here is the medal of a prominent Vicentine figure, the legalist Aurelio dall'Acqua (121), who commissioned from the Pedemuro workshop the magnificent High Altar of the Cathedral (Marzari, 1591, p.163; Puppi, 1973, p.237). B.B.

121 Obverse: Aurelio dall'Acqua in profile to the left. Around, MAGN·AVRELIVS·AB·AQVA·VICENTINVS IVRISCONSVLTVS· EXCEL·COMES·PAL·ET·EQVES
Reverse: Justice seated, holds a balance. Around, IN·MEMORIA·AETERNA·ERIT·IVSTVS·OP·IV·TVR·
By the amateur medalist and doctor of laws, Giulio della Torre.
Bronze: diam. 11.8
Lit: Armand, 1883, I, p.130, no.2
Lent by the Victoria and Albert Museum (7133–1860)

122 Obverse: Andrea Gritti (1523–38), wearing ducal robes and crown, in profile to the right. Around,
ANDREAS·GRITI·DVX·VENETIAR.
Without reverse.
Bronze: diam. 11.6
Lit: Armand, 1883, II, p.173, no.1.
Lent by the Victoria and Albert Museum (311–1910, (A))

123 Obverse: Doge Hieronimo Priuli (1559–67) in profile to the right. Around, HIERONIMVS·PRIOL·VENE·DVX·ANO·P·VIII· AE·LXXX· and, in the field, 1566.
Reverse: Two classically draped figures embrace. Around, IVSTITIA ET PAX OSCOLATE SVT.
Lead: diam. 9.9
Lit: Armand, 1883, II, p.225, no.3; Hill-Pollard, 1967, p.95, no.498 with a different reverse).
Lent by the British Museum (Box 31)

124 Obverse: Doge Marcantonio Trevisan (1553–4) in profile to the right. Around, MARCVS·ANT·TRIVISANO·DVX·V·
Reverse: Within a decorated border, the words, MARCVS ANTONIVS TRIVIXANO DEI GRATIA DVX VENETIARVM ET C. VIXIT ANO·I IN PRINCIPATV·OBIT·MDLIIII·
Bronze: diam. 6.3
Lit: Armand, 1883, II, p.224, no.1; Hill-Pollard, 1967, p.95, no.504.
Lent by the British Museum (Box 30)

125 Obverse: Alessandro Vittoria (1525–1608) in profile to the right. Around, ALEXANDER·VICTORIA·SCVLPTOR·
Reverse: Bernardino India (c.1528–90) in profile to the left. Around, BERNARDINVS·INDIVS·PICTOR·V·
By Alessandro Vittoria.
Bronze: diam. 5.3
Lit: Armand, 1883, III, p.118, B; II, p.274, no.5 as two medals
Lent by the British Museum (726–92)

126 Obverse: Catterina Chiericati in profile to the right. Around, CATTERINA·CHIERIGAT· and, in smaller letters, the initials A·V
Without reverse.
Bronze: diam. 5.3
Lit: Armand, 1883, II, p.298, no.2; Cessi, 1960–1, p.50.
Lent by the British Museum (725–92)

127 Obverse: Pietro Aretino (1492–1556) in profile to the right. Around, ·DIVIVS·PETRVS·ARETINVS·
Reverse: Aretino enthroned on left receives tribute from a warrior and other figures. Around, I PRINCIPI TRIBVTATI DA I POPVLI·IL SERVO LORO TRIBVTANO·
By Alessandro Vittoria.
Bronze: diam. 5.7
Lit: Armand, 1883, II, p.297, no.1; Cessi. 1960–I, pp.58–9.
Lent by the British Museum (724–92)

128 Obverse: Jacopo Sansovino (1486–1570) in profile to the right Around, IACOPVS SANSOVINVS SCVLPTOR·ET ARCHITECT.
By Lodovico Leoni.
Lead: diam. 6.3
Lit: Armand, 1883, I, p.252, no.7.
Lent by the Victoria and Albert Museum (0983–1860)

129 Obverse: Cardinal Pietro Bembo (1470–1547) in profile to the right. Around, PETRI BEMBI CAR·
Reverse: Pegasus with the fountain of Hippocrene.
Bronze: diam. 5.7
Lit: Armand, 1883, I, p.146, no.1 without legend; Hill-Pollard 1967, p.93, no.484b.
Lent by the Victoria and Albert Museum (717–1865 & 243–1910(A))

30 Obverse: Andrea Gritti, wearing ducal robes and crown, in profile to the left. Around, ANDREAS·GRITI·DVX·VENETIAR,· ET·C·
Reverse: An elevation of San Francesco della Vigna. Around, DIVI·FRANCISCI·MDXXXIIII· and, in the exergue, the initials of the engraver Andrea Spinelli, ·AN·SP·F·
Bronze: diam. 3.7
Lit: Armand, 1883, I, p.155, no.4; Hill-Pollard, 1967, p.77, no.413; Tafuri, 1969, pp.18–25.
Lent by the Victoria and Albert Museum (6018–1857 & A244–1910)

131 Obverse: Cardinal Cristoforo Madruzzo (1512–78) in profile to the left. Around, CHRISTOPHORVS·MAD·ET·C·CARD· TRIDEN·LAV·PAR·
Reverse: The phoenix rises from its pyre. Around: RIVIXIT·LP·LP·
By Lorenzo Fragni.
Bronze: diam. 4.2
Lit: Armand, 1883, I, p.278, no.1.
Lent by the Victoria and Albert Museum (7138–1860)

132 Obverse: Valerio Belli (c.1468–1546) in profile to the left. Around, VALERIVS BELLVS VICENTINVS.
Reverse: A Quadriga.
By Valerio Belli.
Bronze: diam. 4.9
Lit: Armand, 1883, I, p.135, no.1; Hill-Pollard, 1967, p.131, no.385a.
Lent by the Victoria and Albert Museum (7138–1860)

133 Obverse: Cardinal Ippolito II d'Este (1509–72) in profile to the left. Around, HIPPOLYTVS·ESTEN·S·R·E·PRESB·CARD·FERRAR· and, beneath the relief, the initials of the engraver Gian Federico Bonzagna, FED·PARM·
Gilt bronze: diam. 4.7
Lit: Armand, 1883, I, p.222, no.5; Hill-Pollard, 1967, p.70, no.374.
Lent by the Victoria and Albert Museum (727–1865)

134 Obverse: Don Nicola Vicentino (c.1511–72) in profile to the left. Around, NICOLAS VICENTIVS.
Reverse: An organ and an archicembalo. Around,

PERFECTAE MVSICAE DIVISIONIS·Q·INVENTOR.
Bronze: diam. 5
Lit: Armand, 1883, II, p.229, no.24; III, p.271, f; Hill-Pollard, 1967, p.96, no.508.   B.B.
Lent by the Victoria and Albert Museum (A321–1910)

Palladio's long working life is documented from when he was apprenticed at the age of thirteen to his death at the age of almost seventy-two in 1580. There is disappointingly little information about his personality or beliefs and feelings about anything other than architecture. A mass of documents testify to his constant, unremitting activity and to the fact that until late in his life he was poor – it was not until he was fifty that he entered even the lowest taxable bracket (Zorzi, 1962, p.21). His personal history is one of amazing ability which enabled him to turn to the best advantage his undoubted luck in the contacts which he made and which were made for him. It is also one of an extraordinary rise from obscurity to a fame which was not, however, ever accompanied by the material rewards which caused architect Antonio da Sangallo to say, 'I may be called Master Antonio, but I would not exchange my life in Rome with anyone whatsoever', and to build for himself a palace larger than those of many of his patrons (Frommel, 1973, p.292ff; Sacchetti-Sassetti, 1958, p.12).

Palladio was born on 30 November 1508, St Andrew's Day, hence his name, Andrea. His father, Piero dalla Gondola, who was dead by 1528, is described in documents as a hat maker and latterly as a miller. His grandfather was a greengrocer. Until 1540, by which date Trissino had given him his splendid, memorable, antique-sounding surname, so appropriate to his architecture, Palladio was called simply and humbly Andrea di Pietro, Andrew son of Peter. His mother Marta was lame and the family lived in Padua (Rigoni, 1970, p.324). Palladio was born into a relatively humble world of boatmen and millers, but right from the start there are indications that useful contacts were available: his godfather was Vincenzo de' Grandi, a Vicentine who later made a very successful career for himself as a sculptor (109), and his first master, the Vicentine Bartolomeo Cavazza, was a stone mason responsible for works of high quality in Padua (Puppi, 1973, pp.7–8). The contract stating the terms of Andrea's apprenticeship to Cavazza in 1521

has survived: he was to study 'the stone mason's art' for six years, get his food and dress (except shirts) from Cavazza, sleep at home, and get a ducat a year spending money. Andrea and his father however left Padua for Vicenza, thus breaking the agreement, which was renegotiated in April 1523. Either the attraction of Vicenza was great, or Cavazza an intolerable master, because a year later, in April 1524, Andrea was formally inscribed in the guild of stone masons of Vicenza as the apprentice of Giovanni da Pedemuro and Girolamo Pittoni, the partners who headed Vicenza's most important stone masons' workshop. Within this workshop Palladio was assured not only of the best training available in Vicenza, but also of contact with the city's most important patrons. The workshop itself probably brought him into contact with leading architects (above all Sanmicheli) and with drawings of ancient and modern buildings.

Already by the mid 1530s, there was a small group of works where Palladio's presence, if not always documented, is almost certain because of the involvement of the Pedemuro workshop (Puppi, 1973, pp.237–8). At this stage Palladio, although his apprenticeship would have been over, was still an employee of the shop, and lived in Giovanni da Pedemuro's house. By 1534, however, he was married to Allegradonna (literally Cheerfulwoman), a carpenter's daughter, whose dowry was provided by a widowed noble lady. This consisted of a bed, 'almost new', a pair of sheets, three new shirts, three used ones, handkerchiefs, clothing, and lengths of material, to a value of lire 177-4-6 (Zorzi, 1916, pp.183–4). The list is a very short one if one compares it with the contents of Palazzo Barbaran (*Interior*, Introduction). Allegradonna had probably been a servant of Angela Poiana, who lived in the street in which Palladio later lived: his move there may in fact have coincided with his marriage.

The next years saw the beginning of the transformation of the stone mason Andrea into the architect Palladio. He probably designed the portal of the Domus Comestabilis in 1536 (13), the Villa Godi in 1537, and Palazzo Civena in 1540 (45). He was recorded in Trissino's own house in 1538 (Zorzi, 1949, p.152), and in 1540 was called Palladio for the first time (*ibid.*).

In 1541 he went with Trissino to Rome, from 1542 was involved with the Palazzo Thiene, and concurrently with a whole group of other projects, for some of which his drawings survive (Villa Valmarana at Vigardolo, the villa at Bertesina, Villa Pisani at Bagnolo, the Ridolfi entry in 1543). In 1545–6 he was studying in Rome; in 1546 he presented a project for the logge of the Basilica; in 1547 he was back in Rome (164) putting the finishing touches to his reading of ancient architecture. Other projects were underway: the Villa Saraceno, the Villa Caldogno, the Villa Thiene, Poiana, and in 1549, crowning a decade of study and development, the final design for the Basilica. Work began at once on the Basilica and provided Palladio not only with fame and recognition, but also, for the rest of his life with a salary of five *scudi* a month, which he probably was never rich enough to regard as a negligible contribution to his income. Two major palace projects followed immediately, the Palazzo da Porto-Festa and Palazzo Chiericati. These works, and those of the next few years can be regarded as defining his mature style (Villa Pisani in 1552, Villa Cornaro, 1553 – both jobs from Venetian patricians, opening up a new area of employment – the Villa Chiericati in 1554).

In 1554 he was back in Rome, with Daniele Barbaro, and Palladio's fresh and individual vision of ancient architecture was revealed in print in the illustrations to Barbaro's *Vitruvius* of 1556 (178). By this time Palladio had probably been working for many years on his own architectural treatise, but his own perfectionism still delayed its publication till fourteen years later. The second half of the 1550s saw a filling out of typologies which he had created in the last half dozen years: the Palazzo Antonini at Udine of 1556, the Villa Badoer of the same year, the Villa Thiene at Cicogna (destroyed), his involvement with the Villa Barbaro at Maser, and the Repeta and Mocenigo villas.

From 1558 Palladio began to emerge as a major architect, working not just in Vicenza and the *Terraferma*, but in Venice itself. By the year of Sansovino's death (1570), Palladio was indisputably Venice's leading architect, and he received the successive national acclaim of membership of the Florentine Academy of Design (1566) and several pages in Vasari's *Lives* (1568). From the mid 1560s, Palladio could and probably did think of himself as one of Italy's greatest architects, and wrote

of his own Basilica, 'I do not doubt that it should be compar to ancient buildings and numbered among the greatest a most beautiful structures which have been made from ancie times up to the present day, both for its size and its ornamen tion'. Vasari wrote: 'a man of singular genius and judgeme . . . for the counts of Valmarana he has completed another m superb palace . . . marvellous and most notable (the Carità) . a stupendous and most beautiful work (San Giorgio Maggior . . . many details of beautiful and strange caprices [not the w in which Palladio is usually seen but worth pondering] . still young . . . one can hope for greater things from him eve day' (Vasari, 1881, VII, pp.527–31). Praise of that sort m have been a stimulus to produce 'greater things every day Stupendous and most beautiful indeed were the works these years: the Villa Malcontenta (1559–60), the Carità (156 61), the façade of San Francesco della Vigna (1562), the Vil Emo, and the great church of San Giorgio and the Palaz Valmarana in Vicenza, both designed in 1565. The Vil Rotonda was designed in 1566–7 and right at the end of t decade, the Villa Sarego and the Palazzo Barbarano. In 157 closely linked to the new developments of these years, was t project of the Loggia del Capitaniato.

The feeling for the visual qualities of stone, the knowledge structure and building, acquired laboriously in the worksho and on the building site; the slow, intelligent evolution types, and of drawing and design procedures; the study ancient buildings, Vitruvius, and Alberti, all had been fuse into an architectural system, which will be explored in th final section of this exhibition and which Palladio himself de cribed in his book of 1570. His achievements up to that dat and after it, were the result of hard and exhausting work, muc of it concerned with the direct supervision of the physica execution of his buildings.

Numbers of projects were always in hand concurrently, an when he was in Venice, he was being called to Vicenza, an vice-versa. He also needed to keep up a correspondence an produce drawings for clients, concerning problems of all sort In Venice in February 1565, he wrote to Vincenzo Arnaldi i Vicenza about the vaults of his villa, 'Before it will be necessar to do anything, I shall be in Vicenza because I have complete making this blessed theatre (for a play in Palazzo Dolfin), i which I have done penance for all the sins I have committed or will commit' (Puppi, 1973, p.355). The year before he wrote to clients of 'the many other occupations which have detained me' (Zorzi, 1966, p.82). Early in 1572 he was crippled with sorrow at the terrible blow of losing his sons Orazio and Leonido within a few weeks of one another (143). They, with another son Silla (his son Marc'Antonio was a sculptor), had handled their father's correspondence for him, and Orazio, probably to his father's great pride (Fabio Monza was delighted in similar circumstances) had graduated as a Doctor of Laws at Padua in 1569 (Zorzi, 1962, p.31). Family preoccupations appear again late in 1572: he excuses himself for a delay in sending drawings, 'because of great travails as my wife has been in great danger of her life with fever, though, praised be the Lord, she has now made an excellent recovery' (Zorzi, 1964, p.303).

It was difficult to find Palladio in Venice, as he was either out visiting sites or engaged in discussions, or dining in patrician houses. The Vicentine representative in Venice looked for him on 27 February 1572: 'I went to the lodging of messer Andrea Palladio and they told me that I should find him at the Morosini house where he had gone to dine. I looked for him in the court of the Doge's palace and in the Piazza, but I didn't find him. I will call on his house very early tomorrow morning...' When he did find him the next day, Palladio, who was still deeply affected by the loss of his sons, said he would have come back to Vicenza three or four days ago had it not been that 'he lacked the spirit to make the journey, above all with the roads as bad as they are' (Fasolo, 1938).

In Palladio's last ten years of life his circumstances obviously improved. Very often he collected his salary late, instead of having to ask for advances on it, or have his wife asking the foreman to ask one of the building commissioners to pay it to her when he was away. The improvement must have begun in the 1560s, but two heavy strains were put on him in that decade: the 400 ducat dowry for his daughter Zenobia (Magrini, 1845, pp.XLI-XLII), and the publication of the *Quattro Libri* (Zorzi, 1964, pp.308-12). This last decade was a busy one, but there was a change in the character of his activities. He was largely concerned with public and ecclesiastical projects, but had little to do with palace building, and none it would seem with villas. War with the Turks at the beginning of the decade,

and the consequent taxation, and then plague in the middle of the decade (reducing the population of Venice and affecting the market for agricultural produce) must have discouraged private building. Scamozzi's early activity however makes it clear, that there was still some demand for new palaces and villas. Palladio's residence in Venice and the demanding character of his work there would have limited his possibilities of undertaking private commissions, while advancing age must have made him less willing and able to move constantly between the two cities. Three of Palladio's major concerns in the '70s derived from disasters: the fires in the Doge's palace and the palace in Brescia, and the great plague of 1575-6 in Venice, which prompted the decision to build the Redentore. This great work and the Teatro Olimpico, designed in the last years of Palladio's life show that his grasp and inventiveness were as great as ever: only in the design for the rebuilding of the Ducal Palace and in some of the San Petronio designs is there a slight suggestion that Palladio's system was hardening, trapping him into solutions which did not adequately take account of site and scale. But even in the case of San Petronio, Palladio once more broke through the conventional solutions, and like Michelangelo at St Peters, proposed a huge free standing portico (Zorzi, 1966, p.113).

Palladio was almost universally liked; the one documented episode of an attempted political vendetta against him failed, and probably had its origins in the feuds of the nobility, rather than a personal antipathy (Zorzi, 1964, pp.309ff). Vasari who met him in 1566, and kept in touch with him through Cosimo Bartoli (188) writes that, 'I will not hide that to such ability he adds such an affable and pleasant manner that it makes him most likeable to everyone'. Gualdo, in his reliable biography of 1616, says that, 'Palladio was very pleasing and amusing in conversation, so that the gentlemen and lords with whom he dealt took a great taste for him, as also did the workmen whom he used, always keeping them cheerful, and treating them most agreeably so that they worked very cheerfully' (Zorzi, 1959). His tone of voice comes across in many of his writings. Sometimes it is sad and weary, as when he writes of the death of his son, or in asides which reveal the resignation of one who knows only too well the difficulties of life, and of his profession, 'if happiness can be found here below' (Palladio, 1570, I, p.6): 'but often it is necessary for the architect to adjust himself more to the desires of those who are spending than to that which one should observe' (*ibid*, II, p.3). The lucidity and honesty of his buildings appears in his writing; he was ready to cross out 'truly' and replace it by 'I believe' in describing the dimensions of an ancient temple (195). He was courteous and considerate in praising other architects' projects submitted to him for comment (Zorzi, 1966, p.88) and courteous even in calling attention to blatant plagiarism at his expense (I, p.15). Nothing suggests that Palladio was not a serious, thoughtful and agreeable man. Even a Venetian satirical verse of the 1560s underlines this:

> Palladio does not visit prostitutes for any bad reasons
> And even if now and again he does visit them,
> He does it in order to urge them to build
> An ancient atrium in the middle of the brothel district.
> (Puppi, 1973, p.36)

There is a slack in every system, which those who are paid by the establishment to manage the arts and the media can turn to their own ends, and use for good or for bad. Palladio used the available space for manoeuvre to achieve sensible, useful, and beautiful buildings. He gave form where it had not existed before, as when he pulled the whole of a villa complex into a single, rationally functioning, aesthetically pleasing whole, or transformed the character of Vicenza's central piazza, so that even today it is a very enjoyable experience to walk through it. Whatever he did, he did honestly and well, and often brilliantly well, as one can see by reading his book and noting how his text and illustrations work together, or by considering his bridge for Bassano. The quality and moral and intellectual commitment of his work have few parallels in the history of architecture. For anyone seriously concerned with creating some degree of happiness for himself and for others 'here below', Palladio's achievement will always repay study and reflection. H.B.

135

FRANCESCO ZUCCHI 1692–1764 after Giovanni Battista Mariotti c.1685–1765

*135 Portrait of Andrea Palladio
Engraving: 15.8 × 10.1
Lent by the Visitors of the Ashmolean Museum, Oxford

The engraving appeared first in Muttoni's *Architettura di Andr* *Palladio* (Venice, 1740–8) and subsequently in Temanza's life o Palladio (Venice, 1762); Arnaldi, *Delle Basiliche antiche e specialmente di quella di Vicenza* (Vicenza, 1769); and Bertotti-Scamozzi, *Le Fabbriche e i Disegni di Andrea Palladio* (Vicenza, 1776–83). It is based upon what seems to have been a medium length portrait of the architect which Temanza identified as by Maganza and in the possession of the Capra family at the Rotonda (Temanza, 1762, p.lxxix). Magrini, (1845, p.335) mentioned the owners of the painting as the Conti family in Vicenza and used an engraving similar to the present one, but reversed, for the frontispiece of his book. The present whereabouts of the painting are unknown (Puppi, 1973–III, pp.182–8). B.B.

BERNARDO LICINIO, Bergamo and Venice, c.1489–c.1560.

5 Portrait of an Architect

Canvas: 111 × 84 (relined)
Signed and dated on the parapet, left: B.LYCINII./OPVS./ ANDREAS./PALADIO./A./ANNOR(VM)./XXIII./M.DXLI. The third, fourth and fifth lines are additions of clearly distinct date and quality.
Prov: from the collection of Consul Smith; in the last century at Windsor (Windsor Castle inventory, 1872, no.1152); more recently at Hampton Court (no.1272).
Lent by Her Majesty the Queen

When the portrait was in the Consul Smith Collection it was engraved as the likeness of Palladio, which cannot be correct. The attributes of set-square and dividers do normally, however, identify an architect. No sensible suggestion for this one's name has yet been made; the successful candidate must be born in 1518 and active in the Veneto in 1541. Licinio's customary disinclination to particularize makes an approach on grounds of likeness practically impossible; and in addition the face is much rubbed and retouched, notably in the shadows, so that its forms are only trustworthy in general terms. The portrait bears better witness, through the costume of long black coat and broad fur collar, to the social status claimed even by a minor architect, if he was a professional, or alternatively to the respectability of the practice of architecture, if he was a gentleman. J.S.

137 Note of the Payment to Palladio for his work for the entry of Cardinal Ridolfi, 1543

Photograph from A.T., b.124

The payment reads 'Master Andrea Palladio for his architecture, *Troni* 36, 16'. This small payment (just under 7 *scudi* when a subsequent 12 troni was added), for making

137

designs, was in line with the very modest recompense which Palladio received on other occasions; 4 *scudi* for the Palazzo Chiericati, 25 ducats for the facade design of San Petronio (Zorzi, 1964, p.312).The Ridolfi entry, like the construction of the 1539 theatre in the Colleoni-Porto palace, was probably a decisive point in the formation of a taste for up-to-date architecture in Vicenza. Behind the idea of welcoming the city's bishop, Cardinal Nicolo Ridolfi (an absentee since his appointment to the see in 1524) with triumphal arches, obelisks, and statues of river gods, lay Trissino's and Ridolfi's nostalgia for the great days of Leo X. The whole programme, even down to an inscription on the arch, JUGUM MEUM SUAVE, echoed the splendid decorations for the procession in which Leo took possession of his see at the Lateran, or for his entry into Florence in 1515. Trissino was probably behind the programme, and he probably put Palladio forward, for the first time, in the role of the city's public architect. Trissino had visited his old friend Ridolfi at Bagnaia in 1541, and Ridolfi stayed with him at Cricoli immediately before entering the city itself. The committee in charge of the decoration was significant: two of its members were among the first commissioners for the execution of the Basilica logge (Valmarana and Capra), and the third, Stefano Gualdo (though his role needs clarification) was, with Trissino, perhaps the city's most trend-setting private architectural patron in these years (900). Maganza and Girolamo Pittoni were also paid for work on the decorations. The event diffused the new style in the city in the most concrete way: the committee recouped some of its expenses by selling off bits of the wooden architecture and Antonio Valmarana bought the columns from the triumphal arch outside Porta di Castello for 20 *troni* (A.T., b.124; Zorzi, 1964, pp.167–9). H.B.

*138 An autograph receipt for Palladio's monthly salary, 1564

A.T., *Summarii* of the expenses for the Palace, *Liber Segnato*, N.38, p.116
Photograph

[handwritten note at top of page, in Italian]
adi 28 agosto del 1564 · 115
io andrea palladio dal conte marcho trisino p[re]sidente sopra la fabrica dal palazo p[er] la mexa del mese de se[tte]mbr[e] scudi 2

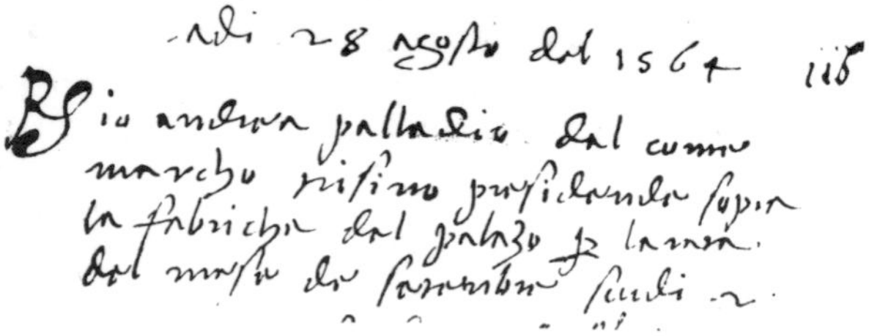

Palladio has written 'I Andrea Palladio have received from the Count Marco Trissino president in charge of the building of the Palace for the instalment of the month of September 2 scudi'. The account books kept by the successive commissioners (*Provveditori*) appointed to supervise the construction of the logge of the Basilica survive. The commissioners were appointed by the City Council from its own membership for a two year term. Each commissioner kept the accounts personally for about eight months. Many of Palladio's patrons worked closely with him in this capacity: Girolamo Chiericati, Girolamo Godi, Giacomo Angaran, Giuseppe Porto, Giuliano Piovene, all held this office, which must have contributed greatly to the architectural education of the local patriciate. Palladio's monthly salary of five *scudi* began in May, 1549, and continued till the end of his life. If this is compared with the figures for builders working on the Scuola di San Rocco in Venice, it emerges that Palladio, with a monthly salary of 700 *soldi*, would in 1550 have been earning a sum close to that of a master craftsman (30 *soldi* a day, for a working month of probably about 22 or 23 days), and his salary, which remained fixed, in the last decade of his life would definitely, with inflation, have fallen behind that of masters (Pullan, 1968, p.157). Palladio however was better off than master craftsmen. He could always get advances on his salary, to see him through a difficult moment and he was usually paid in gold. Palladio was under no obligation to be present all the time (Zorzi, 1969, p.253) and his responsibilities which included design, selection of stones at the quarries, supervising and evaluating the execution, still allowed him to be involved with work on several other buildings. The fact that his salary was frequently collected by his wife, sons, or nephew is an indication of this. In March 1555 he explicitly asked for permission to go off to execute 'certain services in the service of some Venetian gentlemen'. As work progressed his presence became less

necessary, and at the same time his growing influence and contacts at Venice, which could be of use to the city in all sorts of ways, politically and in matters like obtaining good specialised workmen, or a length of rope from the Arsenal to hoist a new bell into place on the clock tower (Fasolo, 1938, pp.260–6), made the continuation of his salary worth while. H

GIOVANNI BATTISTA MAGANZA, AGOSTINO RAVA, BARTOLOMEO RUSTICHELLO
*139 La prima-quarta parte de le rime di Magagno, Menon, e Begotto. In lingua rustica padovana. In Venetia, appresso Bolognino Zalterio. M.D.LXIX.
Lent by the British Library Board (11431.bb.27)

The works of these three Vicentine dialect poets were published in four parts (the first editions came out in 1558, 1562, 1568, and 1583). The poems themselves reflect the taste dialect verse revealed in a mass of anonymous contemporary publications (000) and follow the much esteemed model, of real literary stature, of the dialect poet Ruzzante, whose patron was the Paduan architectural enthusiast and land improver, Alvise Cornaro.
Of the three poets, Maganza was the one closest to Palladio, to whom he often refers, as 'the architect who is the honour of Italy', in dialect as 'Palabio', or simply as 'Barba Andrea', 'Uncle Andrew, what he earned, he spent'. Maganza's career and contacts paralleled Palladio's very closely; so closely indeed that one cannot help thinking that Palladio must have introduced his friend to many of his patrons. Trissino had Palladio and Maganza with him in Rome in 1547. Maganza, like Palladio, was constantly in the Thiene house at Santa Lucia, he executed the frescoes in the Villa Repeta, and his poems are addressed to or mention, not only Vicentine personalities like Mario Repeta, Teodoro Thiene, Leonardo Valmarana, but also the Venetian nobles who played important roles in Palladio's career: Francesco Pisano, Daniele Barbaro, Leonardo Mocenigo, Giacomo Contarini. As much and more than Palladio, Maganza was a 'functionary' (cf. Puppi, 1973–II, *passim*) of the local ruling class. He celebrates their buildings, their houses, their banquets, and their deaths. Palladio designed the temporary architecture for the entry of Cardinal Ridolfi in 1543, and Maganza did paintings for it. He was trotted out, almost as predicatably as the *Rua*, to recite verses when an

more servile than he really was, almost in the attempt to pass off his dependence as a joke. By the 1570s Palladio probably considered himself as almost a gentleman, and so he appeared to others: Fabio Pepoli in 1572 found him 'a gentleman and easy to deal with' (*galantuomo e trattabile*; cf. Zorzi, 1964, p.316). Maganza was without these compensations. His tone however was a true reflection of a situation which Palladio also shared, at least for most of his life. Tips and charity always had their importance: Maganza wrote of a generous patron, lately dead, 'to help some poor man /he would have pawned his coat and sold his home./ Ask Palladio or Magagno about it' (Zorzi, 1964, p.308, and passim; Zorzi, 1968; Bandini, 1969–70; Mantese, 1974, pp.1253–4). H.B.

ANONYMOUS VENETIAN PAINTER, 16th century

140 Portrait of G. B. Maganza
Photograph: Private collection, Vicenza

The sitter is identified by the inscription. The portrait was exhibited in Vicenza in the Palazzo Barbarano da Porto (*Mostra dell'Arredamento*, 1973, p.8)

*141 Palladio's copy of Books I–V of Serlio's 'Architettura' 1559–62
Lent by the Kunsthistorisches Institut, Florence

important visitor was in town (Zorzi, 1964, pp.171; Marzari, 1591, p.201). Like Palladio he mixed with the patricians in the Accademica Olimpica. He was no better off than Palladio, and did not have the same certainty of knowing that he was indispensable, and that however much he had to work, and however little he earned, he was all the same creating for himself a lasting fame. His poems with their assumed, heavy dialect (which covers but does not hide a wide culture and a literary style), his somewhat exaggerated servility with respect to his *Paron* (Guv'nor), and his praise of peasant simplicity and and peasant wisdom are self-assertions and thinly veiled protests against an unsatisfactory, at worst humiliating situation of social dependence. He compensates for being a cultural odd-job man, by pretending to be even humbler and

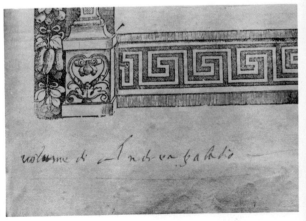

141

The title page of this collection of the first five books of Serlio (Gio. Battista Sessa et Marchio Sessa Fratelli, Venice) carries the note *volume di Andrea paladio* in a sixteenth century hand. Though the hand is not that of Palladio, or of a known member of his circle, there is no reason to doubt that the book did belong to Palladio, and is thus the only volume of his library known at present. There are no notes and drawings attributable to him, which is hardly surprising, as Serlio's books had appeared long before, and Palladio had long since absorbed and passed beyond what they had to offer. H.B.

VINCENZO SCAMOZZI

*142 Annotation in the index of his copy of Daniele Barbaro's 'Vitruvius', 1567
Photograph

Vincenzo's father Giovan Domenico Scamozzi (cf. Barbieri, 1973, pp.44–5) was probably the only architect working in Vicenza in Palladio's time who had an independent style (modelled above all on that of Serlio). Like Palladio's sons Silla, Leonida, and Orazio, or Sansovino's son Francesco, Vincenzo received a literary education, which considerably facilitated his finding a place in the world of the cultured establishment. Scamozzi was an immensely well read architect. His reading weighs down his massive architectural treatise (Scamozzi, 1615) and is recorded in a notebook of his in the Marciana (Barbieri, 1952) and in the annotated books from his library (a Vitruvius in the Avery Library at Columbia University, and a copy of de l'Orme's treatise in the British Museum) as well as this volume in the Vatican Library (Cicognara, IV, 718), which carries the autograph inscription 'Dei libri di Vincenzo Scamozzio' on the title page. Despite (or because of) his enormous stylistic debt to Palladio, Scamozzi was less than fair minded in his suppression of mention of Palladio in his writings. That he was privately acutely aware of the reputation of his great predecessor emerges from the way in which, in the index of Barbaro's book, he writes 'much

praised' against Palladio's name, summarising Barbaro's laudatory reference to Palladio in the main text. (On this seco edition of Barbaro's Vitruvius, see Puppi, 1973–III, p.175.) Palladio's reputation was spread not only by word of mouth and direct acquaintance with his work, but by references to him in contemporary publications, not least his own. He is referred to by Doni (1555), Barbaro (1556 and 1567; 1568), Maganza (139), Barbaran (1566), Ceredi (000), Bassi (000), Benedetti (265), and Marzari . What counted most and must have pleased him most, was the inclusion of a survey of his work in Vasari's Lives (1568), which was a recognition that Palladio had a place in the Pantheon of the great Italian architects. H.B.

143 Palladio's letter to the Deputati of Vicenza, reporting t death of his son, Leonida, 1572
Photograph of the original in the Museo Civico, Vicenza

Like all Palladio's surviving letters this is not an autograph, bu was written for him, in this instance by his son Silla. Leonida' death, referred to here, was followed in March 1572 by the death of his son Orazio. The letter (Fasolo, 1938, p.264) reads
  Magnificent Sirs,
I have understood what your Magnificences write to me, and certainly I should not have omitted to execute everything immediately, but as I have lost my eldest son, so that I find myself impeded and afflicted both in mind and body, and all t more as he has not yet been given burial, I have not found eith the time or the means to do anything at all, but one of the day of this week I will come to Vicenza, and will do everything ye shall command. Wishing you every happiness,
  From Venice, 6 January 1572
  To the Magnificent Sirs, Deputati of Vicenza
  Your affectionate servant,
  Andrea Palladio

Andrea Palladio Architetto. lo٠٠٠ ٠٠. **64**
Ante.   ٠115
Analemma , & discorsi sopra da 366 fin 403 .
142 *Anguli , & circonferenze fatte da i circoli ,*

Giangiorgio Trissino 1478–1550

Palladio in the foreword to the *Quattro Libri* (I, p.5) described Trissino as the 'splendour of our times', a tribute not only to Trissino's wide culture and achievements, but also an implicit recognition of his own debt to him.

Trissino's noble birth and his literary gifts had brought him a distinguished career, fame, and many highly placed friends. In 1542 he sketched his career in a letter to his son Giulio 'Pope Leo [X] who cherished me so much, and honoured me, sent me as Nuncio to the Emperor, and when I was away, had all my possessions restored to me, which had been confiscated by the Venetians [for his taking the Imperial side in 1509], without my knowing anything about it. He sent me as Nuncio to Venice . . . and many of the things which he offered me, such as the Governorships of Cities, and Bishoprics, Cardinalates, and similar things, I turned down . . . Pope Clement [VII] accepted you as a chamberlain . . . and sent me as Nuncio to Venice, and honoured me at the Coronation [of Charles V] ordering that I should carry his train, and similar great honours . . . I would have you know with what kindness Cardinal Ridolfi gave you the Archipresbyterate [of Vicenza]' (Morsolin, 1894, pp.504–505). Trissino had known Raphael in Rome, and the architecture of Bramante and Raphael. This, and not the traditional palace types of the Veneto, must have remained with him as a model of good architecture. He knew most of the leading literary and princely figures of his time: he was a friend of Cardinal Bembo; he borrowed his old friend Isabella d'Este's gardener to tell him how to lay out his garden at Cricoli; the Duke of Ferrara wrote to him asking advice as to whom he should appoint as tutor to his children (Morsolin, 1894, pp.487, 494, 497ff). He was in touch with Pope Paul III and Cardinal Farnese, as well as with literary figures in the Farnese circle.

Trissino's own career, his culture and his contacts gave him ideas about architecture which he was able to transmit to his fellow citizens, and to Palladio. Trissino's familiarity with the upper levels of the political and cultural hierarchy, was only one side of him. His active, constructive character was also important. He was a man who wanted to improve and change things: hence his proposal to reform the alphabet (147), his interest in the music of the ancients (Morsolin, op. cit. p.283), his desire to 'correct and systematise currencies, weights and measures throughout Italy' of which he spoke 'at length' to Pope Paul III in 1541 (Morsolin, p.501). He was not prepared to pursue reform or change in the field of religion to a point where it would upset the social order, or imperil his income (Morsolin, p.504), in the 'safe', world of culture and architecture he was an activist, whose modernisations of his residences were characterised decades later by his son Ciro as 'worsenings rather than improvements' on account of the radical demolitions he undertook in order to strip away out of date but useful logge and balconies (Mantese, 1974, pp.922–3). Trissino's brief jottings on architecture bring out two aspects of his personality: on the one side a conventional enumeration of categories, on the other an incisive and practical approach, which owes much to Alberti and Quattrocento humanism and parallels the much more forcefully expressed views of Alvise Cornaro (Fiocco, 1965). Thus Trissino declared a desire 'to be of benefit to people' and said 'Vitruvius is very badly understood and does not teach anyone enough about this art', because 'religions and times and ways of life have changed' (Puppi, 1973-VI, pp.79–86).

His connection with Palladio also had two sides to it. It fell within a scheme of safe, elegant, aristocratic culture (Puppi, 1973–II, pp.45–7) and probably was partly motivated by the desire to train a local man to provide Vicenza with a new and more splendid architectural face. It was however also a reflection of Trissino's real concern with architecture and probably, too a real personal benevolence. It was also likely that in the last decade of his life he would have been in particular need of loyal friends and dependents like Marco Thiene, Maganza and Palladio. His relations with Giulio, his son by his first marriage, Archpriest of Vicenza but deeply involved like his cousin Alessandro Trissino with heretical ideas, got steadily worse. The origin of the dispute was Trissino's second marriage to the famous widowed beauty Bianca Trissino and the subsequent birth of a son, Ciro, to challenge Giulio's rights to the inheritance. Already in 1533 Giulio and friends armed with arquebuses had sacked the Trissino villa at Cornedo where Bianca lived and carried off the graim (Morsolin, p.313). In the mid 1540's Giulio obtained a sentence against his father in the courts, according to Trissino by 'bribing notaries and everyone else who favoured me and helped me: then through the powerful relations of his mother, and through the nature of the City of Vicenza, which favours evil doers and holds in hatred the good' (Morsolin, p.512). Matters reached a scandalous climax on Christmas Day 1542, when Giulio tried to evict his father from his city house, where he lay ill in bed, actually pulling the bed clothes from the old man (Morsolin, p.384 and 517).

Palladio's debt to Trissino is hard to overestimate. He took Palladio to Rome with him three times. Through Trissino Palladio probably had contact with Antonio da Sangallo and with Ligorio (Burns, 1973-II, n.12). Trissino had a copy of Vitruvius with him when he died (Morsolin, p.524) and there is no reason to doubt that Trissino 'himself decided to explain Vitruvius to him' (Gualdo, 1959). This systematic study of Vitruvius later served Palladio well, both in his works and writings, and in the help he was able to give Daniele Barbaro. Trissino almost certainly also brought Palladio into contact with Alvise Cornaro and Serlio (Puppi, 1973, pp.11-2), figures themselves of the very greatest importance for Palladio's development.   H.B.

VINCENZO CATENA C.1480-1531
144 **Portrait of Giangiorgio Trissino, c.1525**
Canvas: 73 × 64
Photograph: Musée du Louvre

The sitter is shown in a black cap and gown, holding a richly bound volume. The painting is traditionally held to be Giangiorgio Trissino (it was formerly in the collection of the Counts Trissino in Vicenza). It has been attributed to Catena on the basis of its closeness in style to the *Portrait of a Venetian Senator* in New York, and dated c.1525 because of the apparent age of the sitter. There is a drawing most probably after the painting in the Arthur Sambon collection in Paris (Suida, 1930; Robertson 1954, p.67 no.46), and a copy at Valdagno (*Mostra dell' Arredamento* 1973, p.4).   L.F.

GIANGIORGIO TRISSINO 1478-1550
145 **La Sofonisba**
L. de gli Arrighi: Roma, 1524
Lent by the British Library Board (1073. h.15)

This is one of the two first editions of Trissino's very popular tragedy published in Rome by the famous Vicentine calligrapher and designer of type faces, Lodovico degli Arrighi. Arrighi's connection with Trissino probably has its roots in the fact that he came from Cornedo, where Trissino had his principal estates (Mantese, 1974, p.949). Morsolin (1894, p.XIX) records seventeen editions printed before 1600, and the *Sofonisba* was performed in the Basilica in Vicenza in 1562 (74).   H.B.

GIANGIORGIO TRISSINO
146 **Dialogw intitulatw Castellanw nel quale si tratta de la lingua italiana**
T. Janicolo: Vicenza 1529
Lent by the British Library Board (C 76.d.9 (3))

The first edition of one of Trissino's contributions to the lively contemporary debate on the Italian language.   H.B.

GIANGIORGIO TRISSINO
147 **ABC, abc**
T.Ia(nicol)o: Vicenza 1529
Lent by the British Library Board (c.107.R.8)

The purpose of this sheet was to summarise the proposals for the reform of the Italian alphabet and Italian spelling, which Trissino had already put forward in his *Letter to Clement VII* and his *Grammatical Doubts* (Morsolin, 1894, pp.177-8). The most striking aspect of his alphabet was the introduction of a *k*, and a Greek omega and epsilon. Trissino employed these letters in his own printed works, and often in his own notes and correspondence, but his system was not taken up by others. H.B.

*148 **The Villa Trissino at Cricoli, 1532/5-8**
Photograph

In May 1531 Trissino wrote to a friend 'last year ... I decided to come home, wearied with working and having had enough of court life, so I find myself honoured and esteemed in my native city more than anyone else here, and the business of my properties after many upheavals is almost settled, and I find myself less poor than I have ever been before.' (Puppi, 1973,

p.11, and Trissino MSS, 8/1, p.150).

Trissino used his retirement and improved circumstances to rebuild the suburban villa at Cricoli, inherited from his father. In July 1537 he wrote that he had already spent 'many thousands of ducats, and all the same continues spending, and employs a great number of workers' on the villa. Though he certainly exaggerated, as he was submitting evidence in a legal case, just as he exaggerated when he wrote in 1532 that Vicenza was 'small and poor' (Trissino MSS, 8/1, pp.44–8) there is no doubt that his outlay had been considerable, and that the work was well enough advanced for him to have asked for the advice of Isabella d'Este's gardener already in April 1537. Work was clearly finished by 1538 (Puppi, 1971, pp.79–80) and given the extent of the changes, probably had been begun not later than 1535. To these changes Trissino's son refers disapprovingly in his will, 'it appears to be built in the modern style because that which was demolished, in my judgment, was very notable for its columns and doorways of red stone which it had in the logge and other rooms' (Mantese, 1974, p.921).

Though Palladio may have been employed on the villa, its design was certainly Trissino's responsibility. The façade with its towers and central ground floor loggia combines a traditional aristocratic Veneto formula (Villa Porto Colleoni at Thiene) with the Roman suburban villa formula of the Farnesina. The specific solution of the central element was taken straight from a design which Serlio published in 1540 as a Raphael project, altered by himself, of the Villa Madama (Puppi, 1971). Trissino clearly did not use the unpublished book (his façade had been in existence for at least three years when the plate appeared) but must have been shown the drawing by Serlio himself, with whom in any case it is certain he was in contact (Olivato, 1971, pp.84ff). Serlio specifically points out that he had added the little side niches, and perhaps this addition emerged in the course of discussions with Trissino. The use of a Vitruvian Ionic base on the façade could have been prompted either by Trissino's studies, or by Serlio (Burns, 1975, p.158 n.58). The plan in its combination of large loggia, salone, and two sequences of large middling, and small rooms can be seen as one of the points of departure for Palladio's own planning (compare one of his early projects, R.I.B.A. XVII/2 for Vigardolo, and more elaborate, XVII/18 for the Villa Pisani; and later still the plan of the Palazzo Antonini, and the Villa Emo). The proportions (1:1; 2:3; 1:2) also anticipate Palladio. H.B.

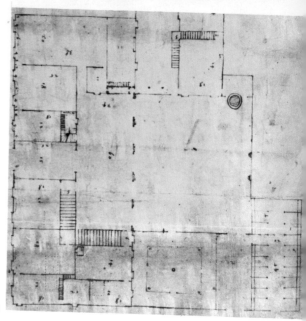

149

GIANGIORGIO TRISSINO

*149 **Project for modernising his house in Vicenza**
Pen and ink : 259 × 272
Photograph: MS Castiglione 8/1, p.39a, Bilioteca Nazionale Braidense (Brera), Milan

Three autograph drawings are preserved among Trissino's papers in the Brera (MS 8/1, pp.37, 38, 39a, 40), which are clearly related, and whose purpose is indicated by a note on the verso of p.37 'Some plans of the house in Vicenza for building it'. All three have been reproduced (Puppi, 1971, p.81). The drawings have been known for some time, and conjectures have been made as to whether they are in fact studies for Cricoli, or for Trissino's town palace (Puppi, 1971, p.83). However the weight of evidence indicates that these drawings are for the town house (Trissino invariably refers to the villa as 'la mia casa di Cricoli'). They probably date from the mid-1530s, and certainly before 1540.

The drawings are for a very extensive site: 39a has a frontage of 115 ft, 37 of 119 ft, and the third drawing of 93 ft (about 15 ft, to allow for wall thicknesses, should be added in each case). The site, as far as it is shown, is of the depth of about 130 ft, 150 ft, and 140 ft in the three different drawings. Trissino in his will does not mention his town houses, but his son Ciro, in his will of 1579 does. His main house had a frontage of a little more than 62 ft, and stood on the present Corso Fogazzaro. He owned another house on the Corso Palladio, and another two houses on the '*Viazola di San Marcello*', which runs parallel to Corso Fogazzaro. One of these was contiguous with the main house, which would mean a potential site of a depth at one point of at least 65 metres, more than the 52 m. needed for the deepest of these projects. It would seem that Trissino was considering an operation of a sort which he would have been familiar with from the Palazzo Farnese and other Roman palaces: the unification in one scheme of extensive and scattered properties, possibly partly by purchase and demolition. The variations in dimensions, and the irregularities at the back of site indicate he was not decided on how much to take in. One constant, the enormous amount of open space left in the middle of the site, is confirmed by the hollow square appearance of the block as shown in the 1580 map.

This drawing shows a frontage on two streets (presumably Corso Fogazzaro, and the alley which runs towards San Marcello) on the lesser of which was the entrance to the stables. The large loggia, articulated with pilasters towards the cortile, recalls Cricoli. At the far end of the cortile is a portal with half columns. The layout is less geometrically lucid than the drawing on p.37 (Puppi, 1971, fig.116), with its sequence of interrelated measurements (12, 18, 27, 30, 42) which leave little doubt as to where Palladio's proportional formulae come from. In its imperfections this plan may well be closer to the pre-existing building. In many of the rooms Trissino marks the position of the bed, that important fourth element (alongside the doors, windows and fireplace) which domestic architects had to fit into place. The indication of beds with dotted lines Trissino had possibly learned from Serlio, who uses the same convention in his *Sixth Book* (Rosci, 1966) having learned it from Peruzzi, who took it from Francesco di Giorgio. Even though Trissino never carried through these schemes, he did alter the house, as his son pointed out, 'and because it could be that in the future somebody . . . should speak of

improvements, I say and do declare that rather it has been worsened than improved because there were some balconies or walkways which were very beautiful . . . which walkways together with some small structures were demolished by my father' (Mantese, 1974, p.922), undoubtedly to make it conform better to his idea of good architecture.   H.B.

GIANGIORGIO TRISSINO
*150 La Italia liberata da Gotthi
T. Ianiculo: Venezia 1547
Lent by the British Library Board (G10744)

This is one of the three editions published, two at Venice, one in Rome (Morsolin, 1894, p.XVIII). Trissino's verse epic, *Italy freed from the Goths*, was in his own eyes his great work, on which he laboured for more than twenty years. The twenty

150

seven books into which the work is divided served as a receptacle for Trissino's studies of many aspects of ancient Roman life, above all ancient military matters. Some of his preparatory notes and sketches of Roman encampments and military tactics have survived to show the seriousness with which he approached these matters (Puppi, 1973–II, fig. 4) and he transmitted his interest in ancient military matters to Palladio (67, 206). In the book Belisarius' guardian angel was called Palladio (Wittkower, 1952, p.52). In July 1547 Palladio returned from a vist to Trissino in Rome carrying a printed copy of the first nine books for Trissino's son Ciro to present to Charles V (Morsolin, 1894, p.331). Palladio made one direct and hitherto unnoticed contribution to the printed edition. At the back of the third volume is Trissino's *impresa* (allegorical device) surmounted by a Greek inscription, taken from Sophocles, 'that which is sought is found'. He had used it since 1529 (Morsolin, 1894, p.198). In the *Italia Liberata* it was contained within a tabernacle, derived from that of the Pantheon, but clearly betraying Palladio's hand, as can be seen by a comparison with the tabernacle windows appearing on his drawings of these years (R.I.B.A. XVII/19: note especially how the bases are joined by a curving moulding to the cornice of the pedestal). The same tabernacle appeared on the title page. H.B.

152

151 Rutilius Taurus Aemilianus Palladius

Translated by P. Marino
B. Vercellese, *Vineggia*, 1538
Photograph

By 25 February 1540 Palladio had acquired his new name (Zorzi, 1949, p.152). The name appeared in Trisssino's *Italia Liberata* but would have been familiar to both Trissino and Palladio as the Italian version of Palladius, the ancient writer on agriculture and the villa. H.B.

*152 The portal of the Thiene palace in Contrada di S.Lucia

Photograph

The Thiene house was on the far side of a courtyard, approached through this undocumented portal, which probably should be dated about 1540, and has been associated by Cevese with the influence of Sanmicheli in Vicenza (Barbieri, Cevese, Magagnato, 1956, p.321). It is also very close to a portal published by Serlio. VI. 1619, fol.11. The palladian/Sanmichelian character of the profile of the cornice does leave open the possibility that this is an early ecclectic work of Andrea, designing a feature, an isolated portal, which in itself allows for experiment and variety. The palace had a loggia facing the cortile, and the 1580 map shows a formal garden behind the palace.

In Palladio's time much depended on where people lived. Though country neighbours could be murderous enemies, in the town neighbours were usually friends, relatives by marriage, or if socially inferior, trusted semi-dependents who would be called in to witness legal documents, or if cultured and educated, could stand in for one at a baptism ceremony, as Palladio's son Orazio did for Teodoro Thiene (Zorzi, 1962). Angela Poiana, who in 1534 provided Palladio's wife with her dowry, lived in the same street as the Thiene, and it is likely that Palladio either rented accommodation in her house, or settled nearby. In 1552 Giacomo Angaran, the friend of Palladio to whom he dedicated the first two books of the *Quattro Libri*, bought the present Palazzo Angarano on the corner of the street towards the river (Zorzi, 1962; Mantese, 1966–7, p.255; 1969–70, p.89). Another friend, Fabio Monza, closely linked with the Angaran family, lived nearby. Not in the same street, but in the same quarter, lived other figures closely connected with Palladio, Girolamo and Pietro Godi. Across the river lived Girolamo Chiericati (Palazzo Chiericati) whose son and heir Valerio (associated with Palladio at the Basilica, at the Teatro Olimpico, and during the visit of Henry III to Venice, where he was in charge of the ordinance) was married to Dorotea, a sister of Odoardo and Teodoro Thiene. Further marriage relationships of the Thiene family carry one outside the quarter, but underline how closely some of Palladio's most important contacts follow the alliances of the Thiene family. Ludovico Thiene, brother of Odoardo and Teodoro's father Francesco Thiene, had a daughter Lucia and a son, Marco. Lucia married Gian Giorgio Trissino's son Ciro, and Marco Thiene, together with Maganza and Palladio was in Rome with Trissino in 1547, and wrote home about Palladio's studies of ancient buildings. This Marco Thiene was a much loved and respected figure, and Teodoro Thiene in his will asked that a marble bust of him, to be made after a drawing by Maganza (often present in the Thiene house), should be placed in the church of Santa Corona. Odoardo and Teodoro's sister Attilia in 1573 married Leonardo da Porto, son of Giuseppe da Porto, for whom Palladio designed the Palazzo da Porto. The Thiene/da Porto connection was already welded by the marriage of the sister of Marc'Antonio Thiene, (belonging to another branch of the family), who commissioned the Palazzo Thiene, to Giuseppe da Porto himself (Zorzi, 1964, p.190, and fig.165). Odoardo Thiene was married to Diamante Pepoli, sister of Fabio Pepoli, a prominent figure in Venice, whose dinner with Palladio in 1572 opened the way to Palladio being asked to make designs for the facade of San Petronio in Bologna. Fabio's uncle Giovanni was the President of the building committee. (Zorzi, 1964, p.316; Mantese, 1969–70, p.85).

A final aspect of Palladio's close relationship with the Thiene is the fact that Odoardo Thiene was a central figure in two local Academies, which were founded for gatherings connected with religious reform. Odoardo for reasons of prudence and Protestant conviction went abroad between September 1567 and March 1568, and in 1576 became like Alessandro Trissino a citizen of Geneva. At the very least Palladio must have been broadly sympathetic to the religious views which were so widely held by, or in, the families of his Vicentine noble friends and patrons. These views had their roots not only in the diffusion of Protestant literature and teaching before the clamp down in 1560s, but also in the survival in the Veneto of a Quattrocento and Albertian humanism, which saw the role of culture and cultural activity as that of creating a better world, and of contributing to the good of one's neighbour and of mankind: 'man . . . is not born for himself alone, but also to be of help to others' (Palladio, 1570, I, p.5; Puppi, 1973, p.11).

H.B.

153 The Villa Repeta, Campiglia dei Berici (Vicenza)
Photograph: *Quattro Libri*, 1570, p.61

The presence, one after another in the *Quattro Libri* of the Repeta, Thiene (at Cicogna), and Angarano villas does not look accidental. All three families were linked by friendship and the heretical beliefs of their members. Francesco Repeta (who died in 1556 and whose will was witnessed by Fabio Monza) and Francesco Thiene held dinner parties every Saturday evening, alternately in the villas at Campiglia and at Cicogna. Though the purpose of these meetings was passed off by a witness called before the Inquisition as being the 'reading and interpreting of Petrarch's sonnets' and 'so as to find themselves at table together with their ladies', the religious concerns of the dining group are fairly clear. Francesco's son, Mario Repeta, who bored Maganza with a paper he read to the 'Costanti' on Plato and Aristotle, was denounced to the Inquisition in 1569 as a 'Despiser of the Church and of masses' (but apparently nothing came of the charge) and carried his outspokenness into the political field by asserting in a memorandum drawn up in 1577 that there was 'much injustice in dispensing (justice) and administering public affairs'. This boat-rocking, which again seems to have brought no unfortunate consequences for Repeta (though he was murdered by a member of the Poiana family in 1589), led the Deputati of Vicenza to nominate a special ambassador to go to Venice to defend the city against charges which were aimed at 'disturbing the pacific state' of the city.

Mario Repeta was also a close friend of Paolo Almerico, owner of the Villa Rotonda (Zorzi, 1968, pp.120ff.).

His villa (destroyed by fire in 1672) was one of the most unexpected of Palladio's designs; apart from the corner towers, it consisted only of a ground floor, and had no central block for the owner's residence. Palladio felt constrained to give some account of this peculiarity, 'and as the portion for the owner's residence and that for agricultural functions are of the same design, so much as the former looses in grandeur, as not being more prominent than the latter, so the whole villa gains in its ornament and dignity . . .'. Different rooms had decorations(by Maganza) related to different virtues. The whole scheme may well be a reflection of Repeta's heretical and possibly anabaptist, egalitarian ideas (Tafuri, 1969–II). The villa was possibly designed about 1557 and was under construction in 1566 (Puppi, 1973, pp.318–20). It was probably, on the basis of new evidence, never completed according to the published scheme (Kubelik, 1974).   H.B.

Drawing, study trips, measuring, surveying

Drawing was an essential skill for Palladio, both for the elaboration of his ideas, their presentation to his patrons, and for the communication of his instructions to the men who actually laid the bricks and cut the blocks. Its role in his design and working procedures will be discussed in the final section. Palladio's graphic methods emerge fairly clearly if one looks closely at his drawings. He often, and always in the first stage of designing a project, drew free hand, and usually in pen and ink. The pen would be an ordinary quill pen(154). When producing neat scale drawings he would first draw the main elements with a stylus and compasses without ink, and only then draw in ink over these incised lines. Construction lines of this sort appear on most of his scale drawings. He would sometimes also make a first drawing in red or brown chalk (163), or in lead and only then trace over it in ink. On the whole in his earlier drawings where there is underdrawing, it is in red or brown chalk, and in his later drawings, it is in lead. He was a very neat and precise draughtsman as a comparison with drawings by his less meticulous collaborators underlines (55 and 77). Even in his most highly finished drawings many small detailed elements would be drawn without any underdrawing, though this is scarcely surprising, as Palladio would have drawn Corinthia capitals thousands of times.

His basic drawing equipment would have consisted, apart from quill pens, of holders for drawing with chalk and lead, compasses and dividers of various sizes, straight edges for ruling and possibly also proportional dividers, protractors, and paralle rulers. All these instruments appear in the two sixteenth century sets of drawing instruments which are illustrated here (155–6) He would also have had set squares, and probably would have had a travelling set of instruments, complete with an inkwell to take with him when studying Roman ruins, or visiting a site for a new building. Palladio probably used, just as Scamozz advised, an ivory or wood stylus for making incised lines or a metal one with a rounded point (a sharp metal one scratches the paper and hence causes blots when ink is applied) and the rulers with their edge cut obliquely on one side, so as not to cause blots when ruling lines (Burns, 1973, p.134).

Five trips of Palladio to Rome are recorded (in 1541, 1545–6, 1547, 1549 and 1554). These were of the greatest importance for his stylistic development, as they brought him in touch with the full range of ancient and modern architecture. Palladio frequently copied existing measured drawings of ancient buildings, thereby saving himself time and expense, and at most added only supplementary drawings and measurements himself (Lotz, 1962; Burns 1973, and 1973–II). In other cases however, above all those of the great bath complexes, or of the great temple complexes at Tivoli and Palestrina, Palladio made careful personal surveys which changed his view of ancient architecture, and with it his own style. Such surveys were complex and difficult undertakings. Serlio notes (1540, p.XLV) that he had not measured the inside of the temple of Romulus (194) 'because it was very filled up (with earth), and also because there were cattle inside'. As one can see from Heemskeck's view (159) even the Forum was deeply buried by centuries of accumulated earth and debris, so that the pedestals of a monument as famous as the Arch of Severus were hidden. Architects if they could not afford to hire workmen to dig, or were not lucky enough to coincide with a hunt for ancient statuary undertaken by some important personage, could only guess as to what was buried. The French architect Philibert De L'Orme (1567, p.131) recalls that, 'being in Rome when I was a very young man, I measured the ruins and antiquities, which I did normally with great labour, expense and outlay, as far as my limited means permitted, for ladders and ropes and to excavate the foundations . . . All this I could not do without a certain number of men who followed me, some to earn two *giulii* or *carlini* a day, and others to learn . . .' Palladio recalls excavations he witnessed on the site of the vast temple on the Quirinal (IV, p.41). He refers several times to the 'greatest diligence' he has observed in measuring ancient buildings and to his travels in and outside Italy to draw them (I. p.5). As his drawings of cornices suggest, Palladio measured projecting elements inwards from a plumb line. Mouldings he either drew by eye, or used a thin strip of lead which could be bent into the curvature of a base, a method traditionally employed in Vicenza (oral communication, G. Girardello). Compass bearings noted on some of his 'on the spot drawings' (164) indicate that he obtained reasonably accurate surveys by employing a circumferentor (166), an instrument with a compass located in the centre, which is the precursor of the modern theodolite.

Palladio also gave attention to the 'modern classics' of the city, the works with which Bramante, Raphael, Giulio Romano, Peruzzi, Antonio da Sangallo the Younger, and by the time of his second visit in 1554, Michelangelo, had adorned it (Lotz, 1973). Drawings by Palladio of Raphael's Villa Madama (163), of Bramante's Tempietto (162) and San Biagio (161) survive. The relation between Giulio Romano's house and the Palazzo Thiene has been discussed (47). The cortile of Palazzo Farnese clearly was in Palladio's mind when he designed the Carità, and it looks as if he may have had an elevation of Peruzzi's Palazzo Massimi facade in front of him when he designed the cortile elevation of Palazzo Valmarana. Sangallo's thermal windows became part of Palladio's vocabulary, as did the basic formula of Bramante's House of Raphael. The scale, conviction, and the flair in the design of detail of the growing St Peter's, the Cortile del Belvedere, and the Villa Madama must have remained unforgettable points of reference for Palladio throughout his career.

Alongside the drawing instruments three beautiful small devices for telling the time have been included. These would have been useful when travelling or in the country, and Palladio probably carried something of the sort. The magnificent

astrolabe (175), signed by no less a mathematician than Egnazio Danti serves to call attention to the extent of the range of interests of Palladio and his close acquaintances. Gualdo writes that 'Trissino observing that Palladio was a young man of great intelligence and very much inclined towards the mathematical sciences' decided to explain Vitruvius (Gualdo, 1959, p.9). An 'astrolabe with four plates' was listed in the inventory of Trissino's effects drawn up at his death in Rome (Morsolin, 1894, p.524). Rucselli speaks of Daniele Barbaro's mathematical interests which were made public in his book on perspective (179). Both Cosimo Bartoli (190) and Silvio Belli (192) published books on surveying, and the latter lectured on mathematics and astronomy at the Accademia Olimpica, to which Valerio Barbarano had presented 'a metal astrolabe, damascened in silver, with a sighting-rule' (Ziggiotto ms, fol.11). H.B.

PIERO DI COSIMO 1462–1521(?)

154 Portrait of Giuliano da Sangallo (detail)
Photograph from the original in the Mauritshuis, The Hague

On the ledge in front of the distinguished Florentine architect (1443–1516) are his basic tools: a well worn quill pen and a pair of compasses. H.B.

*155 A set of drawing instruments, Milanese (?) c.1540
Steel damascened with gold and silver
Prov: Stowe, Drake and Arnold collections
Lent by the Museum of the History of Science, Oxford

The decorative technique of damascening, although known in Europe seems to have been practised during the Middle Ages only in the East. Reintroduced into the West by the 1540s, it had become a fashionable technique especially for decorating arms and armour (Blair 1971, pp.152–3). Damascening is achieved as follows: 'having heated the steel until it changes to a violet or blue colour, they hatch it over and across with a knife; then draw the design or ornament intended on this hatching with a fine brass point or bodkin. This done, they take fine gold wire and conducting it or chasing it according to the figure already designed, they sink it carefully into the hatches of the metal with a copper tool' (Chambers,

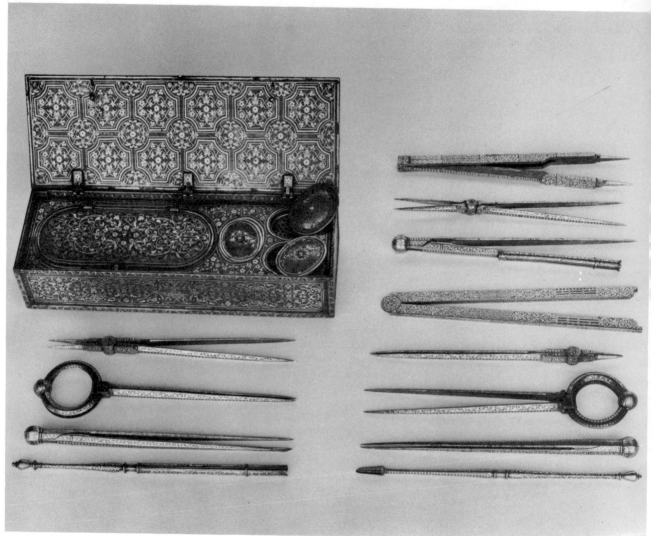

1788 cited by Blair). The popularity of the technique and its wide practice make it difficult to be certain that the set is Milanese, though Milan was a very important centre for this type of work. The set is close however to a casket in the Museo dell'Etai Cristiana in Brescia, and an inkwell in the Victoria and Albert Museum. It has been suggested that the crescents in the decoration of the box indicate that the set may have belonged to Diane de Poitiers (Museum catalogue card). Whether this is true or not, such an exquisite set of instruments certainly belonged to a very rich person, rather than a working architect. The set contains a casket with inkwells, and a pounce box, a charcoal holder, a lead or chalk holder, six pairs of dividers, a graduated folding rule, a pair of compasses for chalk, proportional dividers, and compasses for use with ink. L.F.

156 Drawing instruments, German c.1589
Gilt brass in a green leather case with a red leather lining trimmed with gold braid:
One instrument is signed and dated: MARCVS PVRMAN FECIT, MONACHIO 1589
Lent by the Royal Institute of British Architects, London

This set of instruments, probably made by different makers is the type which was in general use among architects, cartographers, suveyors, sea captains, gunners, etc. The set includes parallel rules, a half foot rule marked with Rhineland, Viennese, Nurnberg, Augsberg, Strasbourg and Munich feet, a sector, a ruling pen with a stylus on the end, two pairs of dividers, a pair of compasses with three heads (one for chalk or lead, one with a tracing wheel, and the other with a stylus), a compass, a protractor a set square and levels. L.F.

157 The Porta de'Borsari, Verona
Pen and ink: 43.4 × 29.4
Lent by the Royal Institute of British Architects (XII/16)

This drawing of the complex and bizarre second century *Porta de' Borsari*, which still exists in Verona, raises problems which have not yet been fully resolved. The attempt to attribute this and the other related drawings to the Veronese architect Falconetto (d. 1535) is unjustified, and the attribution to Palladio's nephew Marc'Antonio is demonstrably incorrect (Zorzi, 1959; Spielmann, 1966, p.172; Burns, 1973, and

1973–II). The note in the bottom right is in Palladio's mature handwriting, the other notes in a hand which neither corresponds with this, or with the 'epsilon handwriting' which appears on Palladio drawings which can be securely dated between 1541 and 1547. There are certain resemblances with the 'epsilon' and 'mature' handwriting, and probably this is in fact an autograph drawing from the 1530s, copied after an original by another artist, who might be Falconetto. H.B.

158 Section of the Temple of Venus and Rome, Rome
Pen and ink over brown chalk: 23 × 43.2
Epsilon handwriting
Lent by the Royal Institute of British Architects (XI/25)

Like the preceding drawing, this impressive study is almost certainly a copy after another artist's survey, with Palladio at the most adding the two measurements he gives. The building is shown reconstructed, but an unforgettable feature, the criss-cross pattern of the great niche is not drawn – a further indication that it does not derive from Palladio's on the spot studies. Whenever a building is shown in a perspective section or in elevation, there is the near certainty that he is copying: in this case (on analogy with the Codex Coner) probably from a lost Roman drawing of about 1515. H.B.

MARTEN VAN HEEMSKERCK 1498–1574
159 The Roman Forum
Pen and ink: 13 × 20.3
Lent by the Trustees of the Chatsworth Settlement

Heemskerck's drawing shows the Forum as Palladio knew it, and it includes many ruins which Palladio drew and reconstructed. The drawing, probably executed in the 1530s (Egger, 1931, II, p.12, no.9; cf. Huelsen-Egger, 1916, II, p.44, fol.79v), gives a view of the Roman Forum from a vantage point between the columns of the Temple of Vespasian (left) and those of the Temple of Saturn (right). Beneath the columns of Vespasian the ancient basilica of SS. Sergius and Bacchus, destroyed under Pius IV (Huelsen, 1927, p.462), can be seen, and next to it, Heemskerck records the attic of the Arch of Severus with its mediaeval tower. During the Middle Ages, a number of Roman monuments were either buried in dirt and debris or absorbed into later buildings. Also a number of houses had been built in the Forum, like those seen here between the Dogana di Grascia and the Column of Phocas (left and right in the middleground). Further in the distance is the portico of the Temple of Antonius and Faustina as well as the arches of the Basilica of Constantine and the Coliseum (cf. Lugli, 1970, pp.211–82). B.B.

MARTEN VAN HEEMSKERCK 1498–1574
160 View of the Old Piazza of St Peter's
Pen and ink: 13 × 20.3
Lent by the Trustees of the Chatsworth Settlement

Among Heemskerck's drawings of old St Peter's, the present one offers an extremely full account of the Piazza in Palladio's time (Egger, 1911, I, p.25, no.18) as seen from the *Porta Sancti Petri* on the north side of the square (cf. Duperac's Map of Rome of 1577). Old St Peter's was a rambling complex of buildings of varying age, as Heemskerck's sketch shows. On the extreme left is the old palace of the archpresbyters with its simple façade and single loggia. On its right was the forecourt of old St Peter's masked by the three portals built by Nicholas V. The Benediction Loggia, from which the pope gave his Easter blessing, stood between the old basilica and the apostolic palace on the right. In the right foreground is the wall of Boniface IX and the outbuildings of the Palace (Magnusson, 1958, pp.98–159); a portion of the Logge di San Damaso, begun by Bramante and finished by Raphael is also visible (Bruschi, 1969, pp.931–7). The level of the piazza itself was very uneven, being flat in front of the stairs of the basilica and gradually rising to the right. Heemskerck has also included what would have been a common sight, a cardinal and his retinue proceeding across the piazza towards the papal palace (Dickinson, 1960, pp.66–7). B.B.

161 Longitudinal section through Bramante's San Biagio
Pen and ink: 20.7 × 26.5
Epsilon handwriting
Photograph: Museo Civico, Vicenza D.11

There is no doubt that this is not an ancient structure, but instead the interior of Bramante's San Biagio, designed to stand on the far side of the cortile of the Palazzo dei Tribunali in Rome (Burns, 1973, p.152; Frommel, 1973, pp.327ff). Palladio

probably recalls the solution of the altar end of Bramante's small church in his plan of the Redentore. H.B.

162 Elevation of Bramante's Tempietto
Pen and ink over incised construction lines: 44.2 × 291
Epsilon handwriting
Photograph: Museo Civico, Vicenza (VIC.D.26v)

Palladio like Serlio before him, gave Bramante's *Tempietto* (1502) an honoured place among the works of the ancients. It was the only modern building which he published in his book dedicated to ancient temples, for as 'Bramante was the first to reveal the good and beautiful architecture, which from the Ancients up to the present time had lain hidden, it seemed to me reasonable to give a place to his works among those of the ancients' (IV, p.64). The Vicenza drawing, even down to the flag at the top, served as the basis for the right half of the elevation in the *Quattro Libri* (the other half shows the interior). H.B.

***163 Plan of the Villa Madama**
Pen, ink and wash over brown chalk: 33.8 × 46.8
Lent by the Royal Institute of British Architects (X/18)

This is the only plan of a modern building to be found among Palladio's drawings. Palladio shows the complex as it existed in his time, and not Raphael's complete project, which was for a large block, with a circular courtyard in the middle, and a Vitruvian theatre on the hillside above the cortile. Like Serlio (1540, p.CXLVIII) Palladio makes the loggia symmetrical whereas it has an apsidal ending only towards the hill. Apart from this 'improvement' Palladio's drawing is exceptionally accurate. He shows the layout of the whole lower level of the villa (and notes the location of the kitchen) combining this (without any explanation) with the plan of the upper level. Of all the modern buildings which he studied, the Villa Madama is probably the one which made most impression on him, and which has most in common with his subsequent style. It provided him with an instantly convincing reading of ancient architecture which was not to be found elsewhere. It focused his attention on features like the triangular stair arrangements of the Pantheon; the original appearance of Roman interiors; the plastic, densely packed character of ancient planning; the

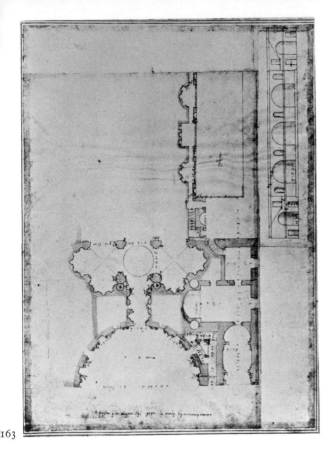

163

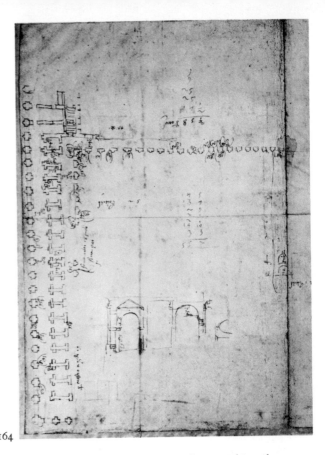

164

juxtaposition of columns and bases of different scales. The taste which created the façade of the Redentore (256) was probably decisively influenced by the hemicycle of the Villa Madama. Right at the end of his career Palladio cited the bulging pedestals of Raphael's villa in his façade designs for San Petronio.   H.B.

164 Plan of the Temple of Hercules at Tivoli
Pen and ink over chalk under drawing: 42.7 × 57.4
Epsilon handwriting
Lent by the Royal Institute of British Architects (IX/13V)

This free hand sketch plan was most probably made in May

1547, when one learns from a letter of Marco Thiene that Palladio was 'occupied in going to Tivoli, Palestrina, Porto, and Albano' (Zorzi, 1958, p.18). The note in the bottom left 'per austro per gradi 19', 'towards south at 19 degrees' shows that Palladio was using a surveying instrument like the one exhibited here. He has not shown the whole courtyard and has not attempted a restoration of the centrally placed temple. The sketch in the bottom left is a section through the arcades and central chamber.

The recto of the sheet shows a sketch of the 'Academy' of the nearby Hadrian's Villa, and like the verso was made on the spot. Many details are noted with much greater accuracy than in modern publications, but Palladio, like Pirro Ligorio who also drew this area, because of the unfamiliarity of the complex, curvilinear plan of the atrium, as well as its half-buried state, simplifies and rationalises it (Salza Prina Ricotti, 1973, p.21). H.B.

165 Plan of the Temple of Herucles at Tivoli

Pen and ink, and wash, over chalk underdrawing and incised construction lines: 28.2 × 42.5
Epsilon handwriting
Lent by the Royal Institute of British Architects (X/16)

This is a fair copy of the sketch plan, RIBA IX/13V, and the two taken together illustrate Palladio's working procedure in his study of ancient buildings. He indicates what he (mistakenly) believed to be the function of the building 'This is an ancient palace and it is at Tivoli' and makes a slip in his transcription of the bearing, writing '10' when it should have been '19'.   H.B.

*166 Italian circumferentor and case, 1612

Brass
Signed: LVD.SEM.FEC. A.D.1612
Prov: Lewis Evans Collection
Lent by the Museum of the History of Science, Oxford

The original wooden case is covered with gold tooled leather. There is a separate brass cover for the compass. The plate is divided into the eight winds: TRAMONTANA, GRECO, LEVANTE, SIROCCO, OSTRO, GARBINO, PONENTE, MAESTRO. These same eight winds are inscribed round the edge of the 1580 map of Vicenza, and are indicated by their initial letters on a sheet (168) in which Palladio records a series of bearings, undoubtedly by using a similar instrument. Each wind was subdivided into 45°, so that bearings are expressed in terms of a wind and degrees, and not in terms of 360°. An arm fitted with sights, swivels around the compass, and enables one to establish the bearing of landmarks or posts by moving the arm so that they are centered in the sights. The flat bar, which bears the inscription, Tartaglia explains, is useful if one wants to take the bearing of a wall: it is simply placed against the wall surface. He illustrates (167) an instrument with a similar cross piece. It is not clear exactly when instruments of this sort were first invented, though compasses had long been in use by miners (oral communication, Juergen Schulz). Its invention should probably be placed between about 1450, by which time Alberti had proposed a

166

method of surveying Rome *without* mentioning the use of a compass, and 1473 when Luca Fancelli was making a land survey with one. Given Fancelli's connection with Alberti, and Alberti's interest in instruments and surveying, it is not impossible that Alberti had some part in the elaboration or diffusion of the method. At the beginning of the sixteenth century Leonardo used a circumferentor to prepare his famous plan of Imola (Clark and Pedretti, 1968, p.10) and Raphael describes the use of one to survey ancient buildings in his letter of 1519 to Pope Leo X. From that time on compass bearings o architectural drawings become relatively common, probably a direct result of Raphael's adoption of the method. The use of these instruments permitted fairly accurate surveys to be made of antique complexes like the Baths, or Hadrian's Villa, and Raphael's, or Palladio's understanding of large scale antique planning in part depends on their circumferentors (Burns, 197 p.139). The circumferentor was also the basic working tool of surveyor and cartographer like Cristoforo Sorte (280).   H.B.

NICOLÒ TARTAGLIA
*167 Quesiti et inventioni diverse

V. Ruffinelli (for) N. Tartalea: Venetia. 1546. 4°.
Lent by the British Library Board (534.g.21)

Tartaglia wrote on a wide range of mathematical and applied

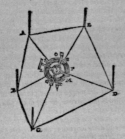

mathematical topics (*Storia di Brescia*, 1963, II, pp.598–617). His
Queries and Inventions has a notable importance as being the first
systematic treatment of the subject of ballistics. Another subject
which he discusses is surveying, and he explains, with
illustrations, the use of a circumferentor. This already had been
done by Raphael, but Tartaglia seems to be the first to explain
the use of the instrument in print. He shows that to make an
accurate plan it is only necessary to take the bearings of
successive points, measure the distance from the sighting
position to each point in turn, and then draw the whole thing
out to scale, reproducing the angles correctly (the
circumferentor itself, as Raphael says, can be used as a
protractor). Cosimo Bartoli also describes the use of the
circumferentor (190).   H.B.

168 The Imperial Fora, Rome, surveyed with a compass
Photograph: RIBA xiv/4v (detail)

In the bottom half of the sheet Palladio has sketched the plan of
the Forum of Augustus and the Forum of Nerva, indicating
some dimensions and bearings (i.e. G g 14 indicates Greco at
14°, or as we should say a bearing of 59°). A smaller area is
surveyed in more detail at the top of the sheet.   H.B.

169 L'antichita di Roma
V.Lucrino: Roma, 1554
Lent by the British Library Board (575.c.7)

Written during Palladio's last visit to Rome with Daniele
Barbaro and other Venetian gentlemen in 1554, probably
between February and July, (Puppi, 1973–III p.176), this is
Palladio's first publication. In the preface to his readers Palladio
says that he was spurred on to write the book by reading *Le
cose meravigliose di Roma*, the marvels of Rome, a popular guide
which had its origins in the Middle Ages, 'which was full of
strange lies'. So he devised this little book, drawing on ancient
writers and modern manuals (Biondo, Marliani, etc.) as well as
his own observation and measurements. The book does not set
out to describe Roman architecture as such, an enterprise already
in hand in the preparation of Barbaro's *Vitruvius* (1556).
Instead, in a simple, direct way, Palladio sketches the layout of
the city, its streets, gates, clocks, temples, public and domestic
building as well as the offices and functions of state, including
such things as coinage and festivals. The book was immensely
successful and went into several editions and translations (Pane,
1961, p.23).   L.F.

170 Descrittione de le Chiese . . . brevemente raccolta
Vincenzo Lucrino Roma 1554
Lent by the Royal Institute of British Architects

This little book, a pilgrim's guide to Rome was published
either with *L'antichita* (169) or shortly afterwards. After a brief
history of Rome to the conversion of Constantine, Palladio
outlines the early history, relics and liturgy of the seven most

important early Christian churches (San Giovanni in Laterano, San Pietro in Vaticano, San Paolo fuori le mura, S.ta Maria Maggiore, San Lorenzo fuori le mura, San Sebastiano and S.ta Croce in Gierusalemme). Dividing Rome into districts, he lists the other early Christian churches and at the end of the book gives a calendar of feast days and stations of the cross. Palladio does not specifically describe the architecture, unless he is reporting the case of the re-use of ancient materials (for example Honorius I's re-use of the gilded bronze tiles from the temple of Jupiter on the Capitoline to cover St Peters), nor does he describe modern churches. Bramante's Tempietto at San Pietro in Montorio is mentioned only for its sacred site as 'that round temple outside the said church is on the site of St Peter's cross'. Only three copies of this edition are recorded (oral communication Paul Quarrie).   L.F.

HIERONIMUS VULPARIA (Girolamo della Volpaia)

171 Ring dial, 1566

Gilt brass: outside diam. 6.2; width 1
Inscribed: HIERONIMUS.VVLPARIA FLORENTINUS. FA. ANO.D.C.
LXVI. AD.
Lent by the Museum of the History of Science, Oxford
(Lewis Evans Collection, I.5)

A simple form of portable sundial made for use in one latitude only in this case 43° 13′. The ring is pierced by a single hole tapering from the outside to the inner circumference. The inner circumference is engraved with a series of hour lines for the different months of the year. The hour lines on this dial are for Italian hours, that is, hours determined by dividing the time from the sunset on one day to sunset on the next into 24 equal hours. In use the ring dial is suspended by the little suspension ring and directed towards the sun so that sunlight passing through the hole in the circumference falls on the hour line for the appropriate month on the inner circumference. The position of the spot of light indicates the time.   F.M.
The maker of the ring dial is most probably related to Benvenuto della Golpaia (or Volpaia) a member of a family of instrument makers, who during the siege of Florence in 1529 surveyed the city at night using a magnetic compass. He made and sent a model prepared on the basis of the survey to Clement VII (Vasari, 1881, V, p.62; Pedretti, 1962, p.24, n.10).   L.F.

172 Horizontal pin-gnomon dial, Italian, 1585

Gilt brass with pasteboard case covered with gold tooled leather and lined with silk
Diam: 8.8 (of the plate)
Inscribed: *Romae Anno dni* 1585
Lent by the Museum of the History of Science, Oxford (Lewis Evans collection 1.60)

This sundial is made for use in two latitudes. Either side of the circular plate may be used; one side is engraved with hour-lines for Italian hours for use in latitude 42°, the other with similar hour-lines for use in latitude 45°. In use, the sundial is placed in its case with the appropriate side uppermost, the whole placed on a horizontal surface and aligned on the meridian by means of the small compass. The shadow cast by the tip of the small vertical gnomon then indicates the hour.   F.M.

173 Astronomical Compendium, Italian c.1600

Gilt brass: 5.2 × 5 depth 1.3
Lent by the History of Science Museum, Oxford (Lewis Evans collection I. 103)

This little book-shaped compendium includes two sundials: a vertical pin-gnomon sundial for Italian hours in the inside of the lid and a horizontal cup-shaped sundial (called a *scaphe*) also for Italian hours in the main body of the compendium. This compendium is used in a similar manner to the Italian pin-gnomon dial described above. With the aid of the small compass the compendium is aligned on the meridian with the lid opened vertically towards the north. The shadows of the *tips* of the pin shaped gnomons indicate the time in Italian hours. The marking of the tropics on the dials gives a rough indication of the declinination of the sun throughout the year. The table engraved on the inside of the lower cover gives the hour of midnight through the year in Italian hours – it will be seen to vary from the 7th to the 4th and back to the 7th hour since Italian hours are counted from sunset, the end of the first hour after sunset being 1 o'clock in Italian hours.   F.M.

Attributed to HENDRIK VAN BALEN 1560–1632

174 The measurers
Panel: 29.1 × 52.5 (visible surface)
Lent by the Museum of the History of Science, Oxford
(Lewis Evans Collection, I.C.180)

The painting shows the various types of measurement and the instruments associated with them. On the right a woman measures cloth with a rule and at her feet are scissors and scales. In the centre a geometrician draws with his compasses, around him are a drawing board, a plumb line, a sun dial (?), a right angle, levels, dividers and a globe. On the left a child reads music. In the background bales, liquids and grain are being measured. In the far distance on the left are two surveyors at work. The principal units of measurement used in Vicenza were displayed under the loggia of the church of San Vincenzo.
L.F.

EGNAZIO DANTI 1536–86

175 Astrolabe c.1580
Gilt brass: diam. 40.8
Signed on the *mater*: . F.EGNATIVS DANTES
Prov. Roussel collection
Lent by the Museum of the History of Science, Oxford
(Lewis Evans Collection, I.C.180)

The common type of planispheric astrolabe consists essentially of a star map moving over a stereographic projection of the horizon at a particular latitude and circles of altitude between the horizon and the zenith. On this astrolabe the single plate forming the body of the instrument is engraved for latitude 43° 40′, probably for Florence. Other astrolabes usually have a selection of plates which can be placed in the body of the instrument so that the plate for the appropriate latitude is on top of the pile. The star map is the cut-away sheet of metal (which can rotate above the plate) in which the zodiacal circle is marked, together with the positions of various fixed stars by the tips of curved pointers. An astrolabe is basically a calculating device which enables certain problems connected with the relative positions of the sun and the fixed stars, and the rising and setting of these heavenly bodies to be solved. By rotating the star map over the plate, one imitates the apparent rotation of the stars about the celestial pole. By making an observation with the alidade (or sighting rule) of the angular altitude above the horizon of the sun in the daytime, or of one of the stars marked on the *rete* (star map) at night, and then rotating the star map until the position of the sun in the zodiac (on the day of observation) or the appropriate star (depending which had been observed) lies on the altitude circle on the plate below corresponding to the observed altitude, the star map has been rotated to represent the heavens at the moment observation.

Having done this it is possible to ascertain the time of day or night at which the observation is made, the position of any of the other stars at that moment of time, and various other astronomical data. The back of this astrolabe is engraved with a special form of planispheric astrolabe which may be used in any latitude.   F.M.

Egnazio Danti came from a family of artists, his father was an architect and a friend of Peruzzi, his brother Vincenzo a prominent sculptor, who published a book on proportion (Burns, 1975, p.149). Danti himself was a mathematician and cartographer. He supervised the design of the Gallery of the Geographical maps in the Vatican (20), for which he was awarded the bishopric of Alatri. He also edited and provided a substantial commentary to Vignola's book on perspective.   H.B.

Palladio's contacts with artists and writers

Palladio was associated with artists from the very start of his life, when Vincenzo de' Grandi acted as his godfather (109). His contacts with painters, sculptors, and writers on the arts were continuous and almost as important for him as his contacts with other architects.

In considering Palladio's first two decades in Venice, one artist stands out as someone from whom Palladio could have learned much. In Vicenza Valerio Belli in the field of the arts was the equivalent of Trissino in that of literature and diplomacy: a great figure, with great achievements at the Papal court behind him and with immense knowledge to make available, if he chose, to younger artists. There is no direct evidence of contact between Palladio and Belli, but Girolamo Pittoni's son Battista (20) witnessed Belli's will, and Palladio was later on close terms with Valerio's son Elio and his nephew Silvio.

Palladio must have seen Belli's famous collection, on which Vasari says he spared no expense, 'hence his house in Vicenza is full with such varied things, that it is a marvel' (Vasari, 1880, V, p.382). Belli's will gives some idea of these varied things: '... all my marbles, that is statues, and other similar antique and modern things and also all those which are of bronze or other metal and those of plaster, large and small, or of other materials which are to be found in my studio ... all my medal dies which may be 150 in number and all the drawings which are in the books or elsewhere, and above all the drawing of Trajan's column.' (Mantese, 1964, p.639). One cannot help wondering how much in the way of architectural drawings Belli owned, in addition to the volume of Lombard antiquities drawn by the Milanese painter Bramantino and seen and copied by Vasari (1881, V, pp.511-13). His drawings of Trajan's column (that is, of the reliefs, not just the column, or he would not have specifically mentioned them) could possibly have some relation to the decoration of Palazzo Chiericati with scenes from the column, or to Palladio's studies of wooden bridge structures (000). Nor is it to be excluded that Belli owned architectural drawings by, or derived from, Raphael. He could therefore be the source of the drawing for the Villa Madama (000) or, less conjecturally, of 'the book [of drawings?] of Rafael d'Urbino', and the 'other book of antiquities of Rome with *figure* (either figures or illustrations)' in the Accademia Olimpica (Ziggiotti ms, fol.11). The decoration of his buildings constantly brought Palladio into contact with other artists: Vittoria, India, Brusasorci, and Zelotti are among the most frequently recurring names (he mentions them all in the *Quattro Libri*) and examples of their work are exhibited here. Palladio regularly frequented the company of other artists, especially in Venice, as Cosimo Bartoli's letters make clear, and discussed artistic and design problems with them (188). He was also in close contact with experienced authors of illustrated or architectural books (Salviati, Barbaro, Cosimo Bartoli, Silvio Belli) and discussions with some of them must have contributed to the successful design of the *Quattro Libri*.   H.B.

PAOLO VERONESE 1528–88
*176 Portrait of Daniele Barbaro, 1514–70
Canvas: 121 × 105.5
Lent by the Rijksmuseum, Amsterdam (2529, B.6)

The usual attribution is plausible, but the painting has not received the attention which it deserves (*Catalogue of Pain* 1960). In his left hand Barbaro holds open his *Vitruvius* of (178) and the volume in the background is his book on perspective of 1568 (179), though its size indicates that this manuscript, and not the printed edition, and hence is not a reliable indication of date.

The portrait compactly summarises Barbaro's situation; h dressed as an ecclesiastic, but is shown with the books of w he was proudest. Barbaro belonged to a famous Venetian noble family and studied in Padua from 1537 to 1545, wh was put in charge of the creation of the botanic garden the His Aristotelian studies of these years had a very great infl on the character of his commentary on Vitruvius. Like his brother Marc'Antonio (278) he seemed to be destined for distinguished public career, and in 1549–51 was ambassade England and Scotland. While he was away, to ensure a cer and politically dependable succession, the Venetian govern brought about his nomination as successor to the Patriarch Aquileia, Giovanni Grimani, who in fact outlived him. He enjoyed the title of Patriarch Elect, but was without pastor administrative responsibilities. His studies together with th embellishment of his villa at Maser (351) from whose estat much of his income was derived, were therefore the only f of activity open to him, as a career in government service now debarred. His relations with Palladio were obviously and very amicable in the years leading up to the publicatio the Vitruvius, and Palladio travelled to Rome with him in 1554. The evidence for a later cooling between the two as result of Veronese's work at Maser is not conclusive (cf. Pu 1973–III, p.175) especially given Barbaro's probable role i obtaining the S.Francesco della Vigna commission for Pal (Puppi, 1973, p.347).   H.B.

DANIELE BARBARO

177 Della eloquenza, Dialogo . . . : nuovamente mandato in luce da Girolamo Ruscelli

In Venetia, appresso Vicenzo Valgrifio. MDLVII.
Lent by the British Library Board (75.a.5)

This publication of an early work of Barbaro, written when he was a student in Padua, is chiefly of interest for Ruscelli's dedication to the aristocratic *Accademia dei Costanti* established the year before in Vicenza, probably in reaction to the socially much more widely based *Accademia Olimpica* (Puppi, 1973–II). Ruscelli stresses Barbaro's nobility, the quarterings of his parents, his links with other noble families, as well as his learning. The same combination of nobility and 'noble and virtuous exercises; as in arms, letters, music, and every other honoured pastime', he sees as distinguishing the forty *Costanti*.
H.B.

DANIELE BARBARO

178 I dieci libri dell'architettura di M. Vitruvio tradutti et commentati da mons. Barbaro patriarca eletto di Aquilleggia. In Venetia per Francesco Marcolini. 1556

Lent by the Royal Institute of British Architects

Barbaro's translation and commentary on Vitruvius was the most thorough and, from the point of view of a working architect, most useful discussion of Vitruvius to have been produced. Although Fra Giocondo (1511) had made the Latin text much easier to understand and had provided helpful illustrations, his woodcuts were crude, and he provided neither commentary nor translation. Cesare Cesariano's beautiful commented translation (1521) was already out of date when it appeared in relation to the advances made in Rome in the study of Vitruvius and ancient architecture.
Raphael, Sangallo, and Peruzzi had given thought to an annotated translation of Vitruvius, but their labours did not lead to publication. The need for a new translation was obviously widely felt and is expressed in the often cited letter of Claudio Tolomei to Agostino de' Landi (Tolomei, 1547, pp.81ff.). Tolmei writes of the usefulness of a translation of Vitruvius into good Italian, accompanied by illustrations. It is perhaps not fortuitous that in the very same year in which Tolmei's letter were published (in Venice), Barbaro began

work on his Vitruvius (Zorzi, 1958, p.113). He furnished an accurate translation and a more than ample commentary. He says himself that he had no collaborators, "except that in the drawings of the important illustrations I have used the work of Messer Andrea Palladio from Vicenza, who . . . has aimed at the true architecture, not only understanding the beautiful and subtle ideas behind it, but actually realising it in practice . . .' (Zorzi, 1958, p.114). Palladio had studied Vitruvius closely from the time of his association with Trissino and, so far from being a mere illustrator, was able to provide Barbaro with insights which he could not have obtained elsewhere. The splendid plates with which the book is illustrated are the first clear, published statement of Palladio's distinctive interpretation of the essential character of ancient architecture, and they revealed him 'as he who . . . has with judgment chosen the most beautiful styles of the ancients . . .' (Barbaro, *ibid*, p.114). Many of Palladio's great themes are presented in the Vitruvius: the ancient theatre reconstruction, on which the Teatro Olimpico is based; the giant columns with balconies strung between them, as at the Villa Sarego; and the house with a pedimented portico. H.B.

DANIELE BARBARO

*179 La Pratica della Perspettiva . . . Opera molto utile a Pittori, a Scultori, & ad Architetti.

In Venetia, appresso Camillo, & Rutilio Borgommieri fratelli al segno di S. Giorgio. MDLXVIII.
Lent by the British Library Board (536.m.21)

Barbaro's straightforward account of perspective, which relies heavily on Serlio's for its illustrations, is an indication of his continuing artistic interests. It was a useful manual, and important as the first publication of the *camera oscura*. Palladio seems to have had no part in its production, but Barbaro does cite Palladio's book two years before its publication, 'the swelling in the middle of the column called *entasis* in Greek is made with the methods Vitruvius describes. Or as Andrea Palladio says in his book on private houses' (p.137). H.B.

VALERIO BELLI C.1468–1546

80 Three plaquettes and one mould
Lent by the Victoria and Albert Museum

Born into a respected Vicentine family, Valerio Belli belonged to the Vicentine establishment. Among his friends were Trissino, the Archbishop Lodovico Chiericati, and the antiquarian and art patron Girolamo Gualdo (Morsolin, 1878, p.13; Barbieri, 1965, pp.682–4; Puppi, 1972, pp.35–7, 55). Belli trained as a goldsmith and developed a talent as an engraver of crystals and dies. He acquired considerable fame in the field of engraving at the court of Leo X, where he knew Trissino, Pietro Bembo, and the future Cardinal of Vicenza, Nicolio Ridolfi (Zorzi, 1920, pp.186–7). For the second Medici Pope, Clement VII, Belli created his masterpiece, the crystal casket with twenty-four scenes from the life of Christ, now in the *Museo degli Argenti*, in Palazzo Pitti, Florence. After 1530 Belli spent most of his time in Vicenza, returning to Rome briefly in 1539, where he may have entered the service of Paul III in the papal mint (Zorzi, 1920, p.190, note 7). In Vicenza Belli amassed a large collection of antiquities and casts which were sold by his heirs to Cardinal Madruzzo of Trent in 1546 (Zorzi, 1915, pp.253–7). His will is published by Mantese (1964, p.639).

As an artist Belli showed his Venetian origins in a relief style with classically draped figures seen against an architectural background, a style brought to perfection by his contemporary Tullio Lombardo. Belli was, however, strongly influenced by the figural style of Raphael and of Michelangelo, and most of his known works bear the impress of his Roman years (Kris, 1929, pp.49–56; Puppi, 1972, p.22). His facility enabled Belli to work quickly, and Vasari observed that Belli had flooded the world with his own works (Vasari, 1881, V, p.381). This is borne out by the Mantuan artist Giovanni Battista Bertani, who, in a letter of 1563, says that the figures in the background of his *Nativity* for the Duomo of Mantua are taken 'from those of Valerio Belli which are sold in all the piazzas of Italy' (oral communication, L.F., 1975). Indeed, facility may be responsible for the most conspicuous aspect of Belli's art, namely that once he found his idiom he never altered it. The plaquettes exhibited here illustrate Belli's formulae. All of them are casts after original crystals and are dictated by a simplified classical style. The fourth object is, in fact, the means by which Valerio Belli multiplied his labours. It is a brass mould for casting plaquettes, based on one of the panels from the Pitti Casket. B.B.

(a) The Incredulity of St Thomas
(878–1904)
Bronze: 6.2 × 9.95
Lit: Molinier, 1886, p.202, no.282. Maclagen, 1924, p.64. Pope-Hennessy, 1965, p.10, no.353.

(b) The Adoration of the Shepherds
(6968–1860)
Gilt bronze with handle to form a pax: 8 × 6.7
Lit: Fortnum, 1876, p.72. Molinier, 1886, p.191, no.258. Maclagen, 1924, pp.61–2. Pope-Hennessy, 1965, pp.10–11, no.13.

(c) The Adoration of the Magi
Verso: The Presentation of Christ in the Temple. (A.477–1910)
Bronze: 7.1 × 5.05
Lit: Molinier, 1886, pp.192–3, no.262. Maclagen, 1924, p.62. Pope-Hennessy, 1965, pp.8–9, no.4.

(d) Christ and the Woman taken in Adultery
(M.197–1929)
Brass mould: 5 × 5.8
Lit: Molinier, 1886, p.195, no.268 as a plaquette. B.B.

179

181

182

183

*181 Relief of Valerio Belli

Marble: 54.1 × 44.8
Lent by the Victoria and Albert Museum (A.4–1932)

In the seventeenth century, the Gualdo collection in Vicenza contained three portraits of Valerio Belli: a small tondo, supposedly by Raphael; a marble relief, attributed to Michelangelo; and a relief in gesso, by Belli's close friend Archbishop Lodovico Chiericati (Puppi, 1972, pp.21–2, 35, 47). In addition to these portraits, several other likenesses of Belli existed in his own lifetime, among them a portrait in the museum of Paolo Giovio, now lost (Rovelli, 1928, p.193, no.354), and a drawing of Belli in the Boymans Museum, Rotterdam, most recently attributed to Parmigianino (Popham, 1971, I, p.178, no.569; cf. Kurz, 1937–8, p.38). The drawing in Rotterdam served as the basis for a number of medallic portraits cast by Belli himself; it was also copied for Vasari's woodcut of Belli in the 1568 edition of the *Lives* (Prinz, 1966, p.132). There was also a marble relief, possibly the one from the Gualdo collection, which George Vertue saw in the Museum Trevisianum, Venice, in the eighteenth century Walpole Society, 1938, XXVI, p.12).

The present relief is approximately the same size as both the Gualdo relief and the one formerly in the Museum Trevisianum. It may have come from the Gualdo collection, though Girolamo Gualdo's attribution of the relief to Michelangelo, with whom Belli was acquainted (Barocchi-Ristori, 1967, II, p.270, 291), is clearly erroneous. A more recent suggestion by Popp that Ammannati may have carved i (Pope-Hennessy, 1964, p.498) would also be unlikely, for the artist of the relief appears to be Venetian and conversant with the style of Tullio Lombardo, to judge from the precise, classical treatment of the hair and features. Puppi has recently suggested that the relief may be a self-portrait (1972, p.47, note 2), but, despite the plausibility of such a suggestion, comparative material is insufficient for a positive identification of Belli as the artist. B.B.

ALESSANDRO VITTORIA 1525–1608

82 Self-portrait
Terracotta bust: h. 80
Lent by the Victoria and Albert Museum (A.12–1948)

The two terracotta busts exhibited here come from a group of six, purchased from the Manfrin collection, Venice, as by Alessandro Vittoria (Pope-Hennessy, 1964, pp.531–4). Recent thermoluminescent tests by Dr Stuart Fleming of the Research Laboratory for Archaeology, Oxford, date the firing of the present bust to between 1550–1710 and that of its companion to between 1525–1680 (written communication, Charles Avery, 1975). These findings and the high quality of the works themselves support the traditional attribution of both busts to Vittoria. Both have, in addition, the appearance of casts after original models, for they lack the crisper treatment of features, hair, and drapery found in hand modelled clay. Like most casts, the present busts have been covered with a mixture of water and clay, in order to give them a more polished surface. That accounts for their unexpectedly light colour; the natural red of the terracotta can still be seen underneath the surface coating.
An inscription on the base, painted by a later hand, identifies this bust as a portrait of the sculptor Alessandro Vittoria. The terracotta is almost identical with the marble portrait bust on Vittoria's tomb in San Zaccaria, Venice (Cessi, 1962, p.25, pl.44), with slight differences in the arrangement of the dress. Although Vittoria's monument was under construction between 1602–5 (Predelli, 1908, pp.145–7), the lateral figures had been finished by 1566 (Gerola, 1924–5, p.343). The self-portrait may have been executed in the early 1590s as Vittoria appears to be in late middle age. The present bust must have been cast after a portrait of Vittoria, presumably the model used by the artist for his tomb.   B.B.

BERNADINO INDIA 1528–90

183 Madonna and child with St Anne
Pen and ink wash: 24 × 15
Lent by the Trustees of the British Museum

This drawing was discovered by Philip Pouncey and identified as a study for the altarpiece for the Cappella Pellegrini in San Bernardino, Verona, of 1579. It is of great importance,

alongside the drawings in the Scholz collection, as a certain example of India's drawing style. It also establishes that India was the author of some of the figures on Palladio's drawings in Vicenza (oral communication, Ballarin, 1973; Magagnato, 1974).   H.B.

DOMENICO BRUSASORCI 1516–67

184 Madonna in Glory with St Sebastian, Sta Monica, a bishop and S.Rocco
Pen, ink and wash heightened with white: 43.3 × 27.5
Lent by the Trustees of the Chatsworth Settlement (no.230)

This cartoon (which is not definitive) is for the altarpiece in S. Eufemia, Verona. It is a key work as together with a drawing in the Uffizi (1672 ORN) it provides the basis for the reconstruction of Brusasorci's graphic *oeuvre* (Ballarin, 1971, p.105).   L.F.

DOMENICO BRUSASORCI 1516–67

185 Diana and Mars
Pen, ink and wash: 20.4 × 28.2
Lent by the Visitors of the Ashmolean Museum, Oxford (no.690)

This drawing was already placed in the Veneto with Parker's attribution to Giuseppe Salviati (Parker, 1956, II, no.690), and has now been convincingly assigned to Brusasorci on the basis of a survey of Brusasorci's whole development (Ballarin, 1971, p.110). The study is, as Parker suggested, probably for decoration over a door.   H.B.

GIOVANNI BATTISTA ZELOTTI 1526–78

186 A woman fleeing through a wood to the right, turns back to a child on the left
Wash heightened with white: 28.5 × 19.8
Lent by Her Majesty the Queen

The drawing tentatively associated with Schiavone (Popham and Wilde, 1949, p.332, no.921) has been convincingly attributed to Zelotti, and related to one of the oval monochrome frescoes flanking the Council of the Gods fresco in the Palazzo Chiericati. It is suggested that the drawing was one of a repertory of designs which could be inserted into various decorative schemes or paintings, and that the drawing probably originated in the designs for the frescoes on the Monte di Pietà façade of 1558 (Ballarin, 1971, p.112).   L.F.

GIOVANNI BATTISTA ZELOTTI 1526–78

187 Design for a frieze(?)
Red chalk: 237 × 396
Prov: Carlo Ridolfi, General Guise
Lent by the Governing Body of Christ Church, Oxford

The attribution was made by Byam-Shaw and accepted by Mullaly (1971) and Ballarin (1971). This very lively and characteristic drawing was most probably for a frieze round the top of a room. Dimensions are marked, and the profiles of the mouldings clearly indicated. The subject of the central relief has been identified as Pompey's head being presented to Caesar (Mullaly, 1971) and both the antique subject and the decorative language are comparable to Lorenzo Rubini's stucco panels above the ground floor windows of Palazzo Barbaran (Zorzi, 1964, p.257).   H.B.

188 Portrait of Cosimo Bartoli (1503–72), c.1565
Woodcut: 21.5 × 15.3
Lent by the Visitors of the Ashmolean Museum, Oxford

The page with the portrait has been removed from Bartoli's *Del modo di misurare le distantie* (190) and could well be based on a drawing by one of his artist friends in Venice (Giuseppe Salviati?).
Cosimo Bartoli came from a family of Medici supporters. His father was a friend of Michelangelo, and he himself, in addition to literary studies, developed an interest in architecture and mathematics. In 1540 he obtained a living (*prepositura*) attached to the Florentine Baptistry; in 1560 became secretary of Cardinal Giovanni de' Medici; and from 1562 to 1572 was permanent Florentine agent in Venice (de Blasi and Cantagalli, 1964, pp.561–3). His official despatches and his letters to Vasari (Frey, 1930) give a very full picture of life in the city, as well as of Bartoli's own life and circle of friends. These included Palladio, Rusconi, Salviati, Vittoria, and Danese Cattaneo, whose greetings Bartoli customarily sends in his letters to Vasari in the period 1568–71 (Frey, 1930, pp.383, 396, 402, 403, 427, 434, 593). His house seems to been a meeting place for this group of

friends, all of them very aware of what Vasari had written about them in his *Lives*. Bartoli writes to Vasari that he had no asked Salviati to acquire some artists' materials for him, but another painter friend instead, as Salviati 'is complaining a bit about you, as in your book on painters you put him after Zuccari' (Frey, 1930, p.572).   H.B.

LEONBATTISTA ALBERTI

189 L'architettura, tradotta in lingua Fiorentina da Cosimo Bartoli, Gentilhuomo, & Academico Fiorentino . . .
In Venetia, Appresso Francesco Franceschi, Sanese. 1565
Lent by the Royal Institute of British Architects

Alberti's book on architecture was one of Palladio's basic sources, and many passages in the *Quattro Libri* derive from it. An Italian translation was published in Venice in 1546, and Bartoli brought out the first edition of his translation in Florence in 1550, adding illustrations to the previously unillustrated text. Already in its early years the Accademia Olimpica possessed Barbaro's *Vitruvius*, the 1550 edition of Vasari's *Lives*, and Alberti's '*Architettura*' though it is not clear in what edition (Ziggiotti ms, fol.10v). Bartoli wrote to his friend Giorgio Vasari on 14 August 1564, 'we shall reprint Leon batista, in such a way that it will be more sought after than the first time, because it will be much more beautiful. And I shall also see that it is printed more correctly and with a type face which is not less beautiful than the original one; and perhaps I shall decide to print it in 4°, so that it will be company for your work on the Painters' (Frey, 1930, p.107). Bartoli's comments on his forthcoming publication provide an interesting insight into the experienced and professional circle of publishers and authors of architectural and illustrated books with which Palladio was connected in Venice. Their discussions and collective experience in part lie behind the high quality of the design of the *Quattro Libri*, which was printed by the Franceschi, who also printed Bartoli's books.   H.B.

COSIMO BARTOLI 1503–72

190 Del modo di misurare le distantie . . .
F.Franceschi, Venetia, 1564
Lent by the British Library Board (531.g.5)
Bartoli's book is a general treatise on all aspects of surveying. He includes a section on the use of the circumferentor.   H.B.

191 Regola di far perfettamente col compasso la voluta et del capitello ionico et d'ogn' altra sorte per Iosephe Salviati ritrovata

In Venetia Per Francesco Marcolini
Lent by the British Library Board (Cup. 1247. p.46)

Salviati in this short work explains a method for constructing the spiral of the Ionic volute, based on a half finished antique capital he had seen, where the construction was still visible. The book was published by Francesco Marcolini, who produced a number of illustrated works of the highest quality and was a very important innovator in the field of architectural publishing. He published Books III and IV of Serlio (200 and 201) and also Barbaro's *Vitruvius*.
Salviati's intimacy with Palladio emerges not only from Bartoli's letters, but also from Palladio's mention of him in his contribution to Bassi's *Dispareri*. H.B.

193 I Quattro Libri dell'Architettura

Venezia, per Dominico de' Franceschi, 1570
Lent by the Royal Institute of British Architects

Neither Palladio's fame nor his influence would have been so great were it not for his *Four Books on Architecture*, first published in 1570. These set out his principles and procedures with admirable lucidity, as well as constituting (in Books II and III) a spectacular retrospective exhibition of his own works, of a richness and range which no other architect published and few could have produced at this time. The nearest contemporary parallel for a 'retrospective' of this sort is a book on the planning of menus, whose author published the menus of a long series of banquets and dinners which he had arranged while at the Ferrarese court (Rossetti, 1584).
Palladio's book derives from the mainstream of Renaissance architectural writing. The range of topics covered, and the starting point for the discussion of building materials, the orders, and town and country houses was provided by Vitruvius. Palladio drew very heavily on Alberti's mid-fifteenth century *Concerning Building* (*De Re Aedificatoria*), which his friend Cosimo Bartoli had translated into Italian in 1550, and re-issued in Venice in 1565 (189). Alberti filled out and amplified Vitruvius' basic message that buildings should be

functional, lasting, and beautiful (Palladio, 1570, I, p.6) and showed how this idea could be applied in the day to day business of design. This, and Alberti's expansion of the Vitruvian idea that buildings should be appropriate to their site, their function, their owner, etc (*ibid* II, p.3) are fundamental to Palladio's whole outlook. Palladio did not restrict his reading to Vitruvius and Alberti. He also drew on ancient Roman writers on agriculture, and the very popular fourteenth-century writer on villa management, Pietro Crescenzio and even repeats Crescenzio's recommendation that the threshing floor should be visible from the owner's residence (II, pp.46 and 294).
Palladio's book has illustrations on most of its pages; many pages carry full page plates. His combination of text and illustrations, as well as his provision of sections dealing with ancient buildings, with the orders, and with domestic architecture derives from and brings to its greatest perfection a long Renaissance tradition of *illustrated* architectural books. (Alberti's book immensely influential though it was, had no illustrations until Bartoli provided them for his editions.) Filarete's treatise of about 1460 was illustrated (Spencer, 1965) but too bizarre and rambling to have much influence. The writings of the Sienese painter, sculptor, engineer and architect Francesco di Giorgio are a different matter (Maltese, 1967). Although Francesco, who wrote in the last two decades of the fifteenth century, was unable to understand the Vitruvian system of the orders, his writings although never published, were widely known and often copied. One of his manuscripts was owned by Leonardo. He knew Bramante, and his pupil Peruzzi was a prominent architectural personality in Rome between 1505 and his death in 1536. Peruzzi's unpublished notes and drawings were in great part inherited by his disciple Serlio, who made ample use of them in the series of architectural books he brought out from 1537 onwards, and it has been shown Trissino (and hence Palladio) was in touch with Serlio in the years immediately preceding Serlio's departure for France in 1541 (Olivato, 1971).
Palladio would have been aware of Francesco di Giorgio's innovations in the field of architectural writing both in Serlio's adaptation and almost certainly through the direct consultation of copies of his manuscripts, which Barbaro cited for his section on ancient fireplaces, and which were drawn on heavily, but without acknowledgment of the fact, by Pietro

Cataneo, with whom Palladio was in touch in Venice (000). One should note that there is also a volume of copies after Francesco di Giorgio in Vicenza, and another in New York has a probable Vicentine provenance (Puppi, 1973–II, p.71). Francesco was perfectly aware of the need to supplement a written text on architecture with illustrations, and sought to provide a comprehensive range of examples of different sorts of buildings, in part based on his own designs (Burns, 1975–II) which other architects could then adapt to the particular circumstances which confronted them. He presented ancient buildings in plan and elevation, with measurements, and a short explanatory note. Both these aspects of Francesco's writings were adopted by Serlio. Palladio then merely modified this basic approach. In representing ancient buildings he facilitated consultation by putting all the dimensions on the illustrations whereas Serlio's readers had to search through the small print for them. He completely redrew all the material he had gathered on ancient buildings, to ensure uniformity of presentation. Serlio's plates in Book III betray the fact that they are based on drawings by different architects, using different conventions, but one would never know that Palladio's plate of the *Tempietto di Clitunno* was based on a drawing by Pirro Ligorio (Burns, 1973, p.153). He also gave great attention both to reconstructing ruined buildings, and showing their details accurately: in this he is emulating and improving not on Serlio, but Labacco (1552), whose merit was to have reproduced drawings and reconstructions by Peruzzi and Sangallo without making them crude or distorting them in the process.

In discussing domestic architecture Palladio did not seek to create a whole hierarchy of types, from the one-room dwelling to the royal palace, as Francesco di Giorgio and Serlio had done. Instead he presented his own works as models. He altered them, ironing out for instance the irregularities imposed by the site in the case of Palazzo Valmarana, so as to make them more generally useful as models. But he offered a more substantial architectural education than does Serlio, as he points out the specific character of the site and of the commission (the Rotonda on a hill, the Palazzo Chiericati on a piazza, and liable to flooding, etc) which had called forth the solutions he publishes. Palladio's book is truly educational. Serlio offers innumerable models but no coherent explanation of what an architect should seek to achieve. He is only too obviously swayed by what he has seen last, or whom he has spoken to most recently. Hence his complete turn-around from Peruzzian criticism of Vitruvius in 1537, to rigid Vitruvianism in 1540 (Burns, 1975, n.83). But Palladio develops, and progressively illustrates a single reasonable message. He takes care to write clearly and simply, 'to discuss Architecture in as orderly and clear a fashion as I can . . . And in all these books I shall avoid long windedness, and will simply provide the comments which I think most necessary, and I shall use those terms, which craftsmen normally use today'. Thus he simply calls the bulge in the middle of the column a swelling, not *entasis*. There is no trace of stylistic or pedantic affectation in the book, and even the dedication of the first half to an old friend, Giacomo Angarano, not even one of the richest of the Vicentine nobility is a reflection of this overall tone.

The *Quattro Libri* is one of the most impressive of Palladio's creations. The plates, with their placing of the plan and elevation on the same page are exceptionally well designed, and sometimes have an audacious quality like the double spread of stairs (I, pp.62–3) or the Roman road (III, p.10) which is both surprising and attractive.

The first stimulus to write the book probably came from Trissino, who roughly scribbled some pages on architecture himself (Puppi, 1973–II) and from Serlio's books. Palladio did not rush into print. He probably began collecting material in the early 1540s, and his manuscript was notable enough to be cited by Doni in 1555 and Barbaro in 1556 (Puppi, 1973, p.443). Barbaro referred to it again in 1568. In the mid-1560s with substantial help from his two sons Silla and Leonida as far as the physical work of writing went, he brought it up to date, incorporating his more recent designs. There are numbers of drawings and drafts of chapters for the *Quattro Libri* among the sheets at the R.I.B.A., and a complete draft of the second book (without illustrations) is in the Correr Library in Venice (Zorzi, 1958, pp.163–93). It was probably this draft which was seen and used by Vasari (1881, p.531). The allegorical figure of architecture in the Villa Emo, though the fact seems to have passed without comment, is holding what appears to be a copy of Palladio's manuscript (196). Palladio was obviously working up to the last minute on the book, and in fact his final design for the plan of Palazzo Barbarano, after the enlargement of the site, was not ready in time for the block

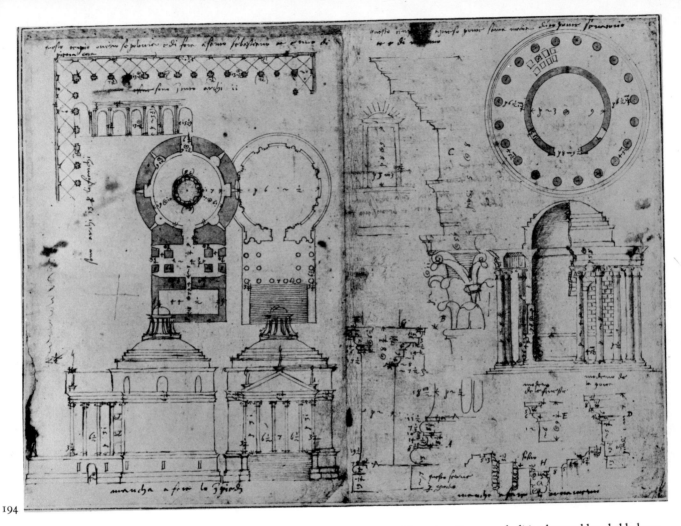

194

cutter and the book went to press without it (II, p.22). The standard of the woodcuts is high, though there are some lapses and mistakes in execution. But Palladio was rightly satisfied with the result 'having finally reduced them (his books) to the greatest perfection of which I am capable' (I, p.3).

Palladio planned other books (on Arches, and Theatres and Amphitheatres, Baths, etc) but never got round to publishing them, even though much of the material was ready, and in part still survives. In a second edition he would probably have added new material to that already published, and one interesting potential addition of this sort has recently been discovered by Lynda Fairbairn, who publishes it here (205). Palladio's publishers were the de' Franceschi family, the same printing firm which published Silvio Belli and Cosimo Bartoli and which printed the second edition in 1581 for Palladio's son Silla. There is no record of the financial agreement, but it was probably much the same as that which Silla obtained, that is 100 copies in lieu of payment (Zorzi, 1962, p.52).   H.B.

*194 The Temple of Romulus, outside Rome and the Temple of Vesta, by the Tiber

Pen, ink and wash: 29.4 × 40.8
Lent by the Royal Institute of British Architects (VIII/I)

This sheet is one of several drawings of ancient buildings, which despite a certain freedom and sketchiness, are not to be mistaken for on the spot drawings. Instead it is one of the drawings made by Palladio on the basis of his earlier sketches and represents a stage in the preparation of the plates of the *Quattro Libri*.

On the right is the Temple of Romulus, near S.Sebastiano on the Via Appia, of which only the ground floor level survived. Palladio drew the plan of this, and to show that it really exists has filled it in with wash. He then reconstructed the missing upper level, first in plan (the relationship with Sanmicheli's Pellegrini Chapel and Palladio's own later Tempietto at Maser is obvious) and then reconstructed the façade and side elevations, following the model provided by the Pantheon. At the bottom of the page he has written as a memorandum to himself 'the section is still to be done'. As in the case of the Baths, Palladio's enthusiasm for ancient buildings, even when ruined, are in contrast to Serlio's indifference to what was not ready made or to what did not fit in with his architectural preconceptions, 'I did not measure it' Serlio writes, 'and also because it has no architectural beauty, I paid no attention to the

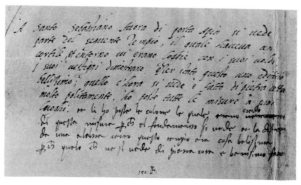

195

196

elevation' (1540, p.XLV).

In the drawing on the left Palladio sketches plan and elevation, and details of the round temple by the Tiber, probably using the drawing now at Cornell (Burns, 1973, p.141) as his point of departure. He reconstructs the dome on the basis of that of the Pantheon.   H.B.

*195 Draft for the text for the Quattro Libri

IV, p.88 R.I.B.A.VIII/IV
Photograph

The text refers to the drawing on the verso. The first half is written by Silla Palladio, and the second half by his father. Palladio initially wrote 'the columns which were truly of this dimension', and then has replaced 'truly' with the more prudent 'I believe': an interesting minor instance of Palladio's scrupulousness as a writer.   H.B.

GIOVANNI BATTISTA ZELOTTI 1526–78

196 Allegorical figure of Architecture, Villa Emo
Photograph

Zelotti's figure of Architecture, part of the fresco decoration of the 'Stanza delle Arti' holds a large book in her hand, and indicates in it a plan of the villa. As the frescoes were executed between 1565 and 1570 (Bordignon Favero, 1970, p.35) the book is a rendering of Palladio's still unpublished manuscript. H.B.

*197 Plan of Diocletian's Palace at Spalato
Pen, ink, and wash, over incised lines, and underdrawing in brown chalk and metalpoint: 360 × 292
Prov: Inigo Jones (probably); Talman; Burlington
Lent by the Trustees of the Chatsworth Settlement

The drawing style and the abbreviations used for feet and inches leave no doubt that this unpublished and unnoticed drawing is by Palladio. There is no evidence that Palladio ever visited Spalato, but his Venetian contacts would have put him in the way of drawings of the famous late antique complex, and in fact a plan of the octagonal mausoleum, not by Palladio but with additional sketches by him, survives in R.I.B.A.VIII/2 (Spielmann, 1966, p.177). Palladio's associate in his last years, Zamberlan, probably derived the scheme for his church at Rovigo from his knowledge of Palladio's drawings of the mausoleum at Spalato (cf. Barbieri, 1967), but Palladio, for whatever reason, did not include it in his *Fourth Book*. The development of rapidly sketched centralized structures along the central axis recalls Palladio's reconstructions of the Baths of Agrippa. H.B.

JAN VAN DER STRAET (Stradanus) 1523–1605
198 Printers at work, 1550
Pen ink and wash heightened with white: 18.5 × 27
Inscribed: *Ioan Stradan invent. Phlps Galle exud.* 1550
Photograph: Royal Collection (Windsor no.4761)

The drawing was for an engraving by Adriaen Collaert which was published with the title '*Impressio Librorum*', as plate 4 of the *Nova Reperta*, a book about new inventions, published without a date in Antwerp by Philip Galle (Puyvelde, 1942,

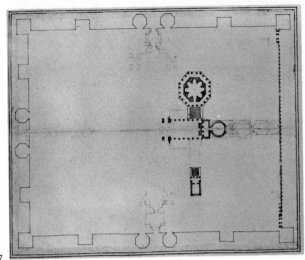

197

p.24, no.158).
The printer's workshop is located in an arcaded vaulted room on the ground floor. On the right the compositors are setting the type following texts which are on stands in front of them, while others read and check the text. On the left there is the printer at his press, and behind him another spreading ink on the type face. The printed sheets dry on lines and an apprentice spreads out the dried sheets on a table. In the background bundles of sheets lie on a table and are carried off to the binders(?). The book is signed on the title page, *Aloysio Alamannio Floren(ti)no Stradi invent:* which may indicate that Stradanus was living in Florence at the time of making the drawing (*ibid.* p.24), though the architecture in the background is northern. L.F.

199 Books III and IV of the 'Quattro Libri'
'sent to me by the Author'
Lent by the C.I.S.A. (Raccolta Cappelletti)

This unbound copy of the last two books of the 1570 edition is identical to the full publication. Its great interest lies in the note at the bottom of the title page of Book III, *Mandatomi dall' Autore li 24 Sett.re* 1571 *Mag.*(?) *Capra.* A clue to the reasons for Palladio sending these two books to an unidentified member of the Capra family (the first name is difficult to read, and seems also to have defeated Puppi, 1973–III, p.177) is possibly offered by the fact that these books are dedicated to Emanuele Filiberto of Savoy, in whose service the recipient declares himself to have been (Puppi, 1973, p.380). On the last page is the note (probably but not certainly in the same hand as that on the title page) '1580, on the 27th of August Saturday at 13½ hours my horse fell on top of me and broke the shin bone of my right leg, and next to this disaster, on the 30th of the same month on Tuesday at 20 hours for my greater misfortune my serene lord the Duke E.Filoberto of Savoy passed to a better life, may the Lord God receive him among the blessed, I, Piolo (?) Capra Vicentine (?)'. The Duke was in Vicenza in 1566, and Palladio was certainly in Turin in June 1568 (Parronchi, 1971, p.220).   H.B.

SEBASTIANO SERLIO

200 Regole generali di architettura . . . sopra le cinque maniere degli edifici, cioe Toscano, Dorico, Jonico, Corintio e Composito con gli esempi delle antichita, che per la maggior parte concordano con la dottrina di Vitruvio
Francesco Marcolini, Venice 1537
Lent by the Royal Institute of British Architects

This was the first of Serlio's books to appear, part of a series which he had been planning for many years (Dinsmoor 1942; Olivato, 1971; Howard, 1973). It provided for the first time in print a clear exposition of the use of the orders, as well as a considerable range of doors, windows, and complete façades which contemporary architects could imitate. The exposition of what Vitruvius says on each order, the comments on this, and the examples of the orders taken from ancient buildings undoubtedly reflect, and in good part reproduce Peruzzi's unpublished material. So probably do the basic designs of doors and windows. But the more elaborate doors and all the complete facades are Serlio's own invention, added as an after thought to the initial Peruzzian scheme (IV, 1540, fol.26v).   H.B.

SEBASTIANO SERLIO

201 Il Terzo Libro di Sabastiano Serlio Bolognese, nel qual si figurano, e descrivano le antiquita di Roma, e le altre che sono in Italia e fuori d'Italia.
Impresso in Venetia per Francesco Marcolini da Forli. appresso la Chiesa de la Trinita ne gli anni del signore MDXXXX. Del mese di Marzo
Lent by the Royal Institute of British Architects

This was the second book which Serlio published. It was the first publication of the equivalent of an architect's sketchbook, in which were collected drawings of ancient and modern architectural classics. The text plays a subordinate role and is little more than an expansion of the notes which architects often added to their drawings from the antique. The core of the material was provided by the notes and drawings which Serlio inherited from Peruzzi, who had planned a publication of this sort. But Serlio enlarged his portfolio by adding his own drawings, and drawings from a variety of other sources. Unlike Palladio he made no attempt to translate his material into a uniform unit of measurement, or a uniform convention of architectural representation. The book however is very attractively designed, and attractive too in the variety of its contents and comments. Serlio says that because of its overhead lighting people look larger and more beautiful in the Pantheon (p.V); he recalls that the finger of the Colossus conserved on the Campidoglio 'is so large that I have sat comfortably on its nail' (p.XXII); and he publishes the Great Pyramid and the Sphinx ('of ugly aspect') from drawings given him by Marco Grimani, Patriarch of Aquilea, who had personally measured the pyramid (p.XCIIII).   H.B.

*202 The interior of the Pantheon
as illustrated by (a) Serlio (1540)
and (b) Palladio (1570)
Photographs

Palladio must consciously have set out to improve on the well known architectural publications of Serlio. Palladio's *Book IV* covers much the same ground as Serlio's *Terzo Libro* (1540). Palladio (1570, IV, pp.82–3) and Serlio (1540, III, pp.XVI–XVII) represent an elevation of the interior of the Pantheon (only of the lower order in Serlio) and some of its details. Both books

202a

202b

were illustrated with woodcuts, and Serlio's block-cutter was capable of producing as fine lines as Palladio's. The difference between the two is nevertheless enormous. The conventions of representation differ: Serlio, betraying the fact that much of his material went back to the second decade of the century, introduces prespectival elements, whereas Palladio remains consistently orthogonal. Palladio is more accurate and includes much more information, without making the plates difficult to understand or unpleasingly crowded. He does so partly by excluding the text, which he concentrates on a page by itself. Much of Serlio's text is, in fact, taken up with giving measurements, and Palladio, more economically and more helpfully, simply enters these directly on the elevations.   H.B.

203 I Quattro Libri dell'Architettura
Venice, 1581
Lent by the Trustees of the Chatsworth Settlement

Like many surviving copies of Palladio's book, this was not just kept on the shelf but read, used, and reacted to. The late sixteenth-century annotations reveal a Veronese patriot, who marks every reference to his native city, corrects references to Zelotti as *Venetiano* to *Veronese* (II, p.6), recalls that not only Sansovino, but also Falconetto was responsible for introducing good architecture into the Veneto (I, p.5) and stands up for the importance of the architect as against the patron. Where Palladio (I, p.61) refers to Alvise Cornaro's buildings in Padua, the annotator comments, 'these buildings were designed by Messer Jovan Maria Falconetto so that they should rather be attributed to the architect than to the patron who spends'.   H.B.

INIGO JONES 1573–1652
204 Manuscript notes in a copy of the 'Quattro Libri', 1610
Photograph: Worcester College, Oxford

Inigo Jones on his extended second tour of Italy in 1613–4 with the Earl of Arundel, took with him this copy of the *Quattro Libri*, which he annotated extensively during his journey and throughout his lifetime. The volume was first published in facsimile in 1970. His manuscript notes record some of Scamozzi's opinions and information about Palladio's work (47). Jones jotted down in the site descriptions and drawings of Palladio's buildings, thus giving the earliest first

hand account of the state of the executed building which did not always correpond to the plate in the *Quattro Libri*. An instance is that of the Villa Thiene at Quinto. His notes in the *Quattro Libri* also provide important first hand evidence of the early collecting of Palladio's drawings. Jones notes that he had seen preparatory drawings for some of the plates for the *Quattro Libri* in the collection of the English ambassador to Venice, Sir Henry Wotton, (234); some of Wotton's drawings survive: R.I.B.A. VI/10 VI/11, X/6 and Jones himself almost certainly acquired most of the drawings in the Burlington-Devonshire collection, except the drawings of the Baths which were acquired by Lord Burlington at Maser (Tait, 1970; Harris 1973, p.64; Burns, 1973, p.133).   L.F.

205 Anonymous copy after Palladio
Manuscript addition to the *Quattro libri dell'Architettura*
Bartolomeo Carampello, Venice, 1581
Lent by the British Library Board (50.f.10)

This copy of the *Quattro Libri* from the collection of Consul Smith, contains on the blank verso of the last page of the first book, a note headed *Aggionta del Palladio* (Palladio's addition). It is written in sepia ink, in a neat late sixteenth century hand. It is the only manuscript note in the book. The passage formulates rules relating to the proportions of superimposed rooms and their ornament, and in summary reads: If there are two superimposed rooms the height of the upper one should be one fifth less than the one below, and a third floor should be one sixth less than the one below it. To determine the proportions of the façade, the distance from the ground to the first floor is divided into eleven modules, and one module will be the diameter of the column, two modules will be the height of the architrave, freize and cornice and the other nine will be the height of the column, capital and base. This lower order should be Ionic. On the second storey the distance from the entablature below to the one above should be divided into twelve modules. The diameter of the column will be one module, the architrave, freize and cornice will be two modules and the column with capital and base, ten. The order will be corinthian. The third order should be composite and divided in the same way as the order below. On each storey the bases of the orders should stand on a little socle, but not on pedestals, as this would tend to hide their membering. If the palace is pre-existing, the heights of the storeys will probably not follow this rule, but all the same, the façade can follow the rule given for new buildings. Rooms with wooden ceilings should rationally have only an architrave, because the beams of the ceiling will represent the freize, and the architrave is the member which goes naturally below the freize. The height of the architrave should be $\frac{3}{4}$ of a module (the module is obtained by dividing the height of the wall from the floor to the underside of the beams into ten). Palladio also provides a rule for those who want to follow the irrational practice of some contemporary architects, who want to place a full entablature below the ceiling beams. The height from the top of the chests or benches round the walls to the ceiling should be divided into six parts, one of these will be the height of the entablature, and the others will be the height of the column, base and capital. The chests or benches will then act as a stylobate.

The neatness of the note (there are no corrections) indicates that this is a copy, and the absence of any other annotations suggest someone close to Palladio, with access to his unpublished writings but (remembering Scamozzi's tendency to annotate his books), probably a non-architect. The handwriting does not appear to correspond to that of persons known to have had access to Palladio's papers after his death; it is not that of Giacomo Contarini who inherited Palladio's papers, nor that of Silla Palladio who did not include the note in the 1581 edition of the *Quattro Libri*, which he saw through the press. But there are other possible candidates (Marc'Antonio Barbaro for one). Though there is no definite proof that the note is by Palladio, the style, the formulation by reference to his own practice and observation, of rules which can be applied according to the taste and circumstances confronting individual architects, and the conciseness leads one to believe that this is in fact a copy made from a note by Palladio for a revised edition.

Barbaro's Vitruvius (1556) does not provide the precise source for these rules, though Vitruvius does say that an upper order should be a quarter less than the order below (Bk.V, ch.1). The note implies that the writer's source is architectural practice and observation, and characteristic of Palladio is the appeal to nature (also ultimately derived from Vitruvius): he compares the reduction in the height of the columns to the way in which the 'knots' on cane get closer together nearer the top. Palladio's studies of the ancient piazze in the *Quattro Libri* (1570, III, pp.32ff.) have a proportional system in the superimposed

orders which is close to the one described in the note. In Palladio's practice the heights of the superimposed rooms (that is, a room over a room as opposed to a loggia) usually follow the one sixth rule given in the *Quattro Libri* (1570, I, p.53), and in the absence of measured sections the use of the one fifth reduction is hard to establish. The system of proportions for superimposed orders determined by the height of the storeys is used by Palladio, for instance in the Palazzo da Porto Festa and the Villa Cornaro at Piombino Dese. The use of the three superimposed orders, a scheme which is rarely found in Palladio's projects before 1570, obviously was a major preoccupation in the last years of his life (San Petronio, the Palace at Brescia, the rebuilding of the Palazzo Ducale, the *Teatro Olimpico*). The addition seems to reflect these preoccupations: the Palazzo Ducale project (279) has no pedestals, and has the sequence of orders recommended by Palladio. L.F.

Aggionta del Paladio

Essendosi parlato molto distintamente: In tutto questo primo libro de gli ordini dell'Architettura, et de membri d'ogn'un d'essi particolarmente: sara bene che aggiongiamo anco quell'altra pratica, o per li lochi che s'haveranno da fabricar da novo o racconciar sul vecchio. Perche pressuposta una altezza, o di Casa fatta che si voglia racconciare, o di casa che s'habbi da fare bisogna sapere la regola che s'ha da tenere, in far le altezze delli solari, poi le base, li Capitelli et altezza delle colone, et di che altezza doveranno esser gli architravi frisi, et Cornici, per che data questa Regola ogn'uno da per se possa applicar li termini dell'Architettura alla necessita, et volunta sua . . . Qui s'hanno da far due consideratione, cioe ò nelle faccie, o negli ornamenti dentro s'ha da por mano. Parlando prima delle faccie se si hanno da far da novo, se saranno In doi solari il solaro di sotto dovera esser la quinta parte piu alto di quel di sopra, et se si fara In tre l'ultimo dovera esser la sesta parte meno di quel di mezo, con questa proportione per esperienza rende una simetria di grandissima satisfattione all'occhio, non altrimenti che si veda nelle canne che piu che si vanno alzando piu si accortano li nodi, essendo che le cose piu alte devono mostrar maggior debolezza, et percio e necessario, che siano piu raccolte. Se la necessita poi portasse che volendo racconciar il vechio non vi fosse questa proportione nell'altezza de piani, bisogna che li membri che si faranno a detta faccia nel raconciamento sijno auitati Con le misure, le quali si sentiranno cosi nel far da novo, come nel raconciare il vecchio. Dal primo della terra fin alprimo solaro si dovera divider in undici moduli, et de un modolo sara la grossezza della colona, doi sara l'altezza dell'Architrave, friso et Cornice, et de. 9. la colona Capitello et bassa et questo ordine dovera esser Ionico, Dalla prima travatura alla seconda si dovera divider In XII. moduli la grossezza della colona uno. Doi Architrave, friso et cornice, et dieci basa Colona et Capitello, et sara fatto di ordine Corintio. Al terzo ordine si richiede Composito Il qual dovera esser diviso pur In XII modoli et il Compartimento de membri dovera esser come L'ordine Corintio, avertendo percio che Intutti 3. questi ordini sotto la base si dovera poner un zoccolo a descrittione dell'architetto che Commanda per sublimar la base delle Colone, la qual dovera venir fin sul Zocco senza piedestillo, accio che meglio si possano goder i membri. et questo basti a chi s'Intende dell'Arte In proposito delle facciate.

Hora veniamo alli ornamenti delle Camere et sale. Io soglio fare Immediate sotto i travi nascer l'architrave per che li travi servono per friso, che e secondo ragione : et questo architrave dovera esser alto $\frac{3}{4}$ di modolo dividendo il muro dalle casse fin sotto i travi In X. modoli : ma perche l'uso de tempi presenti non si contenta delle ragione dell'arte, ma vole alcune cose, che trapassano la scienza, poi che molti vogliono sotto i travi Cornice friso et Architrave, percio per dar regola anco di questo, accio si faccia piu secondo l'arte che sia possibile, si dividera tutto il spacio del muro della sala overo Camera dalle Casse, o banche. o scagni fin sotto i travi In sei parti, et una di esse dovera esser l'altezza dell'Architrave friso et Cornice, et le cinque per la Colona et sui membri, et quell'altezza delle casse si potra finger un bassamento : o vogliamo dir piedestallo, secondo che parera a chi fara questa opera.

NOTE: Abbreviations have been expanded, and some alterations made in punctuation to clarify the sense. L.F.

*206 I Commentari di Giulio Cesare . . . ,
In Venetia, appresso Pietro de' Franceschi.
MDLXXV.
Photograph

The interest of this edition of Caesar's *Commentaries* lies not in the Italian translation (which was not by Palladio, and had been in print for many years), but in Palladio's prefaces and in the illustrations, which are based on drawings made by Palladio's sons Leonida and Orazio before their deaths, early in 1572. The volume was partly commemorative 'to achieve some honoured memory for the name of my sons', as Palladio writes in his introduction (Puppi, 1973–III, p.181). Trissino had set Palladio off on his studies of ancient military matters, 'I had my grounding in them from Sig. Giangiorgio Trissino, a most learned gentleman, . . . who had . . . a perfect understanding of this science . . .' as one can clearly see from his *Italia Liberata*. Palladio would have been further encouraged in his conviction that ancient military manoeuvres were relevant to present day armies by the similar interests and beliefs of Valerio Chiericati, a leading figure in Vicenza, and a commander of the Venetian land forces, who himself was an author of a treatise on military tactics (Puppi, 1973–II, p.72). He is specifically mentioned by Palladio in his introductory essay on Roman legions.

The plate exhibited here, of Caesar's bridge over the Rhine, is derived from the plate in the *Quattro Libri* (III, p.14). H.B.

TORELLO SARAYNA
207 De origine et amplitudine civitatis Veronae
Verona, 1540
Lent by the Royal Institute of British Architects

Sarayna's book presents in the form of a dialogue a discussion of the principal Roman monuments of the city, which are also illustrated by woodcuts after drawings by the Veronese painter Giovanni Caroto. The reconstruction of the Roman theatre is the most impressive of these. Caroto later republished his illustrations (*De le antiquitate de Verona . . .* Verona, 1560) and a volume of his drawings for these books is preserved in the Biblioteca Communale in Verona, and will soon be published by Schweikhart. The possibility that Caroto made use of lost drawings by Falconetto in preparing this material is not to be excluded (oral communication G.Schweikhart). The figures on the façade of the Palazzo Valmarana were possibly suggested to Palladio by Caroto's book (Burns, 1973, p.139). H.B.

*208 Reconstruction of the Roman theatre, Verona
Pen and ink : 27.8 × 54.6
Lent by the Royal Institute of British Architects (IX/10)

This highly finished drawing was probably made as part of Palladio's preparation of a book on Theatres, one of the series of books which he intended to publish after the first *Quattro Libri* (I, p.6). The theatre is shown completely restored. Every feature except the upper two terraces, and the monumental loggie facing the Adige are solidly based on surviving parts of the building, though for some of these Palladio seems to have made use of another artist's surveys (209). The general scheme of the reconstruction obviously derives from Caroto's reconstruction (207), though Palladio models his temple which crowns the complex on the Pantheon and the logge on Bramante's logge in the Vatican (160). The arcades at the side of the temple recall the solution at the Villa Emo, and the drawing explains why Palladio associated the site of the Rotonda with that of a 'very large theatre'. The riverside arcades, surmounted by an order, of the Palazzo Piovene in Vicenza (Zorzi, 1964, fig.352) were perhaps suggested to Palladio by Caroto's, or his own reconstructions of the theatre at Verona. H.B.

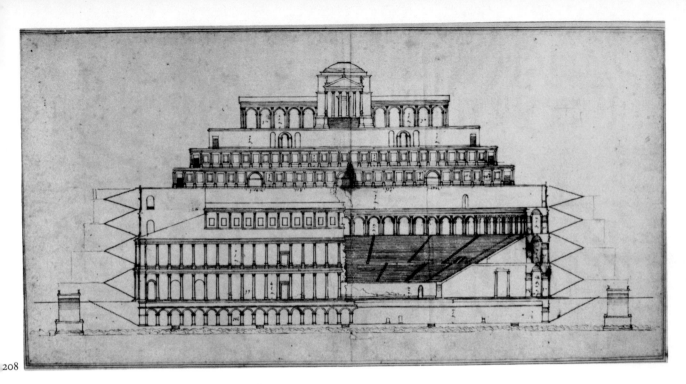

208

209 Elevation of an upper terrace of the Roman theatre, Verona

Pen and ink: 29 × 43.3
Lent by the Royal Institute of British Architects (XII/22V)

This very handsome drawing is probably copied by Palladio
from someone else's survey. This is suggested not by the
character of the drawing (a precise, orthogonal elevation, of the
sort habitually employed by Palladio) but by the unit of
measurement, the Roman foot, not Palladio's usual unit,
the Vicentine foot, which is slightly larger. Palladio in fact at a
later stage (in his mature, post 1550 handwriting) has converted
two of the measurements into Vicentine feet. Given the unit
of measurement, the precision and resemblance to survey
drawings by Antonio da Sangallo with whom Sanmicheli had
worked in Rome, it is possible that Palladio was copying from
a lost drawing by Sanmicheli.   H.B.

Venice in Palladio's time was one of the great cities, not only of Italy, but of the known world. Its commerce, its wealth, the remains of its Mediterranean empire, its publishing houses, its complex oligarchical but constitutional government, made it unique. Palladio himself, echoing a Venetian commonplace, described Venice as the sole 'surviving example of the greatness and magnificence of the Romans' (1570, I. p.5; cf. Chambers, 1970, pp.26ff.). If Palladio's ambitions of reinstating the architectural system of the ancients was concentrated on the ruins of Rome, his ambitions of realising it in practice were necessarily largely centred on Venice. Already in 1554 he applied unsuccessfully for the job of salaried architect (proto) of the Salt Magistracy, the Venetian state agency which financed public works and in 1555 submitted a project for the Scala d'Oro in the Palazzo Ducale (Zorzi, 1964, p.137). In this same period he submitted a design for the Rialto bridge (221).

These early attempts to establish a place in the Venetian architectural world, though they probably had the backing of Daniele Barbaro (178), did not bear fruit. It was only with the S.Pietro di Castello commission of 1558 (Puppi, 1973, p.321) and the very important works which followed it that Palladio became established in Venice, so that by the 1570s 'our faithful Andrea Palladio' (Zorzi, 1966, p.133) became the almost automatic choice for works, like the temporary architecture for Henry III's visit or the Church of the Redentore, in which the reputation and revenues of the state were deeply committed.

Venice was far larger (a population of 170,000 in 1563) and far more complex than Vicenza, and it is much more difficult to define the role of architecture in the city or the reasons for Palladio's Venetian success. In the complex interaction of institutions, assemblies, committees, and individuals which lay behind Palladio's achievements in Venice, it is hard to assess the weight of different contributions and different motivations. The Collegio (234), the Senate, the Council of Ten, the Procurators of St Mark's, were all potential architectural patrons as were the Scuole (275) and religious bodies. Although the patronage of all these in the long run fitted into a pattern of enhancing the prestige of the commissioning body and of the State, and had the tacit or explicit approval of the powers that were, considerable contradictions were present. The energy and expenditure of the Procurators on the Library contrasted with the delay and miserliness which characterized the history of the Rialto bridge, a monument in which the prestige of the State was certainly involved. There are also stylistic contradictions. The relationship between tradition and innovation in Venice was much more complex than in Vicenza, where the rejection of that 'outmoded usage of building' (II, p.4) was swift and decisive. The lingering of architectural traditions in Venice was not just a matter of 'Venetian conservatism'. Physically Venice was a very particular environment, and structural and planning solutions adapted to it over centuries still remained valid, as the notorious collapse of Sansovino's Library vault somewhat brutally showed (Howard, 1975). Thus the Senators voted overwhelmingly to restore the Ducal Palace exactly as it was before the 1577 fire (275); Palladio's details (276) and his church façades contrasted with Sansovino's, and Palladio even in 1570 still found it worthwhile (probably thinking of the Scuola di San Rocco) to attack the carving of garlands round the middle of columns (I, p.52). The difficulties which the understanding of the Venetian architectural scene presents can be put in perspective by recalling the difficulties that even informed contemporaries found in unravelling the contradictions that lay behind the consensus façade of Venetian politics. The Florentine agent Cosimo Bartoli (188), a friend of Palladio, wrote to Florence in May 1571 (ASF, Med. del Princ., f.2980) suggesting that the delays of the Venetians in concluding the alliance against the Turks (283) were to be explained by trading interests of relations of the Doge and of the influential future doge, Niccolò da Ponte (233), which could be harmed by war. Some aspects of the role of architecture in Venice are clear enough. In 1496, despite a shortage of cash brought about by war, 'nevertheless, so that it shall not appear that the country is completely broke', work on the Clocktower in the Piazza was begun (Malipiero, 1443-4, p.699). In 1520 Doge Loredan is described as being 'so much recovered that . . . he wanted to go and see the progress of building at Rialto and San Salvatore' (Micheli, *Diarii*, f.339). Doge Gritti played an important role in securing Sansovino's services for Venice (Howard, 1975). The state was ready to settle a massive debt to the Corner family to rebuild their magnificent palace on the Grand Canal, after it had been destroyed by fire (Gallo, 1960, p.97ff). The Senate in 1535 voted 131–41 to appoint two commissioners to look into the embellishment of the city, which from 1537 onwards was also notably furthered by Sansovino's work in the city centre. Public building in its widest sense, including churches, church façades, scuole, and even private palaces on prominent sites, like the Palazzo Corner, all were seen as contributing to the presentation of a favourable image of the state, for both internal and external consumption. Guide books, above all those of Francesco Sansovino, son of the architect (1562 and 1581) offered keys to the intepretation of the city's architecture. The state, which closely controlled the activities of the scuole and did its best to control the activities of ecclesiastical institutions, would have intervened had it not at least tacitly consented to the expenditure by both of huge sums on buildings. This tacit consent was forthcoming even though the scuole were publicly criticized for using for display the money which should have gone to charity (275). The state gave permission to the monastery of S.Giorgio to cut 1000 of its oaks (which would normally have been reserved for ship building) for the foundations of the new church (Zorzi, 1966, p.64). Several of the buildings on which Palladio worked (Palazzo Ducale, S.Giorgio, the Redentore) were directly connected with the processions and ceremonies which expressed not only the magnificence but the cohesion of the State, as they involved not only representatives of the government and the nobility, but also of the scuole, the guilds, and the clergy, and, at least as spectators, the populace as a whole. In the procession to the site of the Redentore to give thanks for the end of the plague, or in the spontaneous celebration of the victory of Lepanto, these Venetian public occasions were more than formal events, and had to do with the very survival of the city. This emerges in a contemporary description of the arrival of the news of Lepanto in 1571: 'on the 19th October . . . while everyone was intent on his business and when least one expected any good news . . . behold there appeared an angel from heaven (i.e., the galley, the *Angel Gabriel*), behold a galley, and when it was scarcely sighted in the distance, everyone knows, everyone understands what it carries before anything is spoken, and everyone cries to the heavens, 'Victory, Victory, Viva, Viva'. . . and in a moment

all the city knows it, everyone cries out and everyone runs the Piazza; everyone goes mad, everyone tells of joy, becau of which some laugh, some weep, some run, some leap, ever one embraces everyone else, the poor man and the non-noble is the comrade and the brother of the rich man and the nobl they kiss one another, there is no difference of age of sex rank, all render thanks to God, and they compete in their desi to get close to the galley. All the gondolas are not enough . . the air echoes with questions as to how it happened . . . every one like a madman, not content with seeing, touches, kisse embraces the oars . . . Others then in great numbers run to th Collegio (239) and . . . open the well closed doors and face th doge . . . some kiss his hand, some kiss his foot, some kiss th counsellors. Behold, there appears the great messenger of s much good, the Magnificent Giustiniano, captain of the galle behold, they carry him bodily, and he is so tired and squeeze that he can say and repeat nothing else save, in a broken voic "A very great victory, most serene Prince, the enemy navy defeated, it is captured and burned, and ours is safe". No on waits any longer, everyone shouts out, "To the church", and s the doge, the Senate, the whole city, all to the Church of Sa Marco, where there is at once sung a Te Deum, a most solem mass, and afterwards a procession . . .' (BM Add. MS. 10, 815 f.106).

Palladio, alongside his private satisfaction in Venice ('. . . th church of San Giorgio, which fabric I govern, and I hope to achieve some honour from it'); (Zorzi, 1966, p.89) and hi private sorrows (143) also participated in the city's triumphs an sorrows in the 1560s and 1570s: The Turkish War, whicl involved many he knew (Ippolito da Porto, Valerio Chiericati Fabio Pepoli), the fires in the Ducal Palace of 1574 and 1577 the visit of Henry III to Venice in 1574, the great plague ol 1575–7 were all events which he would have followed closely and in some he was directly involved. Cosimo Bartoli cites hin as the source of political information (Parronchi, 1971, p.220 and he probably took a considerable interest in politics anc events. His friends in Venice would have enabled him to do so. They included the Florentine agent Cosimo Bartoli; Leonardo Mocenigo (392), related to the Doge (and also described by Bartoli as 'very much my friend', f.2980, cit, fol 178v); Giacomo Contarini, made a senator by Henry III and join author of the programme for the redecoration of the Sala del

Maggior Consiglio after the 1577 fire (Wolters, 1966), and Marc'Antonio Barbaro (278), Venetian representative in Constantinople during the war, who after his return was one of Venice's most influential statesmen.

Palladio's rise to the position of Venice's leading architect depended on a number of factors. His works in Vicenza brought him fame, and villa commissions early in the 1550s from Venetians (345 and 346). But still in the mid 1550s, despite the probable backing of Daniele Barbaro he failed to achieve a post or commission in Venice itself. At that date Sansovino was still in his prime, and his principal political backers were still the natural choices for committees dealing with architectural matters. The procurators Vettor Grimani and Antonio Cappello who were particularly close to Sansovino were thus appointed to be Commissioners for the new Rialto bridge (221). Until his death in 1559 Michele Sanmicheli, who was a well known and trusted architect in Venice, with years of state service behind him, was also available. Palladio got into Venice by the convenient back door of virtually private commissions, the façades for San Pietro in Castello and San Francesco della Vigna, which were almost certainly put in his way by Daniele Barbaro (Puppi, 1973, p.323). The success of the Vigna façade, and the advancing age of Sansovino and his supporters, as well as the progressive rise in government service of Palladio's Venetian noble friends (above all Marc'Antonio Barbaro) account for his continued success.

The broad trends of Venetian architectural policy were obviously in general widely supported, and this appears in the usually clear Senate decisions on architectural questions. There was a general desire to embellish and adorn the city, which in part had political motivations. Finance was usually the key issue, and major public works were not usually undertaken unless they were ultimately self financing (the Fondaco dei Tedeschi), or essential to the prestige or the security of the State (Sansovino's Zecca, or Sanmicheli's fortress of S. Andrea al Lido). The State could delay for decades, as in the case of this Rialto bridge, but once it did commit itself the projects were usually finished, even though the costs (witness the Redentore) far outran original estimates.

The larger State committees and assemblies could not make complex planning choices, or decide between alternative designs unaided. They depended on those of their members who had a particular interest in architecture, and a particular experience of administering architectural projects. This was not something new in Venice: Marc'Antonio Barbaro filled a role similar to that filled by Bernardo Bembo, with his interest in Alberti and his contact with Pietro Lombardo, many decades before. It was the normal practice to elect commissioners (*provveditori*), initially to report back their findings on decisions like the site of the Redentore or how the Ducal Palace was to be restored, and then to administer the construction itself. Some nobles made a public career by being architectural experts, with a term in the Salt office (which administered public works) as a frequent preliminary to becoming *provveditore* of some important project (278).

The architectural ideas of these influential experts were decisive in determining the sort of designs which were chosen. It is worth stressing that the ideas of Daniele and Marc' Antonio Barbaro and their contemporaries were close to Palladio's own, and quite different from those of Sansovino and (one can conjecture) his chief patrician supporters. The approach of both the Barbaros to architecture was systematic, and characterised by an Aristotelian preoccupation with defining ends and functions. This coincided in great part with Palladio's own concern with functions and naturalistic justifications of the design even of details, and with his vision of good architecture as a total system, not just a combination of sensible, basically traditional solutions, decked out with a correct and if possible striking use of the ancient orders. The Barbaros' and Palladio's approach to architecture was in contrast to that of Sansovino. Whereas Palladio offered a theoretically justifiable architecture, consistently antique even down to the smallest details, Sansovino displayed a brilliant visual opportunism, which turned to its purposes the classical orders, reminiscences of Donatello and Michelangelo, and quotations from the Venetian tradition. The range of his resources and his skill and inventiveness in combining them, rather than new schemes or innovatory planning solutions characterise his work. His major projects are spectacular and exhibitionist, and excellently suited to reflecting the splendour and majesty of the Venetian State. But they could not be justified point by point, in every aspect of their design as

Palladio was able to justify his projects (cf. Tafuri, 1973). As justifications came to count for more than panache, and as Palladio's use of the orders was just as correct, if not more so than Sansovino's, Palladio was increasingly favoured at Sansovino's expense. Sansovino by indulging a taste for traditional Venetian motifs, novel and interesting to him with his Florentine and Roman background, increased the visual richness of his style, and at first probably rendered his designs more accessible and acceptable to his Venetian clients. In the end it was Palladio, who had abandoned all anecdotal Venetian elements, and stripped down the Venetian architectural tradition to a hard core of principles and systems which were for him identical to the basic message of ancient architecture, who won the approval of a younger generation of well educated patrician architectural experts.

Venice provided Palladio with opportunities which Vicenza could never have offered him. It revealed him as an architect whose originality and capabilities could extend well beyond the field of villa and palace design. Venetian problems of scale, and of the design of façades and façade detail to be seen at a considerable distance, before long had their effect on his Vicentine commissions as well: the solutions for the Palazzo Valmarana, the Loggia del Capitaniato, and the Palazzo Porto-Breganze were all spin-offs from the extension of his range and ideas provoked by his Venetian commissions.   H.B.

210 Mariegola of the confraternity of boatmen at Mestre, 1508
Vellum: 30.5 × 43.2 (open)
Prov: John Ruskin
Lent by the British Library Board (B.M. Add. MS. 42125)

In Venice and the Veneto in the sixteenth century there existed a large number of associations with a partly religious, and partly social and charitable character. The richest and most famous of these were the Venetian 'Scuole Grandi', with a large middle class and artisan membership, and impressive and immensely expensive buildings (275). But there were also many smaller organisations, many of them with the character of both trade guild and confraternity. Some of these had buildings of

their own (Palladio was involved with the building of the Scuola dei Mercanti in Venice) others met in churches and chapels.

In 1508 the boatmen of Mestre established a guild confraternity to be dedicated to St Nicholas. They met in the church of S.Girolamo in Mestre. The rules, which include regulations stating that the members were not to speak badly of one another, and that adulterous members should be expelled, were officially approved by the Podestà of Mestre, and by Bernardo de Rossi, Bishop of Treviso. Both these authorities affixed their seals. The volume is bound in red velvet, has an illuminated title page, a miniature of the crucifixion on fol.17v, and of Christ and St Nicholas on fol.18.

The name of Palladio's father 'Piero della Gondolla' indicates some family connection with boats, and his uncle Nicolò was a boatman (Rigoni, 1970, p.324).   H.B.

GIROLAMO FRANCESCO MARIA MAZZOLA (called PARMIAGIANINO) 1513–40
211 Figures in a ferry boat
Pen ink and brown wash: 22.9 × 20.3
Lent by the British Museum, London (1895–9–15–753)

Although the figure of the ferryman seems to be an ideal type, the passengers could be drawn from life. Popham relates the drawing to one now in the Louvre of a man on the gunwale of a boat (1971, no.406 plate 437) and suggests that the two drawings are reminiscences of the same occasion. The boat, which is considerably larger than a gondola has an oar rest like a gondola, and probably is of the type which had another oarsman at the front (212b). Venice could only be approached by water, and boatmen had great importance in the life of the city. The government, for instance, tried to hold down the number of beggars (213) by forbidding the boatmen to ferry them in. Water provided an alternative means of transport in a large area of north Italy, and was especially useful when luggage or heavy goods were involved. In 1562 the Duke of Ferrara travelled all the way to Venice by water, and in September 1576 at the height of the plague in Venice the young architect Scamozzi drew up a contract with a boatman to transport the sculptor Vittoria (182) and all his family right to the port in Vicenza (Predelli, 1908).   H.B./L.F.

**2 Scenes from Venetian life from Giacomo Franco's
'Habiti d'Huomeni et Donne Venetiane . . .'**
Venice 1610
Photographs

The dedicatory letter of this volume of engravings is dated
1 January 1610. Giacomo Franco's engravings are the most
important contemporary visual account of Venetian costume
and official and popular life.

a. The battle of the bridge
The Venetian state encouraged aggressive sports in order to
develop a strong proletariat for enrolment into the militia when
necessary. One of these sports was group boxing matches held
on bridges without parapets. Teams of rival factions from
different quarters of the city faced each other on the bridge and
fought violently until they fell into the water. Alessandro
Caravia in 1550 published a poem about one of these faction
fights: *La vera antiga de castellani, canaruoli egnatti, con la morte di
Gurco e Gnagni, in lengua brava*. The battles were held between
September and Christmas, and took place from 1292 until the
eighteenth century when they were forbidden by law
(Molmenti, 1905, II, p.204). L.F.

b. The women's boat race
There was a long tradition of boat races in Venice. They are
thought to have developed from the races held between youths
of fifteen and over, who by law had on all feast days to practice
shooting with a cross bow, at San Nicolò al Lido. These youths
in training to fight raced from the Piazzetta to the Lido to
develop their oarsmanship, so that they could handle the oars of
a war galley in time of war. This developed into regular boat
races and by 1493 even the women had begun to compete in
their own races in light boats. (Molmenti 1905, pp.206ff.). The
women compete enthusiastically and attract a good number of
spectators. The mens' races were more formal events. Franco's
engraving shows them competing in varying sized boats with
different numbers of oars. The spectators watch from balconies
with carpets draped over them. L.F.

c. Girls in gondolas
Here the marriagable girls go in their canopied gondolas to
visit their relatives in monasteries. They are wearing the typical
dress of aristocratic young ladies, like that worn by the ladies in
the painting of the ball (81). Their hair is dressed in the same
way. L.F.

d. Workers coming out of the Arsenal
The workers are pouring out of the main entrance of the
Arsenal at the end of a day's work: a scene which is familiar in
fully industrialized societies, but would have been considered
remarkable in Palladio's time. Other workers are being paid at
the grill on the left. The large, well organized labour force of
the Arsenal was employed for fire-fighting in grave
emergencies, like the Palazzo Ducale fire in 1577 (277).
Palladio is recorded as visiting the Arsenal in 1574, to borrow a
long length of strong rope for hoisting a new bell into place on
the clocktower in Vicenza (Fasolo, 1938, p.262). H.B.

GIROLAMO PORRO, active 1574–1604
**213 Le Bararie [*sic*] del Mondo (Beggars and good-for-
nothings)**
Signed: *Hieronimus Porro Fecit*
Photograph: Royal Collection

Girolamo Porro illustrated a number of books, including
Porcacchi's *Funerali Antichi* (1574), and a book of his own on
the botanical garden in Padua. His sight was defective, but all
the same he was such a skilled engraver that he could inscribe
long texts on small silver coins. He also invented a flying
machine (Porcacchi, 1591, pp.3–4). Porro was in touch with
Palladio's friend Giacomo Contarini, and so may have had
some contact with Palladio himself (Barbieri 1952, p.127).
The engraving attacks cripples and beggars, who are
represented as doing well out of charity. One man says 'I earn
more in the year with one hand than you can do with two in
the whole year', and the 'bravo' in the centre says 'with
audacity, menaces and with the sword, everyone honours me
and makes way for me.' In contrast the honest working man in
the top right says 'I am a woodcutter, with great labour I
barely manage to nourish myself.' Pullan (1971) offers a
complete survey of Venetian state policy towards beggars, and
cites some bizarre cases of fraudulent begging, including a
beggar who had an income of 45 ducats p.a. from state funds
(pp.302–7). H.B.

Money in Venice

Venice based her coinage upon that of the Byzantine empire, her predecessor and in some ways her prototype as a Mediterranean power. The doge and St Mark replaced the image of the emperor and archangel of Byzantine coins, and this combination of titular ruler and patron saint appeared on most denominations, embodying the central myth of the Republic: the Evangelist's concern for the affairs of the Venetian state. Money was issued from the *Zecca* or mint, an impressive building by Sansovino, facing the water, to the left of the two columns on the Piazzetta. Coins were struck by hammering a prepared metal flan between two engraved steel dies; a correct alignment depended upon the eyesight of the craftsman involved. It was an ancient technique, but it had the merit of swiftness, once the dies were engraved.

The Venetian system of coins corresponded to the old British pounds, shillings, and pence. Twelve *denari* made one *soldo*, and twenty *soldi* made one *lira*. The ducat of account, in which business was conducted, was valued for much of Palladio's lifetime at six *lire* four *soldi* (= 124 *soldi*). At the top of the monetary pyramid stood the gold ducat or *zecchino*, first struck in 1284 and one of the most respected coins in mediaeval Europe (Ives, 1954). During the sixteenth century, a scarcity of gold and an abundance of silver from America and central Europe meant that the zecchino steadily increased in value until it reached two hundred soldi by 1593. Silver, in fact, replaced gold as the most common legal tender. This was given tangible expression by the silver ducat, which was first minted in 1562 with a value of 124 *soldi* stamped on its reverse (Lane, 1973, p.327).

The conservative nature of the Venetian coinage allowed little scope for the splendid artistry that distinguished the coins of other Renaissance states. There were, however, two exceptions: the *osella* and the silver ducat. The *osella*, a cross between a coin and a medal, had first been issued under Doge Antonio Grimani (1521–3). It had the value of a quarter ducat and was given to the Venetian nobles by the doge in lieu of a traditional present of game birds (*uccelli*). Under Alvise I Mocenigo (1570–7) and Sebastiano Venier (1577–8), the design of the *osella* became more ambitious, commemorating among other

things the war against the Turks and the foundation of t Redentore (256). The silver ducat, with its comparatively lar format, encouraged a more ambitious treatment by engrave and became one of the handsomest coins of the Italian Rena sance.

Recent years have seen considerable attention given to t Venetian economy in general, but little to what the individu earned and spent. The disparity between rich and poor cou be enormous, and when bad harvests made food prices ri sharply, it meant sometimes the difference between life a death as bread took a major portion of a poor man's income. rise in the price of bread coupled with low wages led in 1581 Arsenal caulkers breaking into the public granary and removir twenty-five bushels of flour (Pullan, 1968, pp.164–6). At or end of the social scale, a Vicentine noblewoman could bring dowry of many thousands of ducats to her marriage whi Palladio's wife brought to their marriage a dowry worth on 177 lire (Zorzi, 1916, pp.183–4). Some idea of the cost of life mid-century can be gained from the account books of Loren: Lotto (Zampetti, 1969). Food and artistic provisions natural made up a large part of Lotto's expenses. A pair of *calzoni* trousers of Hungarian cloth was expensive at 3 lire 12 sold over half a ducat, and a pair of cloth shoes for a woman fetche a good price at 28 soldi. Candles cost 14 soldi a pound whi sealing wax cost a ducat an ounce. A psalter went cheaply about one soldo. Transport was a major expense. Lotto pai 22 lire 18 soldi for moving house from Venice to Trevis (30 km). Perhaps by way of consolation a *sechia* of wine (10. litres) cost 4 lire.

Lotto never seemed to manage on his earnings, for he ofte borrowed money, sometimes from his friend Sansovino. Ev Palladio, who received the steady if unspectacular salary of fiv scudi (worth five ducats three lire) a month as architect of th Basilica in Vicenza, often had to ask for advances on his wag in order to make ends meet. B.B.

Note on the coins exhibited

These are arranged in descending value, from the gold *zecchino* to the alloyed bagattino worth one *denarius* or penny. All gold coins were valued according to the current purchasing power of the *zecchino*. Silver coins were based upon the *mocenigo* or *lira* (in Vicenza usually called a *tron*), first minted under Doge Pietro Mocenigo (1474–6). By 1525 its value had risen from 20 *soldi* to 24 *soldi*, and the *marcello* or half *lira* also rose from 10 to 12 *soldi* (Papadopoli, 1907, II, pp.177–8). The copper alloyed coins were all multiples of the denarius, with the *sessino* at 8d., the *quattrino* at 4d., and the *bagattino* at 1d. Despite the variety of coins, Venice did not produce enough money to meet her own commercial needs. Foreign coins were accepted as legal tender, and tariffs were published from time to time, listing and illustrating the coins permitted as well as giving them a value in Venetian terms. Divergencies between the two examples of each denomination are noted in the second entry.   B.B.

14 Gold and silver Venetian coins lent by the Trustees of the British Museum

(a) Zecchino
Obverse: St Mark standing to the left gives his standard to the kneeling doge on the right. Behind the saint, the letters ·S·M·VENET· and behind the doge, his name FRAN·VENE· and along the standard, DVX.
Reverse: Christ as Redeemer, framed by a mandorla of twelve, five-pointed stars, gives a blessing. Around, SIT·T·XRE·DAT·Q·TV REGIS·ISTE·DVCAT.
Gold: 2.1

(b) Zecchino
Obverse: As above with the doge's name LAV·PRIOL.
Reverse: As above.

(c) Scudo
Obverse: A cross terminating in a floral design within a circle. Around, + ·PETRVS·LANDO ·DVX·VENETIAR
Reverse: On a shield decorated with leaves, a winged lion of St Mark. Around, + ·SANCTVS·MARCVS·VENETVS·
Gold: 2.6

(d) Scudo
Obverse: As above, with the doge's name
+ ·FRANC'·VENERIO·DVX·VENETIAR.
Reverse: As above.

(e) Silver ducat
Obverse: St Mark enthroned on the left blesses the kneeling doge on the right, who receives the standard. Around, S·M·VENETVS·HIER·PRIOLO·DVX·
Reverse: The winged lion of St Mark, facing left, supports his gospel. Around, DVCATVS·VENETVS· and in the exergue *124*
Silver: 3.9

(f) Silver ducat
As above.

(g) Half ducat
Obverse: St Mark enthroned on the left blesses the kneeling doge on the right, who receives the standard.
Around, S·M·VENETVS·HIER·PRIOLO·DVX.
Reverse: The winged lion of St Mark, facing left, supports his gospel. Behind the lion, a hill and tower. Around, MEDI'·DVCAT'·VENET'· and in the exergue *62*
Silver: 3.5

(h) Half ducat
Obverse: As above with the doge's name ALOYSVS MOCENIGO.
Reverse: Around, DOMIDIVM DVC·VENET

Silver
(i) Quarter ducat
Obverse: St Mark enthroned on the left blesses the kneeling doge on the right, who receives the standard. Around, S·M·VENETVS HIER·PRIOLO·DVX.
Reverse: The winged lion of St Mark, facing left, supports his gospel. Behind the lion, a hill and tower. Around, QVARTVM DV·VE· and in the exergue *31*
Silver: 3.0 (one example only)

(j) Mocenigo
Obverse: St Mark standing to the left gives his standard to the kneeling doge on the right. Behind the saint, the letters

·s·m·venet· and behind the doge, his name ·andreas·griti and along the standard, dvx.

Reverse: Christ as Redeemer blesses with His right hand and holds an orb surmounted by a cross in His left.
Around, ·tibi·soli·gloria.
Silver: 3.3

(k) Mocenigo
As above.

(l) Marcello
Obverse: St Mark standing to the left gives his standard to the kneeling doge on the right. Behind the saint, the letters s·m·venet and behind the doge, his name ·pet·lando and along the standard, dvx.
Reverse: Christ enthroned gives a blessing. On either side, ic xc and around, tibi·soli·gloria·
Silver: 2.7

(m) Marcello
Obverse: As above with the doge's name lavrentivs priolvs·
Reverse: As above.

(n) Six soldi
Obverse: Madonna and Child enthroned on the left bless the kneeling doge on the right, who holds the standard.
Around, ·ave·g·pl· fran·don and along the standard, dvx.
Reverse: The winged lion of St Mark within a circle of pearls.
Around, + ·s·marcvs·venetvs·
Silver: 2.1

(o) Six soldi
Obverse: As above with the doge's name, pet·lavr·
Reverse: As above.

(p) Four soldi
Obverse: St Mark standing to the left gives his standard to the kneeling doge on the right. Behind the saint the letters s·m·venet and behind the doge, his name fran·don·dvx.
Reverse: Christ as Redeemer stands on a pedestal, in the act of benediction. Around, tibi·soli·gloria·
Silver: 1.7

(q) Four soldi
Obverse: As above with the doge's name, hier·pri·
Reverse: Around, lavs·ti· bi·soli.

(r) Two soldi
Obverse: St Mark standing to the left gives his standard to the kneeling doge on the right. Behind the saint the letters ·s·m·ven· and behind the doge, his name fr·don and in the exergue ·dvx·
Reverse: Christ in torso length gives a blessing. On either side ic xc.
Silver: 1.5

(s) Two soldi
Obverse: As above with the doge's name hier pr·
Reverse: As above.

(t) Soldo
Obverse: St Mark standing to the left gives his standard to the kneeling doge on the right. Behind the saint the letters ·s·m·v· and behind the doge, his name pe·lan· and in the exergue ·dv·
Reverse: Christ as Redeemer stands on a pedestal, blessing w His right hand and holding an orb in His left.
Around, lavs tibi·soli.
Silver: 1.4

(u) Soldo
Obverse: As above with the doge's name hie·pr.
Reverse: As above. New soldo. Obverse: A cross of balusters with four spokes within a circle. Around,
+ ·petrvs·lando·dvx· Reverse: The winged lion of St Mark Around, *s*marcvs*venet*
Silver: 1.4

(v) New soldo
Obverse: A cross of balusters with four spokes within a circle
Around, +petrvs lando dvx.
Reverse: The winged lion of St Mark. Around,
*s*marcvs*venet*
Silver: 1.4

(w) New soldo
Obverse: As above with the doge's name +HIER·PRIOLO.
Reverse: Around, +S.MARCVS·VENETVS.

(x) Bezzo or half soldo
Obverse: A Pisan cross within a circle. Around,
+PET·LANDO DVX.
Reverse: The lion of St Mark, facing left, supports its gospel, and by the gospel is a cross. Around, ·IN·HOC·S and in the exergue VINCIT.
Silver: 1.3

(y) Bezzo
Obverse: As above with the doge's name FRANC·DONAT·
Reverse: As above.

5 The smaller denominations of the Venetian Coinage
Lent by the Trustees of the British Museum

(a) Sessino or eight denari
Obverse: A Pisan cross with a squared centre, decorated by pearls, three on each arm of the cross and four around the centre. Around, +·FRANC·DONATO·DVX·VEN·
Reverse: The winged lion of St Mark within a circle.
Around, +·SANCTVS·MARCVS·VENET·
Alloy: 1.8

(b) Sessino
Obverse: As above with the doge's name HIERON·PRIOLI·
Reverse: As above.

(c) Quattrino or four denari
Obverse: Within a double circle, the outer one of pearls, the kneeling doge holds his standard. Around,
+·FRANC·DONATO·DVX.
Reverse: The winged lion of St Mark within a circle.
Around, +·S·MARCVS·VENETI·
Alloy: 1.6

(d) Quattrino
Obverse: As above, with the doge's name PETRVS LAVREDAN·
Reverse: Around, +·S·MARCVS·VENETVS·

(e) Half quattrino or double bagattino
Obverse: A Maltese cross within a circle.
Around, +M·ANT·TRIVISANO.
Reverse: The bust of St Mark within a circle of pearls.
Around, +·S·MARCVS·VENETVS·
Alloy: 1.4

(f) Half quattrino
Obverse: As above with the doge's name HIER·PRIOL·
Reverse: As above.

(g) Bagattino or one denarius
Obverse: The Madonna and Child enthroned on the left bless the kneeling doge on the right, who holds a standard without a banner. Around, PE·LAN RE·CE·L and along the standard DVX.
Reverse: The monogram IHS and beneath it, two leaves united at the stem. Alloy: 1.8

(h) Bagattino
As above.

216 Oselle
Lent by the Trustees of the British Museum

ALVISE I MOCENIGO 1570–7
(a) Obverse: St Mark enthroned on the left gives his standard to the kneeling doge on the right. Around,
S·M·V·ALOYSIVS MOCENIGO·D·
Reverse: A three-masted ship with the lion of St Mark on the stern. In the exergue AN·VII.
Bronze: 3.2

(b) Obverse: St Mark enthroned on the left gives his standard to the kneeling doge on the right. Around,
·S·M·VENETVS·ALOY·MOCEN· and along the standard, DVX.
In the exergue ANNO II·
Reverse: Within a decorated border, M·D·LXXI / ANNO MAGNAE / NAVALIS / VICTORIAE DEI / GRA· CONTRA / TVRCAS.
Bronze: 3.4
This osella celebrates the Victory of Lepanto.

(c) Obverse: St Mark enthroned on the left gives his standard to the kneeling doge on the right. Around, S·M·V· ALOY·

MOCEN·D· and in the exergue ANN·VI·
Reverse: The *Bucentaur* or state barge surrounded by gondolas.
Bronze: 3.2

(d) Obverse: In the centre Christ as Redeemer with banner. Santa Giustina to the left and the doge to the right, both kneeling. Around, PARCE·POPVLO·TVO· and in the exergue 1576. Reverse: A classical temple façade with a six-columned portico and a triangular pediment. Acroteria are placed on the corners of the pediment and additional figures are on the stilobates. Through the temple's portal a statue can be seen. Around, ALOYSII MOCENI·CO PR·MVN and in the exergue REDEMPTORI VOTVM·
Bronze: 3.3
This osella, **e** and **f** below commemorate the decision to build the Redentore.

(e) Obverse: The kneeling doge on the left prays to the Redeemer who appears in the sky. The winged lion of St Mark with its gospel stands on the lower right. Behind, a view of the Bacino and the Piazza. Around, ALOYSII MOCENIGO PR. MVNS· and in the exergue ·ANN·VII·
Reverse: A central plan temple with portico and multiple domes. Through the portal can be seen a statue on a podium. Around, REDEMPTORI VOTVM and in the exergue MDLXXVI.
Bronze: 3.2

(f) Obverse: Christ enthroned on the left gives the standard to the kneeling doge on the right. Behind the doge, the lion of St Mark. Around the border ALOISI MOCENI·P·MVN·
In the exergue MDLXXVI.
Reverse: A rectangular temple with statues along its sides and another statue on the attic level. Above the pediment, the winged lion of St Mark faces right. Around, REDEMPTORI VOTVM·MDLXXVI·
Bronze: 3.3

SEBASTIANO VENIER 1577–8
(g) Obverse: St Mark enthroned on the left gives the standard to the kneeling doge on the right. The doge holds a palm and is crowned by an angel. Around, ·SEB·VENIERIO·P·MVNVS· and in the exergue ANNO·I.
Reverse: A view of the Bacino and the Piazza. Christ appears in the sky, blessing Venice. Around, MAGNA·DEI· MISERICORDIA·SVP·NO·1577.
This celebrates the delivery of Venice from the Plague.
Bronze: 3.3

217 Some comparative costs in Vicenza and Venice

245,537 duc.	Cost of the construction of the Rialto bridge 1588–92 (220)
111,297 duc.	Annual tax yield of Vicenza to Venice in 1554 (Vicenza, introduction)
72,100 duc.	Cost of the construction of the church of the Redentore, 1577–92
60,000 duc.	Total cost of the construction of the Basilica logge, 1544–1616
31,000 duc.	Wage bill and running costs of a great galley 1601 (oral communication John Hale)
30,000 duc.	The Podestà of Padua's estimate of the revenue of the monastery of Santa Giustina (sister house of S.Giorgio Maggiore) in 1554 (ASV, *Relazioni*)
18,500 duc.	The price paid by Conte Odorico Capra in 1591 for the Villa Rotanda (Monza, 1888, p.3
13,002 duc.	The price for which Giovanni Pisani bought the Bagnolo estate in 1523 (Dalla Pozza, 1964–5, p.206)
10,000 duc.	The dowry promised by Teodoro Thiene, owner of the villa at Cicogna, on behalf of his sister Attilia, for her marriage to Leonida da Porto, son of Giuseppe da Porto, for whom Palladio designed the Palazzo da Porto Festa. (Mantese, 1969–70, p.82)
7,000 duc.	An estimate for tax purposes of the income of the Pisani estate at Bagnolo, made in 1572 (*ibid*, p.205)
4,000 duc.	Dowry in 1568 of a daughter of Palladio's friend and patron Conte Giacomo Angarano (Monza, 1888, p.18)
400 duc.	Dowry of Palladio's daughter, Zenobia
60 duc.	The price paid by Fabio Monza to obtain a pardon for a relation who had killed two peasants (Monza, 1888)
50 scudi	Payment to Giulio Romano for his consultation on the Basilica

20 duc.	Palladio's monthly salary at the Ducal Palace in 1574
7 scudi	Price of having a statue in the Teatro Olimpico (73)
5 scudi	Palladio's monthly salary as architect of the Basilica. H.B.

VENETIAN SCHOOL early seventeenth century

18 Expulsion from the temple

Canvas: 38 × 50 in
Lent by Sir George Weidenfeld

The rendering of a religious subject in terms of a realistic portrayal of a scene from every day life is in the tradition established by Jacopo Bassano, but on the evidence of the figures this painting was probably executed outside his circle. In the foreground is shown the merchantile activity of Rialto. A merchant counts his money and a messenger is delivering a letter. He is surrounded by a pile of oriental carpets, as well as packing cases, a cask, and a trussed bale all marked with merchant's trade marks (Mantese, 1969–70, p.96). The porters manhandling a bale on the left recall the activity shown in the engraving of the courtyard of the German merchants trading house, the Fondaco dei Tedeschi (Lieb, 1958, fig.114), and the building with the towers in the background in front could be a reminiscence of the Fondaco itself.   L.F./H.B.

218

DUTCH SCHOOL 17th century

219 The poultry market at Rialto

Pen, ink and wash: 19.8 × 30.5
Lent by the Witt Collection, London (311)

The biggest food markets of the city were concentrated in the Rialto area. The poultry on sale (including birds both alive and dead, and exotic birds like peacocks) hangs from posts or is laid out on the top of the cases in which they were brought to town. A poem written in 1445 by Iacopo d'Albizzotto Giudi confirms the diversity of the market at Rialto and described the poultry market:
'And so many of them come to us
From Autumn to Carneval
That he who hears of it takes it for a lie . . .
A good hundred thousand lire no mistake
the birds are worth
and even more, it cannot be denied . . .'
(Cessi and Alberti, 1934, p.440).
Though merchants and nobles would often purchase poultry low wage earners probably did so rarely (cf. Braudel, 1972, pp.458–9 and 517ff.).   L.F.

JACOPO DE' BARBARI C.1440–C.1516

*220 Bird's eye view of the Rialto bridge, 1500

Photograph

This detail is from de' Barbari's large engraved bird's eye view of Venice which shows the whole of the city with astonishing precision (Schulz, 1970, pp.19–22). The old wooden bridge, which had repeatedly given way, only to be patched up again, remained in existence throughout Palladio's lifetime. The form which it has in de' Barbari's engraving, with shops lining the route across, and a central section which could be raised to allow taller vessels to pass, was established in 1458. It is interesting that even at that date a sizable minority in the Senate, 'esteeming the honour and beauty of the bridge more than the income which can be derived from it', opposed the construction of shops, which blocked the view (Cessi and Alberti, 1934, p.169). This was the only bridge over the Grand Canal, and hence the only land connection between the governmental centre at the Piazza of San Marco and the commercial centre at Rialto. All the same, the proponents of

220

half-measures, temporary repairs, and postponement of decisions had their way until the present stone bridge was constructed between 1588 and 1590. Immediately above and to the right of the bridge appears the old Fondaco de' Tedeschi, the great warehouse and residential hostel of the German merchants operating in Venice. The building shown here was destroyed by fire in 1505 and was at once rebuilt and is now the Central Post Office. On the same side in the foreground is the campanile of San Bartolomeo. On the other side of the bridge is the Rialto area, as it was before the great fire of 1514 (*ibid.* p.86). Immediately to the right of the bridge is the large loggia frequented by the nobility. Although it no longer existed in Palladio's time, it is a surprising anticipation of his pedimented porticos. Further away from the bridge is the piazza of Rialto, the centre for business transactions. What the view does not show is the overcrowding and confusion of the area. Nobles and merchants, transacting business, were mixed up with peasants in from the country to sell their produce, as well as with those who had come to buy silk and books and expensive goods, or simply to do their ordinary shopping at the various food markets (219) packed into this area, which was also a centre for prostitution and low life generally. Not least of the problems was that of parking: though certain areas of the embankment were nominally reserved for gentlemen and merchants (the Vicentines too had their special mooring), boatmen often blocked access, so that in 1487 there is the complaint that many people had to return home by foot (*ibid.*, pp.74–5). H.B.

*221 a and b Project for a new Rialto bridge

Pen, ink, and wash: 47.7 × 76
Photographs: Museo Civico, Vicenza (D.25)
a) Side elevation (D.25r)
b) Plan (D.25v)

Palladio's project combines the scheme of the old wooden bridge with that of his favourite antique bridge, that of Augustus at Rimini (III, p.22). From it he has taken the five arches and the tabernacles applied to the piers. Like the wooden bridge, the sides are lined with shops, which present a blank wall to the outside, and a view over the canal is only available in the middle, though in this case the central opening is dignified with a pedimented loggia, whose scheme was possibly suggested by that of the Tempietto di Clitunno (IV, cap.xxv). The figures are not by Palladio, and the three above are executed in darker ink. They might well be by India (183) and could date from the time when he was engaged on the decoration of Palazzo Thiene (see 125, the medal by Vittoria which implicitly commemorates the work which Vittoria himself, India, and Canera did on the palace). The style of the project is that of the 1550s rather than the 1560s (Puppi, 1973, p.301), and this dating is consistent with the available documentation. After nothing had come of the appointment in 1525 of commissioners to consider rebuilding the bridge, three new commissioners were elected on 17 January 1551, with authority to seek opinions and designs. Two of these, Vettor Grimani and Antonio Cappello were particularly experienced in architectural matters. Francesco Sansovino (1562; cf. Howard, 1975) singled out Cappello as the moving spirit behind his father's Loggetta and Grimani in relation to his Library. Many architects, including Michelangelo, seem to have made designs, and in 1588 Marc'Antonio Barbaro implies that these were presented in 1554 (Cessi and Alberti, 1934, pp.186–7). Palladio's position as architect of the Basilica would of itself have been sufficient reason for the commissioners to consult him, but Puppi is probably correct in his suggestion that Palladio's involvement was the result of Barbaro's efforts to launch Palladio and his radically antique style in Venice itself (1973, p.301).

The decoration is fairly predictable. The statues in the niches derive from Sansovino's statues for the Loggetta, the river gods are always a stand-by for bridges, and Justice (see 227) and

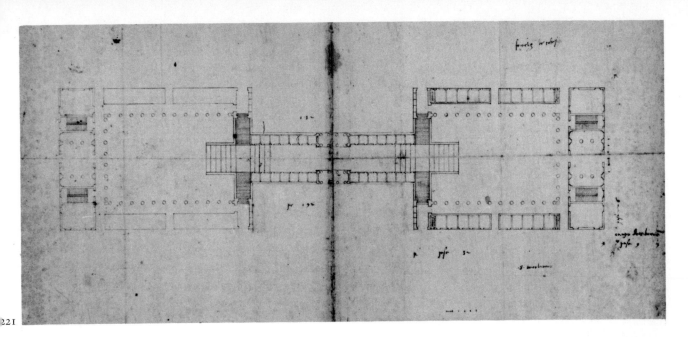

221

Fortitude and Prudence belong to the standard language of Venetian state iconography (compare India's project, now in the Metropolitan Museum (Sotheby's, 13 December 1973, fig.17). The plan of the project is of the greatest interest. It is in fact the only large scale urban project by Palladio to survive. The bridge is approached from colonnaded piazze, each entered through a large room with its beam ceiling carried on four columns. The scheme owes much to Palladio's studies of ancient fora, and the steps of the bridge project into the area, like the steps in front of a temple into its precinct (Puppi, 1973, fig.389). The scheme almost certainly had an upper floor and is connected with Palladio's reconstructions of the Piazze of the Greeks and the Latins (III, pp.32–7; note the tetrastyle entrance to the Piazza of the Greeks). There are also points in common with the Carità (251). The scheme is perfectly functional and in keeping with Venetian tradition. The piazze could be locked at night and resemble the closed piazza/cortile of the nearby Fondaco de' Tedeschi. There is the same sort of attempt to rationalize the confused Rialto area, which Fra Giocondo had unsuccessfully proposed after the 1514 fire, and which Palladio could well have described to Vasari in 1566 (Puppi, 1973, p.299;

Burns, 1973, p.154). Large rooms are provided which could be used for customs or other administrative purposes, and the shops are all arranged so that they face outwards and not on to the piazze. This means that shoppers would not have been mixed up with those who met in the piazze to transact business. The main drawback to the scheme was the substantial demolitions which it would have required on both sides of the canal. H.B.

222 Design for a bridge

Photograph from the *Quattro Libri*, III, pp.26–7

'Most beautiful in my judgment is the design of the bridge which follows, and very well suited to the site . . . which was in the middle of a city, which is one of the greatest and most noble in Italy . . . and there is an enormous amount of trade . . . and the bridge came to be exactly in the spot, where the merchants gathered to do business' (III, p.25). Though Palladio does not specifically mention Rialto, he makes it perfectly plain that it is to Rialto that he is referring. However his circumlocution, and the fact that he does not give any measurements is odd: he usually presents even his theoretical designs and reconstructions with the dimensions fully worked out. This peculiarity led Selva to argue, and attempt to demonstrate, that the project was simply too large for the site, to which Rondelet (1837) convincingly replied that it was not (Magrini, 1845, pp.140–4). The reason for Palladio's evasiveness about the measurements is not that the bridge would not have fitted its site. It is a splendid project, beneficial to the state for the large income from shop rents it would have brought and with fine views over the canal. It goes some way to provide the loggie for merchants and gentlemen which Palladio's earlier project provided for in the piazze on either side of the bridge. It has only one defect: if one calculates the dimensions, as Rondelet did, on the basis of the width of the Grand Canal at Rialto, the column screens giving access to the bridge, similar to screens in the Baths (442) or between choir and presbytery in San Giorgio, become grave obstacles to transit. The columns would have had a 2 foot diameter, and the clear spaces between them, once the bases (projecting to trip one up) are allowed for would have been about three feet wide. The only access to the bridge would have been through these three narrow openings. One need only think of the congestion of the bridge today, or the size of bales and objects which porters would be carrying over it (218), to see that this would not do. Palladio understandably could not bring himself to exclude his 'most beautiful design', but he was too good an architect and too conscious of practical factors (30) and could not bring himself to write '3 ft.' between the columns of his project. H.B.

223 Project for a new Rialto bridge

Pen, ink, and wash: 50.7 × 43
Photograph; Museo Civico, Vicenza (D.20)

This project was published by Zorzi (1966, fig. 141) as a project for a celebratory arch at Venice. There can be no doubt, however, that it is a variant on the project for the bridge published in the *Quattro Libri* (Burns, 1973, p.153). Its decorative programme is like that of Palladio's earlier Rialto project (221): Justice (this time with St Mark's lion) and virtues. Its width (almost 80 ft.) is close to that of the *Quattro Libri* project. The drawing shows the end of the bridge, as it would have presented itself to someone about to climb the

steps and cross to the other side (cf. Zorzi, 1966, fig. 244). Like the *Quattro Libri* project, it provided for six rows of shops and three thoroughfares: the two inner rows consisted of shops placed back to back. Unlike the published project, there are no column screens to impede access. The side entrances have a width of about six feet, and that in the centre of just over eleven. The Senate on 7 September 1569 decided to appoint three commissioners to examine the 'many models and designs' for the bridge already in existence, and to report back (Zorzi, 1966, p.249). There is, therefore, no reason to date either the *Quattro Libri* project or this as late as 1569, and a date around 1565 is likely for both (cf. Puppi, 1973, p.302). The *Quattro Libri* loggie flanked by closed bays with niches recalls the elevation of the end of a choir, as one looks towards the main body of a church (Zorzi, 1966, fig.88). The Museo Civico drawing has a central element just like a church façade drawing of this period (244) with the same grouping of columns and the same tall attic. It also resembles the façade design (244) of this period in the way in which a rectangle is cut out of the wall to make an opening. The composite order and the swags are a standard feature of Palladio's vocabulary at this time (38). The massive basement zone is in the spirit of the San Giorgio façade, and the side units, ending without any column or pilaster, recall the façade solution of the Casa Cogollo (59). This is an extraordinary invention, almost grotesque on paper. If executed, the composition, with vast pedestals supporting further pedestals, and the towering attic would have been very powerful and impressive.
Once more India is the most likely suggestion for the author of the figures. H.B.

VINCENZO SCAMOZZI 1552–1616
*224 Project for the Ponte di Rialto

Pen and brown ink over metalpoint and incised construction lines: 46.3 × 73.8
Signed: *Vicenzo Scamozzi Ar.*
Lent by the Royal Institute of British Architects

Scamozzi shows the complete elevation of the bridge above and its basic structure below. The drawing, with its neat, finely ruled lines, is typical of him. In December 1587 five projects for a new bridge were presented, and late in the month Scamozzi was one of those whom the building commissioners

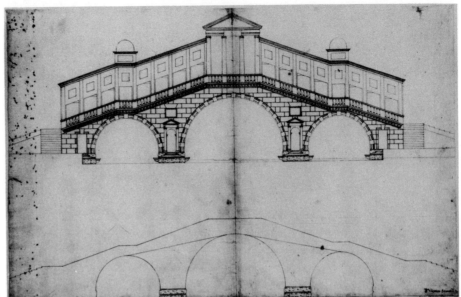

224

225

consulted on the problems which the designs raised. On 31 December Scamozzi presented a memorandum in which he came out strongly against a single arch solution and in favour of three arches, on both structural and aesthetic grounds (Cessi and Alberti, 1934, pp.364–6). By 11 January 1588 Scamozzi himself had presented a 'model' (it is not clear whether this was three-dimensional or merely a drawing), and this was strongly criticised by Gugliemo di Grandi in a written report (*ibid.*). There is little doubt that di' Grandi was referring to the RIBA design, which was also published in a contemporary woodcut (Zorzi, 1966, fig.248). Like Antonio da Ponte's executed bridge, there were three 'roads'. Those at the sides enjoying a view over the canal and were not closed on both sides by shops, as in Palladio's later projects (222 and 223). In all sixty-four shops are provided for. The central pedimental loggia is an echo of Palladio's schemes though its precise design, with the tablet inserted in the frieze derives from Scamozzi's Rocca Pisani (358) which in turn derives from the Rotonda. Di Grandi's criticisms illuminate other aspects of the scheme. The central piers were not to be solid, but divided into two parts, with a cross vault between them: a solution which di Grandi said would set up a turbulence which would be dangerous for small boats. The piers on the banks were also to be hollow and would function as landing stages, though di Grandi points out that 'they will be the hang-out of dirty men and also the dumping place for a great deal of refuse, which will bring it about that no gentleman's gondola will ever arrive there'. His other criticisms are much graver. He argues that it would be impossible to found the piers securely on the canal bed and that subsidence would inevitably follow. He also argues that Scamozzi had got his dimensions wrong, and had calculated that fifteen feet more were available for the width of the bridge at either end than was in fact the case. Scamozzi, after a determined struggle in which he was energetically supported by Marc'Antonio Barbaro who was one of the commissioners, was overridden on the question of the number of arches. He did, however, also produce a design with a single arch (Zorzi, 1966, fig.249), and hence there is some justification for the credit which he claimed for the bridge as executed (Temanza, 1778, pp.426–7; Scamozzi, 1615, II, p.330). Antonio da Ponte's design, executed between 1588 and 1592 at a total cost of 245,537 ducats (Cessi and

Alberti, 1934, pp.207–23), did coincide in certain respects with Scamozzi's projects and was probably influenced by them. It rises towards the centre (which none of Palladio's schemes did), has the same disposition of shops and the same bold cornice and balustrade. H.B.

GIOVANNI ANTONIO CANAL (CANALETTO) 1697–1768

*225 Caprice view with Palladio's design for Rialto
Canvas: 90.8 × 130.2
Signed at lower right
Lent by Her Majesty The Queen

One of a series of thirteen overdoors dated 1743–4 representing views of Venice, commissioned by Consul Smith. They are listed in his inventory as 'the principal Buildings of Palladio', and in a separate note as 'the most admired Buildings at Venice (Levey, 1964, no.408). Smith's collection was acquired by George III in 1770, and nine of this present series survive in the Royal Collection. Joseph Smith was an art dealer, who settled in Venice c.1709, and supplied English patrons with works of art. In 1744 he became British Consul there. As he became richer he acquired a large collection of books and his collection formed the nucleus of the King's Library in the British Museum. He also collected drawings and paintings, mainly by modern masters and was one of Canaletto's most important patrons and his agent before 1730. Initially Smith commissioned works from him which evoked both the beauty and the daily life of Venice. However with the acquisition of his new palace on the Grand Canal, Consul Smith commissioned a series of paintings to be conceived as part of the decoration of the palace (they were overdoors) and in so doing, created a new theme in Venetian painting, where the city is seen in terms of monuments. Here Canaletto has replaced the actual Rialto bridge with the bridge project published by Palladio in 1570 (222) and presumed to be for Rialto. L.F.

ALESSANDRO LEOPARDI active 1482–1523

226 Standard Base from the Piazza di San Marco, Venice (Copy)
Lent by the Victoria and Albert Museum

Alessandro Leopardi was largely responsible for perfecting the technique of large-scale sculptural bronze casting in Venice. Among his first major commissions was the completion of Verrocchio's equestrian monument to Bartolomeo Colleoni, which Leopardi cast and for which he designed the base (Pope-Hennessy, 1971, pp. 298–9). Leopardi's most inventive work, the three bronze standard bases for the Piazza di San Marco, was produced over five years, the first appearing in the Piazza in 1501, the second and third in 1505 (Sansovino, 1581, 105v). Aside from its durability, bronze was the most splendid material for such a purpose and could be elaborately moulded. Each of the standard bases bears the profile of the doge, Leonardo Loredan; beneath it a collar with the names of the three procurators of the Basilica of St Mark, responsible for supervising the work; then the winged lion of St Mark, symbol of the Republic, in high relief. A second collar follows with the doge's name and the fourth year of his reign (both inscriptions are absent from the electrotype). At this point the programme was varied to include three relief scenes, one for each of the standards. The first contains the bounty of the earth brought to Venice from her colonies across the sea. The second, seen here, shows Justice, Minerva, and Abundance as titulary guardians of the Venetian empire. The third relief witnesses Neptune receiving gifts of wine, symbolic of its cultivation in the dependent provinces of Verona, Vicenza, and the Friuli. As examples of sophisticated bronze casting, the standards can be compared with the exclusive use of bronze in the Zen Chapel of St Mark's, with which Leopardi was associated (Paoletti, 1893, pp. 244–7, 268–9). As symbols of Venetian grandeur, they anticipate the iconographic programme of Sansovino's Loggetta (Sansovino, 1581, pp. 111r–112r). B.B.

GIUSEPPE PORTA SALVIATI C.1520–75
*227 **Justice**
Canvas: 90 × 125
Lent by the Trustees of the National Gallery, London

Giuseppe Porta came to Venice in 1539 with the Florentine painter Francesco Salviati, his teacher and namesake (Vasari, 1881, VII, pp.45–7). He was a friend of Palladio, and of Cosimo Bartoli (188). Porta settled in Venice and found a place in the circle of artists and scholars that included the publisher

227

Marcolini, the architect Serlio, and Daniele Barbaro. It was to Barbaro that Porta dedicated his treatise on the Ionic volute (191), published by Marcolini, who also published Barbaro's *Vitruvius* (178). The *Justice* (originally 87 × 104 cms.) may have been painted for a lunette in the Zecca or public mint, commissioned by Tommaso or Paolo Contarini, whose family arms appear in the lower left-hand portion of the canvas and who were overseers of the mint in 1542 and 1558 respectively (Gould, 1975, pp.231–2). A date of circa 1558 would seem most likely for the composition as the figure style is very close to the print of *Lucretia and her Maids*, signed and dated 1557 (Jaderosa-Molino, 1963, p.168) and to the tondi of the Libreria Marciana ceiling, datable to 1556 (Ridolfi, 1914, p.242; written communication, D.M., 1975). B.B.

GIUSEPPE SPORTA SALVIATI C.1520–75
228 **The reconciliation between Pope Alexander III and the Emperor Frederic Barbarossa**
Pen, wash, and chalk: 35.4 × 37.7
Lent by the Trustees of the Chatsworth Settlement

Of the three known drawings for Giuseppe Porta's fresco in the *Sala Regia* of the Vatican palace, those in the Louvre (Tietze and Tietze-Conrat, 1944, p.244, no.1383) and in Hartford, Connecticut (Vitzthum, 1970, pp.26–9; Sutton, 1974, p.277) seem to represent earlier stages in the design and are less finished than the Chatsworth drawing (Tietze and Tietze-

129

Conrat, 1944, p.244, no.1376). The theme of the fresco was the legendary submission of the Holy Roman Emperor to the authority of the pope through the mediation of the doge of Venice, Sebastiano Ziani in 1177. To this legend Venice owed some of her authority as a power in Italian politics, and 'The Reconciliation' became one of the central themes in Venetian state mythology, appearing in the decoration of the ducal palace in the early fourteenth century (Wolters, 1965–6, p.276). As the episode also stressed the authority of the Pope it was chosen for the fresco cycle of the Sala Regia, the chamber in which the Pope received ambassadors (cf.Pastor, 1950, p.558, note 5). Giuseppe Porta was at work on the fresco from 1563–5 (Vasari, 1881, VII, p.46) and included portraits of Pius IV, who had commissioned the work, and the current doge Hieronimo Priuli (214e) as the chief protagonists in the scene. B.B.

229 Venetorum Nobilium Liber, 16th century

Paper: 28 × 20.3
Prov: Sir Henry Wotton (?)
Lent by the Provost and Fellows of Eton College (193)

As well as containing a miscellany of documents relating to the Venetian nobility, the volume contains a brief history of leading Venetian families arranged in alphabetical order. On the left hand margin of each page the coats of arms of the families are drawn and coloured (James, 1895, pp.119–20). Many such collections of Venetian heraldry exist (for instance B.M., King's MS, 150). The volume is shown open at the page showing the Barbaro arms, borne by Daniele and Marc' Antonio: a red ring on a white ground. The origin of the device is that after a standard had been captured, Marco Barbaro removed the bloodstained handkerchief which he had put on a head wound, and fixed it on to a stick to make a new flag. L.F.

230 Promissione of Doge Antonio Grimani, 21 July 1521

Vellum: 32.5 × 45.8 (open)
Prov: Consul Smith
Lent by the British Library Board (B.M. Add MS.18000)

The *Promissione* (Promise) was the official oath containing the rules governing his office which had to be sworn by the new Doge. These rules were revised by a committee of leading political figures after the death of each Doge (Marc'Antonio Barbaro served in this capacity in 1577) and it was often from the handful of 'correctors' of the oath that the new Doge was elected. The *Promissione* was always magnificently decorated and bound (Grimani's has an eighteenth century binding bearing the arms of Consul Smith). The first double opening fully illuminated. On the left St Mark as the patron saint of Venice and with his lion places his hand on the kneeling Doge head. On the right the text begins, with the title in gold letters on deep red, surrounded with gold trophies and putti. The rest of the text is written in a neat hand with illuminated capitals. The manuscript has been attributed to the circle of Benedetto Bordon, who in the early sixteenth century renovated the decoration of official documents, abolishing border decoration and replacing it by a fully illuminated frontispiece. (Canova, 1968, p.331 and fig.8).

Grimani was famous in Venetian history for living down his disgrace (and with it the risk of execution) in 1499, to become Doge twenty years later (Chambers, 1970, p.96). A broken di from the service of Doge Grimani is exhibited here (99). L.F

231 Berretta of Doge Domenico II Contarini

Gold silk trimmed with silk braid
Lent by the Visitors of the Ashmolean Museum, Oxford

Although this Ducal *berretta* (also called *corno*) dates from the seventeenth century, the shape was traditional, and is identical to those worn in the sixteenth century. Francesco Sansovino (1663, p.471) records that from 1367 the Doge was obliged to wear the ducal *berretta* whenever he went out in public. He wore a silk version of the gold crown kept in St Mark's and used only for the coronation. The *berretta*'s horn shape at the back and the gold braid are an allusion to the golden original. Under the *berretta* the Doge wore a cap of fine cambric, which helped the *berretta* to stay firmly on the head and covered his head should he take it off. L.F.

232 Umbrella of Doge Domenico Contarini II, 1666

Silk and wood
Inscribed on the support: FV INDORATA DI ME IACINT(O) PATRIA DI V.(enezia) MDCLXVI
Photograph of the original at Waddesdon Manor

The umbrella is ogee-capped and crowned by a vase finial, and the support is of carved, gilded and coloured wood. The canopy is made of crimson brocaded damask with a pattern of stylised flowers and foliage in gold thread and trimmed with a gold fringe. It is lined with white silk painted with gold stars and arabesques. The umbrella has a wooden strut structure similar to that of modern umbrellas, and it opens and closes by means of pulling a cord (de Bellaigue, 1974, pp.676ff.).

When the Doge went in public procession he was accompanied by regalia conceeded to the Doges (according to the mythology of the Venetian State) by the Pope and Emperor as symbols of his sovereignty. These were: eight silk standards, silver trumpets, a white candle, a sword (233), a throne, cushions and an umbrella. Although this umbrella belongs to the seventeenth century the shape, like the berretta (231) which belonged to the same Doge, was traditional. Matteo Pagan's woodcut of the mid sixteenth century shows the Doge in procession beneath a similar umbrella (Chambers, 1970, fig.44; de Bellaigue, 1974, p.678). ᐟ L.F.

3 Hand-and-half sword and scabbard, German (Munich), c.1580

Sword is of steel: overall length 124.5 weight 5 lb 2 oz
The scabbard is made of wood covered with tooled leather: length 96.5 weight 1 lb 2 oz
Mark: that of the bladesmith Cristoph Stantler of Munich on each face of the forte
Prov: Norton Hall Collection
Lent by Her Majesty's Armouries, Tower of London

The hilt, originally gilded, is in the form of two shells. The guards are inscribed: NEC TEMERE and NEC TIMIDE. The broad straight blade is etched at the forte with the symbol of Venice, the Lion of St Mark holding a book inscribed with the Venetian motto PAX TIPI MARCEE (*sic*) VAN/IEEL/STA MEVS. On the reverse there is a panel containing the standing figures of a bishop (?) and a Doge. Between them, and touched by both is a standard. Above the panel there is a tablet inscribed NICOLAVS DE/ PONTE DEIGD/ A DVX VEN/TIA BEGT (Catalogue file).

This sword like the Doge's umbrella (232) was part of the processional regalia of the Doge. The sword, as the inscription indicates, belonged to Nicolò da Ponte, Doge from

233

1578–87. As procurator he was one of Venice's leading diplomats and several times represented the Venetian State at the Council of Trent, and with Marc'Antonio Barbaro was a negotiator of the peace treaty with the Turks. He reigned in a period of peace and relative prosperity. L.F.

ODOARDO FIALETTI 1573–1638
234 Doge Leonardo Donato giving Audience to Sir Henry Wotton
Canvas: 174 × 264.8
Lent by Her Majesty The Queen

The subject, identity of the doge and the painter of this painting is given in Wotton's inventory (Pearshall Smith, 1907) and on this basis is datable 1606–10 (Levey, 1964, p.79). Paintings of this subject are common, probably because of their interest as souvenirs. The composition reflects Giacomo Franco's engraving in *Habiti d'Huomeni e Donne . . .*, (1610). The ambassador, with his hat on, is on the Doge's right, and is being received in the *Sala del Collegio* in the Palazzo Ducale (one of the rooms damaged by the fire in 1574). The drawn curtains conceal Veronese's *Thanksgiving for the Victory of Lepanto* (281). Sir Henry Wotton was a friend of A. Foscarini who had shared lodgings with Marc'Antonio Barbaro in Venice. He published a treatise on architecture, *The Elements of Architecture* (1624) and owned drawings by Palladio. L.F.

LEANDRO BASSANO 1557–1622
*235 Portrait of a Procurator
Canvas: 113.9 × 102
Lent by the Visitors of the Ashmolean Museum, Oxford

The Procurator is shown in an open loggia overlooking an unidentified port. The sitter wears a rich red robe and the Procurator's stole (236). The ornately bound volume on the table, which he indicates with evident satisfaction, is almost certainly his *Commissione*, or official document of appointment as a Procurator. The Procurators administered public property, and private individuals often appointed them as their trustees. The office, which was held for life, was regarded as second only in honour to that of the Doge, though by the second half of the sixteenth century it was often awarded not for merit, but for a large cash payment. L.F./H.B.

235

236 Part of a stole as worn by a Venetian Procurator
Italian 16th century
Pile-on-pile red silk velvet: 143.5 × 33
Lent by the Victoria and Albert Museum (T317–1910)

The pattern of the stole is traditional and represents crowns and stylised roses. The stole was part of the official dress of the Procurators, and an identical stole is worn by the sitter in (235). L.F.

ALESSANDRO VITTORIA 1525–1608
237 Bust of a Navagero (?)
Terracotta: h.77.8
Lent by the Victoria and Albert Museum (A.10–1948)

The present bust carries an inscription that identifies the subject as a member of the Navagero family; on the border of the left shoulder are carved the letters A.V.F., a formula often used by Vittoria in signing his works (see the lateral figures on the

Mercers' altar in San Giuliano). The subject wears the robes and *stola* of a procurator. He appears to be an as yet unidentified member of the Navagero family who served as a procurator *de citra* or *de ultra* during the second half of the sixteenth century. Vittoria's connections with the Navagero family went back to 1553 when the sculptor rented a house in the *Calle de la Pieta* from Antonio Navagero (Predelli, 1908, p.41, n.1). Like its companion in this exhibition, the bust of Navagero was purchased from the Manfrin Collection in Venice (Pope-Hennessy, 1964, pp.531–4).   B.B.

CIRCLE OF ALESSANDRO VITTORIA 1525–1608
238 Bust of an unknown man
Marble: h. 70
Lent by the Visitors of the Ashmolean Museum, Oxford

The subject's head is turned slightly to the right and has a full beard. Some weathering and abrasions are evident on the features. The base of veined marble is cut in the form of a toga with braiding on the left shoulder. The pedestal is modern. The bust is similar to a number of portraits by Vittoria during the 1570s and 1580s and is probably the work of a contemporary sculptor, well versed in Vittoria's style. The treatment of the high forehead, the hair, and the well defined cheekbones invites comparison with the terracotta and bronze portraits of Tommaso Rangone (in the Museo Correr and the Ateneo Veneto respectively), which were probably commissioned from Vittoria in the 1570s (Cessi, 1961–I, p.38, pls. 37 and 38). The deep cut of the features and beard also resembles the bust of Giulio Contarini in Santa Maria del Giglio, Venice, completed by Vittoria before 1576 (Gerola, 1924–5, p.350; Cessi, 1962, pl.2). Like the Contarini monument, the present bust may have been intended for the wall of a church, possibly an exterior portal, which would explain the slight weathering. The last quarter of the sixteenth century would seem a reasonable date for its execution.   B.B.

JACOPO PALMA IL GIOVANE 1544–1628
239 Portrait of Nicolò Cappello
Canvas: 182.9 × 101.6
Lent by the Trustees of the Chatsworth Settlement

The attribution of the portrait to Palma Giovane was first made by Berenson, who compared it with a second portrait of Cappello, also painted by Palma and now in the Louvre (Berenson, 1947, pp.22–4). More recently Ballarin has placed it among the earliest of Palma's portraits, assigning it to the 1570s (oral communication, 1975). Nicolò Cappello came of a family with a long history of distinguished service to the Venetian navy. His grandfather Nicolò served as *provveditore* (commissioner) of the fleet in the war over Cyprus (1488–94), and his uncle Vicenzo was elected captain-general of the navy five times (Zarbarella, 1670, pp.26–7; Cigogna, 1824, pp.160–1). The inspiration for Palma's portrait was Titian's painting of Admiral Vicenzo Cappello, now in Washington, who is also seen in armour and with a baton in his right hand (Wethey, 1971, pp.83–4, no.17). The inscription, NICOLAVS CAPPELLVS TER CLASSI PRAEFECTVS, probably indicates that Nicolò Cappello held the office of *provveditore* (*praefectus*) three times. In the background are Venetian war galleys of the type which fought at Lepanto.   B.B.

BERNARDO LICINIO
240 Portrait of an ecclesiastic
Canvas: 92 × 76.8 signed and dated 1524
Lent by the York City Art Gallery

The sitter is shown holding a choral book, and his silk clothes, which are not vestments, suggest that he is an important ecclesiastic, perhaps a bishop or a canon.   L.F.

241 Breviary, late fifteenth century Venetian
Vellum: 15.9 × 25.4 (open)
Prov: Robert Curzon, Parham House, Sussex
Lent by the British Library Board (Add. MS. 39633)

The Breviary follows the liturgy of the Benedictine Congregation of Santa Giustina, Padua, and contains a feast of particular importance to the Venetian monastery of San Giorgio Maggiore, namely that of the hermit Saint Cosmas (f.179v), whose relics were venerated in the church. The only illumination in the book is of the Martyrdom of SS. Cosmas and Damian (f.189v), whose relics were also preserved at San Giorgio. Thus it has been suggested that the breviary may come from the Monastery of San Giorgio, whose library was

242

Neither the purpose nor the artist of this drawing have been securely identified although it has recently been attributed to Andrea Michiele il Vicentino (de Rothschild, 1975, no.28). The scene is of a church interior, with a group of well dressed Venetians listening to a sermon by a Dominican monk. In the background is a free version of Titian's *St Peter Martyr* which hung in the Dominican church of SS. Giovanni e Paolo in Venice, until it was destroyed by fire in 1867 (Wethey, 1969, pp.153–5, no.133). The scene may have been prepared for a genre engraving like those in the *Habiti* of Giacomo Franco (212). B.B.

243 The facade of San Francesco della Vigna, Venice
Photograph

Construction of a new church for the Franciscan Observant order in Venice began in 1534 under the patronage of Andrea Gritti, after a design by Jacopo Sansovino (Tafuri, 1969, pp.18–25; Howard, 1975, pp.64–74). Gritti, whose palace stood next to the convent of San Francesco, took great interest in the church, bequeathing it his ducal robes for vestments and the handsome sum of 1000 ducats towards a chancel tomb for his family. In April 1535 the learned and noble friar Francesco Giorgi submitted a critique of the newly begun fabric (Wittkower, 1962, pp.155–7; Zorzi, 1966, p.35; Puppi, 1973, pp.345–7). Giorgi, who together with Zuanne Barbaro, uncle of Daniele, supervised the construction for the monastery, broadly accepted Sansovino's design while recommending proportional changes in the length and width of the nave and chapels, all to be based upon the 'first and divine' unit of three *passi* (approximately 6 m.). Giorgi's harmonic proportions were accepted (they had, in fact, been formally approved by Titian, Serlio, Fortunio Spira, and Sansovino himself), and work on the amended design proceeded over the next five decades, with the consecration of the church taking place in 1582 (Cornaro, 1749, VIII, pp.55–6). After the death of Doge Gritti in 1538, the Grimani family assumed a dominant role as patrons of San Francesco, purchasing in 1542 the right to build the façade as a memorial to Doge Antonio Grimani (230; Howard, 1975, p.69). The Grimani family had close connections with Palladio's most influential patrons; Cardinal Marino Grimani had been a friend of Trissino (Morsolin, 1894, p.131) and Bishop

dispersed in 1806, when the order was suppressed (British Museum, 1933, pp.104–5; cf.Cigogna, 1834, pp.241ff.). Recently Alexander has suggested that the illumination is by the same hand as the *Brooke Antiphonal*, now in the collection of the Society of Antiquaries (Alexander, 1969, pp.385–7), the latter having been attributed to Girolamo da Cremona, who was active in Venice from 1474–6 (see Levi-D'Ancona, 1964, pp.76, 92–3). B.B.

ANONYMOUS LATE SIXTEENTH CENTURY VENETIAN ARTIST
*242 Dominican preaching to his congregation
Pen and brown ink and wash: 15.8 × 12.0
Lent by Kate de Rothschild

Giovanni had appointed Daniele Barbaro his successor as patriarch of Aquileia in 1550 (Laven, 1967, pp.184–205). There would also have been an opportunity to study an earlier design for a church façade by Palladio, the one approved for San Pietro di Castello in Venice, probably with an intervention by Daniele and Marc'Antonio Barbaro (Magrini, 1845, pp.xvii–xviii; Puppi, 1973, pp.321–3). Thus the Grimani decision to commission a design for a new façade from Palladio and not from Sansovino and for a family tomb on its interior wall (245) had substantial reasons behind it.

Clearly, when the façade was being considered, around 1562 (Tassini, 1933, pp.284–5), Sansovino's model would have seemed out-dated. The elevation on the foundation medal (see 130) shows a large order of four evenly spaced columns, above which appears a mezzanine with a three light window, topped by a triangular pediment. Sansovino's design received oblique criticism in Giorgi's memorandum, for Giorgi recommended a façade that would reflect the proportions and the internal divisions of the church itself. Giorgi's memorandum displays a humanistic bias which generally coincided with Palladio's more practical approach to the same problems, as exemplified in his judgment on the model for the new cathedral at Brescia (1567; cf. Zorzi, 1966, pp.88–9).

Palladio's solution for San Francesco della Vigna had been anticipated in the San Pietro design and was later to be reconfirmed in San Giorgio Maggiore, the Brescia letter, and the Redentore (252 and 256). It had the advantages of being strongly classical in flavour as well as reproducing the structure of the church behind it. In San Francesco and in the contemporary project for the Carità (251), Palladio introduced a new element into his architectural vocabulary, the large column order as a unifying motif. The large Corinthian order defines the high, broad area of the nave while the smaller Corinthian order is proportioned to the height of the lateral chapels. The blending of large and small order in the façade of San Francesco looks forward to the façade of Palazzo Valmarana (418), in which the entablature of the small order runs across the façade behind the large order; in both façades the podium becomes an imposing element, breaking forward beneath the large order.

Today, the grandeur of San Francesco overwhelms its small *campo*, but in the early 1560s it represented the most important church commission in Venice, worthy of a formidable

exterior. The façade was revolutionary, without precedent in ancient or contemporary architecture. As elaborated in San Giorgio and the Redentore, it became the point of departure for Venetian church façades of the seventeenth and eighteenth centuries. B.B.

244 Design for a church facade
Pen and ink over incised construction lines: 31.2 × 41.2
Lent by the Royal Institute of British Architects (XVI/10)

The composite and Corinthian orders are shown as alternatives, and instead of the normal pediment Palladio has experimented with a tall attic, based on those of triumphal arches. The little panels between the columns are quoted from the Arch of Trajan at Ancona (cf.284). The large rectangle would have been intended to contain a portal, probably with a window above it, as at San Francesco della Vigna. The formula for a façade employed here is similar to that of San Francesco, with a single pedestal zone below large and small orders. The side sections are not however set back in the same way. An incised scale on the drawing, not visible on photographs, enables one to establish the dimensions, and to exclude the possibility that this drawing is directly connected with either San Francesco della Vigna or San Giorgio Maggiore, which are both bigger. The maximum width is just over 61 ft, the pedestals to the top of the plinth are 6 ft, the width of the central opening is 13⅔ ft, its height 24½ ft. H.B.

ANDREA PALLADIO and FEDERICO ZUCCARO C.1540–1609
*245 Project for the Grimani Tombs in San Francesco della Vigna, Venice
Pen, ink and wash: 48.4 × 38.7 cms
Photograph: Museo Civico, Vicenza, D17

This drawing has been generally associated with the unexecuted wall tomb of Bishop Domenico Bollani, which according to a document of 1579 was to have been erected in San Giorgio Maggiore, Venice (Zorzi, 1963, pp.99–103). But it can be much more plausibly related to the Grimani tombs formerly in San Francesco della Vigna, Venice, as Magrini (1845, p.303) first tentatively suggested.

The three editions of Francesco Sansovino's guide to Venice (1581, p.14; 1604, pp.115–ff; 1663, p.48) say that the Grimani

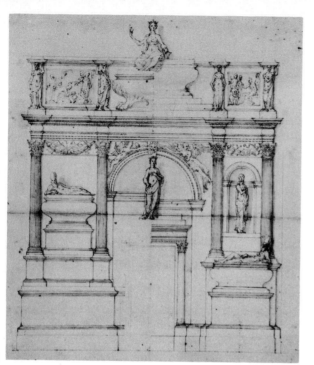

of the pen and ink, especially with regard to the characteristic use of a spidery pen line to suggest drapery and dark blots to accent individual features of the figures (cf. similar drawings by Federico Zuccaro published by Gere, 1966, figs. 30 and 42). Federico Zuccaro was in Venice between 1563–5, and again in 1582 and 1603. During the first visit he was principally engaged in the execution of fresco decorations on the staircase of the Grimani palace at Santa Maria Formosa and in the Grimani chapel in San Francesco della Vigna, both works commissioned by Bishop Giovanni Grimani, who in 1562 had also commissioned Palladio to design a new façade for the same church. Otherwise Vasari (1881, VII, p.100) confirms that for a time Zuccaro and Palladio were in close association, Palladio designing the wooden theatre and Zuccaro the *apparato* for the Compagnia della Calza's carnival performance of 1565 and the two subsequently travelling together to Cividale in Friuli and then through Lombardy.   D.M.

246 The Refectory, San Giorgio Maggiore, Venice, 1560–3
Photographs

The plan for the rebuilding of the whole monastery, drawn up soon after 1520 (253) already shows a refectory projecting on the right, in roughly the same position, and of roughly the same dimensions as the existing one (Timofiewitisch, 1963; Puppi, 1973, p.338). Work was begun on a new refectory in 1540, but not carried to a conclusion. On 3 July 1560 a contract was made with Berton di Bon and his son, builders, 'for building our new Refectory already begun in our orchard, with the attached buildings, that is the Refectory, wine cellar and kitchen as shall be shown to them by messer Andrea Palladio *proto*' (i.e., salaried supervisory architect). It is clear that the greater part of the walls were already in existence and the builders were even to do some demolition of what had already been built. Their main task was to be the construction of the vaults. By 1563 the refectory was finished, complete with its vestibule with the two monumental wash basins, the two great portals, the red and white paving stones, and the carved benches (247) and tables round the walls where the monks ate (Zorzi, 1966, pp.59–64; Puppi *ibid.*). On 6 October 1563 Paolo Veronese wrote out the receipt for the 300 ducats he had received for his *Marriage at Cana* (249). Palladio had been faced with a long rectangular room (the

monument in San Francesco della Vigna contained three sarcophagi, those of the two Cardinals, Domenico and Marino Grimani, and the Patriarch of Aquileia, Marco Grimani, and that it was located on the inside of the façade wall. The drawing shows alternative solutions for such a wall monument erected over a large door, with one sarcophagus placed on either side of the central door, and a third above it. Since Sansovino does not mention any sculpture, apart from the figures of the two Cardinals reclining above the door, the left-hand solution may have been the one more closely followed. And while the Grimani's association with the façade of San Francesco della Vigna has been clarified by Deborah Howard (1975, pp.69–70), it has not yet been established exactly when the tombs were built, or demolished.
The figures in the drawing were attributed by Zorzi (1963, pp.102–3) to Paolo Veronese, but they are clearly by Federico Zuccaro. This is as evident in the elongated figure type, with over large hands and rather vacant heads, as it is in the handling

present refectory is about 10 × 30 m) preceeded by one or two smaller rooms (one cannot be sure what changes were made to create the two successive vestibules). Out of this very simple but inflexible starting point he created a work from whose novelty and impressiveness one should not be distracted by the church itself. The two successive flights of steps, and the two huge doorways lead up to the Refectory, whose end wall was originally filled by the vast rectangle of Veronese's *Marriage*, with a great semicircular thermal window above it. Two other thermal windows (now only visible from the outside) in the middle of each side wall set up a strong cross axis, which was emphasised by the use of a cross vault at this point. Cross vaults of this sort, inserted into a barrel vault, was a formula which Palladio would have acquired from the Baths, in 1541, and had often employed since then (for instance at Vigardolo, 320). The establishment of a cross axis as a way of enlivening a rectangular space by means of a vault solution in combination with thermal windows, he would have known from Sangallo's Cappella Paolina (493). The smaller round topped windows were probably inherited from the existing structure, round topped windows, even in Venice, did not come naturally to Palladio (Puppi, 1973, p.397). In the inside he brings them into line with the bold, massive scale of the room, by giving them heavy flat topped surrounds, with jutting consoles. On the outside he leaves them simple, and merely adds a personal antique touch in the panel which serves as a sill, modelled on the sills of the windows of the 'Temple of Vesta' at Tivoli. As is usual in refectories, the windows are too high to see out of, and provide no distractions from eating and listening to the day's reading. H.B.

PIETRO, IACOMO and FRANCESCO ZUANELLI and FRANCESCO DI MATTEO DA BROZZI (?), all active in 1560
247 A section of the refectory benches from S.Giorgio Maggiore, Venice (?)
Walnut: 221 × 111.5
Restored
Lent by the Victoria and Albert Museum (9–1881)

In the accession note of 1889 the throne is stated as coming from the monastery of San Giorgio Maggiore, though no confirmation of this provenance has appeared. It does have the appearance of late sixteenth-century church furniture from a rich foundation, though it is not related to the choir stalls still in place in the Church. Zorzi published a seventeenth-century engraving of the refectory (1966, fig.50), which shows the original continuous benches in the Refectory as decorated with terms, cartouches, and a projecting cornice supported by consoles, all very much like this 'throne'. The benches were designed and executed by Pietro Zuanelli and his sons Iacomo and Francesco, and Francesco di Matteo da Brozzi, a Florentine, and paid for between July 1560 and July 1562 (*ibid.* pp.59–60, docs. 3 and 4). These benches no longer exist in the monastery. At some date following the suppression of the monastery in 1806, they were dismantled and probably made into saleable single items. The carved decoration of the cornice does not continue on the sides, which further suggests that the 'throne' has been put together in this way. L.F.

248 The portal of San Salvatore at Spoleto
Pen and ink, over brown chalk and incised construction lines: 43.5 × 28
Epsilon handwriting
Lent by the Royal Institute of British Architects (IX/17)

This elegant and fairly accurate drawing shows the central portal of the façade of San Salvatore, details of its volutes, and in the top right, a capital in the interior of the church. There is no certainty that the drawing is based on Palladio's own on the spot sketches, and the repeated quotation of this same door by Sanmicheli (Gazzola, 1960, figs.54, 76, 147) suggests who Palladio's source might be. Following Sanmicheli's example, and probably on the basis of this very drawing, Palladio designed the outer of the two doors which led into the refectory at S.Giorgio. H.B.

PAOLO VERONESE 1528–88
249 The marriage at Cana (copy)
Canvas: 151 × 209.6
Private collection

The Marriage at Cana was commissioned for the refectory of San Giorgio on 6 June 1562 (Zorzi, 1966, pp.61–2). It marked the completion of the new hall and kitchen for the Benedictine monastery, which had been begun some thirty years earlier. In 1560 Palladio had furnished the design for the thermal windows and cross vaulting that covered the refectory (Puppi, 1973, pp.338–9), and it is possible that he was consulted on the design of Veronese's painting. Certainly Veronese had to be aware of Palladio's architecture when calculating the effect of his painting. Thus the symmetrical massing of columns to the left and right of the central scene may have been dictated by the dimensions of the thermal window – now closed – directly above the painting. The luminous sky that dominates the upper half of the canvas may also have been in response to the brilliant effect achieved by the thermal windows and vaulting. The painting was finished in just over a year, a heroic feat considering its dimensions (6.7 × 9.9m.). For his labours Veronese received the modest sum of three hundred and twenty-four ducats, a cask of wine and his meals while working on the painting. B.B.

*251 The Convent of the Carità, Venice
Photographs

From the turn of the sixteenth century, the Lateran Canons of Santa Maria della Carità sought to rebuild their convent as they had earlier rebuilt their church (1441–5). Building activity of an unspecified type was under way in the 1540s, but a decision to reconstruct the monastery appears to have been taken some years later, presumably in 1560. By 7 March 1561 Palladio is recorded as having been paid ten *scudi* for a 'modelo de la fabrica'. During the next year the architect received forty *scudi* for supervising the construction, but after May 1562, Palladio is not mentioned again in the documents until 1569–70, when he briefly returned to direct repairs to the coffering of the atrium. Work advanced slowly thereafter until a disastrous fire in 1630 destroyed not only part of the fabric, but also the possibility of further expansion. That portion which survived – the sacristy and oval staircase, the southern wing of the cloister – underwent later restorations which saw the destruction of two bays of the cloister and its reconstitution as the Accademia di'Belle Arti (Bassi, 1971; Puppi, 1973, pp.333–6).
If completed, the convent of the Carità would have been Palladio's most impressive Venetian commission, just as the boldness of its design marked him as the most promising 'new' architect in Venice. Vasari described it in some detail in his biography of Palladio (Vasari, 1881, VII, p.529), and Palladio himself gave three plates to it in the *Quattro Libri* (II, 1570,

pp.29–32). Next to the church, Palladio intended to build a Roman atrium, open to the sky and surrounded by a large order of Composite columns which supported a terrace on the third floor of the fabric. Opening onto the atrium was the sacristy, called *tablinum* by Palladio after the room adjacent to the atrium of a Roman house. From the sacristy an oval staircase leads to the upper floors of the monastery. As Palladio wrote elsewhere in the *Quattro Libri* (I, p.61), such stairs were compact and could be constructed around an empty shaft, thus allowing them to be lit by a skylight. A cloister of three orders lay beyond the atrium. Of its three storeys, the first two were open loggias, the third contained the cells of the monks. The side of the cloister opposite the atrium was filled by a new refectory; begun in 1574, it was to have been a double square in length, two storeys high, with a cellar beneath and additional rooms on the third floor above. The rest of the plan indicates a second cloister beyond the refectory and other buildings to contain the kitchen and outbuildings.
The plan is so large that it would have encroached upon a public way and upon buildings not owned by the monastery, both major obstacles in a city as compact as Venice. The symmetrically ordered design in the *Quattro Libri* could be a later version for publication. Its starting point was, of course, the ancient houses which Palladio and Daniele Barbaro had reconstructed from Vitruvius and from the evidence of ancient monuments, chiefly the Roman baths. The ancient house, as Palladio conceived of it, could only have been recreated in terms of a large establishment like a monastic foundation or, to a lesser degree, in an important private commission like the Palazzo Porto, whose design in the *Quattro Libri* shows points of similarity with the Carità (413). The plan of the Carità demonstrates the assimilation of Roman architecture that allowed Palladio to achieve novel effects, such as the use of large and small orders in sequence or the bizarre conjunction of a Corinthian frieze (from the Temple of Vesta at Tivoli) with the Doric order of the cloister. The sacristy or *tablinum* remains one of the purest examples of Palladio's practical application of classicism. Its columnar screen and apsidal termination were probably inspired by the remains of similar chambers bordering on the frigidarium of the Baths of Caracalla and used by Palladio in his reconstruction of other thermal complexes (445). It was however also functional as the Doric columns helped to

251

support the wall mass on the upper floors.

The Carità was not only impressive as a design, but also successful in its combination of monastic requirements with classical formulae.   B.B.

*252 San Giorgio Maggiore
Photographs

Already by about 1520 the Benedictine monastery of S.Giorgio was considering rebuilding not only its church, but the greater part of the monastery buildings. By then the complex was obviously, despite the fairly constant renovations throughout the fifteenth century, out of line with the position of the foundation in the city's life (it was visited annually by the Doge, on St Stephen's day, see Damerini, 1956) and with its abundant resources. Though there is no clear indication of the monastery's income, in 1554 the annual revenue of the sister house of Santa Giustina in Padua was estimated at 30,000 ducats, and when building began on the church, one of the monastery's first steps was to cut 1000 oak trees on an estate in the province of Treviso for use as foundations (Zorzi, 1966, p.64): a detail which gives some idea of the monastery's wealth. Considerations of prestige involved ecclesiastical as much as private or civic building. By 1520, of all the great Venetian monasteries, San Giorgio was probably the most indecorously housed. The Franciscans at the Frari, and the Dominicans at San Giovanni e Paolo had their vast late gothic churches, adorned with the tombs of Doges and statesmen. Between 1458 and 1500 the nuns of San Zaccaria had rebuilt their church, and from 1505 the monastery church of San Salvatore was under construction. The design of 1521/22 (253) however lacks the force and conviction of the interplay of domes and barrel vaults at San Salvatore, and more closely resembles Santa Maria Formosa. It probably closely reflects the early designs for Santa Giustina in Padua (Timofiewitsch, 1963; Puppi, 1973, pp.363-4). By the 1560's this design was outmoded, and lagged far behind what had been achieved in other foundations of the order to which S.Giorgio belonged, the Benedictines of the Montecassino congregation: the church of San Benedetto Po had been skillfully and magnificently modernised by Giulio Romano in the late 1530's and early 1540's, and by 1555, under the direction of Moroni, the whole of the apse and crossing

area of Santa Giustina was complete (Rigoni, 1970, p.271). In Venice the Franciscan Observants at San Francesco della Vigna had a new church designed by Sansovino, and its façade, following Palladio's design was under construction from 1562 till about 1570. The public character (and site) of S.Giorgio also called for an architecture which was more in keeping with the new public style which Sansovino had created just across the water.

Palladio's design was translated into a wooden model between November 1565 and March 1566, and in that year work began under Palladio's direction. The early contracts with masons all stipulate that details are to be executed 'according to the profiles and measurements' provided by Palladio. The main structure, including the dome, seems to have been finished by 1576, but the façade was not built until 1607-11 (Puppi, 1973, pp.363-9). The façade is in fact the only portion of the church which has aroused doubts as to its fidelity to Palladio's project, but neither in the 1609 contract, where it is stated that the masons must follow the model exactly, nor in the overall solution or details is there the slightest indication of the intrusion of another designer. It is likely however that Palladio retouched his façade design, and also that he considered, probably in the late 1570s, the construction of a huge free standing portico (Puppi, 1973, p.366 and 430). San Giorgio was probably the most complex and demanding design problem that had confronted Palladio since that of the Basilica. Moreover it was his first commission for a complete church. His design represents a very complex mediation between the needs and demands of the Benedictines, recent developments in church design, and his own architectural system. The result is complex, and even today remains a surprising, even mystifying creation. The immediate effectiveness of every detail, and the beautiful condition in which the church is maintained only increases a feeling of bewilderment and marvel at a work which seems so absolute and self contained, and seemingly so without references to anything beyond itself. It is possible to make some conjectures as to how Palladio arrived at his design. The wealth of S.Giorgio, and the example (to be outdone) of the other monastery churches of Venice and of the Cassinense order, as well as the scope for a greatly enlarged church which the site provided, dictated the scale. Liturgy and function sketched in the principal parts of the plan: monk's choir, presbytery,

252

crossing, nave (Murray, 1966; Puppi, 1973). The need for a dome as an attribute of an important church was already ingrained in Venetian tradition (S.Marco, San Zaccaria, the Miracoli) and confirmed by the projects for St Peter's in Rome. The cruciform plan had tradition, convenience, and obvious symbolism on its side (IV, pp.6–7). All these features were embodied in S.Giustina in Padua, which must have been indicated to Palladio as a model, and which in any case he would have known well. In Palladio's plan the different parts of the church are made more distinct, the assembly of small units at S.Giustina is abandoned, as is the interlocking grid of domes and barrel vaults. The choir is larger and simpler; the presbytery is clearly defined by the antique formula of a cross vault, over a space decorated with four fluted columns; and the crossing itself reflects the unified simplicity of Michelangelo's design for St Peter's. The sequence of distinct but connected spaces, strung along a strong central axis derives from Palladio's studies of the Baths, as do specific solutions (the semicircular windows, the vaults, the column screen between the choir and the presbytery). The use of half columns goes back to the Basilica design, as do the paired pilasters on the sides of the piers, though these also resemble the paired pilasters which Moroni used on the side of his piers at Santa Giustina. The proportions of the church demanded the use of pedestals under the columns, as Bramante and Raphael had intended for St Peter's. The crossing piers are adaptations of the corner piers of the Basilica. The design of detail is immensely important here, and at every point is calculated to avoid the tediously predictable, and provide visual variety and give a living character to the interior. The sides of pilasters are not parallel, but taper with a gentle curve, like the columns. The pilasters also gather in energetic clusters reminiscent of the gothic portal of San Lorenzo in Vicenza. The column bases flow with a curving moulding into the pedestals and in general there are a very few vertical elements which are not slightly curved. The main cornice provides a massive conclusion to the lower part of the elevation, and the entablatures above the pilasters, with bulging friezes and their cornices scored with lively lines of shadow, establish a secondary horizontal division. Particularly attractive is the way in which when these entablatures run round the transept arms the cornice becomes flat and contrasts with the gentle curve of the frieze.   H.B.

UNIDENTIFIED ARCHITECT, 1521–2

253 **Project for rebuilding the church and monastery of San Giorgio Maggiore, Venice**
Pen and ink
Photograph from ASV, Misc. Mappe 744

This is clearly an outline project for rebuilding the church and monastery. The church is to be larger than that which preceeded it, and seems to reflect the contemporary projects for S.Giorgio's sister house, S.Giustina in Padua (Timofiewitsch, 1963; Puppi, 1973, p.363). Although Palladio church extended much further back, its site is already defined in this drawing, as well as the layout of the two large cloisters, of the 'laurels' above and of the 'cypresses' below. The latter was built, to Palladio's design, from 1579 onwards (Puppi, 1973, pp.428–9). The large rectangle of the refectory projects on the right, not far from it is the kitchen oven (a circle) and in the bottom right and top left are what appear to be latrines.
H.B.

*254 **Project for the facade of S.Giorgio Maggiore, Venice**
Pen and ink over incised lines: 293 × 425
Lent by the Royal Institute of British Architects (XIV/12)

The sheet consists of two different drawings stuck together. On the left is an elevation of an octastyle temple, which it has been suggested is the Temple of Venus Genetrix (Spielmann, 1966, p.152, n.93). The other drawing is clearly for S.Giorgio as it provides for one of the two Doge's tombs which had to be placed on the façade (Damerini, 1956; Wittkower, 1952, p.85). The grouping of the pilasters on the side portion corresponds closely to the executed façade (and not to the scheme in the ASV plan, cf. Puppi, 1973, p.369) but differs from it in not having pedestals below the larger columns, which as in the Redentore façade, rest on the same level as the smaller order. The drawing may well belong to an early stage in the evolution of the design: the little sketches in the top right have some resemblance to the pier and bay system of the actual church, but differ substantially from it, and the order shown is Doric. The solution later adopted by Palladio (and here one must disagree with Wittkower, 1952, pp.84–5) was obviously chosen because it reproduces the system of the interior, with the columns on high pedestals, and the pilasters resting on the ground. The dramatic contrasts of scale are controlled and deliberate, as well as backed by the logic of the interior, and are another demonstration of Palladio's independence not only with respect to contemporary church façades, but even in relation to his antique sources. The façade, legible at a distance and marvellously adapted to its site totally belies Ruskin's abuse: 'it is impossible to conceive a design more gross, more barbarous, more childish in conception, more servile in plagiarism, more insipid in result . . .' (Ruskin, 1904, III, p.381). H.B.

254

PALLADIO or assistants

255 Plan of the church and monastery of San Giorgio
c.1577/80
Pen and ink and wash:
Photograph from ASV Misc. Mappe 857

The completed church (but without any indication of the altars) appears on one side, and on the other Palladio's project for the 'Cloister of the Cypresses' with its paired columns (Puppi, 1973, p.403). Added in another ink is the indication of a massive free standing portico, though the whole façade treatment is obviously a single conception, not unlike that of the Worcester College project for San Petronio. The side elements recall those of the Vigna façade. H.B.

*256 The church of the Redentore, Venice
Model and photographs

The plague in Venice began in the late summer of 1575, and by February 1576 there had been 3,700 deaths. But this was only an introduction to the terrible mortality of the summer of 1576, which reached a peak in early August. By the end of February 1577 there had been 43,000 further deaths, and the total up to July 1577, when the plague was officially declared over, was more than 50,000. This was an enormous figure in relation to contemporary populations: it almost equalled the total population of Verona, and was more than twice the population of Vicenza, and probably about 30 per cent of that of Venice itself (Pullan, 1971, p.324).

The Venetian government was well advised by the Paduan doctors Mercuriale and Capodivacca that the best course to take was to evacuate the poor from their unhealthy dwellings, and see that they were properly fed, and some steps were taken in this direction (*ibid.*, pp..316–24). Alongside administrative measures, which almost inevitably were inadequate, the Venetian Senate resolved, on 4 September 1577, to build a church to the *Redentore* (Redeemer), to cost 10,000 ducats, 'not using stones of marble, but making a solid building, appropriate to a devotional church'. Two building commissioners were appointed on 18 September, and given three days to consider possible sites, and to report back. On the 22 November the present site was chosen, in preference to one on the Grand Canal on Campo S. Vitale, and the dimensions of the site were

laid down. Palladio must have begun elaborating alternative designs for the chosen site (258) in his role of 'engineer' in charge of work at the Palazzo Ducale, where he was again at work, if not earlier, at least early in 1577 (Zorzi, 1964, p.150). At no stage is any architect but Palladio mentioned in connection with the designs, though Rusconi was involved in surveying the possible sites (Zorzi, 1966, p.132) and it is likely one of the *oselle* (216e) commemorating the dedication derives from his project (Timofiewitsch, 1969, pp.61–2). Marc' Antonio Barbaro, and possibly Palladio himself favoured a centralised (or circular?) solution, but this was turned down by the Senate on 1 February 1577. One perhaps should not seek to read too much theoretical or iconographical significance into this decision: a longitudinal church was simply larger and grander than a centralised one, as one can see by comparing Palladio's centralised projects (258) with the actual building. A week later 'a design by our faithful Andrea Palladio in quadrangular form' was approved by the Collegio, by 21 votes to nil. The day after it was decided to enlarge the site. The foundation stone was laid on 3 May, and the liberation of the city from the plague was celebrated by the procession to the site across a bridge of boats on 20 July, an event which became annual. Building went ahead swiftly, and the church was dedicated in 1592. Costs escalated on the project: the original decision to spend 10,000 ducats, grew to 12,000, and by the end 60,100 had been spent over and above this original 12,000 (Zorzi, 1966, pp.121–41; Timofiewitsch, 1969; Puppi, 1973, pp.419–23).

Palladio's design provides for all the functions of the church, ceremonial, votive, and monastic (Timofiewitsch, Puppi). The choir is austere (unlike that of S.Giorgio), in keeping with the character of the Capuchins, an offshoot of the observant Franciscans at S.Francesco della Vigna, and dedicated to the strict observance of the Franciscan rule. The Capuchins in fact protested that the church was too grand for them, and even sent representations to Rome to make this point (P.D. da Portoguaro, 1957). Whether he was instructed to do so or not, Palladio did base his design on Observant Franciscan models. In terms of distribution (chapels with altars in the nave, a large crossing area, a deep choir) he followed the basic scheme of S.Francesco della Vigna, where the crossing arms are contained by the total width of the nave. His plan very closely follows Genga's project for the Observant Franciscan church of

S.Giovanni Battista in Pesaro, which Palladio would have certainly noted when he passed through the town on his way to Rome (he actually recalls a visit to Pesaro in a draft letter on R.I.B.A. XVI/9) and which he would have been reminded of by the high praise which it received in Vasari's Lives (Pinelli and Rossi, 1971, pp.260–4). Even more clearly than S.Giorgio the solution owes much to Palladio's studies of the Baths. On a single sheet, IX/14v, one can find precedents for the nave and its chapels, for the triconch solution, for a radiussed column screen, and for the segmental end wall of the choir (cf. Puppi, 1973, p.423). The structural system, in which the walls between the chapels are extended upwards to act as buttresses for the nave vault goes back to Alberti's S.Andrea, and was standard by this time (cf. Vignola's *Gesù*). The nave elevation, with its paired order, and thermal windows reads like a transcription of Sangallo's UA 67 (Frommel, 1964, fig.13). More than S.Giorgio, the different parts of the building contribute to make a unified effect. This is partly the result of the design of details: the massive entablature, the presence of columns right round the perimeter. It also depends on skillful calculation of viewpoint, something which ultimately derives from Palladio's scenographic experience, and is clearly present in the church and refectory of S.Giorgio (Wittkower, 1952, p.88). The façade derives from years of experiment in adapting ancient schemes to modern churches. But it is even less conventional than Palladio's previous façade ventures, and presents without dilution or compromise what Palladio considered to be the original appearance of those ancient buildings which combined temple fronts with massive brick and concrete structures, just as Palladio himself was doing here (compare Palladio's reconstructions of ancient façades: IV, pp.13, 37, 76–7). The lively and unorthodox side elevation owes much to the baths: particularly telling is the drawing cited by Puppi (1973, fig.601).   H.B.

JAN VAN DER STRAET (STRADANUS) 1523–1605
257 Death is welcome to the Poor
Pen, ink, and wash, heightened with white: 19.5 × 28.5
Signed: *Ioan. Stradanus inveniebat 1565*
Photograph: Royal Collection

This is a design for an engraving by de Sadeler (Puyvelde, 1942, p.24). It shows a living space with a bed, the fire for cooking, a spinning wheel, and agricultural instruments. It gives some impressions of the conditions which leading medical authorities identified as fostering the spread of plague: dirty, overcrowded housing and undernourishment (Pullan, 1971, p.318). Mercuriale repeated his observations to the Venetian government, in his book of 1577 (pp.59, 95–6). Another contemporary writer (Gratiolo, 1576) reached the same conclusions in a chapter entitled 'That the true cause of this plague is the dirtiness of houses' (pp.29–30). He suggests that the air in interiors had been poisoned by putrifying silk worms 'so dear and familiar to women' (300), and matters had been made worse by keeping the windows closed during a cold May, to prevent the worms dying. He goes on to say 'visiting a sick man, I found him in a narrow room, full of silk worms, for the most part dead and putrifying, with only a hole in the place of the window . . . moreover there was a large pig just next to the kitchen, which together with the other smell produced the most abominable stink which I have ever smelt in my life. A short time afterwards the sick man died, together with all his family. And in these houses it was easy for such putrefaction to grow, as all of them . . . are in the lowest part of the town, in narrow, more densely built up streets . . . without any facilities, either of orchards, or courtyards . . .' H.B.

258 Projects for the church of the Redentore, Venice

a) Plan
  Pen, ink and wash: 41.5 × 28.5
b) Section
  Pen and ink over incised lines: 28.5 × 41.5
c) Façade
  Pen and ink over incised lines: 40.4 × 27.6
d) Plan, without a portico
  Pen, ink and wash: 41.2 × 28.5
Lent by the Royal Institute of British Architects
(XIV/13, 14, 15, 16)

The first three drawings in the group all illustrate the same project and correspond to one another. The second plan however is for a simpler, cheaper alternative, without a dome, and without a portico. The words written on XIV/14 ('side', 'side of the portico', 'altar', 'choir') are not in Palladio's hand, nor are the figures in this drawing, and in the elevation of the façade. All the rest of the drawing including the measurements are by Palladio.

Many features of the Redentore are present in this group. R.I.B A XIV/16 has an arrangement of spiral staircases and sacristies like the existing one (Puppi, 1973, p.432), and a façade whose basic scheme is not far removed from that of the central portion of the executed church. The plan and elevation of the other project have a semicircular column screen, crossing pier and niches like the built church. Various suggestions have been made as to the purpose of these drawings. The site indicated, as well as the difference of scale and plan excludes Maser (ibid. 1973, p.434) and documents exclude S.Nicolò dei Tolentini (ibid, p.433). The church of the Zitelle in Venice is a possibility, but the projects are much larger than the executed church, are not directly associated with a residential structure, and are probably too costly. Much the most likely hypothesis is that advanced by Pane (1961, pp.304–5) and restated and amplified by Puppi (1973, pp.422 and 432) that these are projects for the Redentore. In both the plans the width of the site, including that of the two alleys which flank the church is just over eighty feet. This is precisely the width made available for the church in the Senate decree of 22 November 1576: 'that the Church should be built on the site on the Giudecca next to the Capuchins . . . and there sixteen paces of land should be taken (a Venetian passo or pace equals five feet) for its width on the embankment, and continuing the same width up to a length of 40 paces' (Zorzi, 1966, p.132). No. reference is made in this earlier document to the alleys at the side of the church, but they are mentioned when it was decided on 17 February 1577 to extend the width of the site by twenty feet 'to give with this addition more space to the said church and to the alleys at the sides' (Zorzi, ibid. p.135). In fact the Redentore as built has a maximum width at the front of about 82½ Venetian feet.

Palladio has therefore taken account of the site, which he carefully indicates on both plans. He allows the portico and the steps in front of it to project out across the fondamenta (embankment). The projects are therefore to be dated after the definition of the site (22 November 1576) and before the Senate rejected on 9 February 1577, by a vote of 103 to 54, Marc'Antonio Barbaro's proposal that the church should be centralised (rotonda), rather than 'quadrangular'. If Barbaro really meant round by 'Rotonda', and not just centralised, these drawings would in any case have to be before the enlargement of the site on 17 February (Zorzi, 1966, p.133). The group of drawings illustrates Palladio's normal working procedure: the deliberate and systematic evolution of alternatives, which even if they were not chosen as they stood, could still be drawn upon in subsequent designs. H.B.

259 Studies for the interior of a church
Pen and ink: 28.3 × 37
Lent by the Royal Institute of British Architects (XIII/18v)

These two sketches have only recently been discovered, as the sheet was previously stuck down on its mount. They show the plan of a chapel, with an altar with a tabernacle frame for an altarpiece, and steps leading up to it. On one side is shown a part of a pier, with (presumably) two half columns on either side of a niche. The sketch could be connected, to mention only two possibilities, with the evolution of designs for the Redentore, or for Palladio's destroyed work for the church of S.Lucia in Venice (Puppi, 1973, p.361). In both of these cases chapels are flanked by a paired order, but also the side walls of the chapels are not flat, and there are not openings at the side of the altar, as there appear to be here. The other sketch is harder to interpret: it appears to show a pedimented door or window frame, flanked by niches. H.B.

260 An ancient tomb in Spoleto
Pen and ink over brown chalk: 44.1 × 29.1
Epsilon handwriting
Lent by the Royal Institute of British Architects (IX/18)

Palladio draws the plan, elevation, and details of this structure, which is fairly clearly a Roman tomb. He indicates that it was square in plan, and writes 'this tower is in Spoleto in the property of messer Silvio notary of the Apostolic Chamber'. The measurements are in palmi which would indicate a copy (from Pirro Ligorio?). The elevation of this structure is so close to that of the lower part of the wings of the façade of the Redentore, that it seems probable that Palladio used the drawing as the basis for his design (Burns, 1973–II). The entablature at the top of the sheet is that of the Temple of Antoninus and Faustina in Rome. H.B.

ANTONIO VISENTINI 1688–1782
*261 Interior of the Redentore
Pen, ink and grey wash: 43.8 × 54
Lent by the Witt Collection, Courtauld Institute of Art

This beautiful drawing is almost certainly for the painting of the interior of the Redentore by Visentini and Zuccarelli (reproduced by Zorzi, 1966, fig.161), now in the Goldschmid Collection Milan, and which may well have been commissioned by Consul Smith (Witt, 1931, p.294). The drawing provides an accurate impression of the interior except that the depression of the nave vault in the actual building has been 'corrected' (Zorzi, 1966, pp.128 and 130). L.F.

Circle of PALLADIO (?) c.1580
262 Design for an altar tabernacle
Pen, ink and wash: 76.1 × 47.3
Prov: John Ruskin
Lent by the Ruskin School of Drawing and Fine Arts, Oxford

This very handsome unpublished and undiscussed drawing was noticed by Hugh MacAndrew, and has recently been skillfully restored by Eric Harding of the British Museum. In the bottom right is the inscription *Dissegno di Andrea Paladio* and there are two other inscriptions on the verso: *Del Paladio* and *Anda Paladio*. All three must be close in date to the drawing itself, and the familiarity of *Del Paladio* and, the use of only one 'l', indicates a contemporary artist or craftsman, rather than a collector. This early attribution needs to be taken seriously.
The drawing is not in Palladio's hand, and the figures are not by any of the figural artists who collaborated with him (India, Zuccari, Marc'Antonio Palladio). The details of the two successive orders, and features like the small decorative panels flanking the lower central arch, and the swags and heads between the capitals all have parallels in Palladio's work (Brescia palace design, side portal of the cathedral in Vicenza). The balustrades are like those of Maser. The masks in the stilobate, and the broken pediment do not have parallels elsewhere in Palladio's work (unless the monument of Triadano Gritti is in fact by him: see Puppi, 1973, p.273). This project is one of those works which puts in question the accepted picture of the range of an artist's personality. If this

261

was a design for a church one could confidently exclude Palladio's involvement. But its shape, the successive allusions to the Holy Ghost, God the Father, and the risen Christ, and the scale of the statuary indicate that it is a tabernacle, probably a large one, but all the same a decorative rather than an architectural work. A much greater figural and decorative component would in Palladio's eyes be permissible indeed necessary, and probably even the mild 'abuse' of the broken pediment (cf. I, pp.51–2) would be seen by him as acceptable. The case is therefore analogous to that of the title page of the *Quattro Libri*, which also has a broken pediment, and also despite its decorative license, employs Palladio's basic architectural vocabulary. The clear presence of Palladio's language in the lower part, the contemporary attributions, the nature of the commission (for which unfortunately no stylistic parallels exist in Palladio's work) prompt a tentative conclusion: that Palladio made the outline design for an important church tabernacle, and this drawing represents a redrawing of this, probably with some changes or interpolations, by an artist with more figurative and decorative experience; or, more probably, that the drawing or the design was made by someone who had worked closely with him in his last years. Here the name Zamberlan suggests itself (Barbieri, 1967). A comparison with Zamberlan's wooden altar (1607) of the 'Rotonda' at Rovigo (*ibid*, fig.24) is illuminating both for its similarities to the tabernacle drawing, and for its clear indication that the drawing is to be dated well before 1607, as it lacks the semi-Baroque elements which Zamberlan was ready to introduce by that date.

The inscriptions on the back of the drawing of Christ (drawn on a separate piece of paper, stuck over the main sheet) do not help towards an attribution. They are in two different hands, and list prices or weights of pharmaceutical substances: *conserve ex accido citri mel ros(arum)* (cf. Mantese, 1969, pp.44 and 46). H.B.

MARTINO BASSI 1541 or 1542–91

63 Project for the reconstruction of S.Lorenzo, Milan
Pen, ink, metal point, grey and brown wash, and white
heightening: 45.6 × 33.1
Lent by the Victoria and Albert Museum (no.613)

In June 1573 the cupola of the huge Early Christian Church of
S.Lorenzo collapsed, making nearby houses shake, as in an
earthquake (Baroni, 1940, p.152; Kleinbauer, 1967).
Reconstruction began in 1574 after designs by Martino Bassi
which had received the approval of the archbishop of Milan,
Cardinal Carlo Borromeo. Bassi was a highly professional
architect, who after the death of Tibaldi and Alessi was put in
charge of some of the city's most important projects
(S.Fedele, San Celso). In 1572 in his *Dispareri* (397) he had
published letters of Vasari and Palladio.
This section is only one of a series of alternative designs by
Bassi for rebuilding the church. There is a plan for the church
in the Victoria and Albert Museum (no.614), and numerous
drawings in Milan (Baroni, 1940, pp.145–6; Bascapè, 1967,
pp.44–6). This solution is close to the executed one as regards
the hemicycles, but differs from it in the use of eight huge doric
columns under the dome, and in having a hemispherical dome
whose decoration was influenced by Michelangelo's project
for St Peter's. It almost certainly should be dated 1573–7 as at
the time of the lengthy and acrimonious debate of 1589–91, in
the end won by Bassi (Baroni, pp.155–82), an octagonal dome
was already decided upon, while by 1581 the building was
complete up to the level of the dome, and there were no
columns in the crossing. The project therefore belongs to the
same years as that for the Redentore and shares with it a
preference for a hemispherical dome, and columns in the
crossing. Bassi wrote on his drawing: 'the dome is designed
round, because it will be more beautiful, and of a form which
was more frequently used by the Ancients, who almost never
made them octagonal ... The columns ... in such a celebrated
church should on no account be omitted, as the ancients put all
their greatness and majesty into measureless columns, and also
in all Roman temples one sees the columns were the principal
ornament ...' Bassi however lacked a personal and systematic
vocabulary of the sort which Palladio had developed, and
important details like the entablature over the columns are not
given the attention which Palladio would have given them. H.B.

The visit of Henry III to Venice 1574

The reception offered Henry III by the Venetian State in 1574,
was a demonstration of the Venetians' ability to put on a
splendid show, with very short warning. Henry was in Cracow
as king of Poland when the news was brought that he had
inherited the throne of France. The news was kept secret, and
on the night of the 16th he left, or rather fled southwards,
reaching Vienna on 24 June. He at once wrote to the Venetians,
saying that he intended to pass through the Venetian state on
his way to France. The Venetian Senate on 30 June voted him a
safe conduct, and the preparations were set underway. The
huge Cà Foscari (400) was chosen as Henry's residence, in
preference to Sansovino's Palazzo Corner (273): what it lacked
in modernity, it made up for in its size and magnificent site, on
the turn of the Grand Canal (Benedetti, 1574, f.2v). All the
gilders of the city were put to work on regilding the Bucintoro,
the state barge. Palladio must have designed the triumphal arch
and loggia for the Lido in a matter of days, as they were in
place and decorated with paintings in time for Henry's ceremonial entry into the city on 18 July. His brief stay in the city
saw a series of magnificent ceremonies and receptions, and the
town was packed with spectators from the surrounding
countryside: the Florentine envoy reported how he had over-
heard one of 'these Magnificos' (Venetian patricians) saying to
another in his heavy dialect, 'Look, look, Magnificent Sir,
what a rabble there is here today' (De Nolhac-Solerti, 1890).
The whole occasions reveals how Palladio by this time had
achieved in Venice the same position he had held for many
years in Vicenza. His chief friends and contacts among the
Venetian establishment all had parts in the celebrations.
Giacomo Contarini was one of the two commissioners in
charge of seeing to the execution of the arch and the loggia, and
it was he who Henry was allowed to nominate to the Senate
when he paid his visit to the Maggior Consiglio. Marc'Antonio
Barbaro was one of the six procurators (Nicolò da Ponte, the
future doge, was another) who accompanied the king all the
time he was in Venice and held the gold *baldachino* over his
head. Leonardo Mocenigo's son Luigi was among the young
nobles who attended Henry (De Nolhac-Solerti, 1890, p.58),
and the Vicentine patrician 'Colonel Valerio Chierigato' was
charged with assembling the ordinance for the salutes
(Benedetti, f.2v). H.B.

MONGRAMMIST GDM
264 The landing of Henry III at the Lido
Photograph from the original engraving (Padua, 1574?)

The Bucintoro is drawing up in front of the triumphal arch, and the procession has already entered the loggia, where an altar had been set up. The arch and loggia were almost certainly on axis with one another and would have provided an unfolding vista for the advancing procession, like that offered by Palladio's churches. The loggia is a development of the Portico of Octavia in Rome, and the swags hung between the columns imitate those which appear on buildings in Roman reliefs. Palladio included permanent versions of them on his façade for the Tempietto at Maser (432).
The foreground is crowded with galleys. Sanmicheli's magnificent Fortress of S.Andrea on the Lido, one of his masterpieces and now sadly crumbling, almost forgotten, appears on the left, wreathed in the smoke from the salutes fired by its artillery (Puppi, 1973, pp.407–8).   H.B.

ROCCO BENEDETTI
265 Le feste et trionfi fatti dalla sereniss. Signoria di Venetia nella felice venuta di Hernico III Christianiss. Re di Francia et di Polonia. In Venetia. Alla libreria della stella. MDLXXIIII.
Lent by the British Library Board (811.e.61.)

This is one of several detailed contemporary accounts of Henry III's visit, and one of the many Venetian publications which indicate a considerable demand for publications about contemporary events. Benedetti, like Marsilio Della Croce (Zorzi, 1964, pp.171–5), describes the arch 'built by the most excellent Architect Palladio, similar to that of Septimius made by the ancient Romans at the foot of the Campidoglio', and Palladio's loggia which stood behind it (f.4v).   H.B.

ANTONIO VISENTINI 1688–1782
266 A reconstruction of the plan and elevation of the loggia erected for the entry of Henry III, 1574
Pen and ink and grey wash: 53.4 × 65.5
Prov: Consul Smith
Lent by the British Library Board (King's MS 146)

This drawing is from a group of eight drawings in the British Museum commissioned by Consul Smith in 1756. They reconstruct the ceremonial architecture designed by Palladio for the entry of Henry III (Puppi, 1973, p.407) Palladio's loggia was placed behind the triumphal arch and in front of the churc of San Nicolò al Lido. After the disembarcation, Henry passed through the arch and entered the pedimented loggia, with ten Corinthian columns, and a coffered ceiling. He gave thanks for his safe arrival at an altar placed in the central niche and heard the Te Deum (Sansovino, 1663, pp.444ff). Visentini's drawings are based on contemporary accounts and representations of the decorations, but (as do his drawings of Palladio's surviving buildings) they tend to simplify and refashion Palladio to bring him into line with his own architectural taste.   L.F.

ANONYMOUS VENETIAN Later sixteenth century
267 Festive float in front of the Ducal Palace
Pen and two brown inks with traces of chalk undrawing: 20.5 × 32.6
Inscribed in a later hand: *Tintorette*; inscribed on the verso
Lent by the British Museum (1938–10–8–169)

The drawing reproduced in Tietze (1944, fig.222d) shows a circular float in front of the Ducal Palace on a huge shell and with nude male figures supporting a Doric entablature and a balustrade, surmounted by a tall cone. Given the sketchiness of the drawing and the absence of the prisons next to the Ducal Palace the drawing was probably made as a record of the float (there is no known painting of the composition), and probably dates before 1589 when the new prisons were extended forward.
This type of circular 'theatre' (important foreign spectators were seated inside them) was popular in Venice by the 1530s, and they became a regular feature of official entertainments and musical evenings (Padoan Urban, 1966, pp.142ff). This particular float recalls one of the most famous floating 'theatres' designed by Giovanni Antonio Rusconi for the Compagnia degli Accessi in 1564 and recorded by G.Franco (1598). A similar composition with nude male figures supporting entablatures (with access to the upper storey concealed in the central column containing a spiral staircase), and surmounted by an obelisk, appears in Filarete's treatise

dedicated in 1464 (1972, Book XIV, f.102v). The famous late fifteenth century manuscript of Filarete now in the Marciana was at this time in the Library of San Giovanni e Paolo and Scamozzi mentions that he owned a copy (Scamozzi, 1615, I, p.18). The most famous float of this kind was the one designed by Vincenzo Scamozzi for the Dogaressa Morosina Grimani in 1597 (Padoan Urban, *ibid.*, p.142ff). It is shown in the background behind the Bucintoro in the painting of her arrival at St Mark's (268).   L.F.

ANDREA MICHIELI IL VICENTINO *c.*1539–1614

*268 The Reception of Dogaressa Grimani in the Piazzetta of St Mark's

Canvas: 114.3 × 264.2
Lent by the Trustees of the Chatsworth Settlement

The celebrations for the coronation of Dogaressa Morosina Grimani in 1597 seem to have outdone those of her predecessors (Molmenti, 1887, pp.307–25). They also bore some resemblance to the reception of Henry III of France at the Lido in 1574, an occasion for which Palladio designed the temporary architecture customary for such events (Padoan-Urban, 1969, 145–52; Puppi, 1973, pp.407–8). In the painting by Vicentino two elements of temporary architecture are shown, one the small floating loggia designed by Scamozzi to accompany the state barge (Barbieri, 1952, pp.155–6); the other, the triumphal

arch erected by the Butchers' Guild which commissioned a similar one forty years earlier for Dogaressa Zilia Priuli (Molmenti, 1887, pp.281–94).

After a procession up the Piazzetta, accompanied by four hundred gentlewomen, Councillors, Senators, and one thousand members of the guilds, the Dogaressa was invested with her office in St Mark's and then toured the Ducal Palace. Two further days of festivities followed. In addition to written accounts of the coronation, there is a second painting by Vicentino, originally in the Palazzo Grimani and now in the Museo Correr, Venice (Mariacher, 1957, pp.114–5, no.928) and engravings of the event by Giacomo Franco (Padoan-Urban, 1969, pp.152–4).   B.B.

ALESSANDRO CARAVIA

269 Naspo Bizaro

Apresso D.Nicolini: Venetia 1565
Photograph

This book of four satirical poems written in Venetian dialect, relate the love and jealousy of Naspo Bizaro, a castellan (i.e. from the Castello quarter of Venice) for Cate Bionda (blonde Kate), which ends with their marriage. The engravings accompanying the poems show Naspo serenading Kate while his friend plays the pipes and sustains and refreshes them both with wine. In the plate shown here Naspo continues his

268

serenade while his friend lies back in the boat and picks his
teeth, watched with interest by Kate, who for the first time
opens wide her window. A cloaked figure hovers at the corner
of the house.

Alessandro Caravia (born 1503) was a jeweller at Rialto. His
satirical verse was about the life of the people, and his poems in
their mocking and comic juxtapositions of the expectations of
the rich and the poor, show a genuine sympathy for the plight
of the working classes. He was also a sharp critic of
superstitions and the way in which the Scuole (275) spent their
money on architecture, not charity. His reforming sympathies
led to his being interviewed by the Inquisition (Pullan, 1971,
pp.117ff). In *Naspo Bizaro* he describes the pride which Naspo
and men from Castello had in themselves and in their work:
'When a man from Castello is born, a poet is born
a galley's pilot, an admiral' (1565, f.15v).

He describes the rivalry between the men from different
quarters of the Venice, exploited in the faction fights on the
bridges (212a). Caravia wrote with sympathy for the poor, but
he was in touch with prominent figures. He came to the
attention of Pietro Aretino (Pullan, 1971, p.117). *Naspo Bizaro*
describes the famous 'studio' of Giovanni Grimani Patriarch of
Acquileia (243), with its fine collection of cameos, bronzes and
medals. The description indicates a first-hand acquaintance
with Grimani's collection, and suggests that he may have acted
as an agent in the acquisition of precious objects. He appears as
the witness to a document drawn up by a Vicentine notary
(ASVi, Not B.Massaria, *Carte Volanti*: oral communication,
H.B.).   L.F.

*270 Projects for (a) a Venetian housing development, and (b) for a small palace

Pen, ink and wash: a) 28.1 × 34.1 b) 21.2 × 34.5
Lent by the Royal Institute of British Architects
(XVI/16 a and b)

The drawing for a modest housing development is the only
project of this sort by Palladio which survives. It is clearly for
Venice, as the access from the characteristic *calli* (alleys)
indicates. This type of development itself is typically Venetian
(Trincanato 1948) and was sponsored by the State, and by
ecclesiastical and lay institutions as well as individuals,
sometimes for charitable purposes, but most often to provide

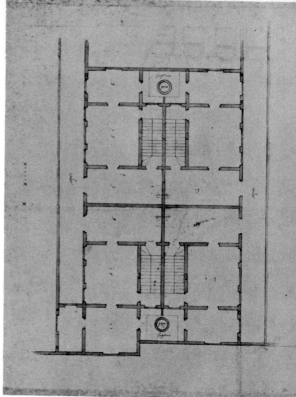

270

income from rents. Palladio was obviously in touch with many
institutions and individuals who might want to sponsor a
development of this sort, which recalls Sansovino's design of
ordinary housing (Gallo, 1957, pp.83–105; Howard, 1975).
The project in its rationalisation of contemporary housing
types also recalls the more modest projects in Serlio's *Sixth
Book* (Rosci, 1966). There are four similar living units (one has
one room more than the others). The windows face on to the
alleys, and the stairs are lit from the small yard, which has a
well, and is shared by two units. It is not clear whether the
project is for flats, or whether each unit consisted of a whole
house. The first of the rooms corresponds to the unheated
main hall of a Venetian palace. The second room is a living
room with a fireplace, and the third smaller room, with access

to the well, could be the kitchen. What may be latrines are sketched in chalk at the centre of the scheme, recalling a solution in Serlio's *Sixth Book*.

The four projects on the left of the sheet are for a small palace or a large house with a total frontage (not counting the thickness of the walls) of 43½ ft. The grouping of the windows in the centre of the façade suggests that it might be for Venice.   H.B.

GIOVANNI ANTONIO DE LODESANIS, IL PORDENONE
1484–1539 (after)

271 Sketch of the facade of the Palazzo d'Anna
Pen and ink: 41.2 × 55.7
Prov: Padre Resta; Lord Somers; Count Morritz von Fries; Sir Thomas Lawrence
Lent by the Victoria and Albert Museum (2306)

Palaces in Venice and the Veneto were often frescoed in order to give those façades, not made of stone, a richer appearance. Most of the great Venetian painters of the sixteenth century had some experience of façade painting, and Ridolfi claims that Andrea Schiavone, when he first came to Venice, made friends with masons so that they might put such work in his way (1914, p.248; see Foscari, 1936, passim.). Pordenone's frescoes for the Palazzo d'Anna (now Volpi di Misurata), of which the present drawing is a record, established his reputation in Venice as a master of foreshortening. On the drawing two later hands have recorded not only the name of the palace, but also its mention in Vasari's *Lives*. The façade was divided into three horizontal bands of decoration, punctuated by typically Venetian fenestration. The two vertical panels on the ground floor are *Marcus Curtius* on horseback to the right and the *Rape of the Sabines* (?) to the left; both partake of the dramatic use of perspective that Pordenone had exploited in the *Conversion of Saul* at Spilimbergo (1524; see Fiocco, 1969, pp.69–70). Across the entrance is the *Rape of Prosperpine*. Of the major panels on the *piano nobile*, the one on the left has been identified as *Mercury, Herse, and Aglauros* while on the floor above, the chief subjects are *Fame* and *Time*. The artist has left a record of the colour of Fame's wings by inscribing *azurro* (blue) on them. Pordenone's frescoes did not survive, but others have, notably in Trent. A very similar decorative scheme can still be seen at the Villa Sernagiotto at

Fossalunga di Vedelago, near Treviso (Mazzotti, 1961, p.305). The present drawing was first published by Hadeln as a copy after Pordenone (1924, p.149), with which opinion Tietze and Tietze-Conrat (1944, p.238, no.A1332) and Popham (1962, p.27, no.50) concur. It would appear to be a faithful copy after Pordenone's design by a contemporary draughtsman.

Two chiaroscuro woodcuts after portions of the façade exist. One is of *Marcus Curtius* (Bartsch, 1866, xii, p.151, no.19; cf. Dodgson, 1920, p.61); the other, by Ugo da Carpi, is of *Time* (Bartsch, 1866, xii, pp.125–6, no.27; cf. Tietze-Conrat, 1939, p.91). At Chatsworth there is also a pen and bistre drawing of *Time* by Pordenone, which may have been a study prepared for engraving (Tietze and Tietze-Conrat, 1944, p.235, no.1299; Popham, 1962, p.27, no.50).

The date of the Palazzo d'Anna frescoes are not known although Ridolfi, following Vasari (1880, V, p.115), places them before the frescoes of the choir of San Rocco, which are documented to the years 1527–9 (Ridolfi, 1914, p.120, n.7). Fiocco has drawn attention to the role of the Flemish merchant Martino d'Anna as *guardiano* or head of the Confraternity of San Rocco (1969, p.150). Thus a relationship between the two commissions seems very likely.   B.B.

GIOVANNI ANTONIO CANAL (CANALETTO) 1697–1768

272 Palazzo Vendramin-Calergi
Canvas: 39.4 × 48.3
Lent by C. L. Loyd Esq.

Dated by Constable (1962, no.326) to the early 1740s. This palace built for Leonardo Loredano (now the Casino), is not shown on Jacopo de' Barbari's view of Venice of 1500, but it was in existence by 1509 (Paoletti, 1893, p.187). This was the largest palace to be built in the new style in Venice, and it represents an entirely new departure for the city, with the application of successive orders of columns and pilasters to the façade. It established a new type for the grand Venetian palace, which strongly influenced Sansovino (Palazzo Corner and Palazzo Dolfin) and Sanmicheli (Palazzo Grimani), and is listed by Francesco Sansovino together with these palaces (1663, p.387) as one of the four finest Renaissance palaces in the city. It is usually ascribed to Codussi, but in the lack of documentation, the names of Tullio Lombardo and Alessandro Leopardi should not be excluded.   L.F./H.B.

273 The Grand Canal and the Palazzo Corner
Canvas: 49 × 63
Lent by the Visitors of the Ashmolean Museum, Oxford

Guardi's beautiful painting shows the Palazzo Corner on the Grand Canal, designed by Jacopo Sansovino for the very rich and important Corner family. This is Sansovino's finest palace, and his son Francesco in his guide to Venice describes it as one of the four most splendid Renaissance palaces in the city (Sansovino; 1581: Howard, 1975).   L.F.

274 Design for a Venetian Palace
Photograph from the *Quattro Libri*, II, p.72

Palladio, unlike Sansovino or Sanmicheli, never built a palace in Venice. This design 'for a site in Venice' adapts Palladio's normal formulae to a long narrow site, typical of Venice. There are four columns in the vestibule. The oval stairs, like Bramante's famous Belvedere stairs, revolve around an open well, bordered by a continuous colonnade. Like Sansovino's Palazzo Corner the cortile is small in relation to the site as a whole, and is at the back of the complex. There are two living floors above the ground floor. This is a Venetian feature (not to be found in Palladio's Vicentine palaces), the result of the need to get the most out of limited sites, and very expensive foundations. The sequence of the orders and the fact that there are no pedestals beneath the columns, resembles the Palazzo Ducale drawing (279). Two Palladio drawings (270 and 379) may also be connected with the Venetian Palace projects.   H.B.

275 Project for the facade of the Scuola Grande della Misericordia, Venice
Pen, ink and wash: 76.5 × 58.4
Photograph: Museo Civico, Vicenza (D.18)

The Misericordia was one of the six 'Great Schools', the wealthy lay confraternities which played such an important part in the public life and functioning of Venice. From their original character as devotional and charitable organisations, they became administrators of considerable incomes, from state funds, properties, and trusts. They were a source of loans to the state in times of crisis, and they bore part of the burden of paying for the crews of the Venetian warships. They made a substantial contribution to the processions which expressed the splendour and cohesion of the Venetian State, and they probably also contributed to its stability by relieving poverty, and by providing a field of public office and public, red-robed prominence to the members of the Venetian non-noble citizen class, to whom political office was closed (Pullan, 1971). The scuole spent vast sums on their splendid buildings, of which those of S.Rocco and the Scuola di San Marco are the most notable. In competition with these the Misericordia obtained a design in 1532 from Sansovino and began pouring its income into a vast structure where costs went far beyond its means. The Misericordia earned the searing criticism of Caravia (269; 1541; Howard, 1975): 'Anti-Misericordia one would like to call this scuola which is so badly governed ... (they) have ruined it, each one to satisfy his fantasy, they wanted to have a regata with San Rocco, when it would have been better to give that dead money to give comfort to poor wretches'. Seen from a less strictly moral and charitable point of view the building did have a function: it gave a great deal of employment, and contributed to the glorification of the State. Francesco Sansovino (1562) describes it as an 'eternal work and worthy of this Dominion on account of its eccessive beauty, if, however, it should ever achieve its due completion'.

The irony with which the architect's own son tempers his praise of the building was justified. It was never finished, and its vast façade, for which Sansovino intended a treatment which took account of the fact that it can be seen a long way off, was never faced with stone. Palladio's drawing preserves Sansovino's basic scheme, which in any case, by that time the drawing was made (presumably after Sansovino's death in 1570) was roughed out on the unfaced brick façade. The drawing does present problems. The figures in the upper and the lower halves are in different hands (that below is much finer, and recalls Veronese) and actually on two different sheets of paper, stuck together. There is a second version of the upper half in the R.I.B.A. (VIII/13). Palladio's involvement with the Scuola is not documented. But the respective contributions of Sansovino and Palladio in this project are quite clear. The basic scheme is Sansovino's with paired columns like the Loggetta, and a smaller order to carry the arches, like the Library. The form given to every detail, however, unmistakably reveals Palladio (Puppi, 1973, p.395; Tafuri, 1973; Burns, 1973 and 1973–II).   H.B.

276   The Ducal Palace and Palladio

Not even Sansovino's Library, which Palladio called 'perhaps the richest and most ornate building since the time of the Ancients' competes in magnificence with the Ducal Palace. Its pink and white mass dominates Venice's grandest face, and expresses the fact that most of the central institutions of Venetian government were housed behind the fretwork of its colonnades. It was the official, obligatory residence of the Doge, and the principal electoral, legislative, and executive assemblies and committees had their richly decorated permanent meeting rooms within its walls. Here the Maggior Consiglio, the assembly of all adult Venetian nobles, met in its vast hall to elect to the Senate and a host of other state offices. Here the Senate debated and voted on matters of general policy, here the powerful and secretive national security council, The Council of Ten, wielded much of the effective power of the state, and in the Collegio, as one can see in Fialetti's painting of the English ambassador Wotton being received by the Doge (234), foreign ambassadors presented their credentials and communicated the views of the rulers they represented. Law courts, government offices, and even the prisons were also housed within the building.
The importance of the Ducal Palace did not however render it immune from fire, which in conservative Venice provided the principal stimulus to architectural improvement. In 1482 the Doge's apartments were destroyed by fire, and was then rebuilt in a grander, up-to-date style. In 1574 the halls of the Senate and the Collegio were gutted by fire, and Palladio was paid 20 ducats a month to act as a consultant on their re-decoration (Zorzi, 1964, pp.137ff) and may, for instance, have given his advice on the placing of Veronese's *Allegory of Lepanto* (281). Then on the night of December 1577 the whole of the upper floors on the sides towards the Piazzetta and S.Giorgio, including the great hall of the Maggior Consiglio with its famous paintings by Bellini, Titian and others, was destroyed. Pozzoserrato's painting (277) vividly illustrates what the written accounts record. The wind blew strongly, fanning the flames, and carrying them dangerously close to the

Library, and the Mint. The Piazza was cleared and armed Venetian nobles stood guard to prevent any attempts at sacking, above all if the Mint should catch fire. The fire itself was fought, and eventually contained, by workers from the Arsenal (212d), whom it was usual to call out to fight fires in public buildings.
Two Veronese drawings for the redecoration of the Palace are exhibited here (281 and 282) as well as Cristoforo Sorte's impressive definitive design for the new ceiling of the Sala del Senato (280). Palladio was among the architects and engineers who were consulted about the restoration of the palace, whose outer walls amazingly had suffered little damage, though the tie bars and beam floors which bound the massive outer walls to the inner part of the building were either destroyed, or gravely damaged. Palladio in his report stressed the seriousness of the structural damage, and furthermore called attention to what he considered as the inherent structural defects of the building, even apart from the situation brought about by the fire. Puppi has perceptively suggested that reading between the lines of Palladio's report, one can detect an antipathy to the whole unclassical style of the palace, but no one so far has taken seriously an early and reliable biographer's statement that Palladio made a design for rebuilding it. The project, hitherto unpublished and unnoticed, survives at Chatsworth, and is exhibited here (279). It is magnificent, and it carries over from the actual building the motif of a large central triumphal arch in the middle of each façade. Palladio's influential friend and patron Marc'Antonio Barbaro used all his eloquence in the Senate to persuade his fellow senators to accept the scheme. But the prudent Senators in the end overwhelmingly voted to restore the exterior of the Palace 'exactly as it was before.' It would be hard to deny that they were right.   H.B.

LUDOVICO TOEPUT called IL POZZERATO
*277   The 1577 fire in the Ducal Palace
Canvas: 61.5 × 96.5
Lent by the Museo Civico 'Luigi Bailo', Treviso

Ridolfi (1648, II, p.86) records this painting, or another version of it, and the composition is also preserved in a contemporary engraving. It is among the earliest works of Pozzoserrato in Italy (Menegazzi, 1963, p.257). Whether or not this is an

277

279

156

eye-witness account, it closely corresponds to contemporary descriptions of the scene, which is rendered strikingly and vivaciously: even the lion on the top of the column looks scared, and the fire-fighters dash about and hastily consult in a wholly convincing fashion. All the top floor of the palace is on fire, and the flames and smoke are blowing towards Sansovino's Mint and Library (which at this stage was still unfinished). The Piazza is cleared and guarded to prevent any attempts at looting, above all if the Mint should catch fire. Disasters of this sort were not uncommon in Venice. The Ducal Palace had suffered severe fires in 1483 and 1574, the Scuola di San Marco was destroyed in 1485, the Fondaco de' Tedeschi burned down in 1505, Rialto in 1514, and the Palazzo Corner (273) in 1532. In each case the building was restored in an up-to-date style. The other Veneto cities were not immune from fires. The Palazzo della Regione in Verona was destroyed by fire in 1541, and the event was recorded in a painting by Cristoforo Sorte, now lost (Schulz, 1961–3, p.206). The palace in Brescia was severely damaged by fire in 1575 (425).   H.B.

LAMBERTO SUSTRIS 1515/6–C.1595
*278 Portrait of Marc'Antonio Barbaro, 1518–95
Canvas: 1.14 × 1.00 metres
Inscribed: MARCVS ANTONIVS BARBARO EQ MDLXXII
Lent by the Gallerie dell'Accademia, Venice (deposited with the Fondazione Cini)

The portrait originally hung in the first of the three rooms occupied by the Procurators of St Mark's in Sansovino's *Library*. There is a payment in the Procurator's account book of twenty ducats, under the date 30 March 1591, to Alberto d'Ollanda for the painting, which had originally been commissioned from Tintoretto, who never got round to doing it. The date 1572, like the dates on the other two portraits for which Alberto was paid in 1591 refers to the year in which the sitter was created Procurator, in Barbaro's case 'for honour, not for money' as Cosimo Bartoli reports in his dispatches (Bartoli, ASF). Alberto d'Ollanda has been securely identified with Sustris (Peltzer, 1950; Ballarin, 1962 and 1962–3; Moschini Marconi, 1962, pp.213–4).
Barbaro had a long and distinguished public career. Like his brother Daniele (176) his first important appointment was as an

278

ambassador (to France, in 1561–4). In the critical period from 1568–74 he was the Venetian representative in Constantinople, and it was he who negotiated the peace with the Turks after Lepanto, and his diplomatic services in these years were rewarded with his appointment as Procurator. He acted as the spokesman for the six procurators who accompanied Henry III in Venice in 1574 (264) and in 1577 was described by Francesco da Molino as one of the three most influential figures in Venetian politics. He served in that year on what was at that time the critical office of Health Commissioner, and also as Revisor of the Doge's Oath (230).
By the same date he had achieved a reputation as the leading expert on architecture in government circles. In his private life he was the joint patron with his brother of their villa at Maser (351) and later of the Tempietto, on the Maser estate (432). His architectural interests were more than superficial: Palladio (I, pp.61–3) publishes a type of spiral staircase invented by him,

and he made a design for the temporary housing of the Maggior Consiglio after the fire in 1577 (Lorenzi, 1868, p.420). Much of his career was involved with architectural administration and architectural policy, a field of considerable importance for the state and one in which able administrators were as important as in any other departments of government. This aspect of his activity began in the usual way with his appointment in 1564 as *Provveditore al Sal*, that is the commissioner for the Salt monopoly, which had the responsibility for financing and adminstering public works. It is worth noting that both the two commissioners for the Redentore, Agostino Barbarigo and Antonio Bragadin also served in this office, in 1572 and 1574 respectively (DBI). Barbaro was closely involved in the debates on the Redentore (256), and on the rebuilding of the Ducal Palace in 1577, and he was a commissioner for the Rialto bridge. In all three cases he ended up as the powerful advocate of a minority view (for a centralised solution for the Redentore, for the total rebuilding of the Ducal Palace, for a three arch Rialto bridge) but it is also clear that he was a diligent and committed building commissioner whose services were always valued, so that in 1593 he was appointed Provveditore for the construction of the new fortress town of Palmanova, in which Scamozzi was also involved (Barbieri, 1952, p.150). The fact that Palladio was backed by a person of such standing must have been very important for his own position in Venice, though it is clear that Palladio had a whole network of friendships and connections working for him. He was also by the 1570s an elder statesman among architects, and had a personality which tended to make him friends rather than enemies. But without adequate political backing there was always the possibility of an intrigue to oust an artist in state service, as the case of Cristoforo Sorte suggests (Schulz, 1961–3, p.207). The support and friendship of Marc' Antonio Barbaro and Giacomo Contarini seem to have passed straight to Scamozzi after Palladio's death.   H.B.

*279 Project for the reconstruction of the Palazzo Ducale

Pen, ink and wash: 45.9 × 105.2
Lent by the Trustees of the Chatsworth Settlement

This large and impressive drawing was brought to my attention by John Harris who recognised it as belonging to the Palladio/Scamozzi area, and was struck by its resemblance to

Inigo Jones schemes for Whitehall and for Somerset House (cf. Harris, 1973, pp.146 and 152). This resemblance strongly suggests that the drawing was bought back to England by Jones himself, though its influence probably goes back even further, to Scamozzi's Procuratie Nuove on the Piazza San Marco.

The information that Palladio made a design for rebuilding the Ducal Palace after the fire in 1577 has long been available in a trustworthy contemporary source. Gualdo in his short life of Palladio (1617, in Zorzi 1959, p.94) writes that in his last years Palladio also designed 'the Public Palace for the Republic of Venice'. Gualdo, it should be noted was in touch with Scamozzi (*ibid.*, p.98) and possibly had the information from him. Zorzi (*ibid.* p.104; 1964, p.164ff.) would not accept Gualdo's statement. But the evidence is overwhelming. Francesco da Molino (MS., p.91) wrote in his chronicle 'the opinions of the best architects in the city were taken, and they all came to the conclusion, that the walls had remained sound . . . only Andrea Palladio the celebrated and famous architect concluded that there was nothing which was still structurally sound, and that the façade towards San Giorgio should be destroyed and demolished, and the whole building substantially renewed, and this opinion of his was fomented by Marc'Antonio Barbaro, Procurator of S.Marco, a most able and prominent orator, to such an extent that although it appeared very extravagant to the whole Senate, all the same arguing with all his ability he kept the proposal alive for many days, and finally had a committee of three set up to consider the restoration of the Palace . . . (Jacomo Foscarini, Alvise Zorzi, and Pietro Foscari) who having for many days consulted with the architects . . . finally came before the Senate, and put the motion that the Palace should be restored neither more nor less than it was before.'

Palladio submitted two very similar reports on the Palace after the fire. The first was verbal, and recorded by a notary, the second was written (Zorzi, 1964, pp.164–7). Although Zorzi passed over the clear trend of Palladio's agreements, recent close readings of the reports (Barbieri, 1967, pp.43–5; Puppi, 1973, pp.424–5) have exposed Palladio's real position, which is in any case more or less explicit: the extension of the Palace is unsatisfactory, structurally and aesthetically, and the fire damage only underlines the need for reconstruction. Palladio refers to the great height of the wall above the loggie, and the fact that the columns which support it have a diameter of only $1\frac{1}{4}$ feet, whereas the wall itself is $2\frac{1}{2}$ ft thick. This in itself, he maintains, will inevitably lead to collapse, and conflicts with a natural principal, exemplified in trees which always become slighter towards the top. He concludes that on the lower level there should be 'very thick piers, and that from these upwards all the openings (i.e. the upper loggie) which are the most dangerous part of the palace should be filled up, making the windows which are necessary for the sala both above and below . . . the wall above . . . should be renewed, and the roof placed on top of it, and those ornaments which shall be appropriate to the rest of the building'. At this stage he visualised 14 bays on each façade, and optimistically estimated the cost at 1,500 ducats per bay. He also significantly invokes the site of the building, and 'public honour and convenience' in favour of his ideas, and assures the Senate that even if his opinion 'is contrary or different to that of other architects' he is not counselling anything which is 'sophisticated or showy rather than certain or secure'.

Palladio's drawing is in line with his reports. The scale of the building; the three orders; the 9 ft openings of the ground floor arcades, corresponding to the actual Palace; the great central triumphal arch with the lion in the pediment (an allusion to the central feature of the existing façades) all leave little doubt as to the identification of the project. The height of the building, from the ground to the top of the crowning cornice is 70 ft, as against 74 ft in the existing building. The discrepancy in width (190 ft as against 225 ft towards the Piazzetta and $219\frac{1}{2}$ towards San Giorgio: see the contemporary plan in Marc. Ital. VII, 10047, pp.295 no.13) is more puzzling. There are also only eleven arches here, as against the fourteen to which Palladio refers in his reports.

Some changes in dimensions would follow from the very considerable internal alterations which the lowering of the upper floor level and the total reconstruction of the outer walls would have entailed. One must imagine that like the salone at Brescia in Palladio's 1575 project, the Sala del Maggior Consiglio would now be lit by two successive levels of windows. But the drawing must be considered not as ready for execution and exactly tailored to the pre-existing structure, but as an 'invention' closely but not precisely reflecting the problems involved. Its purpose could either be to attract interest, or alternatively (like the *Quattro Libri* Rialto project or

the *Quattro Libri* adjusted designs of Palladio's existing works) to offer an improved, regularised version of a design which the real situation prevented from achieving a total regularity and perfection. Palladio for instance may in a more realistic version have been forced to have six bays on either side of the triumphal arch, and have had to abandon the symmetrical arrangement of the window pediments which five bays permitted. He may even have had to place the central arch off centre with six bays in one side and seven on the other. This solution (as the arch openings were 9 ft, and the piers are 5 ft across) would have brought the total width of the building up to its existing dimensions. The drawing is in many respects clearly an ideal project, as it shows the freestanding columns of the lower part of the triumphal arch projecting on both sides. This would in fact have been possibly only one side of either of the two façades.

The points of departure for the design are: 1) the need (so much stressed both in the reports and in Palladio's 'Addition') to decrease the thickness of the walls, and the height and width of the columns and the pilasters on successive levels; 2) the central arch in the middle of each façade, a characterising feature of the Palace; 3) the need to have a closed wall with plenty of windows for light and ventilation on the two upper floors; 4) the formal solution prepared only two years before by Palladio for the rebuilding of the Palace at Brescia (425). Here too there were three orders, arcades below, tabernacle windows in the middle, and statues in front of the upper order. The three orders also resemble Palladio's projects for Venetian palaces, and drawings F-F and E-E for San Petronio (429). The sequence of the orders, the avoidance of pedestals under the columns, and the way in which the order diminishes from the top to the bottom of the building respect the fragmentary 'Addition' to the *Quattro Libri* (205). Together with the 'Addition', the Brescia and San Petronio designs, and the Teatro Olimpico and the drawing for it, the project reflects the final phase in Palladio's treatment of large scale public projects. Palladio clearly did not like the Ducal Palace, though he probably honestly believed that it was structurally doomed. He tried to provide a replacement which was worthy of both site and function. He differentiated his design from Sansovino's Library (268) by choice of order and restriction of decoration, but took account of it in the arcades below and in the introduction of the subordinate order in the first floor, which he enlivened by the

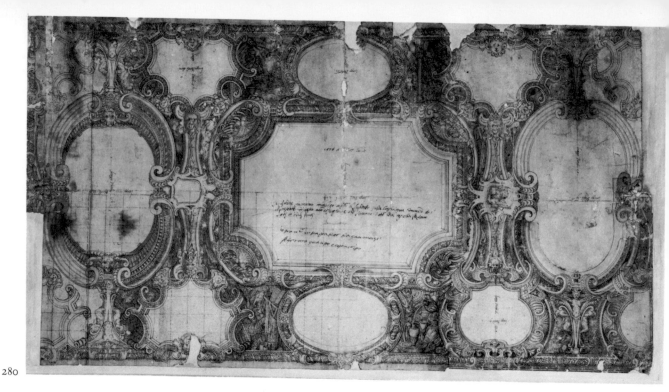

280

use of the spirally fluted columns on alternate windows. The
decision to preserve the old palace was a wise one, but Palladio's
design modelled by light and shade, and pierced by the dark
recesses of windows and arches would have appeared livelier
and less fussy realised in stone than it appears on paper. H.B.

CRISTOFORO SORTE 1506/10–1594 or later

*280 **Project for the ceiling of the Sala del Senato in the Ducal
Palace, Venice**

Pen, ink and wash; traces of underdrawing; squared in black
chalk: 46 × 86.4
Lent by the Victoria and Albert Museum, London (E.509–1937)

In the middle of the drawing is written the date (July 1578) and
the formal undertaking of the craftsmen to abide by the design:
'I Andrea of Faenza undertake to make the ceiling according to
the contract and the present drawing together with the profiles

which will be provided by Cristoforo Sorte and the two
protos'; 'I Francesco wood carver of San Moise undertake
what is written above'. It was usual for craftsmen to make
written undertakings of this sort on the drawings which they
had to execute, though in fact Sorte later complained that both
this ceiling, and the one he designed for the Sala del Maggior
Consiglio were not properly executed after his project
(Wolters, 1961/63; Schulz, 1961/63; Schulz, 1968, pp.112–4).
Sorte's design is extraordinarily complex, and is built up of
intertwining curving elements, grotesque masks and panels of
trophies.

Sorte had a long, varied and interesting career. He came from
Verona, worked under Giulio Romano in Mantua, and records
some of Giulio's working methods in his *Observations on
Painting* (Sorte, 1580 and 1960). For many years he was
surveyor for the Magistracy of Uncultivated Land (313) and in
this capacity had contact with numbers of Palladio's patrons

(315) and almost certainly with Palladio himself (391). He was a fine landscape draughtsman, and a notable cartographer (Schulz, *op. cit.* and forthcoming study). He was employed in the Palace between 1578 and 1582, and in 1587 and 1588 was consulted about the building of Rialto bridge. He also published (1593 and 1594) treatises on the irrigation of the province of Verona. H.B.

PAOLO VERONESE 1528–88
281 Drawing for the painting in the Sala del Collegio
Oil in grisaille over a prepared red paper: 29.7 × 47.0
Lent by the Trustees of the British Museum

The drawing represents a late stage in the design for the votive painting in the *Sala del Collegio* of the Palazzo Ducale (Parker, 1930, pp.66–7; Tietze and Tietze-Conrat, 1944, p.345, no.2092). The painting was probably commissioned during Venier's short reign as doge (1577–8) and appears to have been in place by 1581 (Sinding-Larsen, 1974, pp.95–8). The drawing shows the doge in armour and ducal mantle kneeling before a vision of St Mark and an unidentified saint who are seated on a cloud, St Mark raising his hand in benediction. To the left and right of the doge are Faith and Venice, the latter holding the ducal crown. On the upper right, a host of music-making angels have been tentatively sketched; beneath them are several allegorical figures, including Agostino Barbarigo, Venier's second-in-command at Lepanto, who holds a standard. Two Ionic columns frame the scene on the right while the base of a complementary column can be seen on the lower left. The pediment of the ducal throne, which is beneath the painting, has been anticipated in the drawing. The painting essentially preserves the formula of the drawing although Christ takes the place of St Mark and Santa Giustina is added to the number of intercessory saints around the doge. Also, in the background of the painting is a naval battle, presumably Lepanto at which Venier and Barbarigo distinguished themselves, the latter losing his life in battle. B.B.

PAOLO VERONESE 1528–88
282 Venice Triumphant
Pen, brush, and bistre on brown paper: 52.5 × 35
Lent by the Earl of Harewood

A preliminary design for one of the central panels in the ceiling of the hall of the Maggior Consiglio in the Doge's Palace, Venice, which Veronese began in 1578 (Schulz, 1968, pp.108, 111, n.7). Veronese's composition exploits an imposing architectural framework together with an inventive display of figures, motifs that had been perfected earlier at Maser (351) and in the great canvases for San Giorgio Maggiore and San Giovanni e Paolo (249 and 250). The artist began by incising the architectural background in ink, and only then adding the figures with a brush and bistre (Borenius, 1936, p.40, no.74; Titze and Tietze-Conrat, 1944, p.346, no.2101; Edinburgh, 1969, p.44, no.94). B.B.

PAOLO VERONESE 1528–88
283 Allegory on the Holy League of 1571
Pen, ink, and wash with white and black chalk on a green ground: 43.7 × 58.3
Lent by the Trustees of the Chatsworth Settlement

Long considered a production of Veronese's shop (Tietze and Tietze-Conrat, 1944, p.355, no.2165), the present drawing has recently been restored to a place among Veronese's own drawings (Byam-Shaw, 1973, p.30, no.73). In format, the drawing is comparable to *Venice Triumphant* (282) and many other Veronese compositions which set historical events in a grandiose architectural scene. The Holy League of Philip II of Spain, Pope Pius V, and Doge Alvise Mocenigo of Venice was formed to combat the expansion of the Ottoman empire in the Mediterranean (Lane, 1973, pp.369–74). Its most brilliant, albeit temporary success came with the Battle of Lepanto (21 October 1571) in which the Turkish fleet was defeated. Both the League and Lepanto immediately passed into Venetian mythology and figured in the decoration of the ducal palace after the fire of 1577 (Bardi, 1587, pp.15r–19r; Gombrich, 1967, pp.62–8; Sinding-Larsen, 1974, pp.84–97). The scene represents Faith, with chalice in hand, entreating the rulers, seated on the podium to the left, to do battle against the infidel. In the sky, the apostle-protectors of Spain, Rome, and Venice (SS. James, Peter, and Mark) bestow blessings. Among the minor episodes, a woman (Bellona?) unties the *fasces* on the left while putti hold spears. Soldiers stand in readiness on the podium to the right while others skirmish in the distance.

The drawing shares a number of motifs with works by
Domenico Tintoretto for the Chapel of the Rosary in
SS.Giovanni e Paolo, Venice, and by Palma il Giovanne for
the Confraternity of the Rosary in Brescia, both of which
celebrated the Holy League (Ridolfi, 1924, pp.199, 258).
The absence of Santa Giustina, who became the patron saint of
the Victory of Lepanto, may indicate that this design was
commissioned after the founding of the League but before the
naval victory. The highly finished nature of the drawing
suggests that it was a *modello* for an important commission,
perhaps even for the ducal palace, but not executed.   B.B.

284 Designs for windows or doors
Pen and ink: 22.5 × 32.8
Prov: Anthony Salvin Collection
Lent by the Royal Institute of British Architects (A6/10)

This drawing has been published as by John Webb, perhaps
after an Italian building (Harris, 1972, no.173). John Harris has
suggested to me that it is closer to Palladio, and I feel that it can
be confidently attributed to him. The busts and the figures are
in the same hand as the figures on the projects for the
Redentore (258). A late dating is in any case likely. The
entablature, which consists only of a cornice and architrave, for
instance, resembles that of the side elevation of the Loggia del
Capitaniato.
The building for which these were intended must have been
important, but it is not even clear whether these are designs for
windows or doors. The solutions on the right would seem to
be for doors, and the busts and the statues would need to be
seen from close up. The presence of a step beneath each
opening would tell against their being doors, as paired off in
this way they would probably lead to flights of stairs going
up on one side, down on the other. The indication of an
opening with a dotted line in the arch in the middle is also
puzzling: it could indicate a flight of steps going down, or a
window opening pierced obliquely through a thick wall. The
panel beneath all three elements is often employed by
Palladio as a window sill (Palazzo Valmarana cortile, exterior
of the refectory of S.Giorgio, Brescia Palace designs).   H.B.

VILLAS

Palladio is best known as a designer of villas, and villas constitute the largest element in his production. It is in the field of villa architecture that his originality and the development of his ideas can be most clearly measured. In his villas it is possible to see clearly the relation in his work between tradition and innovation, between old functions and new forms. This part of the exhibition has been divided into sections which explore these contrasts and relationships. The first section deals with the villa and country life, the second with villas in the Veneto before Palladio, and the third with Palladio's villas. Each section has an introductory note.

Villas and country life

Palladio's villas were the country houses of their owners, who almost invariably had town houses as well. The analogy of the English country house can be misleading. In Jane Austen's *Mansfield Park*, Sir Thomas Bertram spends virtually all his time at his country seat: a single prolonged absence is brought about by the need to attend to his West Indian interests. Vicentine and even Venetian nobles might draw the greater part of their income from their country estates, but their personal power and influence derived from their standing in town. There was no equivalent of 'the county' or county society. Careers were made in town, not in the country. The town was the centre for maintaining one's network of friendships and personal alliances, which could only be done by putting in a regular appearance on the Piazza. Pleasant dinner parties at the villa (Zorzi, 1968, p.120) or gifts of game off the estate were only means of consolidating a social and political position which, though it might be underpinned by an income from the country, was essentially town based. In the town, too, one was better placed to influence legal cases which could have great importance for one's position in the country, as Trissino's later history makes clear.

Vicentines and Venetians went often to their country houses (especially if they were in easy reach) for peace and quiet, to escape the hot and unhealthy town, to hunt and hold parties, and to attend to their estates. But they were not country gentlemen in the eighteenth-century sense, and even the organisation of agriculture, that is with share cropping contracts, meant that the one essential time for landowners to be present was when harvesting was under way as those who worked the land on this 'profit sharing' basis had a stake in doing their jobs well. The villa, therefore, had an important part in its owner's life, but it was only a part, and the villa was never an autonomous sphere, any more than was the countryside as a whole, which sold its produce and paid its taxes to the town. The villa's primary function was agricultural. In Palladio's time the word villa had a much more extensive meaning than it does now. It was either a synonym for village or meant a whole estate. Palladio's 'villas' and sometimes even his surviving villa projects (339, 390) include not only what he calls 'the owner's house' (*casa dominicale*), but also a whole series of farmyards, barns, outbuildings, as well as gardens and orchards. The planning of all these elements in relation to one another is what villa architecture meant for him, not just the owner's home, which we call the villa.

Palladio's own general observations on the villa centre round practical, functional matters (II, pp.45–6). His remarks are not original, merely a clear, densely packed summary of the standard writers on the subject (292), based on common sense and contemporary practice. He says that the villa buildings should be as near as possible to the centre of the estate, to facilitate supervision and improvement, and so that 'the produce . . . can be brought in an orderly fashion to the owner's house by the farm workers'. Where maps of estates survive, as for the Pisani estate at Bagnolo (333), one can in fact see how the villa buildings are centrally placed. The Villa Pisani is one of Palladio's villas which is on a river: 'if one can build on a river, it will be very convenient and beautiful, because one can carry the produce at any time at small cost into the city with boats, and it will serve for the use of the house and the animals, as well as bringing coolness in the summer and making a more beautiful view, and with great profit and ornament one can irrigate the possessions and the gardens and orchards which are the soul and recreation of the villa' (II, p.45). Palladio's concern with the access to a river is paralleled with statistical precision by the Podestà of Padua in 1554: 'there are 397 villages in the province of Padua, of which a great number are on navigable rivers and a great number are in easy reach of them. But no village, whether it be in the hills or on the plain is further than four miles from a river' (ASV, Relazioni).

Palladio's remarks about villas reflect their basic organization. There needs to be accommodation for the factor (Fattore, cf. 296), the accountant (Gastaldo), the agricultural workers, stables and cowsheds, agricultural instruments, and produce, including wine, oil, grain, firewood, and hay. His reference to the workers bringing their produce to the owner's house, and his usual description of the villa house as having the granary under the roof and the wine cellars in the basement reflect a concern with the security of the produce on which the owner's income depended. He cites Crescenzio's (292) remark that the threshing floor (294) should be 'not so close to the owner's house, because of the dust; nor so distant that it cannot be seen' (II, p.46). In one of his villa projects Palladio actually notes on the drawing the intended site for the threshing floor (393). The basic facts of villa economy emerge more crudely in Giulio Trissino's scandalous sacking of his father's granaries at Cornedo in 1533 (Morsolin, 1894, p.313, n.2) and in Giulio's later refusal to hand over the keys to his father's granaries in 1544 (ibid, p.317).

The agreements according to which the land was worked, as Mantese has observed (1971-3, p.79) were not much worse than those operating until very recent times. They were all broadly similar, and typical is that concluded between Alexandro Cividale and his 'labourer' (lavorador) Battista in Vicenza on 18 October 1565 (ASVi, Not.M.Cerato, b.780). The agreement ran from St Martin's day 1565 (11 November) to St Martin's day 1566. The labourer was 'obliged to work the said possession well and diligently and sow it with good seed, paying to the owner half of the wheat, transporting the sheaves to the owner's residence (casa dominicale) entirely at his (the labourer's) expense'. If the owner wished, the produce had to be brought into Vicenza. Half the produce of grapes went to the owner, and half of the large firewood. On the other hand, only a third of the 'small grains' (biave menute), which could include millet, rye, barley, and sorghum (cf. Pullan, 1971, p.295) went to the owner

and only a third of the brush wood. Furthermore, the labourer paid a nominal rent in poultry to the owner, whose state obligations were restricted to having the ditches dug on the property. Obviously in large land improvements and reclamation schemes, the capital expenditure was undertaken by the owner. Above all, on the larger estates (and nearly all Palladio villas were commissioned by big landowners) the division of the produce needed careful supervision, which would be overseen by the factor and the accountant (gastaldo) as well as the owner himself. There may have been a small permanent work force, to handle the produce once it had been consigned, as well as to carry out maintenance and improvements. This work, however, could have been carried out by ad hoc agreement with the sharecroppers. The scene in one of the big villa complexes at harvest time is documented in a drawing by Pozzoserrato, with the wagons coming in with the produce and a labourer doffing his hat to the 'paron' and his wife (295). The labourers sometimes lived in the villa complex itself and sometimes in the 'labourers' houses' which are listed on the tax returns of the landowners. These houses, which sometimes appear in landscape backgrounds in paintings, were simplified versions of the villas themselves, with living accommodation and farm functions contained in one structure, usually with a loggia in front, or to one side, of the house (Forster, 1974).

The housing and general conditions of life of country people were probably, when harvests were good, superior to those of the urban poor. During the great plague in Venice, about a third of the population died. In 1578 the Podestà of Vicenza reported 2357 deaths in the city (out of a population of 26,000 in 1570) and only 767 in the province out of a population of 135,440 (ASV, Relazioni). But famine was the plague of the countryside. If the harvest was bad, it affected the pockets of the landowners, but their labourers could die of starvation. The terrible scenes which the Vicentine Luigi da Porto and the Venetian diarist Marin Sanudo describe in 1527-8 are familiar, at least from the television screen. The starving rural poor flooded into Vicenza and Venice in search of food: 'You cannot walk down the street or stop in a square or church without multitudes surrounding you to beg for charity: you see hunger written on their faces, their eyes like gemless rings, the wretchedness of their bodies with the skins shaped only by bones' (L. da Porto, quoted by Pullan, 1971, p.243). Sanuto reports that the starving peasants had come to Venice from as far off as the provinces of Brescia and Verona, and that in the morning, people who had died in the night were sometimes found outside the Ducal palace (*ibid*, p.244). That winter was particularly bad, but not unique. Hard frosts, rain and flood, droughts, even locusts (in 1545; Bortolan, 1887) could tip the balance between prosperity and starvation, and did so every few years. The peasants were reduced to eating grass in 1527 (Pullan, 1971, p.245), and things were no better in the Paduan countryside in 1591, when Fabio Monza wrote, 'I have been to Padua where I did not find any bread in the bakers' shops, and the famine is so great that it horrifies humanity. The peasants are black, emaciated, and weak, and are eating grass . . .' (Monza, 1888, p.35).

The villa owners were not by any means always ready to make a full contribution to relieving distress. Giovanni Pisani, since 1523 himself the owner of the Bagnolo estate (333), wrote to the Venetian government on 4 April 1528 as Podestà of Vicenza that if the Vicentines had obeyed the proclamation that all grain was to be brought into the town, there would not have been such a scarcity. He had noted that on a census of grain holdings, Matheo del Toso, knight, and Nicolò Chiericati (probably the brother of two of Palladio's patrons; Puppi, 1973, p.296) were recorded as possessing 3934 and 1038 bushels respectively. When he sent men to bring this grain into town, they found the granaries empty, and Del Toso and Chiericati could not be traced (ASV, *Lettere*, b.223, f.128). A Vicentine notary's characterisation of successive years fills out the picture further: 'In the year 1556 there was an abundant harvest of everything . . . In 1557 there was a poor harvest of everything . . . In 1558 there was a miserable, most sterile harvest . . . there was in the month of March such water and tempests as had never been seen in the memory of man and the months of June, July, and August and the whole summer drier than ever before . . . And it only rained at the end of October. [In 1559 the price of wheat then mounted from one ducat to the astronomic sum of fifteen ducats in the countryside] . . . In 1561 was a decent harvest . . . Beginning on St Catherine's day 1561, it rained torrentially all winter and did not stop so one could take a breath . . . In 1562 was a sterile harvest . . . In 1563 it began to rain at the beginning of March and rained until the 21st June . . . and there was a lot of hay and the wheat was bad . . . In 1564 the harvest was very sterile in everything . . . In 1565 there was a valuable wheat harvest . . . In 1567 there was a most fertile harvest of everything . . . In November there was so much flooding that great damage was done . . . In 1568 there was a most sterile wheat harvest . . . In 1570 there was a very fertile harvest of everything, but the grain was dear because of the war with the Turks' (Mantese, 1974, pp.749–50). In the spring of one of these bad years, 1559, there was an outbreak of typhoid (as there had been in 1528) which, above all, attacked the young. It is little wonder that on 22 June 1559, the Rectors of Vicenza reported to the Venetian government disturbing symptoms of mass hysteria in the countryside: 'in 18 or 20 villages of this territory, under pretext of Religion and of miracles which it had been put about that the Madonna had performed, the people had risen up to such a point that an infinite number of people had come together in the churches of these places, where they remained day and night, because they said that the Madonna had performed miracles. And in these churches they ate, danced, and kissed each other, the women the men, and the men the women, and they said that the Madonna had ordered them so to do, and they committed other improper acts under this pretext, adding also, as we understand, some heretical things. And to such an extent had these people risen up, that the peasants had totally abandoned the countryside, and the artisans their workshops as they did not want to work any more, saying that as for their livelihood, the Madonna will provide'. The Rectors response to this strange but by no means unparalleled (Cohn, 1970) anarchic reaction to terrible conditions was simple: they ordered that the churches were to be kept locked except during services.

Contemporary popular literature reflects the ups and downs of peasant life. The anonymous *Dialogue of two Paduan peasants*, Venice, 1552, describes the experience of a peasant who made a journey at carnival time to amuse himself in the Venetian brothel district and found 'one who looked like a figure painted in gauche'. The episode ends with a Swiftian touch as her bodice stank so much that he was sick. The main part of the little volume records a discussion between the peasants about a dowry. One says he has no money; the other tells him all the things he can give instead. The long list of clothing and domestic articles reads like the many notary's documents recording peasant dowries, much the same in value and in content as the one which Palladio's wife brought him in 1534. *The Lament of a Bergamasco brought to poverty by the famine*, 1554 (299) needs no comment.

It would be a mistake to think that the countryside was, apart from the villa owners, an entirely anonymous world, without its own organizations or social structures. Alongside walled centres like Lonigo, from which, reputedly, came the best bread in Italy (Pullan, 1971, p.295), there existed rural communes with a measure of autonomy, which were invariably in conflict with the City Council in Vicenza (Mantese, 1964, p.559ff.). In tax returns and censuses, the whole population of Lugo in 1546 is recorded, household by household (AT, b.302). There are only two gentlemen among the 547 inhabitants, Messer Hieronimo di Godi, owner of the Villa Godi (317), and Messer Thomaso Piovene, whose more modest villa was possibly also modernized by Palladio (Puppi, 1973, p.241). Hieronimo Godi and his wife Madonna Romana had ten servants. Messer Thomaso had only three. There were 96 households, with an average of just over five people in each house, and therefore there is no question of 'extended families' living in the same building. Eleven households had servants; twenty paid money rents to Hieronimo Godi. Some families had nephews living with them, and four of these are childless couples, indicating a sharing of the burden of bringing up a family with other members of a family. The husband's mother lived with the family in eleven households. Two families had ten children, one six, but the average was about three. Surnames tend to recur, and the small rural community was probably as densely intermarried as the nobles of the town. The families who paid money rents and had servants probably represent a more prosperous, middle level of rural society.

This small foothill community was dominated only by two families, the Godi and Piovene, represented only by one household each. This is a very different situation from that of the Caldognos at Caldogno (336) or the many Poianas at Poiana. The two 'great houses' of the area confront one another at a close distance, each on top of a small rise. It was hardly surprising that tensions existed between the two, and these came to a dramatic conclusion in 1577, when the then owner of the Villa Godi, Orazio Godi, broke into the Villa Piovene together with armed companions and, after discharging their

arquebuses into a wardrobe in which Fabio Piovene ha[d] hidden, had a carpenter force it open, and killed him (Zor[zi] 1968, p.28).

Vicenza and Venice were the cultural, social, and politic[al] centres for their local nobilities. Palladio's own villa designs, [if] anything, made the country even more dependent on t[he] values of the town, and contributed to the urbanisation of t[he] countryside. Palladio himself, following Alberti, wrote th[at] 'the city is nothing else but a certain large house, and on t[he] other hand the house (he was referring to the villa) is a litt[le] city' (II, p.46).

The countryside, however, and the villa (in its wide sense) pr[o]vided the economic base of the Vicentine nobles, and increa[s]ingly in the sixteenth century a new and profitable field f[or] investment by the Venetians (Woolf, 1968). It was a place f[or] relaxation, whether by hunting (297), or by playing music [in] the garden (363). In the country, surrounded by their servant[s] dependents and tenants, the Vicentine nobles in part returne[d] to their feudal and bellicose origins, so that when they got bac[k] into town at the start of winter, they made trouble (see *Vicenz[a]* Introduction above). Much more clearly than the town, th[e] country reveals the dramatic differences between rich and poo[r.] In time of plague, the rich could retreat to their villas in th[e] healthy country, leaving the poor to die in the towns. [If] attendance on the Venetian Maggior Consiglio dropped in th[e] summer of 1576 from 1300 to 300, it was not because a thousan[d] Venetian nobles had died (Pullan, 1971, p.323). They were i[n] the country. The ordinary country people at best risked bein[g] cheated in the city markets, where they went to sell the[ir] produce (26, 289). In 1554 the Podestà of Padua wrote th[at] 'the contadini are universally poor and are going from bad t[o] worse ... when they sold their wines in the piazza of Padua ..[.] the measures were so rigged that ten *mastella* of wine came o[ut] as eight (ASV, *Relazioni*, 6.32 f.44). At worst they starve[d.] A Vicentine nobleman might die of a hen bite (Monza, 188[.] p.24) or might be killed by a noble neighbour, but he neve[r] died of hunger. H.B.

GIOVANNI ANTONIO MAGINI

285 Map of the province of Vicenza (Bologna?; 1600?)
Engraving, coloured by hand: 35.3 × 43.8
Lent by the Museo Civico, Vicenza

The map indicates the confines of the Vicentino in the
sixteenth century. The area to the south of Vicenza was more
fertile. H.B.

DOMENICO CAMPAGNOLA c.1484–1564

286 Landscape with a reclining figure
Pen and ink: 24.1 × 36.8
Lent by the Trustees of the Chatsworth Settlement (268)

The landscape is rocky and not agriculturally rich. In the
background there is a small village dominated by a castle and a
simple gothic church. The largest houses have three floors, but
most of them one or two storeys; all of the houses have steeply
pitched roofs. A timber foot bridge and a road bridge cross
the river which powers the water mills. This is a romanticised
version of the country in the hilly, wooded areas of the Veneto,
where timber growing, grazing and sometimes mining were
much more important than arable farming. The number of
mills indicates a certain prosperity. A man is approaching the
village on a donkey, the most frequently used means of
transport for people and goods in these regions. L.F.

287 Detail of a map, 1624
Photograph from ASV, Provv. Beni Inculti, Verona, Mazzo 5

Coaches are shown going along the road, which is lined with a
series of farm establishments. H.B.

ANONYMOUS VENETO ARTIST

288 View of a Piazza
Pen and brown ink over black chalk: 19.6 × 20.7
Prov: L. Zatka; W.M. Miliken
Lent by Kate de Rothschild

The piazza sketched in this drawing appears to be a synthetic
creation, using topographical elements from several Veneto
towns. The medieval walls and moat to the left may have been
suggested by Castelfranco while the buildings in the piazza and
their arcading resemble those in the Prato della Valle, Padua.
In the foreground the artist has placed a column with the lion
of St Mark, the symbol of Venetian dominance over the subject
cities of the Terraferma. The treatment of the grander *palazzi*
to the left – the large order portico, the serliane, and the
obelisks – as well as the general character of the drawing seem
to indicate a date in the last quarter of the sixteenth century
(de Rothschild, 1975, no.21). B.B.

LEANDRO BASSANO

*289 A vegetable and fruit market
Canvas: 134.6 × 162.5
Lent by Lord Barnard, Raby Castle

The painting appears to be unpublished. Market scenes of this
sort were among the more common genre themes produced by
the Bassano workshop. The attribution to Leandro is on the
basis of a signed *February* in the Kunsthistorisches Museum,
Vienna, which also shows a market scene.
The traders have set up their stalls and sell their goods from
baskets on the steps of palaces in the piazza of a small country
town. In the background people are going to church. L.F.

289

After JACOPO BASSANO

290 The seasons: Spring, Summer and Autumn
Engravings
Inscribed: Bassan pinxit; Ioan Anton de P.f(ecit)
Photographs

There is a painting by Francesco Bassano of *May* and *June* in the Kunsthistorisches Museum, Vienna (Arslan, 1960, II, fig. 213) which corresponds to the *Spring*. Individual elements in the compositions reoccur in numerous paintings from the Bassanos' workshop. The seasons, representing the agricultural cycle, was a traditional subject, and the Bassano produced many paintings of this theme. The engravings are marked off, probably for copying.

Traditionally Spring is represented by the hunt (297), Summer by the Harvest (292 and 294), and Autumn by the grape harvest (295).

STUDIO OF BONIFAZIO DE PITATI

291 The labours of the months
Canvas on wood: each 13 × 10
Lent by the Trustees of the National Gallery, London

Ridolfi tells us that Bonifazio, like Giorgione before him, made a large number of decorative panels for furniture (1914, I, p.295), amd some of these still exist (Vertova, 1972, pp.175–84, 336). The present series are generally accepted as coming from Bonifazio's studio, with which the young Jacopo Bassano was associated (Arslan, 1960. I, pp.37–51; Westphal, 1931, p.97; Gould, 1975, pp.32–3).

The labours of the months is a common medieval theme which was still popular in North Italian art in the mid sixteenth century in the form not of single figures carrying out the major tasks of the agricultural cycle, but of genre compositions (295). Here the months are represented as single figures, which recall earlier examples like Luca della Robbia's roundels for the Palazzo Medici, now in the Victoria and Albert Museum. The panels have been rearranged and do not follow the sequence of the calendar. The tasks can be identified as follows:

An old man asleep by a stove	January
A youth asleep on a rampart	?
Killing a wild boar	December
A falconer with hounds	May
A man cutting corn	June
Ploughing	August
Threshing	July
Pressing wine	September
Coopering wine casks	October
Pointing vine poles	February
Making vine trellis	March (?)
Vine dressing	April

The man asleep under a tree is a puzzle: if the identifications above are all correct, he would be November   B.B./L.F.

Translated by FRANCESCO SANSOVINO

*292 Pietro Crescentio
Per Francesco Sansovino Venetia 1561
Photograph

This influential treatise on agriculture, based on contemporar practice and so an invaluable source for knowledge of agricultural life in the Renaissance, was written c.1305 and dedicated to Charles II of Sicily. It was copied in manuscript form many times both in Italy and Northern Europe, and published in Latin in 1471, it then went into numerous Italian editions (Fratti; Sorbelli, 1933). As well as giving practical advice to farmers about crops and animal husbandry etc., Crescenzio describes the planning of the villa in relation to its functions (000). Francesco Sansovino as an appendix to his translation, illustrates on four plates the instruments in use on the farm. Illustrated here are: a wooden sieve, a sickle (293c), a pruning hook (296), a scythe, a wooden grain shovel (174), a flail (294), an auger, and a harrow.

Francesco Sansovino was the son of the famous architect Jacopo. After studying at the University of Padua he made his living as a professional writer. He is best known for his very detailed guide to Venice (Sansovino, 1581).   L.F.

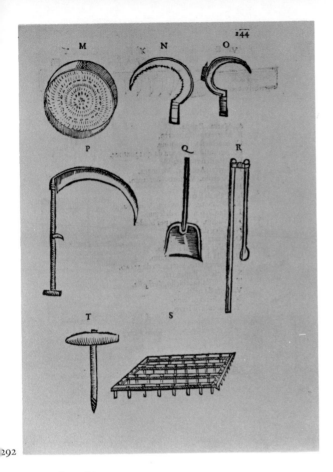

292

293

293 Agricultural instruments
Lent by the Accademia Polironiana

(a) Swing plough
Wood and iron

This plough, although it may not be of the sixteenth century, is just like the one illustrated in Sansovino's edition of Crescenzio (1561, p.243v). This type, widely used in Italy was only satisfactory where the top soil was thin (not the case in most of the Veneto), and is inefficient compared with the heavy, wheeled plough in general use in Northern Europe (Braudel,

1972, p.426). Crescenzio wrote that heavy wet and weedy soil should be ploughed four times, while light dry soil needs only one, two, or three ploughings. He says that 'each ploughing should increase the yield, and as long as the yield is greater than the effort one should continue, but if the effort becomes greater than the yield the place or field should be abandoned' (Crescenzio 1561, p.227).   L.F.

(b) Butter churn
Wood

Olive oil was preferred in Italy and in the Mediterranean for cooking, while butter was generally used in Northern Europe. Oil keeps better in hot climates. Mediterranean people travelling in the North frowned on butter. The Cardinal of Aragon, travelling in the North in 1517 with his own cook attributed his impression that the North was 'overrun with lepers' to its consumption (Braudel, 1972, p.237). Olive oil, however, was scarce in the Veneto, where grazing and milk production was plentiful. Oil was produced, but in small quantities, so the Veneto relied on its being imported. Butter would have provided a widely used substitute, if not for the rich, then at least for the lower paid.   L.F.

(c) Sickle
Wood and metal

The sickle is just like the one illustrated in Crescenzio (1561; (292), and it was used for harvesting corn (291).

(d) Rake
Wood

CIRCLE OF DOMENICO CAMPAGNOLA (?)
*294 Threshing
Pen and ink: 149 × 274
Photograph from an original at Chatsworth (no.241)

This unusual design for a lunette vault shows two men threshing with flails like the one illustrated in Crescenzio 1561 (292), while a putto carries the straw back to the thatched workers' cottage in the background. Crescenzio wrote that the

threshing floor should be outside but close to the villa's outer walls so that it remains in sight of the owner and the grain and straw can easily be carried back to the villa. The floor should made of stone or earth hardened with a paste of sheeps' hooves and water, and it should be prepared and cleaned in June. There should be a covered platform raised above ground where the grain could cool before being carried back into the barns inside the farm. (Crescenzio 1561 p.42v). Palladio while he recommends that the threshing floor should be raised in the middle (so that water runs off it and it stays dry), and adds that there should be porticoes all round or at least on one side), otherwise follows Crescenzio's recommendations and contemporary practice (Palladio 1570, II, p.46).   L.F.

LODEWYCK TOEPUT called POZZOSERRATO C.1550–1610
*295 September
Pen and brown ink and blue wash: 27.5 × 42.0
Lent by the Fitzwilliam Museum, Cambridge

This drawing is similar in size and the vertical division of the composition to the drawing of January and May in the Yale Gallery, and may belong to the same series (*Yale Drawings*, 1970). On the left are the fields, and a navigable water course. On the right outside the villa walls, grapes are being harvested. An ox cart laden with grapes has entered the farmyard through the main gate, and large collection vats stand under the thatched wooden structure on the right.

294

295

In the right foreground the villa owner and his family are saluted by a workman.   L.F.

FRANCIABIGIO (FRANCESCO DI CRISTOFANO) Florence, 1484–1525

96 Portrait of the Factor of Pierfrancesco de' Medici
Panel, 65.3 × 49.5cm.
Photograph reproduced by gracious permission of Her Majesty The Queen

Signed with the artist's monogram on the pruning-hook top right. Inscribed on the left page of the ledger: Mdxxiij; and on the right page (much worn): . . . floren . . ./ogi adi 20 . . ./ . . . si girolamo . . . The Medici arms are on the stone sill.
Prov: Acquired by Charles I, and hung atWhitehall, attributed to Andrea del Sarto (Van der Doort, ed.1960, p.40, No.14: 'supposed to be some harborest of the familye of the house of Medecey . . .'); the brand of Charles I is on the back. Seen by Waagen and others in the nineteenth century at Windsor (Windsor Castle inventory, 1872, No.12). More recently at Hampton Court (No.1168).
Exh: King's Pictures, R.A. 1946, No.238.

The portrait is described by Vasari in his *Vita* of Franciabigio (ed. Milanesi, v, p.197): 'Fece (un ritratto) a un lavoratore e fattore di Pier Francesco de' Medici al palazzo di San Girolamo da Fiesole, che par vivo'. Pierfrancesco (1487–1525) was the father of Lorenzino, the murderer of Duke Alessandro de' Medici. From his father he inherited Cafaggiolo and a small villa at Fiesole, with vineyard, olive-grove and quarry, in the parish of San Romolo (Shearman, 1975, p.17); this villa was not Michelozzo's Villa Medici, which would more naturally be described in Vasari's phrase 'Palazzo di San Girolamo', and it is not clear why the fragmentary inscription would seem also to refer to the latter. Pierfrancesco took little active part in Florentine life and politics, and was mainly concerned with estate-management; he had little success, however, and his factor had good reason to be as worried as Franciabigio makes him appear. The attributes and activity of the sitter refer straightforwardly to his stewardship, save for the laurel-shoots, which are not in the first instance the casual results of his pruning but are familiar symbols of renewal of the branches of the Medici house (McKillop, 1974, p.84); at the date of the portrait Pierfrancesco, the eldest by continual legitimate descent of the younger branch of the family, had a good claim to be its head, and the placing by Franciabigio (or the factor) of one laurel-branch in semi-eclipse under the ledger may refer in the only possible way – that is, obliquely – to this situation.
A replica on canvas from the Corsini Collection (now in Palazzo Barberini in Rome) was once the property of Guido Reni, who believed it to be by Andrea del Sarto; this replica, probably not earlier than *c.*1600, shows a composition taller and wider on the left, but the original appears not to be cut on any side.   J.S.

BERNARDO LICINIO C.1489–C.1560
*297 A nobleman hunting
Canvas: 231.4 × 396.2
Lent by the Earl of Hopetoun

This fine painting has been attributed to Francesco Beccaruzzi (Berenson, 1907, p.87) and to a follower of Paris Bordone or Pordenone (Berenson, 1957, p.206). But there seems little doubt that it is a work of Licinio (A.Ballarin, oral communication). Hunting was a highly valued activity, both as an upper class recreation, often carried on in the hunting reserves (*barchi*) attached to the villas (333), and as a source of varied meat dishes for upper class tables. This relatively early treatment of the theme (probably about 1525) shows a huntsman with his falcon and dogs, one of his sons (?) and an attendant. In the background there is a typical pre-Palladian villa complex, similar to that which existed at Bagnolo (328), with dovecote and barn, as well as the owner's villa itself. On the right is a labourer's cottage with an attached barn. Though there is no reason to accept the identification of the huntsman as the Emperor Charles V, the scene recalls a famous event in Vicentine history, the visit of Charles V to the Gualdo villa at Montecchio Maggiore (437) in 1532, attended by the Captain Nicolò Morosini (10) and Trissino, as well as a host of noble Vicentines. The Emperor with his two hunting dogs caught a hare in Stephano Gualdo's reserve, and ate ten figs from a Gualdo fig tree (Mantese, 1964, p.88). The story about Charles saying to the many Vicentines seeking titles from him on this occasion 'I make the whole lot of you counts' if not literally true, is at least a pointed and witty fabrication

297

(Mantese, 1964, p.88). A Vicentine noble, Francesco Carcano, who died in 1497, was the author of a treatise on falconry and hunting dogs (Mantese, 1974, p.951).   L.F./H.B.

298 Dialogo di duoi villani padoani ...
In Venetia Appresso di Candido Bindoni. MDLII
Lent by the British Library Board (11427. b.34)

The content of this anonymous dialect poem is summarized in the section on country life, above.   H.B.

299 Lamento di un Bergamasco venuto in poverta per la carestia ...
1554
Lent by the British Library Board (11427. b.20)

There is no indication of the author or place of publication of this short poem in the Bergamasco dialect, entitled *Lament of a Bergamasco brought to poverty by the Famine*. There is a crude woodcut of a peasant on the title page.   H.B.

JAN VAN DER STRAET called STRADANUS

300 Preparing the eggs of silkworms
Pen, ink and wash, heightened with white: 20 × 27.5
Mark: G.R.
Photograph reproduced by gracious permission of Her Majesty The Queen

The drawing is for an engraving in *Vermis Sericus* (plate 3) published by L.Renard with neither date nor place of publication, and dedicated by Jan van der Straet to

Constantia Alamannia, the wife of Raphael Medici of Florence. The drawings for all the engravings are in the Royal Library Windsor, and many preparatory drawings for them are in the Cooper Union Museum (Puyvelde, 1942, p.25, no.165 and Benisovwich, 1956).

The setting of the scene is a richly panelled interior with a large canopied fireplace and an ornate bed. Otherwise the furniture, a table, chests, and rush seat chairs (one of the most common types of chair) is very simple. In the centre a woman bathes silkworms' eggs with wine while two others cut silk bags to hold the eggs. On the left two women put these little bags between their breasts to keep them warm so that they hatch. On the right another detaches the hatched worms from the silk.

The silk industry was an important one, providing work for women who supplied the needs of the merchants. Thus Gratiolo (257) attributed the insanitary conditions of the homes of the poor in part to the keeping of silk worms ('so dear and familiar to women'), as many of the worms tended to die and putrify. L.F.

DOMENICO CAMPAGNOLA C.1484–1564
301 Reeling silk
Photograph from the drawing in the Gabinetto dei Disegni degli Uffizi, Florence (1786F)

The drawing, in pen, ink, and wash, measures 25.3 × 42.1 cm. Despite the Giuliesque antique setting and the elegance of the postures, the process of reeling the silk off the cocoons is shown clearly. The older woman in the centre sits at a large vat of water, which is heated by a fire underneath. She detaches the threads which she then passes over the hooks attached to the bar in front of her, and from there the silk is wound onto the frame. There are drawings by Stradanus of this same stage in silk production. H.B.

JACOPO and FRANCESCO BASSANO 1510/15–1592, 1548–91
302 Joachim's vision
Canvas: 38 × 52
Signed on the stairs on the left
Lent by The Methuen Collection

Jacopo Bassano's paintings were especially valued amongst Venetian connoisseurs for their genre content as early as the 1560s (Vasari, 1568, III, p.816). In 1577–8 Jacopo designed a set of genre treatments of biblical themes which had immediate success and were often repeated by his sons to supply a steady demand. The painting must be before Francesco's suicide in 1591. The subject Joachim's vision, has been identified by association with two frescoes by Giotto in the Scrovegni Chapel, Padua (Rearick, 1968, pp.246–7). Here Anna sits making a lace border (probably for a chemise), while her two companions spin and weave wool. The distaff, for making thread, the loom and spinning wheel were standard household equipment in the sixteenth century. On the left of the painting a boy blows on a firebrand while a woman with a salver dispatches or receives news from Joachim. A large-scale drawing by Jacopo Bassano (303) is related to this painting. L.F.

JACOPO BASSANO
303 Boy blowing on a fire-brand
Blue wash heightened with white: 43.8 × 33.5
Photograph reproduced by gracious permission of Her Majesty The Queen

This large scale drawing for the right half of Jacopo Bassano's *Joachim's Vision* was used by his sons in their copies of his paintings and slotted into various compositions (302 and Rearick 1969). The boy is shown kneeling before a typical canopied fireplace with a cooking pot hanging over the fire. Behind him a woman takes or gives a message to a man who has come in through curtains hanging over the doorway. Curtains were often used in this way. L.F.

GIOVANNI ANTONIO DE LODESANIS, IL PORDENONE 1484–1539
304 The Death of St Peter Martyr
Red chalk: 23.9 × 20.2
Prov: William, 2nd Duke of Devonshire
Photograph from an originl at Chatsworth

Ridolfi first mentioned Pordenone as a competitor of Titian and Palma Vecchio for a painting commissioned by the Confraternity of Saint Peter Martyr of SS. Giovanni e Paolo in

Venice (1914, p.167). The commission was won by Titian, whose painting of the *Death of St Peter Martyr* was finished by April 1530 (Wethey, 1969, pp.153–5, no.133). Two drawings by Pordenone for the same theme survive, and the present one is probably a study for the *modello* now in the Uffizi (Tietze and Tietze-Conrat, 1944, p.235, no.1301, p.236, no.1311; Popham, 1962, p.28, no.51). As Fiocco has pointed out (1969, p.102). the inspiration for Pordenone's composition was Titian's fresco of *The Miracle of the Jealous Husband*, painted for the Confraternity of St Anthony in Padua in 1510–11 (Wethey, I, 1969, pp.128–9, no.95). B.B.

This unidealised rendering of the martyrdom in contemporary terms is a powerful reminder of the violence of the period, above all in the countryside (Zanazzo, 1964–5). H.B.

BARTOLOMEO MAGGIO
305 Trattato delle ferite delli arcobugi
Tr. B. Polli
G. Discepolo: Verona 1594
Lent by the British Library Board 783. h. 3 (2)

This treatise on arquebus wounds sought to settle a current dispute as to whether the wound is burned or poisoned by establishing that the wound is poisoned. In the second part surgical treatment and medications are described. The translator Bartolomeo Poli, a surgeon from Montagnana (345), in his dedication to Curio Boldieri says that gentlemen are abandoning the sword as a weapon (still worn for purposes of dress), and using the arquebus to settle private quarrels. The publisher's preface gives the reason for the translation: arquebus wounds were becoming so frequent not only in the army but also in civilian life, in the town and countryside that it had become necessary to make information about treatment available. L.F.

Form and Function of Pre-Palladian Villas in the Venet

The problems connected with fifteenth-century villas in the Veneto are complex and involve a wide range of non architectural matters relating to form, function, typology, and contemporary terminology relating to the villa.

Seen in a broad historical view, the development of rura economic nuclei after the fall of the Roman empire was based on surviving non urban complexes, i.e. the *castrae*, the *massa* and the *villae*. It is within this context, that the primary function of the villa is to be seen: a non urban, partially self-sufficient group of buildings, which might or might not have had another 'primary' function, though this from the point o view of the evolution of the type is of secondary importance It is therefore correct to call farms, convents, priories and hostels Villas, providing they had a certain economic self-sufficiency.

The basic form of these Villas is generally a walled rectangular precinct with peripheral buildings, amorphously grouped around a courtyard. These would include, living quarters, stables, barns, dovecotes and sometimes a chapel, fishpond, and well.

The development of a distinct main residential building, at first most probably for the tenant and later for the periodically present owner, does however go back to the time of the treatise of De Crescentius in the first decade of the fourteenth century. Palladio's villas, at least in their touched-up presentation in the *Quattro Libri*, adhere to this development, giving the residential building a central position, which its predecessors did no thave. It is this formal aspect of the villa's development, in its unification of a vernacular functional tradition with a new formal pattern, based on his study of the antique, which give Palladio his unique position in the history of villa architecture.

The problems, however, of satisfying old functional and new formal requirements lie behind the unfinished state of many of Palladio's villas. These moreover were often to be located directly next to existing buildings and were hence further developments in the vernacular tradition, especially in its functional aspects. M.K.

306 Frontispiece showing the layout of a villa
Piero Crescentio
De Agricultura M.Capcasa : *Venetiis* 1495
Photograph

The frontispiece shows a medieval enclosure within high walls (shown here as wattle fence). The principal court is entered through a covered gateway (which could be locked at night). A villa block with a central tower within a smaller courtyard surveys and is protected by the outer court, containing on the left workers' accommodation, with a woman spinning outside (302), and on the right a kennel and a *teza* (a structure with a roof and no walls). Closing the inner court are stables and a barn. To the left of the villa but outside the walls is a dovecote, and on the right a garden with a pergola, where the choice vines grew, the bee-hives and an orchard. The plate is both simpler than and different from the description given in the book (I, chap.VII), which states that the rectangular court should be divided by a 'street' running from the entrance to the exit gate on the long axis. On one side of the 'street' there should be a U-shaped villa block with the short wings extending back to the pergola and gardens, on the other side of the 'street' the workers' accommodation with a well and oven nearby, while the stables and dung heap should be at the head of the court, as far away as possible from the owner's house. The threshing floor is to be as close as possible to the entrance gate. Both schemes are found in fifteenth century Veneto villas.   L.F.

ANDREA PREVITALI
*307 Farmyard
Photograph from the drawing in the Kupferstichkabinett, East Berlin

This drawing was published by H. and E. Tietze (1944, no. 1370) with the attribution to Previtali. Thatched buildings with steeply pitched roofs were common in the Veneto, even in the sixteenth century (286). There is a drinking trough next to the well, and a four wheeled cart in one of the barns.   H.B.

308 The nests inside the dovecote at the Villa Godi
Late fifteenth century
Photograph

Doves which were an important source of meat during the winter were kept in protective towers. Pietro Crescenzio recommends that the dovecot should be on top of a tower (which should not be too high) with smooth whitewashed walls. It should have *small* holes for the doves to go in and out, since doves are easily caught by birds of prey. Although the doves could nest in baskets suspended inside the tower, Crescenzio by experiment found that doves brood better in straight narrow nests built into the walls of the tower (Crescenzio, 1561, p.199v), precisely like the inside of this tower. Palladio often provided for dovecotes in his villas: see for instance the towers of the Villa Emo (355).   L.F.

309 Villa dal Zotto in Venegazzu (Treviso)
Photographs

Built in the years 1405–12, the Villa dal Zooto is of extreme importance for research into pre-Palladian villas, as it was built in one piece and still remains today, more or less as it was originally conceived. The three bayed portico is typical of the multi-functionalism of this architectural element. It served as shelter against both sun and rain, as a small barn and as a storage place for agricultural tools. The 'saw tooth' cornice, visible in the front façade on the right, is (according to Cevese)

307

a typical decorative element of the fifteenth century. Originally the whole front façade of the villa was covered in frescoes, of which only traces remain today: a Madonna on the left of the loggia, another one on the inside right of the loggia, and balustrade decorations on the wall between portico and loggia (cf. Rosci, 1968). M.K.

310 Villa Sella at Castelnuovo (Verona)
Photographs

The influence of the ecclesiastical architecture is visible in many pre-Palladian villas in the province of Verona. The long row of portico and loggia arches are reminiscent of cloisters. Although the outbuildings are later additions, the complex gives an excellent impression (see plan) of what the layout of this type of villa must have been. Today one tends to see the function of the central courtyard as being both agricultural and recreational/representational. Originally however the two aspects were fused in a single unity, as a careful analysis of the architectural form and contemporary writings on villa life reveals (cf. Prinz, 1974?, pp.40–1). M.K.

311 Villa Agostini at Arcade (Treviso)
Photograph

Built most probably in the years immediately following the peace of Brussels (1516), which brought peace to the Venetian Terraferma after the wars following on the League of Cambray, the Villa Agostini is an excellent example of the development from the amorphous and purely functional conglomerations of buildings visible in fifteenth-century villas to the formally classicised façades of Palladio's villas. The symmetrical placing of the two barchesse to the left and right of the main house and the raised position of the latter illustrate this point. The frescoes still visible on the main façade are a later addition (Corsi, 1960; Rosci, 1968, pp.50–1). M.K.

*312 Barco Povegliani, Longara (Vicenza)
Photograph

This photograph of a small fifteenth-century villa building is a further example of the tradition of superimposed loggie, which influenced Palladio's designs. It also shows how the ground

floor loggie on buildings of this type were probably always used to store wood and hay. This is the sort of jumbling up of functions of which M.K. speaks above: the upper loggia was probably used for eating and sitting about in the shade. The trend of Palladio's villa designs at a functional level was to differentiate within an orderly articulated scheme between agricultural, residential and recreational functions, just as in his Rialto scheme (221) there is a separation of the shopping and business areas. H.B.

313 A note on the Provveditori sopra i beni inculti
This note is offered as an explanation of numbers of photographs of maps exhibited here (328, 340, 455)

(a) The office
Founded and constituted by two decrees of the Venetian republic of the years 1545 and 1556, the office of the *Provveditori sopra i beni Inculti* (Commissioners for uncultivated properties) goes back to a suggestion of Alvise Cornaro to the Doge in the year 1540. It was thought necessary to centralise all efforts to improve lands in Venetian Terraferma. Legally the functioning of the office was underwritten by the declaration that all waters on the mainland were public property. Landowners who wanted to undertake improvements applied to the Commissioners. Thereupon two surveyors were

312

generally sent out to measure the land, submit a suggestion as to how the problem in hand could be tackled, and draw a map showing both the proposed alterations in the watercourses, and the land to be gained through drainage.

(b) The maps

Approximately 5,000 maps in the State Archive of Venice alone survive. They date from the foundation of the office to the fall of the Venetian republic in 1797. This figure does not include the maps of later divisions of this office, which include the *Provveditori sopra i beni communali*, the *Savi ed esecutori alle acque*, the *Magistrato all' Adige, all' Piave*, etc.

The maps were drawn on paper in ink and watercolour. The buildings of the applicants were very often shown in a detailed bird's-eye view, and sometimes those of their neighbours as well. This has led to speculation, supported by other evidence, that the surveyors' job also included setting up some sort of building control on the Terraferma.

Often the maps were drawn in two copies, one for the owner (sometimes to be found in private archives), one for the office (now in the Venetian State Archive).

Their style and accuracy, especially in rendering buildings, varies greatly according to the surveyor involved, and the period in which they were made.   M.K.

MARC'ANTONIO PALLADIO, nephew of Palladio

314 Elevation of a 'Barchessa' at the Villa Thiene at Cicogna di Villafranca Padovana

Pen and ink over incised construction lines: 23.7 × 41.1
Lent by the Royal Institute of British Architects (XVII/20)

The handwriting is that of Marc'Antonio Palladio (34). This barchessa (bam) at Cicogna still exists, and except for the absence of a pediment and the coupled pilasters which are more widely spaced in the building, it follows the design (Puppi, 1973, p.312). This is the only surviving elevation project for a barn by Palladio or one of his assistants. The barchessa forms part of the never completed scheme for the villa of Odoardo and Teodoro Thiene at Cicogna (Palladio, 1570, II, p.62; Puppi, 1973, pp.311–3).   L.F.

315 Letter of Christoforo Sorte to Count Odoardo Thiene, 22 April 1563

Photograph from ASV, *Provv. alla Camera dei Confini*, b.262

This bulky volume, which contains a mass of Christoforo Sorte's (280) notes and sketches relating to his work over many years as a surveyor and cartographer has been recently studied by Schulz from the point of view of cartography and as regards material relating to villas by Kubelik. A few sheets (392) relate to Palladio and his patrons. One of these is a draft (or copy for record purposes) of a letter dated from Verona and sent to Odoardo Thiene, owner of the villa at Cicogna (314). It relates to the 'calculations of the levelling undertaken on your order, and in your presence', obviously to improve the irrigation of the Thiene estate. It is a concrete demonstration of the direct personal interest which many of Palladio's patrons took in improving their possessions.   H.B.

GIUSEPPE CEREDI

316 Tre discorsi sopra il modo d'alzar acque da' luoghi bassi
S.Viotti, Parma, 1567

Photograph

A brief passage in this treatise on 'the way of raising water from low-lying places' indicates that Palladio concerned himself not only with the design of villas and their farm complexes, but also with the technology of land improvement. Ceredi had been shown by Palladio a 'very excellent' and still unpublished 'machine for raising water to a medium height' which 'had already been praised by the most honourable signor Marcantonio Barbaro (278), brother of the most reverend and learned Patriarch Elect of Aquileia (176), to whom rightly these Venetian nobles refer judgement on almost all mathematical works'. Palladio's machine is praised for its practicality by Ceredi, who makes it clear that it is some sort of Archimidean screw. Palladio's concern with such matters is a reflection of the widespread scientific and technical interests of the cultured world (175; Puppi, 1973, p.380).   H.B.

Palladio's Villas

The need for owner's houses on their country estates was felt before Palladio's time. Even the Venetians had begun investing in land and building themselves villas in the fifteenth century above all in the nearby provinces of Padua and Treviso. The conservative diarist Priuli in a famous passage in fact attributes the loss of the mainland territories in 1509 to the softening effect of a land-based way of life, as opposed to the Venetian nobility's seafaring traditions (Woolf, 1968, p.188 and *passim*). By the 1540s however the increase in urban population, above all that of Venice, made investment in land increasingly attractive for the individual, and from the point of view of reducing expenditure on food imports. The reclamation of uncultivated land 313) was persuasively called for by the exponent of 'holy agriculture', the Paduan noble and architectural expert Alvise Cornaro (Fiocco, 1965). Vicentine nobles who had held country estates for generations, and Venetian nobles like Giovanni Pisani who bought himself an estate in the Vicentino in 1523 (327) were equally stimulated to improve their lands (cf.315). At the same time they were under the same sort of social and cultural pressures to rebuild in an up to date and impressive way as were the Vicentine palace owners. Agricultural expansion made available the money for the new buildings, and in part (as in the case of the huge new barns designed by Palladio for the Pisani in the 1560s, 334) the need for them. But the fact that Palladio was called upon for designs, instead of everything being settled between the owner and a building firm (both would know what a barn was like) comes from the increasing penetration of the country by the culture of the town, and the fact that Palladio was also very skilled in providing effective solutions on a functional and practical level. Vincenzo Arnaldi in 1547 gave much thought to how he could improve his villa complex at Meledo Alto (390): 'should one build a door?'; 'should one make another similar loggetta above the one mentioned?' His questions and memoranda go on for pages, and Palladio was the right man to give the answers.

Palladio's first villa was the Villa Godi, designed in 1537 (317). It is revealing both as a first indication of Palladio's capacities, and as a building against which his subsequent development can be measured. The scheme with the living floor raised off the ground, and a service floor below, is like the villa at Cusignana di Arcade (311). The plan also resembles it with a wooden roofed central hall flanked symmetrically by smaller rooms (four on each side at the Villa Godi, instead of two at the pre-Palladian villa). Palladio's insetting of the loggia, his creation of a division between the loggia and the *salone* (on the example of Cricoli?) are departures from tradition. But there is none of the clear division into large (about 18 × 30ft) middling (about 18 × 18ft), and small (9 × 18ft) rooms which one finds in most of his villa projects from 1542 onwards, as well as explicitly recommended in his book (II, p.4).

The effect on Palladio of his visit to Rome in 1541 must have been enormous. He implies as much himself, as Puppi has perceptively noted: 'I applied myself to the investigation of the remains of the ancient buildings . . . finding them worthy of much greater observation, than I had at first thought' (I,p. 5). In 1541 Palladio would have corrected the first impression he had probably received from Serlio's Third Book (1540; 000) as to the indifferent quality of the Baths of Diocletian. 'As for the elevation', Serlio wrote, 'I have not wanted to draw anything for three reasons: first, because of the great ruins, so that one understands little that is complete; second, because of the difficulty of measuring them; third, because this building was not made in that happy century of good architects, indeed one sees here many discordances, and clumsinesses (Serlio, 1540, p.XCVII). Projects for villas drawn up shortly after Palladio's return from Rome (321, 322, 325) are full of motifs from the Baths: their roof line (326), the serliana which Palladio at this time believed was common in the great baths complexes, and even, in one extreme case (XVI/16c), a great cross vaulted hall complete with column screens and a loggia with a radiussed rear wall. Some of these 'thermal' designs were obviously too strange and unfamiliar for Palladio's clients. But these early attempts to combine antique schemes with plans which would fulfil modern functions were of the greatest importance in Palladio's development. It is from this point on that he becomes an architect with something completely new to offer.

The Villa Valmarana at Vigardolo, of 1542 (321) is 'thermal' in its central loggia, its vaulting schemes and its roof line. But the plan follows closely that of Trissino's Villa at Cricoli (148). The large middling and small room system is clearly established, as well as a way of tucking the stairs going up to the attic and down to the cellars into a small space between the loggia at the front of the villa and the room at the back. The cross vault in the small front rooms, derived from the baths, and expressive of intersecting axes also becomes a standard element in Palladio's vocabulary from now on.

Palladio's early villa projects, influenced by the baths both in their interior planning and in their elevation are reflected in only two built works: the Villa Valmarana and the beautiful Villa Poiana (341) which constitutes a fluent reshuffling and elaboration of the elements present in the earlier villa. Comparing the three drawings for Poiana (342, 343, 344) with the building itself one can actually see this shuffling in progress, as the square and small rectangular rooms are moved from the front to the back of the villa. Palladio was already employing a system, which is entirely his own, though its points of departure are Trissino's villa at Cricoli, Trissino's ideas on proportion (149), and elements from the baths.

In the 1540s Palladio was open to other influences (cf. Barbieri, 1970). Most important was that of Raphael (Villa Madama; 000) and Giulio Romano (above all the Palazzo del Te). These buildings suggested villa façade schemes articulated with a single order, and with a centrally placed loggia: the solution adopted at Bertesina (323) and for Quinto (338), commissioned by Marc'Antonio and Adriano Thiene, whose taste for Giulio's architecture was so clearly demonstrated in their town palace (47). For the Pisani at Bagnolo he also designed a central loggia, this time with apsidal ends (an echo either of Sanmicheli's La Soranza or possibly Giulio Romano; cf. Carpeggiani, 1969). The exterior of the loggia reflects one of Sanmicheli's grand manners, and the towers (resembling Cricoli, or the magnificent late gothic Villa Porto Colleoni at Thiene) were probably introduced as a symbol of lordliness, a readily comprehensible expression of the Pisani jurisdiction over the Vicariate of Bagnolo. The idea of a semicircular loggia, based on Bramante's Belvedere hemicycle, internal column screens, and octagonal rooms, advanced in the projects for Bagnolo (329, 331, 332) were rejected either by Palladio himself or the patrons, as being too elaborate or too unfamiliar. The bold semicircular thermal window however was retained to light the central hall.

By the end of the 1540s Palladio had evolved effective and functional villa schemes based on the baths and on a clear set of room sizes. He employed vaults wherever possible, whereas the traditional Veneto villa had no vaults, only wooden ceilings; he had adopted the pediment as a way of giving a central emphasis, and of displaying the owner's arms (II, p.69); and he had consistently raised his buildings well off the ground. This gave ample space for well lit (and dry) service accommodation underneath the main living floor, and increased the impressiveness of houses which were for the most part built in the plain. There were precedents for this solution (311) but it is worth noting that even the villa at Cricoli was only very slightly raised above ground level. Alongside his more expensive projects of these years, he evolved a simpler type with arches and piers in the loggia, as in the Villa Godi (or in the Quattrocento Villa Porto Colleoni) but his usual compact planning of the interior. The Villa Saraceno (335), the Villa Caldogno (336), the Villa Arnaldi (390), belong to this group as does the Villa Zeno, which may however be later (337). The Villa Forni is only superficially similar to these early works, and I feel I should not be dated earlier than about 1560. The Villa Saraceno clearly displays Palladio's characteristic insertion of the villa block into a regular scheme of colonnaded farm buildings. This was not altogether novel, as the Villa Giustiniani (Prinz, n.d., pp.15-7) was designed as a single symmetrical complex. Palladio's inspiration for the schemes which appear in the drawings for the Villa Thiene (338) and the Villa Arnaldi, both closely related, and for the Villa Pisani (327) and for Poiana (341) was only in part contemporary practice. They also reflect his studies of ancient temples and their precincts. It is interesting that he considered the Temple of Hercules at Tivoli to be a 'palace' (165), as the temple stands in the centre of an arcaded precinct.

The 1550s saw the creation of the rest of Palladio's famous villa formulae: the porticoed temple front, and the two storey villa with superimposed logge. Although these were wholly new solutions, at most owing a little to Giuliano da Sangallo's Villa at Poggio a Caiano (designed in the later 1480s) they represented an even closer synthesis than Palladio had achieved before between traditional types and functions and his new architectural system based on the antique. The real development in Palladio's villa architecture from his return from Rome in 1541 is therefore not simply a gradual increase in the antique element in his designs, but rather a sifting out of those antique elements which were best adapted to the reformulation of traditional villa schemes.

Loggie with columns were a standard feature of both farm labourers' houses (Forster, 1974) and of Quattrocento villas. Superimposed loggie were also common in the Quattrocento, and sometimes both the upper and the lower loggia had straight entablatures, with the beams placed directly over the columns (310). The bigger Quattrocento villas were often almost indistinguishable from city houses. All these traditional features are reflected in Palladio's villa designs of the 1550s.

Palladio is, for instance, much less preoccupied with villa and palace typology than many who have written about his architecture. 'The owner's house', he writes 'should be made, having regard to his household, and his status, and one makes it as one does in the city' (II, p.46). Making it 'as one does in the city' of course includes designing in relation to site, but where a town house was not built round a courtyard, and where it had a relatively open view in front of it, its design is often almost identical to that of a villa. The Palazzo Antonini in Udine (417) is a variant of the Villa Cornaro (346). The Palazzo Porto does not have loggie towards the outside, but its plan is very similar to that of the Villa Pisani at Montagnana (345).

In the development of these new types, the Palazzo Chiericati (53) was probably of the greatest importance. Its superimposed loggie at both the front and back connect with earlier Veneto traditions and with Palladio's subsequent villa and villa/palace projects. The experiment, in the planning phase, with a huge central pediment (55) was influential, and so too was the adoption of the Portico of Octavia solution of an arch to close the ends of the loggia. The Villa Pisani at Montagnana (1552) and the Villa Cornaro at Piombino Dese (1552) followed very quickly and consolidated the advances made in the Palazzo Chiericati and in the plan of Palazzo Porto. In this development should be recalled the simple and attractive Villa Chiericati (349) designed for Giovanni, the brother of the builder of the Palazzo Chiericati (Puppi, 1973, p.296). Though the building was not finished until after Palladio's death it is his first known design for a villa façade with a single free standing portico (350). It also connects with the reconstruction of the Roman

house for Barbaro's Vitruvius (1556) which Palladio would have been considering in this period, and to which he gave a massive pedimented portico. Palladio's next, and more ambitious venture with a free standing portico, the Villa Foscari (353) possibly goes back to one of the Villa Chiericati projects in its arrangement of columns, though the drawing could be for the Villa Foscari itself (350b).

Most of Palladio's porticoes, whether of one or two storeys are flush with the façade, as in the case of the Villa Badoer, and the Villa Emo. The interior of his villas present varying combinations of his standard set of rooms. All have a loggia and a central salone, flanked left and right by sequences of rooms of three sizes. Within this scheme a basic planning problem was the placing of the stairs: 'one should be very careful in placing the stairs, because it is no small problem to find a place which is suited to them, which does not get in the way of the rest of the building. However one will principally assign them their own plane, so that they do not get in the way of the other parts, or be interfered with by them' (I, p.60). It was easy enough if the villa had only one main living floor, and so needed only small service stairs to go down to the kitchens, latrines and cellars, and up to the attic. These could be tucked between the loggia and the salone, or at the side of the central hall, into which, as the cross roads of the whole building (cf. Scamozzi, 1615, I, p.304) it was convenient that they should lead. It is thus not surprising that villas which on the outside are very different from one another have more or less identical plans (Poiana and Badoer; Pisani at Bagnolo and Zeno). Villas with two living floors, whatever truth there was in Scamozzi's remark that 'we have seen many which in the upper part are either never inhabited, or rarely' (1615, I, p.272) needed bigger stairs. At Montagnana and the Villa Cornaro Palladio placed large oval stairs at either side and thus kept the centre of the building free. In other cases he placed the stairs centrally, between the loggia and the sala at the Villa Mocenigo (391) or at the side of the sala (Cicogna).

In the later villas and villa projects the motif of curving colonnades was added to the schemes for linking the owner's house with the outbuildings. The source was almost certainly the Forum of Augustus in Rome. The long straight ranges of outbuildings on either side of the house at the pre-Palladian

Villa at Cusignana (311) points to the existence of a distinct type in use in the province of Treviso, to which Palladio conformed in both the Villa Barbaro (351) and the Villa Emo, as Sanmicheli had in part done before in his Villa Soranza.

The owner's needs imposed a certain standardisation on Palladio's projects, and probably he was often asked for a variant on an existing building. But he does not always adhere to his own types. The Villa Barbaro, perhaps because of Barbaro's own involvement, is quite different from the other villas. So is the amazing Villa Repeta (153), and the Villa Sarego (360) can only be very incompletely accounted for by reference to traditional villa types with superimposed loggie. The Villa Rotonda's familiarity offers no explanation either for its beauty or its very novel design.   H.B.

317 Villa Godi, Lonedo di Lugo, Vicenza
Photographs

During the 1530s the Vicentine noble family of Godi acquired large holdings at Lonedo, north of Vicenza, which included a foundry and peasant cottages (Zorzi, 1968, p.25). The Doric barchessa, to the left of the present-day villa, bears a date of 1533 and may have been the first stage in building a villa complex (Hoffer, 1969, pp.16–20; Puppi, 1973, pp.238–40). Shortly after the death of Enrico Godi in 1536, his son Hieronimo turned to the Pedemuro bottega and to Palladio in particular for the design of a *casa domenicale* (owner's residence); it was not, however, their first commission from the Godi. In 1531 Francesco Godi had ordered from the bottega the portal of the Servite church of Santa Maria in Vicenza, and in 1532–3 Enrico Godi entrusted to them the building of his mortuary chapel in San Michele (cf. Puppi, 1973, p.237). Most of the construction work on the Villa Godi must have been finished by 1542, the date inscribed over the portico. This is supported by a tax declaration of Hieronimo Godi from between 1541–2, which listed a residence and fourteen fields of orchard land at Lonedo with a value of 1,600 ducats (Dalla Pozza, 1943–63, p.120). Bertotti-Scamozzi also published the record of several payments to Palladio from 1540 and again from 1549–52 (1778, II, p.29n). The first of these was to 'messer Andrea architetto', a recognition of his new role and status.

With its projecting wings and recessed central block, the Villa Godi marks a juncture between the earlier villa-castello like the Cà Brusa and the Villa Porto Colleoni and the reworking of this type in Palladio's mature villas like Emo (355) and Badoer (424). Although severe in appearance, it contains elements of Palladio's study of the antique and of contemporary architecture. The simple cornice is adapted from that of the Coliseum, which at that date Palladio would have known from Serlio's Book III (1540). The serliana of the *salone* is also a contemporary motif but probably dates from around 1550, and is perhaps connected with the later payments to Palladio and the preparation for the fresco decorations by Zelotti. The hemicyclical garden and stairway to a lower level would also seem to be later additions under the influence of Roman works like Bramante's *Cortile del Belvedere* and are probably contemporary with the well which carries a date of 1555. The differences between the actual building and the plate in the *Quattro Libri* (II, p.65) may have been prompted by the desire to make an outmoded design more presentable. The fame of the building, the importance of its owners, and Palladio's attachment to his first major work would have prompted its inclusion.   B.B.

318 The kitchen of the Villa Godi
Photograph

A contemporary sink profiled like a section of an architrave is on the left, and on the right a series of oven openings. The room is vaulted, and much lower than the living rooms on the floor above: this is typical of the service floor in Palladio's villas. It is lit by windows cut in the vault.   H.B.

319 Bartolomeo Scappi, cuoco secreto di Papa Pio Quinto Opera . . .
Venice, Michiel Tramezzino (1570)
Photographs

This work by Pope Pius V's personal cook describes kitchen arrangements and recipes in considerable detail. The engravings at the end of the book give a clear picture of the layout of a large sixteenth-century kitchen.   H.B.

320 Villa Valmarana, Vigardolo di Monticello Co. Otto
Photographs

The excellent credentials of this neglected and attractive building were established in a masterly fashion by Dalla Pozza (1964–5, pp.229–38). He showed that it was begun for Giuseppe Valmarana in 1541, and that its ground plan corresponded *precisely* to an autograph Palladio drawing, R.I.B.A. (XVII/2). The villa was obviously not completed according to Palladio's intentions, and the whole coherence of the façade is lost in the artless way in which its upper part was finished. But it merits close attention as his second known villa project, and his first villa project after his return from Rome in 1541. The obvious reference in the grouping of rooms to Cricoli (Puppi, 1973, p.246) is less important than the fact that this building combined the Cricoli scheme (148) with features of the baths (cross vaults) which remained in Palladio's vocabulary to the end. The vaulting scheme shown on the drawing was in fact realised in the front half of the building, in the smaller rooms. In these, in the central serliana, and in the regular scansion of the windows down the side, Palladio's touch is already quite distinct. There is no basement service floor, probably because of the damp terrain, and the attic would probably have been used as a granary.   H.B.

321 Project for the Villa Valmarana at Vigardolo
Pen, ink and wash: 40.3 × 25.8
Lent by the Royal Institute of British Architects (XVII/2)

As Della Pozza showed (1964–5, figs.32 and 33) Palladio's plan corresponds exactly to the Villa Valmarana (320). As the villa was begun by October 1541 the drawing cannot be dated later than 1542 and not earlier than Palladio's return from Rome in 1541. The windows in fact exactly correspond to those of Palazzo Thiene (47) save that they are flanked by rusticated lateral extensions, obviously to prevent them becoming lost on the walls they occupy, as happens with the executed windows. The loggia has a cross vault, derived from the baths, but not executed (the present loggia has a beam ceiling). The façade, with its divided pediment, looks forward to the Villa Poiana (341), or even Maser (351), and like most of the later villas the main floor is raised on a high podium, which probably was intended to house the service rooms.   H.B.

322 Plan and elevation of a villa
Pen, ink and wash over incised construction lines: 39 × 24.1
Lent by the Royal Institute of British Architects (XVII/1)

The project presents a centrally planned villa, probably deriving from the Odeo Cornaro in Padua, with the square central salone lit from above by thermal windows. It is close to the project for Villa Valmarana, and must be of about the same date.   L.F.

*323 Villa Gazzotti-Marcello Bertesina (Vicenza)
Photographs

Far from being a palatial building for a nobleman, this little villa was the residence of a salt tax contractor who had invested in land to farm for profit. It has been convincingly dated c.1542 on the basis of the rise in the owner's fortunes and on stylistic grounds (Puppi, 1973, p.250). Palladio's early villa drawings have been shown by Barbieri (1970, p.63ff) to be projects for actual villas rather than theoretical exercises. In most of these projects Palladio explores a scheme which is dependent on Veneto tradition, with a squarish plan, and a central loggia leading to a centrally placed salone. In Palladio's initial proposal for Bertesina (R.I.B.A. XVII/27) this type of plan is rejected in favour of a rectangular single-storey block raised on a basement (used for the services) with a long rectangular loggia, a salone parallel to it, and a sequence of three rooms on each side. This plan resembles Giulio Romano's initial project for the Palazzo del Te in Mantua (Forster and Tuttle 1971, p.267ff). Though there is no reason to suppose that Palladio knew Giulio's *original* project for the Te, both Bertesina and the Villa Thiene at Quinto are ultimately Giuliesque in their inspiration. In another drawing (325) and in execution, the villa was reduced. The rectangular salone was substituted for a T-shaped room (later converted into a cross-shaped room (cf. Barbieri, 1970, p.70), which was a favourite motif in Palladio's designs at this period (see the Villa Pisani at Bagnolo). The three bays on each side of the loggia in the earlier project are reduced to only two bays. As the plan got smaller the ornament, and hence the cost, was reduced. The Ionic half columns shown in the first drawing became composite pilasters, and the rich and varied vaulting systems were abandoned.   L.F.

323

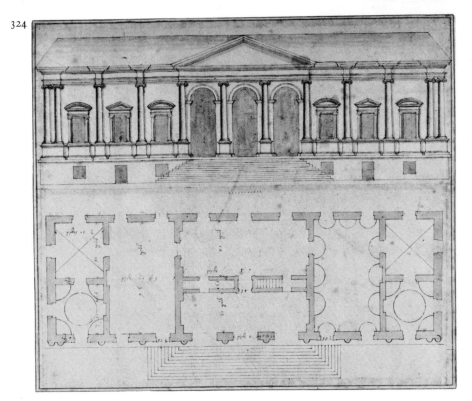

324

323

323

*324 Plan and elevation of the Villa Gazzotti-Marcello at Bertesina

Pen, ink and two brown washes over incised construction lines: 32.6 × 37.6.
Epsilon handwriting
Lent by the Royal Institute of British Architects (XVII/27)

This highly finished drawing could have been prepared for showing to the client or for publication. It is on two sheets joined horizontally in the centre, and shows an unexecuted project for the villa. Vaulting systems are marked on the plan. Palladio's vocabulary in the drawing is rich in reminiscences of his first visit to Rome in 1541. The sequence of Ionic half columns, aediculated windows with alternating segmental and triangular pediments, the basement breaking forward below the bases, and the triple arch loggia all seem to be quotations from Raphael's Villa Madama (491).   L.F.

325 Plan of villas

(a) Pen, ink and wash over incised construction lines: 10.8 × 20.8
(b) Pen, ink and wash over incised construction lines: 17.3 × 25.3
(c) Pen, ink and wash over incised construction lines: 15.1 × 23

Lent by the Royal Institute of Architects (XVI/16)

(a) This little plan is of the Villa Gazzotti, as it was executed (Barbieri, 1970, p.68). A comparison with the alternative project (324) reveals that the dimensions are here considerably reduced (the loggia from 40 to 29 *piedi*). In the larger project there was access to the three side rooms only through the salone. In this final project these rooms can be approached either from the loggia or the salone. The dimensions are very close to the executed villa, the loggia being 36 × 14 ft as opposed to the 13.4 × 36.10 ft given on Bertotti Scamozzi's plan (Zorzi, 1968, fig.92).

(b) The dimensions of this plan (90 × 60 ft) are like those of R.I.B.A. (XVI/18) and they are certainly for the same project (Zorzi, 1968, pp.48–9; Barbieri, 1970, p.68). The plan provides for four similar appartments. There is a narrow rectangular atrium, a narrow vestibule with niches, behind which are staircases, and a square salone inspired by the Baths. In each appartment there is a rectangular sala with two square rooms (camere) off it. The two smaller rooms are self contained, without doors connecting them. All of the doors are axially aligned across the building. Only the four large rooms have fireplaces, which are placed so as to give heat to the smaller rooms. The façade is pierced by evenly spaced windows and the entrance marked by a serliana like that of the villa Valmarana (320 and 321).

(c) This plan, like *b*, shows a façade with a serliana and is divided horizontally into two. The large *sale* on each side of the atrium have wide openings instead of the two small windows shown in *b*. Although this project is small (c. 50 × 75 ft) the design of the central area gives it remarkable spaciousness and monumentality. The *sale* and salone merge into a triple nave vaulted space inspired by the Baths (442). All the doors, windows, and fireplaces are on axis. In the large loggia/salone the fireplaces would have been framed scenographically by the columns.
Barbieri (1970, pp.68–9) has suggested that *b* and *c* and R.I.B.A. (XVI/18) all relate to the Villa Gazzotti at Bertesina, and this suggestion has been accepted by Puppi (1973, p.250). There is however no strong internal evidence to support this view. L.F.

326 Plan and elevation of a villa
Pen, ink and wash over brown chalk and incised construction lines: 32.3 × 23.2
Epsilon handwriting
Lent by the Royal Institute of British Architects (XVII/15)

The project is unidentified but almost certainly was for an actual building. The façades with the three gables/pediments and the serliana are direct quotations from the Baths. The doubling up of the apartments in the plan may suggest that the design was for two brothers. The vaulting systems resemble those of the larger Bertesina project (000). L.F.

*327 Villa Pisani, Bagnolo di Lonigo (Vicenza)
Photographs

The Villa Pisani at Bagnolo was among Palladio's first commissions after his trip to Rome in 1541. It was also his first commission from a Venetian noble family. Giovanni Pisani had purchased the estate and lordship of Bagnolo in the Vicentine territory from the Venetian government in 1523. The estate originally belonged to Girolamo Nogarola, one of the Terraferma nobility who had revolted against Venetian rule during the War of the League of Cambrai (1509–16) and in consequence had had his land confiscated by the Venetians (Dalla Pozza, 1964–5, pp.206–10). The purchase of an important estate in the *Vicentino* marked Giovanni Pisani as an obvious candidate for the office of Podestà of Vicenza, which he occupied in 1528 (see above). While in office, Pisani ordered his insignia from the Pedemuro bottega (Mantese, 1964, p.883, n.35).
The early contact with the Pedemuro bottega did not immediately lead to a project for replacing the palace of Girolamo Nogarola, described at its cessation to Pisani as burned. Rather, the motivation may have been the marriage of Giovanni's son Vittore around 1542 (Zorzi, 1968, p.53, no.7). Palladio names the three brothers as the patrons of the villa (II, p.47), and he probably furnished them with a design for the new fabric between 1541 and 1542 (Cevese, 1971, I, pp.100–3; Puppi, 1973, pp.254–7). The villa was finished by 1544 when a tax return of the three brothers refers to it as 'newly built' (Zorzi, 1968, p.59, no.1). The date of 1544 is also corroborated by Magrini who claimed to have seen the date, later destroyed,

327

in one of the villa's frescoes (1845, p.79).

Judging from recently discovered drawings of the villa before rebuilding (328), the Villa Pisani is approximately the same mass as its predecessor; it also retains the *castello* motif of towers. In plan, the villa shows a synthesis of traditional Veneto building practice with Palladio's studies after the antique and contemporary architecture. The salone, like the *portego* of a Venetian palace, runs the length of the house, and its cruciform shape and groin vaulting anticipate the salone of the Villa Foscari (353, also for a Venetian patron). The symmetrical disposition of small, middling, and large rooms

on either side of the salone likewise follows one of Palladio's central building tenets (II, pp.3–4). The apsidal loggia of the river is the only one of the two planned façades that was actually built. The rusticated Doric pilasters, popularized by Sanmicheli and considered by Palladio for the Basilica arcades (35) would have seemed appropriate in combination with the pediment bearing the Pisani crest and the lateral towers, for the first view of the villa from the roads and from the River Guà. The more grandiose cortile façade, illustrated in the *Quattro Libri* (II, p.47), was never built. Its combination of free-standing portico, elaborate staircase, and loggia would appear to be later than the initial project of the early 1540s, as it has more in common with façades like that of the Villa Badoer (424). Still, the woodcut of the *Quattro Libri* probably represents more than a mere up-dating of an old project, for Vasari, who received his information from Palladio in 1566, mentions the Doric cortile at Bagnolo as especially notable (1881, VII, p.528; Puppi, 1973, pp.341–2). Hence the presence of the Villa Pisani at the opening of Palladio's section on villas of Venetian *signori* may not only reflect the importance of the Pisani family in the Vicentino, but also demonstrates Palladio's continuing interest in the project during the late 1560s. B.B.

ZUAN ANTONIO LOCHA and ZUAN CARERA
328 View of the earlier villa at Bagnolo, 12 September 1558
Detail from a map, ASV, Provv. Beni Inculti, Verona, Mazzo 63

The detail shows the pre-existing structure on the site of the later Palladian Villa Pisani at Bagnolo, which belonged to the

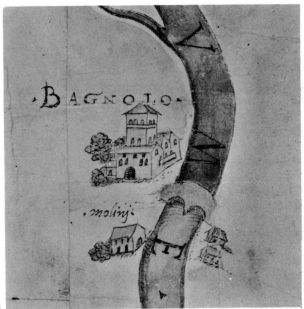

328

Nogarola family and was expropriated from them for the part they played in the wars of the League of Cambrai, the technical reasons used being the height and structure of the tower. The three-bayed building has a balcony onto the river and is crowned by a dovecote tower. Below it is a smaller building used as a mill and expressly mentioned in the deed of expropriation. M.K.

*329 Project for the Villa Pisani at Bagnolo
Pen, ink, and wash: 38 × 25.3
Lent by the Royal Institute of British Architects (XVI/7)

The plan has been generally accepted as an early design for the Villa Pisani (Puppi, 1973, p.255). It includes a design for a spacious cortile, a separate building for the kitchen and oven (marked *cusina*), and a river landing as well as an elaborate project for the villa itself. The main façade of the villa is characterized by a hemicyclical portico with concave-convex stairs, based on Bramante's hemicycle in the Belvedere of the Vatican Palace. In elevation, it would have resembled (332) below. The salone is rectangular and separated by a columnar screen from the cortile loggia, which is distinguished by cross-vaulting, a serliana, and lateral stairways. A similar loggia is indicated on a plan for Poiana (342), and in both cases the inspiration may have been the Tempietto at Clitunno. At the far end of the cortile stands a second loggia that may have been suggested by Serlio's plan for the loggia of the Villa Madama (1619, III, p.120v). It appears to have replaced the hemicycle, which would have been costly to build, as the final solution for the river façade. B.B.

330 Project for the Villa Pisani at Bagnolo
Pen and ink
Photograph of RIBA XVII/2v

The drawing represents a free-hand sketch for the Villa Pisani at Bagnolo (oral communication, H.B., modifying Burns, 1973, p.148). The triangular stairway between the portico and the salone may have been suggested by Raphael's use of the motif in the Villa Madama, or from its original source in the Pantheon. The apsidal salone with cross vaulting and three seliane echoes solutions proposed for the contemporary

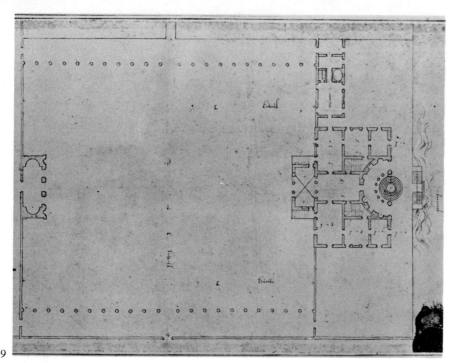

329

Palazzo Civena (45; see Zorzi, 1964, fig.148). There are
slight indications of a monumental stairway beyond the
salone as well as a double stairway on the opposite side of the
house, perhaps indicating a lower level or a river landing.   B.B.

331 Project for the Villa Pisani at Bagnolo
Pen, ink and wash, over brown chalk: 40.8 × 26.4
Lent by the Royal Institute of British Architects (XVII/18r)

Unlike the other designs connected with the Villa Pisani, the
present one has a hemicyclical façade with a single serliana
bordering the stairs, and columns flanking the niches and
windows of the façade. This last motif derives from the cortile
of the Villa Madama. The cross-shaped salone has been recast
as two spaces, one an apsidal loggia and the other square. Both
rooms are cross vaulted and share a columnar screen. Of the
sequence of lateral rooms, the central ones have been given a
traditional Venetian *volta a schiffo*. The distinctive solution for

the central salone was adopted for the corner rooms in the
barchessa illustrated in the woodcut in the *Quattro Libri*
(II, p.47).   B.B.

332 Plan and elevation of the Villa Pisani
Pen, ink, and wash: 41.7 × 27.8
Lent by the Royal Institute of British Architects (XVII/17)

Both the plan and elevation share many features with the Villa
Pisani as constructed, including the cruciform salone with cross
vaulting (here further embellished by a central panel for
frescoing), a thermal window to light the salone, compactly
designed staircases and service chambers between the salone
and the side rooms, rustication in the basement level, and
similar window mouldings on the towers. At variance with the
final design is the elaborate portico comparable to 329 above
and the matching corner rooms with four niches, probably
inspired by the sala of the *Odeo Cornaro* in Padua.   B.B.

ANDREA FISARO

333 Plan of the Pisani estate at Bagnolo, 2 August 1569
Photograph: detail

A detail of this plan was published and discussed by Dalla
Pozza (1964–5, pp.208 and 209). It was produced to show the
whole hydric system in the Bagnolo area, by Andrea Fisaro,
sotto proto all'officio sopra le Acque (Deputy Engineer to the
Water Office). It shows the layout of the very considerable
Pisani estates at Bagnolo, including the rice fields (a new type
of cultivation), one corner of which just appears in the top left
of the detail. Their walled hunting reserve (*barco*), their mills,
and farm workers' houses are also shown. The activities of the
Pisani were on a massive scale. Their tax declaration of 1564
indicates an income of 6,000 ducats from the estates, and in
1572 the Vicentine tax authorities guessed that the estate had
an income of 11,500 ducats (*ibid*, pp.205 and 208). Moreover as
feudal lords of Bagnolo the Pisani called on the men of
Bagnolo to work for them one day a week (*ibid*, p.207). There
was thus no lack of capital or labour to improve the estate, and
its buildings (334).   H.B.

**334 Doric barns at the Villa Pisani, Bagnolo di Lonigo
(Vicenza)**
Photograph

This vast colonnaded farm court, constructed between 1562
and 1569 (it is shown on the map of that year, 333), can
securely be attributed to Palladio (Dalla Pozza, 1964–5;
Cevese, 1971, I, pp.101–3; Puppi, 1973, p.341). It was
destroyed by bombing in 1945, and has been partially
reconstructed. The scale is enormous, with columns eight
metres high, and was made possible by the huge income from
farming enjoyed by the Pisani.   H.B.

*335 Villa Saraceno, Finale di Agugliaro (Vicenza)
Photographs

The date of construction for the Villa of Biagio Saraceno at
Finale has recently been brought forward to the years just
prior to 1545 (Puppi, 1973, pp.258–9). The Saraceno
patrimony at Finale was divided between the brothers Biagio
and Giacomo in 1525, and in 1540 Biagio purchased an

additional field for his own estate. By 1546 a tax return of
Biagio's lists a residence at Finale among his possessions.
Saraceno himself belonged to a distinguished Vicentine family
and lived in the Borgo di San Vito at Vicenza, the same
area in which Palladio had a house (Zorzi, 1968, p.72). His
decision to employ Andrea as the designer of his villa was part
of the Vicentine nobility's growing recognition of Palladio
as 'their' architect.

The Villa Saraceno is one of the most basic of Palladio's villa
designs, and belongs typologically and chronologically to the
early group of the Villa Marcello at Bertesina (323), the Villa
Caldogno (336), and the Villa Pisani at Bagnolo (327).
Like those villas, the main floor of the Villa Saraceno was
reserved for the patron's living quarters, while the upper and
lower storeys were destined for a granary and storage rooms
respectively. To either side of the elevated central block there
were to be identical barchesse with Doric loggias. These
lateral wings would have contained kitchens in addition to the
farm buildings. As it happened, only one small barchessa was
built to the right of the house, and the villa itself underwent
considerable modifications. Muttoni reported that the room
to the right of the portico had been given two extra windows
and was in service as the villa kitchen (1740, I, p.29). The
salone was also divided into three rooms and a small extension
was added to the rear of the house. At some point the

335

189

336

entrance staircase was destroyed and the present stairs improvised. The simple entrance arches, reminiscent of those at the Villa Godi, are not embellished by an order, but they do carry prominent keystones and a finely moulded pediment. The mouldings of the door and windows are in an antique style; the windows of the upper storey exploit the same motif used by Palladio at Caldogno and Bagnolo. B.B.

*336 The Villa Caldogno, Caldogno (Vicenza)
Photographs

The name of the owner, Angelo, son of Loscho Caldogno, appears on the façade of the villa, with the date 1570. The villa however is closely related to works of the 1540s (Villa Saraceno, Villa Arnaldi), and to the Villa Zeno, as it has an arcaded central loggia and an attic above. The plan however is simpler. A very similar scheme however is sketched on RIBA XVI/20. The central room is not vaulted, and there is not the same compact composition of rooms of different sizes. The rooms nevertheless are magnificently decorated, above all the salone with frescoes showing villa life, by Fasolo. Although Palladio's association with the building is not documented, the crisp and effective façade has on the whole been accepted as autograph (Ackerman, 1967; Cevese, 1971, I, pp.134–8;

Puppi, 1973, pp.251–61). The building is not included in the *Quattro Libri*.

Puppi, noting the substantial holdings of Michele (building commissioner at the Basilica, 1566–7) and Ludovico Caldogno in the area, tentatively suggests that the villa passed by way of inheritance or cession, from them to Angelo (*ibid*, p.260). A tax survey of 1541 (BBV, *Balanzon Thiene*, 1541) however clarifies the situation further. Angelo's father Losco had himself very extensive possessions in the area, which included, in Caldogno itself 'a proprietor's house with tiled barn and dovecote, worth 950 ducats'. A slightly later marginal note adds 'for improvements made to the above mentioned owner's house, 237 ducats'. It would not be surprising if Loscho Caldogno was in touch with Palladio in the early 1540s. Angelo his son married Anna, a niece of Hieronimo Godi (of the Villa Godi) and the Caldognos also had properties at Finale, and would thus know of the Villa Saraceno (Puppi, *ibid*). In the 1540s an existing house was probably modernised and regularised. If it was not totally rebuilt, this could account for the regular, but not thoroughly Palladian plan. About 1570 Angelo decided to reface the central portion of the façade, which till then would probably have consisted of simple brick arches, like the rear façade, or like the Villa Saraceno. The side windows (more or less identical to those of the Villa Saraceno) were left untouched. The rustication of the façade arches is only superficially close to the Bagnolo façade of the 1540s (327) and finds its closest parallel in the neat and undisturbing revision (on paper) of the cortile of the Palazzo Thiene which Palladio carried out in preparation for the *Quattro Libri* (52). H.B.

337 Villa Zeno, Donegaldi Cessalto (Treviso)
Photographs

The villa was designed for Marco Zeno a Venetian nobleman who was appointed Podestà of Vicenza in 1559. The commission most probably dates from that time (Ackerman, 1967, p.43). The project was illustrated in the *Quattro Libri* (II, p.49) but only the central block was constructed. It follows the published plan, but the façades have been severely remodelled. The triple arch loggia and the long salone is very close to the Villa Caldogno, but in elevation the treatment of the string coursing as plain bands below the arches and below the attic is very close to the Villa Saraceno (335). The salone, two stories high, and originally lit by a thermal window resembles that of the Villa Pisani at Bagnolo (327).   L.F.

338 Villa Thiene at Quinto (Vicenza)
Photographs

Palladio's description of the plate in the *Quattro Libri* (1570, II, p.64) presents his 'designs' for the continuation by Ottavio Thiene, of a villa begun by Marc'Antonio and Adriano Thiene, and dateable 1545-6 (Puppi, 1973, p.262). The executed villa seems to be part of a much less ambitious project and more or less corresponds to the apartments to the right of the inner court in the published plan. A drawing (339) discovered by John Harris (1971, p.34) is possibly related to Palladio's project and may be similar to the autograph drawing referred to by Muttoni as being in his possession when he was employed on the extension of the villa in the eighteenth century, and which he accepted as the original project, rather than the plate in the *Quattro Libri* (Puppi, 1973, pp.261–2). In contrast to the plan inspired by Palladio's reconstructions of ancient villas with a sequence of an open court, atrium and inner cortile (Palladio, 1570, II, pp.69–70), the drawing shows a simple block of symmetrically arranged apartments of five rooms on each side of a wide rectangular loggia. Attached to the block and projecting towards the river and the piazza are porticoes, and on each side of the block are very substantial farm buildings. The state of the building is recorded by Jones on his visit to Quinto on 13 August 1614, when he sketched the building in his copy of the *Quattro Libri* (204). His sketches confirm the evidence of the Worcester College drawing. Jones drew the elevation of the side towards the piazza showing the loggia and five apartments on the right (this façade was demolished by Muttoni for his extension: cf. Tait, 1970). The discrepancies between Palladio's plan and the *Quattro Libri* plate can be explained in two alternate ways: first that the *Quattro Libri* plan is an elaboration of an earlier project (Harris, 1971, p.34), the second that the Worcester College drawing is a reduction of the initial project illustrated in the *Quattro Libri* (Cevese, Burns, 1973, pp.56–7 and 150). The hypothesis seems untenable in spite of the insertion of a measurement (piedi 70) in Palladio's later (?) hand. The unusually imprecise description of the villa in the

Quattro Libri, and the close agreement between the plan and Jones' drawing leads to the conclusion that the Worcester College drawing represents Palladio's actual project for the villa. The siting of the villa behind walled enclosures with farm courts on either side is like Villa Poiana (341). The rectangular plan with a triple arch loggia, coupled Doric pilasters with niches, and a full storey and a half storey enclosed within the orders, all recall Giulio Romano's Palazzo del Te.   L.F.

339 Plan of the Villa Thiene at Quinto
Pen, ink and wash: 44.4 × 58.7
Lent by the Provost and Fellows of Worcester College, Oxford (HT 89)

The drawing is possibly not by Palladio and it could be by the same hand as the project for the Villa Poiana (342). A dimension 'p[iedi]70' is written in Palladio's hand. The plan shows the relation of the villa to its site with a symmetrical arrangement of walled enclosures. On either side of the villa are streets which cross the river. The porticoes projecting directly out of the villa are drawn in a different ink and are filled with hatching and not wash (Burns, 1973, p.149, suggested that they were additions by Jones). They are however probably part of the original project and this likelihood is reinforced by a comparison with the Villa Arnaldi project which also has projecting porticoes (390; oral communication H.B.). The five rooms on the right of the plan and the loggia were constructed following this design. This is confirmed by Inigo Jones' note in his copy of the *Quattro Libri* (204).   L.F.

340 View of the Villa Thiene at Quinto, 1610
Detail from ASV, Provv. Beni Inculti, Vicenza, Masso, 59B

This crude view, which shows the villa as a square block, is nevertheless sufficiently detailed to show that the Worcester College project for the Villa Thiene (339) closely reflects the actual situation, with large walled farm entrances on either side of the villa. A dovecote appears at the bottom of the drawing (Kubelik, 1974).   H.B.

341

*341 Villa Poiana, Poiana Maggiore (Vicenza)
Photographs

The Villa Poiana was probably designed about 1549 for
Bonifazio Poiana (Puppi, 1973, p.274). It is sited at the junction
of two roads on the plain near Montagnana. Like the Villa
Godi (317) and the Villa Thiene at Quinto (339) the villa block
had to be placed in relationship to the farm buildings. Two

drawings for the villa show proposals for relating villa and
farm buildings. R.I.B.A. XVI/3 (342) follows Crescenzio's
castle/villa scheme (343; Ackerman, 1967, p.63). The villa
block is set well back from the roads in an inner court, behind
a long rectangular porticoed service court with stables and a
barn. On each side of the block there are walled gardens. In
R.I.B.A. XVI/4 (343) the villa is brought closer to the road, so
that it is clearly visible from it. The whole site is regularised.
There is a square walled enclosure in front of the villa, on the
left a huge almost square porticoed service court, and part of
garden is shown on the right. In both these drawings the
central block is without the present wings, which were added
following a new design in 1606 (Puppi, 1973, p.275).
In plan the villa conforms to Palladio's earlier Villa Valmarana.
The rooms are raised on a high basement housing the services
and the plan has a rectangular atrium and a long barrel-vaulted
central hall. The bold façade has novel features as well as other
which were by now familiar in Palladio's architecture. It is an
obvious restatement of the Villa Valmarana façade project (32
The attic windows just below the cornice are standard
elements. The window-sills are low so that one can look out
easily, and so that the sills are on the level of the stylobate. The
striking window frames are unique. It is possible that they are
later additions, but they appear on Bertotti Scamozzi's
elevation (illustrated Zorzi, 1968, fig.127). The serliana on the
façade with oculi cut into the arch to let light into the loggia
ultimately derives from Bramante's Nymphaeum at
Gennezzano. The serliana itself is related to its earlier use at the
Villa Valmarana (30) and his employment of the motif for the
logge of the Basilica (000). The sequence of rooms, of different
heights and sizes, each with a different vaulting scheme is a
particularly attractive example of what by this time had
become Palladio's standard system for interior design. The
large rectangular room is splendidly decorated with frescoes
by India and Canera.   L.F.

PALLADIO WORKSHOP
342 Project for the Villa Poiana
Pen, ink and wash over incised construction lines: 30.2 × 40.3
Lent by the Royal Institute of Architects London (XVI/3)

The handwriting and the drawing style is not Palladio's but there is no doubt that this is a working drawing for the villa. The drawing shows two roads on two sides of the site and a river on the third side. The approaches to the villa are on the main axis through the service court or alternatively through the walled gardens from the river. Because the villa is set back from the road it is raised on a high basement. At the entrance to the site Palladio has placed a T-shaped cross-vaulted entrance gate (a feature of the castle villa, 000), with substantial attached porticoed barns. The entrance loggia projects forward and access is by stairs at the sides. In this respect it resembles the later solution to the Villa Foscari (353), but here two columns form a serliana. The sequence of rooms at the side is exactly as in the executed building (this is true also of XVI/4) though the sequence here begins at the loggia end.　L.F.

343　Project for the Villa Poiana
Pen, ink and wash over incised construction lines: 27 × 38
Lent by the Royal Institute of British Architects (XVI/4)

The site has been regularised and divided into two square or nearly square zones and the villa brought closer to the road. On the left a porticoed farmyard and on the right part of another walled area is shown, and on each side of the villa block there is a small walled cortile or garden area. The villa block, probably for reasons of economy, no longer has the projecting loggia, and the high basement has been abandoned. This was now visually less necessary because of the greater proximity of the villa to the road.　L.F.

344　Sketches of the plan and elevation of the Villa Poiana
Pen and ink: 27 × 38
Photograph (R.I.B.A. XVI/4v)

These sketches, whose clumsiness suggest a collaborator rather than Palladio himself, reflect the scheme on the recto. The plan is exactly the same, except for the partition closing off the room at the rear (a misunderstanding of the plan on the recto?) and the fudging of the serliana. The elevation agrees with the plan, and is close to the executed building. The belvedere on top of the roof (compare 332) is an odd feature, but the plan on the recto would have permitted its realisation. The elevation is probably copied after Palladio.　H.B.

345　Villa Pisani, Montagnana (Padua)
Photographs

Built just outside the medieval walled town of Montagnana for the Venetian noble Francesco Pisani and documented c.1552 (Puppi, 1973, pp.288–9), the Villa Pisani like the Villa Cornaro (346) has the character more of a palace than a villa. The rooms are arranged on two storeys and there are no farm buildings. The closed street façade with Doric and Ionic superimposed half columns, the continuous Doric entablature and the open garden logge are most closely paralleled in the Palazzo Antonini (which also was to have services in an attached wing). The villa is illustrated in the *Quattro Libri* (II, p.52), and the executed villa is very close to the illustration, though only the central block was built. The triumphal arches shown in the plate which connect the service towers to the villa could never have been realised, because they would have invaded the town's moat (Ackerman, 1967, p.58). Cevese (1973, pp.70 and 125, n.86) suggested that the villa was reorientated, and that on the basis of the *Quattro Libri* illustration one arch would then be over the road to Padua, and so on axis with the town gate, while the other arch would be over a minor road which possibly lead to farm buildings. Attractive though this suggestion is, such a project involving the invasion of a public highway would not have been practicable, but similar ideas could have been in Palladio's mind when he reconsidered the villa and its site (at the entrance of a town) when preparing the *Quattro Libri* plates. In plan the villa is the same on both floors. The atrium with four columns as in the Palazzo Porto resolves both functional and aesthetic problems. Palladio wrote of the atrium (II, p.52) 'the entrance hall has four columns, one fifth thinner than those outside, which support the pavement of the sala and make the height of the vault beautiful'. The abstract curving form of the vault, which establishes an axis at right angles to the entrance axis is particularly attractive.　L.F.

346 The Villa Cornaro, Piombino Dese (Treviso)
Photograph

The agricultural holdings of the Cornaro family at Piombino went back to 1422, and at the death of Girolamo Cornaro in 1551, the substantial estate was divided between his sons Andrea and Giorgio. Thereafter the younger son Giorgio entrusted Palladio with the design of a new palace on his portion of the patrimony. The account books for the Villa Cornaro, recently discovered, place its construction between 1552–3, in addition to recording a visit by Palladio in April 1554 to supervise work on the second storey of the house (Lewis, 1972, pp.381–3; Puppi, 1973, pp.292–5). Although habitable by 1554, the house was described as 'unfinished' in a tax declaration of 1573 (Zorzi, 1969, p.197, no.2). The villa seems to have been finished by 1613 when it was shown on a plan of the estate, now in the Museo Correr.

Comparison with a preparatory drawing (347) indicates that fundamental changes in the building's design must have taken place during 1552, before the construction began. Thus the Villa Cornaro was being conceived at the same time as the villa of Francesco Pisani at Montagnana (345; Puppi, 1973, pp.288–90). Indeed, the villas, which appear on facing pages in the *Quattro Libri* (II, pp.52, 53), have a similar central unit with lateral additions. The portico of two orders also reflects the design for the Palazzo Chiericati (53), especially in the Villa Cornaro, where the projecting portico terminates in an arch. Some of the shared elements of the Villa Cornaro and the Villa Pisani are probably related to building traditions of Venetian palaces, as, for example, the double loggie found in Gothic palaces like the Cà Foscari (400) or the use of columns in the ground floor salone to support the salone on the upper floor as in the Scuola di San Marco or the Scuola della Misericordia. The discrepancy between the rectangular windows of the *Quattro Libri* plate and the arched windows of the house as built may also indicate a concession to a Venetian preference. The treatment of the columns in the ground floor salone corresponds to the description found in the 'Aggiunta del Palladio' (205): the columns support an architrave while the roof beams constitute the frieze. The Ionic capitals, carved by the Paduan sculptor Agostino Zoppo (Rigoni, 1970, p.307, note 6), illustrate Palladio's creative use of antique precedents, for the single canted volute was suggested by the Temple of Fortuna Virilis at Rome. Palladio employed the same motif later in the Palazzo Antonini at Udine (417; Puppi, 1973, pp.306–8). B.B.

*347 Preparatory Drawing for the Villa Cornaro
Pen, ink and wash over chalk: 26 × 37.3
Lent by the Royal Institute of British Architects (XVI/5)

One preparatory drawing for the villa of Giorgio Cornaro at Piombino Dese survives and is of considerable interest for the differences shown between it and the finished building. Unlike the final plan, the present one shows a portico which is flush with the wall and not projecting; the salone does not have four columns; and the rear façade lacks a portico. Thus the plan appears to date from the end of 1551 or just before work began on the villa in 1552 (see 346). B.B.

348 Plan of a suburban palace
Pen, ink and wash over incised construction lines: 43.1 × 27.2
Lent by the Royal Institute of British Architects (XVI/15)

The large forecourt is a feature found in numbers of Vicentine palaces, for instance that of the Thiene in Contra S.Lucia (000), especially those in the Borghi, where much more space was available, though just as in this case the sites were usually rigidly limited at the sides. Palladio has taken advantage of

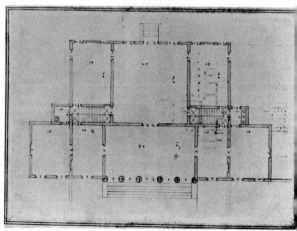

347

the large open space of the courtyard in front of the façade, and inserted a villa-like loggia. Possibly there would also have been a loggia on the floor above. Several palace façades of this sort appear in the *Quattro Libri* (II, pp.74, 76, 77). This is one of Palladio's projects which point to the lack of clear frontiers between his villa and palace types.   H.B.

*349 Villa Chiericati-Porto Vancimuglio di Grumolo delle Abbadesse (Vicenza)
Photograph

This villa was almost certainly a country retreat (without farm buildings). It was designed in 1554 for Giovanni the brother of Girolamo Chiericati, builder of the Palazzo Chiericati, and was not completed until after 1574 (it was finished by 1584). Domenico Groppino was responsible for the construction (Puppi, 1973, p.296). Palladio's design for the villa exists in the R.I.B.A. (350a). Elements in the plan reflect the plan of the Palazzo Chiericati: the arrangements of three rooms on each side of the long apsidally-ended salone (left as a square area in execution), and the free-standing loggia. The importance of the villa in the evolution of Palladio's villa designs, lies in the early use of the monumental temple front portico, which later became his classic solution for the villa façade (353 and 356). The columns on the corners of the loggia are not engaged as they are shown in the drawing (350), but free-standing. The

349

string coursing below the arch, and the key stones are similar to the Rotonda (356). The placing of the windows so near the corner of the façade, contrary to Palladio's normal theory (I, p.55) and practice, is not the result of imprecise execution, but is to be found also in the drawing.   L.F.

350 Projects for the Villa Chiericati
(a) Pen, ink and wash, over incised construction lines: 21.3 × 19.4
(b) Pen, ink and wash, over incised construction lines: 25.5 × 19.6
Lent by the Royal Institute of Architects (XVI/20)

(a) This plan of the Villa Chiericati is close to the executed building. The projecting portico has attached ¾ columns, freestanding in execution. A narrow vestibule leads into the apse ended T-shaped salone. The villa is raised on a basement with only four steps leading up to the portico.
(b) This has been generally accepted as an alternative version of the same plan. The central salone is regularised and turned into a cross with apses on one axis. The whole building is raised on a high basement with a long flight of steps leading up to the portico. The loggia is completely different from (a) and is related to Palladio's meditations for his reconstruction of the upper level of the Temple of Romulus in Rome (IV, p.89 and 194; Zorzi, 1968, pp.159–60). The lower flight of steps leads up to the level of the villa, possibly from a river. This fact, and the resemblance of the portico to that of the Villa Foscari, suggest that the project is not connected with the Villa Chiericati at all, but with the Villa Foscari.   L.F./H.B.

351 Villa Barbaro, Maser (Treviso)
Model and photographs

The Villa Barbaro extends along the line which divides the arable fields of the plain from the hilly pasture lands above (352). Beyond the pastures rise the high barren mountains. With the Villa Godi it is the only one of Palladio's villas to be built on a slope, and it takes full advantage of it. It is the most richly decorated of all his villas and the one which had the most distinguished patrons, the brothers Daniele (176) and Marc'Antonio Barbaro (178). Both were architectural experts, Daniele the author of a translation of Vitruvius for which

Palladio provided the illustrations (1556), Marc'Antonio, ultimately one of Venice's leading statesmen, whose voice was prominent in the discussion of every public building project from 1574 till his death in 1595.

The site, and the illustrious and highly cultivated patrons, who obviously played an active role in the planning of their villa, make it unique in Palladio's work. Many questions connected with it remain open. It is fairly clear however that the villa existed by 1558, probably incomplete, and that Veronese's famous fresco decoration of the interiors falls in the years 1560–2 (for a summary, Puppi, 1973, pp.314–8; Huse, 1974, is not yet available). The sketch of the villa in an early map cannot be taken as firm evidence as to the original appearance of the villa (352).

The villa has an eclectic quality which one meets with nowhere else in Palladio's work, and which certainly derives from the range of Daniele Barbaro's contacts, above all in Rome. His visit to the city in 1554, together with Palladio, is fairly clearly echoed in the design. In 1554 the Villa Giulia was the most spectacular new building in Rome: its stuccoes, its fountains, even the way in which semicircles are repeated throughout its plan is reflected at Maser (cf. Falk, 1971). Barbaro dedicated his *Vitruvius* to Cardinal Ippolito d'Este, and praises his architect Ligorio (498) in the text. There is an echo in the fountain court of the ornately antique fountains and great garden schemes which the Cardinal realised at Tivoli and on the Quirinal. The façade of the central block, with its stuccoes and broken entablature, has almost as much of Ligorio about it as of Palladio. The balustrades of the first floor balconies, which Veronese repeated in his decoration, occur nowhere else in Palladio's work and are lifted from Michelangelo's St Peters. The façade windows though effective in their context were never used elsewhere by Palladio. At the same time the long range of outbuildings on either side of the block conforms to a local tradition (311); the façade and the plan of the main block has points of contact with Palladio's design for his friend Giacomo Angaran (Puppi, 1973, pp.271–2) and the placing of the rooms in the corners of a basically cruciform plan, as well as the double flight of stairs, on either side of an opening resembles the Ragona project. Similar stairs appear in R.I.B.A. XVII/9v, one of the projects for the Palazzo Porto. The use of the Ionic columns of the 'Temple of Fortuna Virilis' (II, p.51 and IV, pp.48–51) as part of a closed wall scheme anticipates the realisation of three dimensional schemes in two dimensions on his church façades. The cruciform central hall is not so very different from that of the Villa Pisani at Bagnolo, and the slightly later Villa Foscari. The design on two levels ('the upper floor is level with the rear courtyard' Palladio explains, II, p.51) itself is related to Palladio's investigations of hillside complexes (447) and possibly also with theoretical projects by Serlio (1619, p.161). The treatment of the rusticated *barchesse* connects with the arcades of the Casa Civena (45), the Villa Arnaldi (390), and a quick scribble on one of Palladio's drawings (437). It would be exaggerated to say that Maser was not by Palladio. He publishes it as his own work, when the owners were there to contradict him. But it is clear that he was here co-ordinating ideas, and even schemes and motifs, which were extraneous to his own vocabulary, rather than mediating largely *on his own terms* between the requirements of patrons, of site, of function, and of the principles of good architecture, as normally happens even in very complex projects for demanding employers (252). Daniele Barbaro obviously suggested, even insisted upon, many elements in the design, and it is not impossible that he obtained at least suggestions from other architects (Ligorio?) which were then worked over by Palladio and incorporated into the overall design (cf. Cevese, 1973, pp.78–81). The programme and co-ordination of the interior decoration were probably completely in the hands of the patrons (Puppi, *loc. cit.*).   H.B.

352 Sketch of the Villa Barbaro, Maser, 1605–33

Photograph from ASV, Provv. sopra i beni communali, b.228, Catastico Asolo

This little sketch, a detail from a large map, is published and discussed by Kubelik (1974 and 1975). The *pascholi* (pastures) are shown rising behind the villa. The dovecotes do not correspond to those shown in the *Quattro Libri*, or to the present appearance of the building, but this difference in my view falls within the margin of error to be expected from a tiny rapid sketch, and is not to be taken as an accurate indication of the appearance of the villa in the early seventeenth century   H.B.

353

353 Villa Foscari Gambarare di Mira, Malcontenta (Venice)
Photographs

The Villa Malcontenta was commissioned by the Venetian noblemen Nicolò and Alvise Foscari, prior to the death of Nicolò in 1560. Two other factors suggest that the fabric of the villa was nearing completion at that time: one is the description of it in the manuscript draft of the *Quattro Libri*; the other is that Battista Franco began to fresco the interior before his death in 1561 (Puppi, 1973, pp.328–30).

The Foscari family wanted a *villa suburbana* on their small-holdings near Venice, a wish that is reflected in the design illustrated in the *Quattro Libri* (II, p.50), with its single domestic block and an absence of farm buildings (Puppi, 1973, II, p.329). The villa lay conveniently on the river Brenta, only a short boat ride from Venice, and like a Venetian palace, its main façade looked towards the water. The elevation is notable for the high basement – a precaution against flooding – and for the imposing portico and staircases. The solution owes something to the earlier Villa Badoer (Puppi, 1973, II, pp.308–10) though the projecting portico with lateral stairways of the Malcontenta may have been modelled after a specifc antique monument, the Temple of Clitumnus at Spoleto, which Palladio had studied (*Quattro Libri*, IV, pp.98–102). By contrast, the rear façade,

which looks southward, appears more utilitarian. The thermal window provides additional light for the vaulted salone, but also, together with the broken pediment, gives a monumental centre to this flat façade. The exterior is enlivened by vigorous rustication in shallow relief, executed in stucco on brick. B.B.

GIOVANNI ANTONIO CANAL (CANALETTO) 1679–1768
354 The Brenta at Dolo
Canvas: 63 × 97
Lent by the Visitors of the Ashmolean Museum, Oxford

This painting shows a small town on the Brenta. Palladio's patron, Leonardo Mocenigo owned properties at Dolo, and Palladio drew up projects for this site (393). In the right-hand foreground there is a dam with its sluice gates and mill wheels. The painting has been dated c.1728. The scene is engraved by G.F.Costa *Le Delicie della Brenta* and etched by Canaletto. (Constable; 1962, no.371). L.F.

355 The Villa Emo, Fanzolo (Treviso)
Model and photographs

Recent evidence indicates that the Emo family held interests in a foundry at Fanzolo from 1535 (Puppi, 1973, 352–3). The estate was inherited by Leonardo Emo as a child, and the construction of a villa probably fell between 1561–4, the years of Leonardo's early maturity. In plan and elevation, the Villa Emo reflects the completely developed language of Palladio's architecture (*Quattro Libri*, II, 55). It is a synthesis of many elements which had been explored before, notably at Badoer and Maser (351; and Puppi, 1973, II, 308–10, pp.314–8). The elevated, separate block of the villa, together with its inset portico reflect the precedent of the Villa Badoer. Similarly the long side arcades for services and agricultural uses and the terminal dovecotes follow the scheme of Maser. In its simplicity, the Villa Emo observes the basic principles of Palladio's architecture: a lucid division into subsections which complement one another and contribute to a harmonious whole; and, in the case of the side arcades, the provision of an attractive solution for a service structure. B.B.

356

*356 Villa Almerico, 'la Rotonda' (Vicenza)
Model and Photographs

Paolo Almerico's 'Rotonda' which according to Magagnò was
built 'in such a short time' (1583, p.98) is documented as
inhabited by 1569 (Puppi, 1973, p.381). According to the sources
it was built after Almerico's return from Rome (Palladio, 1570,
II, p.18; Marzari, 1591; cf. Mantese, 1964–II), where he held the
post of Referendary to Pius IV. This was a highly important

office which involved conducting enquiriesand reporting to the
Pope on petitions received by him. Puppi has found a document
of sale of what may well have been Almerico's city house in
the Contrada del Pozzo Rosso for 2,600 ducats. The sale
indicates Almerico's intention to move to a suburban house,
and so suggests a date of the design and the commencement of
building (Puppi, 1973, p.382). Palladio deliberately lists the
villa in the *Quattro Libri* at the end of his section on city houses,
and not among villas, since it is so close to the town.

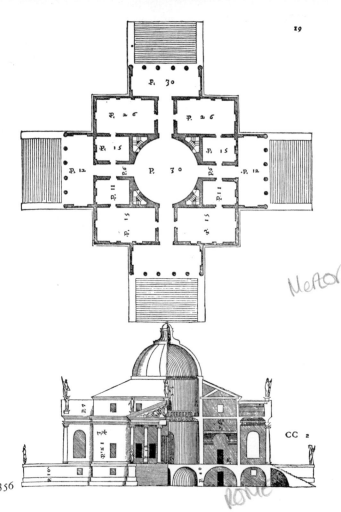

CC 2

356

356

Palladio described the site as a gently sloping hill with the Bacchiglione flowing on one side and hills on the other 'which gave the appearance of a very great theatre'. He was probably thinking specifically of the theatre at Verona, which has a similar setting. The temple at the top of the reconstruction of the theatre (208 and 434) probably suggested the domed solution he gave to the villa. He explains that he put porticoes on all three sides for the better enjoyment of the views. The plan with a circular room inside a square, and entrances on all

four sides is novel, though the round room is just another version of the usual central hall. The notion of the circular room may well derive from Francesco di Giorgio (oral communication H.B.). A similar plan is sketched on a sheet connected with the Palazzo Porto-Festa (000). Although there is no definite reason to connect this sketch with the 'Rotonda' the possibility should not be excluded. Palladio says in his text that the basement (i.e. the ground floor) was 'for the use and commodity of the household'. Above the piano nobile there was an uninterrupted loft area (which in the actual building has been subdivided: Ackerman, 1967, p.69ff).

The plate in the *Quattro Libri* and the executed building differ in one crucial respect. The *Quattro Libri* shows a high pitched roof and dome which in the actual building is low pitched and the dome is stepped. Both of these solutions are shown on the model. After Palladio's death, work continued on the Rotonda under Scamozzi (1615, I, p.266) and it is possible that he executed the low stepped outer covering, though not the vault of the central room itself (Barbieri, 1952, p.125; Ackerman. 1967, p.71; Puppi, 1973, p.383). The rich stucco and fresco decoration of the interior praised by Magagnò (1583; and Zorzi, 1968, p.134) were being executed by Agostino Rubini, Ruggero Bascapè and Domenico Fontana in 1581 (*ibid* pp.133–4). Given the expense involved in the construction of a dome like the one in the *Quattro Libri* it is unlikely to have formed part of Palladio's intention for the execution. The present lantern is not original. Inigo Jones notes that the centre of the dome of the Rotonda was open and covered only with a net (Jones, 1970, II, p.19).

In execution the Rotonda is modest. It is relatively small and built almost entirely of brick and stucco. Only the key decorative elements are carved in stone. The corners of the entablatures are of stone to achieve the greatest clarity of profile, but the rest of the entablatures are executed in brick and stucco. In spite of the modesty of scale and materials, its elegance gave it a high value in the sixteenth century (though it also had an attached estate worth 7000 ducats p.a.) and it was sold for the very large sum of 18,500 ducats in 1591 (Marzari, 1591, p.203; Monza, 1888, p.35). It has inspired many, often expensive, and grandiose imitations.   L.F.

*357 Sketch of a square castle-villa
(A suggestion for the Rocca Pisana?)
Photograph from R.I.B.A. XVII/9v

This small sketch on a sheet otherwise given over to projects for the Palazzo da Porto Festa (000) seems to have been passed

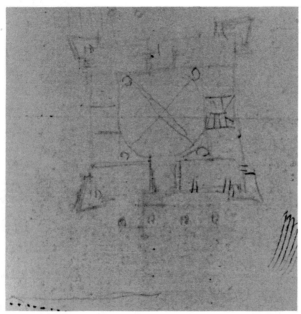

357

over without comment (Burns, 1973, p.136). It is, however, of great interest, above all as there is no reason to date it later than the rest of the sheet (i.e. c.1548/9). The building is square and has angle bastions. There are free standing porticoes on two sides, with steps leading up to them. In each corner, like the Rotonda, there is an apartment which consists of one large and one smaller room. Two alternatives for the central hall are superimposed: one with columns in the corner, carrying a cross vault; the other with a dome over a circular room, like the Rotonda. The villa-castle type is not employed, to my knowledge, at this time in the Veneto, though it is not inconceivable that Palladio could be thinking of a residence within a fortress, like the much later Villa Belvedere in Florence. He would probably know the type, which appears several times in Peruzzi's drawings, through Serlio, or through his visits to Rome. The sketch is important in that it probably advances by a few years Palladio's invention of the porticoed villa and by many years the basic idea of the Rotonda. The suggestion that this was an early idea for a Pisani villa on the hill called the Rocca (castle) outside Lonigo is made below (358). An early design for a centralised villa (R.I.B.A. XVI/19b) derived from the Odeo Cornaro, anticipates the basic scheme and room arrangement of both this project, and the Rotonda. H.B.

VINCENZO SCAMOZZI 1552–1616

358 Plan, section, and elevation of the Rocca Pisana
Pen, ink and wash: 28.5 × 38.8
Lent by the Trustees of the Chatsworth Settlement

This drawing is almost certainly a preliminary study not for the villa itself, but for the plate of it in Scamozzi's treatise (1615, I, 273). The published plate is rather more detailed than the drawing, and does not show the section.

The Rocca Pisana stands on a hill overlooking Lonigo, and it is only a short distance from the Pisani estate at Bagnolo (327), from which it is visible. It was designed by Scamozzi in 1576 (*ibid*, p.272) for Vettor Pisani, one of the three brothers who jointly owned the Bagnolo estate, 'so that he could have a place near Lonigo to enjoy more healthy air; it is placed on top of a hill called the Rocca (the castle)'.

This health and pleasure villa is the earliest and probably the most beautiful of all the villas inspired by the Rotonda.

Scamozzi probably chose it as a model because of the similarity of the two sites, though in fact that of the Rocca is finer, as the hill is prominent and enjoys splendid views. One cannot help speculating that Vettor Pisani and Palladio had considered building on this hill years, even decades before, and that the Rotonda-like sketch by Palladio of about 1549 (000) in fact was an early, unrealised response to this marvellous site. This hypothesis would explain the bastions ,as a mere conceit, probably only projecting as low terraces at the corners, called forth by the name of the hill itself.

It is not surprising that in 1576 Vettor Pisani, alarmed by the plague, should set underway the construction of a really healthy retreat, a veritable castle against infection. (It would be interesting to know how quickly the building went up: Vettor Pisani had the resources to put it up very rapidly indeed). The fact that he did not call upon Palladio cannot be taken as a slight: the long trusted architect of the Pisani was now deeply committed to major projects in Venice, while the brilliant and cultured young Vicentine would have been able to give the project much more personal attention.

Scamozzi obviously set out to improve on the Rotonda, and though his building, a variation on an already established theme, is not on the same level of achievement as Palladio's audacious and innovatory work, there can be little doubt that he here created the most beautiful of all the Veneto villas. The entrances to the central room are wider than in the Rotonda, no longer mere corridors, and the main loggia is brought into a palpable relationship with the central area. The small loggie on the other three sides furnish views, and bring light and cooling breezes into the centre. This, because of its deep corner niches seems much more spacious than the round room of the Rotonda; it is much more of an entity in itself, less of a cross-roads. Its detail, the oval windows, the bold imposts of the vault ribs are magnificently surprising, bold and effective.

H.B.

ANTONIO VISENTINI 1688–1782 and FRANCESCO ZUCCARELLI 1702–88

359 Mereworth
Canvas: 83.8 × 131.1 signed and dated 1746 on the left
Lent by Her Majesty The Queen

One of a series of eleven overdoors commissioned by Consul Smith, showing the classics of English architecture. The architecture is based on Colen Campbell's plate in *Vitruvius Britannicus* (1717–25) of his own design for Mereworth. He follows Palladio's Villa Rotonda (356) in the symmetrical arrangement of the four temple fronts. However the modest elegance of Palladio's villa becomes richer and more grandiose. The dome (except for its lantern) is based on that shown in the *Quattro Libri*. Palladio's strict symmetry in the plan has been abandoned in favour of an axial emphasis, and he gives the villa only two entrances, on the main façade and on the garden façade. Instead of the suites of two rooms in each corner, Campbell designed one long room behind the full length of the garden façade (Levey, 1964, no.675). L.F.

*360 Villa Sarego S.Sofia di Pedemonte (Verona), c.1569
Model and photographs

This unfinished villa was designed for Marc'Antonio Sarego, who was the brother of Annibale Sarego, and brother-in-law of Giovanni Battista della Torre, both patrons of Palladio. It is probably the last villa designed by Palladio, and in the absence of direct documentation has been plausibly dated c.1569 (Puppi, 1973, pp.391–3). The site described by Palladio in the *Quattro Libri* (1570, III, p.66), between two valleys surrounded by hills and springs, was well known in Roman times, and there were beautiful gardens and fountains there. The Sarego family had owned the site since 1313, they had laid out the gardens and constructed the fountains (the last one was constructed in 1555) suggesting that there was already a villa on the site.

The villa described by Palladio remained substantially incomplete and there are inconsistencies in Palladio's description, and the plate in the *Quattro Libri* (1570). Palladio writes that the villa block was to occupy two storeys arranged round a cortile. On the narrow sides there were two salone on the first floor which projected out over the loggie of the cortile. Attached to the villa were two wings containing stables and services, which formed an open courtyard leading to the inner court. The description makes no mention of the colonnaded exedra, and the plate shows one side of the cortile without apartments as a simple colonnade. The villa was extensively restored in 1857, and a reconstruction of its appearance before the restoration depends on the observations of Muttoni, (1740,

360

p.19 and plates): and Bertotti Scamozzi (1781, p.41). It appears that only the left half of the villa was built, though until the nineteenth century bases and shafts are recorded on the south side. Of the executed part only the main block had rooms. The rooms were fitted arbitrarily between the columns in the restoration of 1857 (Puppi, 1973, p.393).

The sequence of open and closed courtyards derives like the Villa Thiene at Quinto from the Roman villa plan in the *Quattro Libri* (1570, II, pp.69–70) and probably in view of the Roman origins of the site, mentioned by Palladio, the adoption of this type of villa is a reference to the history of the site. But here the scheme of the Villa Thiene at Quinto is developed by the insertion of the piano nobile between the giant rusticated columns (at Quinto the upper storey was reserved for services). The rusticated columns, made out of

great cheese-like blocks recall Sanmicheli's Porta Palio in Verona, and they could be a reminiscence of Palladio's visit to Ostia in 1547. He describes them as appropriate for the villa, 'which should have bold and simple things, rather than delicate ones.' L.F.

361 Villa Forni-Cerato Montecchio Precalcino (Vicenza)
Photographs

The attribution of this tiny (only about 45 × 33 ft) and very beautiful villa to Palladio was first made by Muttoni (1740; 362), and has been accepted by most Palladio scholars. Recently Puppi enthusiastically endorsed the attribution and dated it on stylistic grounds to 1541–2 (1973, pp.247–88). Such an early date would however exclude the possibility that the villa was built for Girolamo Forni (5) as Zorzi suggested (1966–II). Forni owned it; no documents refer to the villa before Forni's will of 1610. Zorzi attributed the villa to Vittoria.

In plan the villa is simple, and traditional. It has two floors, a projecting loggia, a long salone running almost the full length of the villa with two rooms on either side, and a staircase on the right. Two small rectangular spaces by the staircase are probably the guardaroba (Zorzi, 1968, fig.426).

Puppi relates the façade of the projecting loggia and the use of the serliana to the Villa Godi (317) and the Villa Valmarana (320) and dates the villa 1542. But several elements would suggest a later date, probably in the sixties. The loggia motif can be read as a simplified version of the Casa Cogollo façade, or another version of the motif on the side arcades of the Villa Barbaro, rather than a motif typical of the 1540s (cf. 437). Window-sills in the form of recessed panels are frequently used in the 1560s (i.e. in Palazzo Valmarana cortile façade or under the exterior windows of the refectory of San Giorgio). The placing of the attic windows immediately below the cornice was probably in part to give the maximum field for fresco decoration. Zorzi plausibly suggested that in 1576–7 Girolamo Forni commissioned the sculptural decoration from his friend Alessandro Vittoria who had moved to Vicenza to escape from the plague in Venice. The decoration consisted of reliefs of the four seasons (now replaced by modern copies), to fill the rectangular panels, and winged victories holding the coat of arms to fill the pediment, as well as the beautiful Medusa's head on the key stone which is original. Nothing indicates that the façade was altered for the insertion of the sculpture. The one-off quality of this façade and its ample provision for painting and sculpture does indicate that it was a special commission and most probably the house of an artist. A commission from Forni, a dilettante painter, and its stylistic affinities point to a date in the 60s or even the 70s. L.F., H.B.

FRANCESCO MUTTONI Active 1704–60
362 Plan and elevation of the Villa Forni
Pen, ink, and wash: 45.2 × 29.2
Signed: Franc(esco) Muttoni Architetto
Lent by the Trustees of the Chatsworth Settlement

Muttoni provides a scale in both English and Vicentine feet, and the drawing carries the inscription 'Palazetto di Paladio in Montechio Precalzino, del R(everen)do D(omin)o Girolamo Cerato'. The building is rendered less precisely than in Bertotti-Scamozzi's plates, and in both plan and elevation there is an attempt to simplify and 'improve'. The stairs, for instance, are made much larger than in the actual building. H.B.

LUDOVICO TOEPUT called IL POZZOSERRATO c.1550–1604/5
363 Music in a villa garden
Canvas: 171.5 × 129.5
Lent by the Museo Civico, Treviso

This very attractive painting is unanimously attributed to Pozzoserrato (Menegazzi, 1963, p.261). The musicians are almost certainly not professionals but are indulging in a cultivated, upper class recreation. There is a similar group included in the scenes of villa life by Fasolo in the *salone* of the Villa Caldogno. The garden is of the most elaborate type, with statues and tabernacles, a secular and pleasurable version of the elaborate north Italian Sacro Monte complexes (Stefani, 1974 and 1975). A near equivalent are the surviving gardens of the Villa Brenzone at San Vigilio del Garda (Puppi, 1974, fig.4 and p.93). Palladio's references to gardens in his book are not very explicit (Zorzi, 1968, pp.161–3), but he says that 'gardens and orchards . . . are the soul and recration of the villa' (Puppi, *ibid*, p.99). H.B.

ADRIANO WILLAERT
364 Musica Nova
A.Gardano: Venetia 1559
Lent by the British Library Board (K.3.m.14 (5) & (7))

These two music books (cantus and Altus) dedicated to Alfonso D'Este contain mottets, dialogues and four, five and six part madrigals composed by Adriano Willaert. Willaert (born in Bruges) became choir master at St Mark's in Venice in 1527 where he remained until his death in 1562. He was one of the most distinguished composers of his time, Cosimo Bartoli (1567), who met him at St Mark's, pays tribute to him as 'one whose compositions are highly praised'.

Skills in music were developed by Italian nobles especially ladies who are often painted with musical instruments (5). The performance of this type of music is often represented in painting (363), and in the portrait of the Valmarana family the elder children hold their madrigal books (6).   L.F.

365   Reconstruction of the Temple of the Sun, Rome
Pen, ink, and wash: 29.1 × 43.8
Epsilon handwriting
Lent by the Royal Institute of British Architects (X/17)

Palladio writes on this drawing, 'I believe that these were gardens in ancient times. They are next to the Arco di Portogallo, next to the Strada Flaminia in Rome'. So little has been uncovered in modern times of this complex that it has not been possible to check the accuracy of Palladio's plan (Crema, 1959, p.521). The round temple in the middle of a rectangular area was a potential model for garden schemes of his own. H.B.

366   Conjectural reconstruction of the Temple of Vesta(?)
Pen and ink: 41.9 × 27.9
Lent by the Royal Institute of British Architects London (XVII/18v)

The round form, and the flame on the central altar suggest that this is a theoretical reconstruction of the temple of Vesta, rather than the rendering of any actual building. The trimming of the sheet at the top has probably resulted in the loss of a dome. Alternatives are shown for the level above the main cornice (that with the balustrades resembles Bramante's tempietto, 162). The reliefs are based on an antique type (457) which Palladio employs elsewhere in his drawings (403). The door which narrows towards the top, on the model of the 'Temple of Vesta' at Tivoli recalls those of the rear loggie of the Palazzo Chiericati (Puppi, 1973, fig.306).   H.B.

367   Project for a monumental garden
Pen, ink, and wash: 30.7 × 42
Lent by the Royal Institute of British Architects (VIII/13)
(a) R.I.B.A. VIII/13

Zorzi associated this sheet with Palladio's visit to Turin in 1566, as well as R.I.B.A. XVI/19b, a plan (in fact certainly of the 1540s) for a centralised villa (Zorzi, 1968, pp.210–3). The suggestion is interesting, but by no means demonstrated (Puppi, 1973, pp.379–80). The drawing, however, does

document some of Palladio's thinking on garden design. The avenues are lined by trees, and there is a theatrical prospect towards the round 'temple'. The existence of a *tempietto* in the middle of the Valmarana garden as early as 1580 (it is shown in the view of Vicenza of that year) strongly suggests that Palladio might have had a hand in its design. Other plans of the garden, also showing this element, survive in Vicenza (BBV, Mappe, 164 and 697). Palladio clearly associated *tempietti* with gardens (365).   H.B.

MARC'ANTONIO PALLADIO, nephew of Palladio
368   Rustic portal
Pen, ink and wash over lead underdrawing: 45 × 30.7
Lent by the Royal Institute of British Architects

The drawing style and handwriting is that of Palladio's nephew (cf. 34). The ornament on top of the wall may indicate that the drawing is for the entrance gate of the Villa Badoer. On the right of the sheet is drawn the profile of the entablature.   L.F.

PALLADIO'S ARCHITECTURAL SYSTEM

The previous five sections have been concerned with establishing some of the outlines of the world in which Palladio worked. *Vicenza* explored the way in which architecture was used by the members of the local establishment to express their individual and collective prestige and standing. It was shown how the culture of certain leading Vicentines, as well as their wealth and needs, provided the broad guidelines within which Palladio worked until he began receiving important commissions in Venice from the late 1550s onwards.

The *Interior* dealt with further aspects of prestige, and it also touched on some of the functions which Palladio had to provide for in his villa and palace designs. *Palladio* presented Palladio's life and development in terms of his contacts, his personal social and economic situation, his studies, and the praise which he received, culminating in Vasari's eulogistic *life* of 1568. *Venice* sketched some of the features of a much wider field for Palladio's activity than Vicenza could offer. It underlined his rejection of the more superficially obvious of Venetian architectural formulae, both the old ones and Sansovino's brilliant adaptation of up-to-date Central Italian architecture to the Venetian context. It also reveals his range and stature as an architect, capable of providing new and satisfying solutions to very complex and individual problems.

Villas is dominated by the question of Palladio's treatment of traditional types and functions. It also established the great extent to which Palladio employed an architectural system, a whole procedure of design, and a whole range of possible solutions which clarified the options and facilitated the achievement of a satisfactory final design. It is with the question of system in Palladio's architecture with which the present section is concerned. An attempt will be made to define his standard procedures and his standard solutions, to suggest how he arrived at them, and how often he departed from them.

The central questions have been discussed before, above all, in the illuminating books of Wittkower (1952), Ackerman (1966), Forssman (1965), as well as in studies of particular aspects of Palladio's architecture (Puppi, 1972; Gioseffi, 1972 and 1973; Prinz, 1969; Forssman, 1969; Cevese, 1968–9; Wilinski, 1969; and many others). What will be offered here will be something between an analysis of Palladio's architecture and a patchy manual of it. The most complete manual on the subject is, of course, Palladio's own *Quattro Libri*.

There is no doubt that Palladio is the most systematic and system conscious of the great Renaissance architects. Brunelleschi, Alberti, Bramante, Raphael, and Michelangelo worked on fewer buildings than Palladio did. The greater part of their commissions, because of the nature of the commission itself (the Florentine cupola, St Peter's, the Villa Madama, the Campidoglio, etc.) or the way they approached it (there was nothing new about medium-sized palaces, only about what Bramante made if one, 407), were exceptional, without precedent, totally one-off. Alberti developed a coherent architectural theory, which Palladio relied upon heavily, but never a coherent body of realised designs. Bramante and Raphael invented a new architectural style and established the ancient orders as a systematically articulated and visually expressive language, but they never devised a whole range of standard solutions. Even Palladio's contemporaries – Giulio Romano, Sangallo, Sanmicheli, Sansovino, Ligorio, Alessi, Vignola – were less systematic than Palladio. This is not only a matter of the commisions which they received. Their training and background differed greatly from Palladio's. With the exception of Sanmicheli (who however became entirely assimilated into the Roman artistic world) these are all artist-architects, certainly concerned with structural soundness, and the correct use of the orders, but not greatly influenced by specifically local needs or traditions (Rome was a rootless new town compared with Florence or the Veneto cities) and preoccupied more with maintaining a high level of artistic *performance* rather than with consistency in the types of solutions employed. At the same time only Ligorio (and his aim was not the establishment of a system) really called into question Bramante's reading of the antique, which saw it above all in terms of wall architecture, articulated with pilasters and niches, not columns.

Every element in Palladio's background, however, contributed to make him a system-conscious architect. Venetian architecture, because of the particular environmental conditions of the city, consisted of a series of distinctive formulae. It was also, as one can see merely by travelling the length of the Grand Canal, an architecture in which standard units (columns, window frames, etc.) were repeated again and again. This was a matter of obvious convenience, when stone had to be ordered from quarries a sea voyage away in Istria. Palladio's initial training as a craftsman habituated him to standard procedures, and rules of thumb, some of which he repeats in the *Quattro Libri*. Trissino and Barbaro, and other Padua educated noble friends and patrons with their Aristotelian habits of mind, reinforced on a higher intellectual level, Palladio's tendency to think in terms of rules and categories. He came relatively late to the systematic study of Vitruvius and the antique. This in part gave him a freshness of viewpoint, and a certain critical detachment, but he also came looking for norms and rules. The problems of designing villas and palaces in the Veneto were also more uniform, because of physical conditions, building materials, and the patrons' needs and expectations, than they were further south.

Much of the interest of Palladio's architecture lies in the interaction of the systematic and standardised on the one hand, and the novel and individual on the other. A systematic approach to architectural design is not a virtue in itself, but circumstances can make it so. Where similar problems recur, and where budgets and available materials are fairly uniform and predictable, there is an obvious advantage (and not only in terms of economy of effort) in seeking to develop a really satisfactory solution, which can be adapted to particular circumstances. Palladio provides the classic example of how an architectural system, providing for demanding functional, structural and aesthetic requirements, can be developed, in theory and practice, without being over rigid, or resulting in too uniform or boring buildings. He also shows how a basic adherence to method and system need not impede, and can facilitate the creation of totally new solutions, whether for small scale works, like the Villa Forni (360) or for monumental structures, like the Logge of the Basilica (30). H.B.

Nature

'Nature, mother and mistress of all good things', as Palladio writes (Zorzi, 1966, p.109), provided his ultimate authority in matters of design, more fundamental even than Vitruvius or the architectural works of the ancients. 'As Architecture, like all the other arts, is the imitator of Nature . . . hence we see that those ancient architects who began to construct buildings, which formerly had been made of stone, established that the columns at their top should be less thick than at their foot, taking the example of trees, which are all thinner at the top than in the trunk, or next to the roots' (I, p.51). The analogy of trees appears several times in Palladio's writings and reports. Thus he cites it in support of the need to diminish the size of columns on successive storeys (205) and in his criticisms of the Ducal Palace, whose upper wall was thicker than the columns which carried it (279; Zorzi, 1964, p.109).

Palladio's appeal to nature involves several aspects of design: structure, function, and appearance. The aesthetic factor is necessarily involved because if a supporting element is seen to be slighter than what it supports, this is unnatural, dangerous, and unacceptable, and as the rejection of it is total, it also automatically comes to be seen as ugly. Palladio also incorporated into his appeal to nature the historical explanation of the classical system of architecture, as given by Vitruvius. Triglyphs thus represent the uses of beams (I, p.51), and actual beams are the equivalent of the frieze (205). The massive and impressive blocks which project to support the balconies of the Capitaniato (38) or the walkways outside the first-floor windows of the Palazzo Valmarana (418) are the equivalent of projecting beam ends and were thus justifiable and satisfactory forms for Palladio, to whom beam construction was a matter of everyday experience. Palladio was against 'that manner of building, which departing from that which Nature teaches us about things, and from that simplicity which one discerns in those things created by her, almost creates another Nature and departs from the true, good, and beautiful way of building' (*ibid*). Hence brackets should not be used to support weights in the place of columns (cf. Zorzi, 1966, p.108 and fig.117: Palladio welcomes the change from cornices carried on brackets, to cornices supported by pilasters).

The reference to Nature also extended to planning: 'but if Blessed God has designed the parts of our body, so that the more beautiful should be in places which are exposed to sight and the less decent in hidden places' so the nobler parts of the building should be made as visible as possible while service areas should be hidden away in the basement (II, p.3).

Generally Palladio's adherence to Nature does make his buildings more satisfying. It seems right and agreeable that bases should look as if they are compressed by the weight of the columns. Symmetry left and right of the main axis, or the tri-partite division of his façades, is satisfying because it connects with other experiences. The fact that he narrowed not only columns, but also pilasters with a gentle curve towards the top, gives a lack of hardness and predictability to his two great church interiors, and does convey a feeling of growth, energy, and a living character, which springs directly from Palladio's own association of columns with trees (205). It should be added, however, that Palladio does use the appeal to Nature as an argument on which to fall back and that the Palazzo Ducale has greater visual merits than his project for rebuilding it. And many of Palladio's most effective inventions (including his church façades and the Capitaniato) are successful precisely because of the way in which they flout the normal 'natural' conventions. H.B.

369 Base of the Loggia del Capitaniato, Vicenza
Photograph

These magnificent bases illustrate Palladio's dictum that 'it is very appropriate that those things, on top of which a great weight is placed, are compressed; (the Ancients) placed bases under the columns, which with their rounded mouldings and hollows appear to be compressed because of the superimposed weight', Palladio, with his word 'appear', makes explicit the pseudo-structural logic which informs much of Renaissance architecture, both in the breach (including the way in which in the Capitaniato the window frames cut into the architrave) and in the observance. In these large scale bases, which can be seen from close to, Palladio increased the number of elements, on the model of the Forum of Nerva (IV, pp.28 and 29) and, even more closely, of the Maison Carrée at Nîmes (IV, p.115). It is

interesting that the former base was also Raphael's model for the pilaster bases of the lower order of the street façade of the Chigi stables (Frommel, 1973, III, pl.70a). H.B.

*370 Palladio's formula for obtaining the curvature on columns
Photograph from the *Quattro Libri*, 1570, I, p.15

Palladio follows Vitruvius in saying that the taller a column is, the less it should narrow towards the top, as the increase in height will itself give the impression that it narrows. As for what he calls the 'swelling in the middle of the column' (rather than the Greek term *entasis*, true to his promise to use terms in everyday use, I, p.6), he provides a simple rule for achieving it. He says the column height is to be divided into three parts, the bottom third is to be plumb, but a flexible rule should be placed against the shaft, so that the lower third is against the vertical portion. The upper part of the rule is then to be moved to point C, the top of the column shaft, immediately below its 'collar'. The resulting curvature will be the outline of the column. The formula can be seen employed, both in Palladio's buildings and in his drawings, where the break between the vertical bottom third of the column and the upper two thirds is often clearly discernible. Palladio concludes, with characteristic finesse, 'I am . . . further confirmed in this invention of mine since it so much pleased Messer Pietro Cattaneo, to whom I had described it, that he put it in a work of his on architecture . . .' H.B.

*371 Side Chapel of the Church of the Redentore, Venice
Photograph

The curving profile of both the columns and the pilasters can be seen. These last, in fact, curve in two planes. Palladio certainly took the idea of giving a curve to a pilaster from Sanmicheli (34), and it appears in the portal of Palazzo Conti in Vicenza, which was probably designed by Sanmicheli in the 1530s (Cevese, 1956, p.151; Puppi, 1973, p.237). H.B.

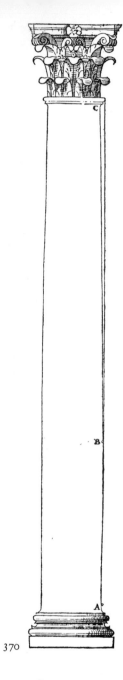

370

371

208

Building materials and structural solutions

Palladio, like Vitruvius and like other Renaissance writers on architecture, begins his book by considering building materials. He briefly discusses the best times to cut wood and quarry stone and what stones are best for carving (I, pp.6–8), and he repeats the prudent commonplace that the building materials needed should be acquired in good time (cf. Burns, 1975, p.155, n.33).

Palladio declared in 1567 that 'buildings are esteemed more for their form than for their materials' (Zorzi, 1966, p.89). He was, however, very conscious of quality and finish and always displays a firm sense, doubtless acquired during his training and early practice as a stone mason, of the building as a made thing. He notes with admiration that the ancient Romans used 'so much diligence in joining together the blocks that in many places one can scarcely make out the joins' (I, p.14), and of his own Basilica (30) he writes proudly, 'it is all of the hardest living stone, and all the blocks are joined and bound together with the utmost diligence' (III, p.42). The stones available to him were, in Vicenza, the white, resistant 'hard stone' out of which the Basilica and the stone parts of most of his Vicentine buildings were built, and the 'tender stone', usually yellowish, very easy to cut, excellent in interiors (13), but friable if exposed to the elements. Vicenza was fortunate in having good sources of stone near the city, which was brought into town on 'mad waggons', specially large waggons adapted to the transport of the blocks (Rodolico, 1953; Dalla Pozza, 1943, pp.124–5). Waggons of this sort were still in use in the early 1950s. In Venice, when Palladio used stone, it was the white, hard-wearing Istrian stone. His basic building material was brick, and he regarded it not as a second best, but as having distinct merits of its own, which were demonstrated by its extensive employment by the ancients. It was strong, durable, resisted fire better than stone and could be harmonized with stone by the simple device of covering it with stucco (Zorzi, 1966, p.89).

Palladio notes in the same passage that it had been used in St Peter's, in the cathedral and Santa Barbara in Mantua, in San Benedetto Po, 'and now in Venice, San Giorgio Maggiore is being built of brick too, which building I direct, and hope to achieve some honour by it'. For the cathedral in Brescia he recommends stone for the piers in the interior 'as high as the hand can reach', and the rest brick, except the cornice (*ibid*). This is the solution of San Giorgio and the Redentore as well as of the façade of Palazzo Barbaran. Even free-standing columns in Palladio's buildings are usually of brick, built out of bricks shaped like slices of cake (375).

The other basic material in Palladio's buildings is wood. Great wooden beams made possible the straight entablatures of his villas (378), and in his sketch for the Villa Arnaldi he even indicates in his drawing that the architrave is to be of wood (390). Some of his visually most audacious solutions derive from the structural use of wood (379), though in this he is merely following Venetian and Veneto traditions.(309). When possible, Palladio employed vaulted ceilings, which diminish the fire risk. But in other important works (Villa Godi, 317; Palazzo Valmarana, 418) the ceilings are of beams, which firmly and flexibly bind the outside walls together. The roof structures of his buildings, of course, are of wood too (341). For roofing Palladio in general used tiles (372), but he proposed lead for important public works (Zorzi, 1966, p.89; I, p.9). For floors Palladio favours Venetian terrazzo work (I, p.53; cf. Fasolo, 1938, p.260) and also tile floors (373). For large churches he recommends 'squares of white and red stone, as one sees used in all churches of some importance, and they succeed very well' (Zorzi, 1966, p.89). H.B.

*372 The Units of measurement of Vicenza, 1583
Photograph of the panel under the loggia of San Vincenzo, Vicenza

The tall slab of red Veronese marble is inscribed MISURE DELLA M(AGNIFICA) COMMUNITA and dated 1583. It shows the standard size for bricks (30.2 × 15.5 cms), the braccia for cloth (69.1 cms) and for silk (63.7 cms), and, at the bottom, the Vicentine foot (35.4 cms here; cf.76) and the standard size for roof tiles. It was common in Italian cities for measurements to be displayed in this way, in or near the central square, where measures being used by traders could be checked against them. H.B.

*373 Floor treatments in the Villa Foscari
Photograph

Palladio writes that 'floors of tiles, as the tiles can be made of
different shapes and of different colours because of the different
clays, are very beautiful and pleasing to the eye because of the
variety of colours' (I, p.53). Different patterns of tiles are here
contrasted; there is a pattern in tiles of different colours in the
salone of the Palazzo Valmarana (418). H.B.

374 Sixteenth-century bricks from the Palazzo Chiericati
Lent by the Museo Civico, Vicenza

**375 Wedge-shaped bricks for the construction of column
shafts**
Lent by the Museo Civico, Vicenza

*376 The loggia of the Palazzo Valmarana during restoration
Photograph

The sala is immediately above the loggia, and both have beam
ceilings. The massive beams are set into the walls at either side
and roughly correspond to Palladio's prescriptions: 'these
beams should be one and a half beams' width distant from one
another, because in this way ceilings turn out beautiful to the
eye, and there remains sufficient wall between the heads of the
beams as to be capable of supporting what is above: but if they
should be made more distant, they will not look well, and, if

372

373

210

376

377

378

less far apart, it will almost divide the wall above from that below, so that if they rot or burn, the wall above will necessarily collapse' (I, p.53).   H.B.

*377 The second floor corridor in the Monastery of the Carità, Venice
Photograph

This shows the structure of the ceiling of the upper corridor of the Carità exposed during the restoration of 1970. The vault is not formed of brick, but of a series of wooden arches to which cane is attached to serve as a foundation for the plaster.   H.B.

*378 The portico of the Villa Badoer
Photograph

The columns, whose shafts are of brick, support a beam architrave, and the ceiling of the portico is a coffered wooden structure, whose central panel emphasizes the axis of the entrance.   H.B.

*379 Project for a waterside palace
Pen, ink, and wash: 44.7 × 58.2
Photograph from the drawing in the Museo Civico, Vicenza (D.27)

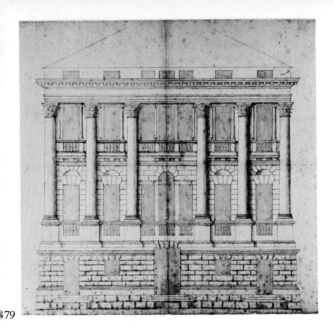

The audacious opening out of the centre of the upper storey would only be structurally possible with a massive beam across the tops of the columns. Large beams make possible many of Palladio's most characteristic solutions, and the structural importance he gives them derives from Venetian traditions and is without parallels in Central Italian architecture.

The destination of the project has not been securely established. The landing stages, which project dramatically out of a rusticated wall indicate a waterside site, and the wide, central opening of the façade and two main living floors could well be for Venice, as was suggested by Ackerman (1966, p.114). The other possibility is that it is an unexecuted project for the Palazzo Piovene all' Isola (54; Puppi, 1973, pp.388–90) destroyed in 1818. This palace as executed had a giant order, spanning two storeys, one towards the Piazza dell' Isola and another with a view of arches between the order, facing onto the river (Zorzi, 1965, figs.351–2). The rusticated lower level in this drawing could correspond to arches giving onto the river in the built project. Though the most obvious parallels for this drawing are the Palazzo Porto-Breganze and the Loggia del Capitaniato, there is no reason why it should not be a work of

the late 1560s. Palladio had already used the giant order in Palazzo Valmarana, and the scheme has points of contrast with the design for the end of the Rialto bridge (223). The odd way in which the voussoirs of the central flat arch break through the string course and end up touching the lower part of the central balcony is exactly paralleled in the central balcony of the Palazzo Schio of 1565–6 (Puppi, 1973, p.375). The lower rustication relates to *Quattro Libri* I, p.13 and also resembles the majestic masonry at water level at the Villa Trissino (453). The flat rustication above is very close to that of the rear façade of the Villa Foscari (353).   H.B.

ANONYMOUS DRAUGHTSMAN, 1467 (?)

380 A Roman Legion crossing a bridge of boats over the Danube

Pen and ink: 24 × 41.2

Lent by the Trustees of the Chatsworth Settlement

The drawing is one of a set of six at Chatsworth (one of them with a piece of paper with the inscription 1467, 11 *novembre* attached to it). The quality of the drawing is low, and indicates that it has been transmitted through probably more than one stage of copying. The six drawings all show reliefs at the bottom of Trajan's column and so are not the result of a daring enterprise like that of Ripanda, who drew the whole column from a suspended chair or platform (Strong, 1913). Trajan's column was much studied, both for its figural style, and for the information which it contained about ancient life. Parts of it were imitated in the stuccoes in the Palazzo del Te and by paintings in the Palazzo Chiericati. Valerio Belli specifically mentions in his will a set of drawings of it which he owned (120). Palladio must have carefully considered the wooden bridge structures which are shown on the column, and they seem to have influenced his own wooden bridge designs, just as the latter influenced even nineteenth-century cast iron structures. Trajan's column was also one of Palladio's sources for his description of the way in which legionaries were armed (Magrini, 1845, docs, p.36) which ends 'and these were the arms with which the Romans subjugated the world'.   H.B.

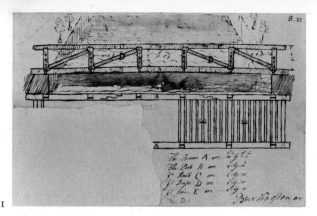

381

206

*381 Garden Bridge
Pen, ink and wash: 19.8 × 31.3
Lent by the Trustees of the Chatsworth Settlement

Perhaps the least attention has been paid to the influence of
Palladio's chapters IV–XV, in his third book, devoted to
bridges. The many abortive projects in the early eighteenth
century for a new bridge at Westminster or Lambeth show
that Palladio could be as seminal a source for bridge design as
for villas. It took modern French engineers such as Labelye
(Westminster Bridge, 1738) to teach Palladio a lesson or two.
Inurred as we are to the term 'Palladian bridge' applied to the
famous colonnaded examples at Wilton, Stowe and Prior
Park, it is often forgotten that architects in the eighteenth
century understood the term to refer to bridges of a more
simple timber construction, in Palladio's words (1570, III,
p.16) 'according to which wooden bridges may be made,
without fixing any posts in the water'. Sir William Chamber's
Palladian bridge at Kew Gardens (c.1760) was of this type, as
was this example by *il Palladio e il Jones de nostri tempi'*, to
quote Scipio Maffei's description of Richard Boyle, 3rd Earl of
Burlington, the great protagonist and patron of neo-
Palladianism in Britain. Although his design is undated, it
seems to be in the hand of Henry Savile, his draughtsman in
the thirties. It could be as late as the 1740s when Charles, 2nd
Duke of Grafton was employing William Kent at Euston Hall,
Suffolk, for landscape and garden temples.   J.H.

*382 The covered wooden bridge at Bassano del Grappa, Vicenza
Photograph

Palladio also published his design for the bridge at Bassano
(III, pp.19–20), which he was paid for in 1569 after the old
bridge had been swept away in 1567. Palladio's friend Giacom
Angaran played a part in organizing the construction. Althoug
the bridge has been repeatedly repaired, it preserves Palladio's
original design (Puppi, 1973, pp.389–90). This, with its covere
loggia and its blade-like piers, is of great visual and structural
elegance.   H.B.

383 Bridge on the River Tesina, Torri di Quartesolo (Vicenza)
Photograph

Palladio's experience of bridge design was not limited to his
production of unexecuted projects for the Rialto (221). In 1559
he was consulted about the rebuilding of this bridge over the
Tesina, 'for the convenience of the public highway which
leads towards Padua, so much frequented in every season by al
the nations of the world' (Zorzi, 1966, p.197). The proposed
improvement to the old wooden bridge formed part of a
general plan of improvement to the province's bridges
proposed by the City Council of Vicenza, as 'the crossing of
them is not only difficult but dangerous . . . with frequent
upsets of waggons and the death of horses and oxen' (*ibid.*).

Palladio's design was not immediately put into execution, but
he published it (III, pp.25–7), and in the end its execution was
set underway in 1580 (Puppi, 1973, p.326). Palladio took as his
model (witness the tabernacles on the piers) the bridge which
he considered 'the most beautiful and most worthy of
consideration', that of Augustus at Rimini (III, pp.22–3).   H.B.

The Site

In drawing up a project, Palladio started with an analysis of the site, and sometimes this had decisive importance in shaping his design. He devotes a long chapter (see above and Forssman, 1969) to the choice of sites of villas, though in most cases the choice would not have been open, as the owner's new residence had to be situated next to older farm buildings. But the chapter does show that Palladio possessed a set of criteria for picking sites which could also serve to get the most advantage out of a given site. Whether the ground was marshy or not, or liable to flooding, would determine whether rooms could be placed in a basement. The nearby presence of a road or a river would usually decide which way the main façade was going to face, and the raised sites of the Rotonda (356) and the Villa Trissino (453) called forth the very particular solutions given to them. He often comments on the site of his villas. The Villa Thiene at Quinto's site 'is very beautiful' (II, p.64), and the Villa Godi is 'on a hill with a very fine view' (II, p.65). In the city, a building site is 'closed within certain established confines' (II, p.45). However, its façade is influenced by the street or piazza on which it stands. The grandeur of the projected façade of the Palazzo Thiene (47) can in part be accounted for by the fact that it was intended for the section of the main street which is nearest the city centre. The monumental character of Cogollo's house (59) was determined in part by its prominent site. A suburban location could lead to a palace being designed following a scheme normally used for villas, the criterion merely being whether there was enough clear view in front of the building to make the construction of loggie on the façade worthwhile (see 53; 348; and the project for the huge space on the Brà, 'a most notable site', at Verona, II, p.76). The other aspect of palace design in relation to site was simply that of fitting all that is needed in a palace into an area which might be awkward in shape. This was an exercise in which Peruzzi had been a master (as in Palazzo Massimi or in his alternative projects for palaces in the Uffizi) and which Serlio expounds in his Book VII. Palladio also published designs for oddly shaped Venetian sites (II, pp.71–2), and three alternative projects survive for creating a new palace for Montano Barbarano on an assymetrical site (386).

Palladio does not attempt to 'harmonize' his buildings with their surroundings, but to dominate them, so that a new façade is set like a jewel in an old street, lined with out of date or modern buildings. At most, in the case of Palazzo Valmarana, he established a change of scale at the outer sides of the façade which makes a transition from the giant order to the ordinary houses on either side (Ackerman, 1966, p.112; 418). He does, however, design the façades he inserts into a pre-existing urban context as elements in a scenographic composition. In Venice he created a broad sweep of scenographic highlights, from the façade of San Giorgio to that of the Zitelle and the Redentore, all designed to be seen at a considerable distance and all gleaming out over the lagoon, in the tradition of Codussi's San Michele in Isola. The Palazzo Chiericati, the Palazzo Porto-Breganze (62) are consciously adapted scenographically to their piazza sites. The Basilica, the Capitaniato, Palazzo da Porto-Festa (413), and Palazzo Barbaran are all designed to look well in a raking view. Palazzo da Porto is startling in its scale and magnificence but has the appearance of being fitted a little awkwardly into the corner which delimits it on one side. Palazzo Valmarana, on the other hand, is marvellously successful from wherever it is seen, and its great pilasters dominate the view as one advances towards it, all the way from behind the cathedral.   H.B.

*384 The facade of the Palazzo Chiericati, Vicenza
Photograph

Palazzo Chiericati (53) provides a clear instance of the way in which Palladio adapted his design to the site. It was possibly Palladio who suggested building the loggia out over the piazza (in his successful petition Girolomo Chiericati says that 'experienced architects' had advised him to do so). Thereby the building was made not only more striking, but gained space on the upper floor. The existence of an open piazza, and not a narrow street in front of the palace, prompted the opening up of the greater part of the façade with loggie. 'The pavement of the first order is raised five feet above the ground, which was done to accommodate the cellars and other service rooms underneath it, which would not have turned out successfully if they were entirely underground, as the river is not far off, and also so that the living floors should better enjoy

the beautiful site in front of the palace' (II, p.6). Palladio does not mention the obvious advantage of raising the palace somewhat above the level of the cattle market which was held in the 'bel sito dinanzi'. Characteristically he uses a beautiful, antique solution (the stilobate, based on that of ancient temples) to meet a functional need.   H.B.

Functional convenience, durability, beauty

In the first chapter of his *First Book*, Palladio paraphrases Vitruvius (I, cap. 2) and writes 'three things in every building (as Vitruvius says) should be considered, without which no building deserves to be praised, and these are usefulness (*l'utile*) or convenience, perpetuity, and beauty'. Functional convenience is achieved, Palladio says, when all the different parts of the building are in their right place. Durability, on which Palladio sets great store, is achieved by having walls which were plumb, thicker at the bottom than at the top, and having solid over solid, and void over void. In this way one could make buildings, 'if that were possible', which were 'eternal' (Zorzi, 1964, p.166) and as durable as those of the ancient Romans (Zorzi, 1966, p.89; Zorzi, 1965, p.108). 'Beauty will result from a beautiful form, as from the correspondence of the whole to the parts and of the parts among themselves and of the parts to the whole, given that buildings should appear one entire and well finished body, in which one part corresponds to another and all the parts are necessary to that which one wants to make' (I, p.6). This definition of beauty underlines the fact that the three aspects of Palladio's architectural aesthetic are bound up with one another. Unnecessary, unfunctional parts to a building make it ugly, and, in Palladio's view, a lack of symmetrical layout makes a building structurally unsound. 'Rooms should be placed on either side of the entrance and of the central hall, and one must take care that those on the right correspond to those on the left, so that the building should be on one side as on the other, and the walls feel the weight equally'. If not then great inconveniences will arise, to the ruin of the whole work' (I, p.52; cf. Ackerman, 1966, p.163).' Palladio here is probably, yet again, revealing his roots in the Venetian architectural tradition. With solid foundations, what he says is somewhat exaggerated. But where subsidence was not just a danger, but a near certainty, it was important that the whole building should have a very equal distribution of weight. The regularity of Venetian palace plans is probably an almost instinctive reaction to the character of Venetian foundations, and it is an instinct which Palladio inherited.' It is also reflected, for instance, in Guglielmo di Grandi's observation that the piers of Scamozzi's Rialto bridge project would subside much more than the bridge's shoulders (274; Cessi and Alberti, 1934, p.381). H.B.

385 The logge of the Basilica
Photograph taken in 1940

Palladio's three criteria for good architecture interlock not only in his theory, but also in his actual practice. The way in which he gave equal weight in a completely unified design to function, structure, and appearance, as well as the creation of an 'image' for the building and its patron, is one of the main reasons for the interest of his architecture. The Basilica is a model example of his approach: structurally robust, impressive, and functional in the access it gives to the broad passageways which cross the building (30). The cylindrical bases of the smaller columns are calculated to facilitate transit: they have no plinths, which might trip one up (Cevese, 1968–9, cf.IV, p.52). Palladio could have justified the form by saying it was derived from the Roman theatre at Verona (209) though in fact similar bases were used in the fifteenth-century buildings in both Vicenza and Padua, and here Palladio, as so often, combines not only the functional and the visually attractive, but antiquity and local traditions also. The photograph shows the Basilica as Palladio built it before it was raised on steps (by lowering the Piazza), to bring it into line with Palladio's own improvement of it in his *Quattro Libri* plate. It is perhaps slightly handsomer as it is now, but also slightly less individual. A little of the edge has been taken off Palladio's solution, in which the logge are immediately accessible covered extensions of the piazza. H.B.

The commission and the patron

'I am confident that, among those who will see the building published below and who know how difficult it is to introduce new methods, above all in building, in which everyone thinks he knows best, I shall be held to have been very fortunate, in having found gentlemen of such noble and generous mind and excellent judgment, who have accepted my arguments . . . and in faith I cannot but thank God . . . that I have been able to put into practice many of these things which I have learned with great exertions because of long journeys and with much study' (II, p.4). Palladio certainly was very lucky to have been accepted relatively soon as the available architect who offered the best sort of architecture. He enjoyed a remarkable initiative with respect to his clients, and after the initial intellectual and professional requalification with which Trissino provided him even his most cultured patrons had little to teach him and much to learn from him. Daniele Barbaro himself owned that Palladio had 'acquired the true architecture, not only understanding the elegant and subtle underlying reasons of it, but also putting them into practice, both in the most subtle and beautiful designs of plans, elevations, and details, and in the execution and creation of many superb buildings in his home city, and elsewhere, which give light to contemporaries and will give reason for marvel to those who will come afterwards' (quoted by Puppi, 1973, p.19). If Palladio was limited by his patrons' wishes, it was more probably by their wanting a fairly close version of an existing work by him rather than by their wanting to override Palladio's architectural principles. Palladio probably had to suffer less than most architects from the fact that 'often the architect has to fit in more with the desires of those who are spending, than with what one should observe' (II, p.3).

Although in two cases one can see the birth of an identifiable project on paper (390 and 392), there is no record of the discussions between Palladio and an individual patron, except the long list of queries which Vincenzo Arnaldi drew up to submit to him (390). One can only make conjectures about the way in which private projects developed, by analogy with those public projects where correspondence exists between Palladio and his clients. The cases of San Petronio (429), the Palace and Cathedral at Brescia (425), and the Palazzo Ducale (279) indicate that the approach to Palladio was often not a direct request for a design, but took the form of a simple consultation. Palladio's way of reacting is quite clear: he begins by praising what has been done, advancing modest, limited recommendations, but then, as he writes (or more often talks) he becomes more involved, almost excited by the problem in hand, and his recommendations become more far reaching, so that he ends up by proposing a design which falls completely within his own typology and by saying that he will send a drawing and the profiles of the details. He probably talked about buildings much as he wrote about them: one knows this from the first version of his report on the Ducal Palace, which consists of notes taken on his oral report by a notary (Zorzi, 1965, p.164-5). Palladio's report on Beretta's model for the new cathedral in Brescia was probably characteristic. He began by praising what he had to comment on: 'He has not been wanting in very beautiful and well proportioned inventions, the layout of his model pleased me in the highest degree', but nevertheless, Palladio goes on to redesign it verbally as another version of San Giorgio, complete with his preferred type of façade, and concludes by saying that he will leave with Beretta 'all the profiles of the bases, capitals, cornices, and the measurements of all the parts of the building which will be noted in the design' (Zorzi, 1966, pp.88-9). The reports on the Ducal Palace and

San Petronio (429) follow just the same pattern. One can imagine that in private discussions Palladio sometimes brought out his drawings from the antique, just as in the reply to criticisms of the 1575 Brescia project (427) he cited (from his drawings) the dimensions of ancient buildings (Zorzi, 1964, pp.108-9). One also suspects that he tended to be grossly over optimistic about the cost of what he proposed: large a sum though it was, 42,000 ducats seems absurdly little considering what Palladio intended to do to the Ducal Palace (Zorzi, 1964, p.167). Palladio was a persuasive, eloquent, likeable talker, and many patrons did believe his arguments. It may well be that the unfinished state of so many of Palladio's Vicentine palaces (they tended to stop when they arrived at the traditional size and even shape for the class of patron who commissioned them) in fact derives from the fact that patron and architect reciprocally encouraged one another, to the expense of a realistic estimate of needs or the available budget, though both of these factors reasserted themselves in the end. Montano Barbaran, interestingly, who went further than most towards completing his palace (386), seems to have undermined his family's whole economic position (Mantese, 1971-3, p.43).   H.B.

386 The Palazzo Barbarano, Vicenza
Photographs

Palazzo Barbarano was constructed between 1570 and 1575 (Puppi, 1973, pp.393-5). Palladio publishes the present elevation of the palace, and also a plan of it, which shows a more restricted site than the present one, as it lacks the whole area to the left, in which stairs, stables, and the loggie of the cortile were constructed. Palladio writes (II, p.22) that Montano Barbarano 'has now bought the neighbouring site, hence one will have the same layout on both sides of the cortile. One has already begun to build . . . I have not shown the design of the plan as it has been most recently decided upon and according to which foundations have already been laid, as I could not have it engraved in time to have it printed'. As well as the large detail of the executed façade, he shows an elevation which resembles that of Palazzo Valmarana.
The building itself raises further problems. The cortile is only completed on one side (there would only have been room for a loggia with no rooms behind it on the other side). The flat wall

of the main block is treated in a simple, abstract way, with giant blocks supporting the balcony and delicate, linear imposts for the openings into the vestibule. The way in which it is inserted into the loggie is startling and not only because of the asymmetry. One cannot help wondering whether even Palladio at this late date would have willingly devised such a brusque transition.

Some explanation, even hypothetical, is called for. There is no reason to doubt (as Puppi does) that the site was extended by purchase in 1570. After the purchase, the initial idea was probably to leave the cortile small as in the *Quattro Libri* scheme. But when work was well advanced on the main block of the building and on the vestibule, the idea of a very magnificent cortile emerged, too late for Palladio to provide a unified solution for the meeting of the loggie and the exterior of the main block, which probably had been designed for a small narrow courtyard. The hypothesis of a later change in plan is supported by the known fact of an earlier change, as the cultured Montano Barbarano abandoned a perfectly good façade scheme in favour of something more novel. This indicates either that he was a very ambitious and demanding patron or particularly ready to believe Palladio's arguments, or probably both. The palace is ambitious and very impressive and successful in its vestibule and its exterior. Despite the lack of one side of the cortile, it is among the more complete of Palladio's projects and went some way towards ruining the Barbarano family (Mantese, 1971–3, p.43). This is in itself an indication of the style of Montano's patronage.   H.B.

387 Three alternative projects for the Palazzo Barbarano

Pen, ink and wash: 53.2 × 42.2
Lent by the Royal Institute of British Architects (XVI/14)

The three alternatives are for an identical site, less extensive on the left than the present one. The placing of the stairs and the stables is similar in all three, but the façades, and the vestibule/cortile areas are treated differently in each case. The project at the top has a long cross-vaulted hall, derived from the Theatre of Marcellus (437) and has no open courtyard. The plan in the bottom left has a four-columned vestibule, and a cortile rather like that of some smaller sixteenth-century Roman palaces. Its façade is of the Villa Pisani at Montagnana type (345). The project on the right corresponds to the plan published in the

Quattro Libri (II, p.22) and also to the executed vestibule and the two front rooms on either side of it.   H.B.

The first ideas on paper

It is possible to follow in Palladio's drawings the whole design process from the first rough formulation of a project to its final form. Sometimes even Palladio's second thoughts about it survive in preparatory drawings for the *Quattro Libri* (52) Palladio, in the initial phase of working out a project, drew very rapidly, and indicated walls with only a single line, and could rapidly cover a whole sheet with tiny alternative sketches (389). In his use of rapid, almost diagrammatic sketches he resembles contemporary figurative artists: a particularly close analogy is offered by Veronese (388). The use of a single line for walls is natural in a rapid sketch and also was a widely employed convention (for its use by Francesco di Giorgio, Burns, 1975–II; in a plan of the Carità, *not* by Palladio; Bassi, 1971, pls.xvii–xix). The sketches exhibited here for the Arnaldi Villa and for the Mocenigo Villa at Marocco, given the context in which they are preserved (among the patron's papers in one case and among the site surveyor's in the other) were probably done on the spot and possibly in conversation with the patron. They are striking in that they appear to indicate an ability to arrive at a more or less final solution in a matter of minutes though it may be that they are recapitulations of a design arrived at previously by a longer process. But in the field of villa architecture, where Palladio combined a firm basic typology with great sensitivity to basic parameters (cost, site, type of subsoil, the number of people to be accommodated, etc.), he could in fact have produced a design as soon as he knew how they affected each particular commission. The design process for churches or public buildings, where more factors had to be taken into consideration and where there was not such a firm set of types to choose from and adapt, would obviously have been more lengthy but would again begin in the same way as some rough sketches for San Giorgio indicate (252). It is not always possible to say whether a quick sketch is *for* a work or a reminiscence of it, perhaps as an explanation in the course of conversation (40). In any case I feel that Palladio's more rapid drawings were very often produced in the course of discussions.   H.B

388 Studies for a coronation of the Virgin
Pen with brown wash on white paper: 30.7 × 20.9
Lent by the Governing Body of Christ Church, Oxford

The recto is devoted to studies for a coronation with groupings
of angels, prophets, and saints to form an oval surround; in the
upper left, there appears to be a study for a flagellation. The
verso contains a number of sketches for a coronation, a n
annunciation, and recumbent figures over portals (Tietze and
Tietze-Conrat, 1944, p.349, no.2128; Parker, 1958, p.35,
no.41; Mullaly, 1971, p.59, no.64). The sketchy quality of the
drawing contrasts markedly with more finished *modelli*, like
those from Harewood House and Chatsworth (282 and 283)
and illustrates an earlier stage in the development of a theme.
Quick sketches of this sort are directly comparable to the first
stage in Palladio's own design procedure. The drawing has
been connected with the late, largely shop-completed
Coronation of the Virgin, now in the *Accademia*, Venice
(Moschini-Marconi, 1962, pp.93–4, no.150). B.B.

389 Sketches for a villa or palace
Pen, ink, in part over underdrawing: 31.6 × 39.3
Lent by the Royal Institute of British Architects (X/22v)

These structures are on a sheet otherwise taken up with
drawings of the 'Temple of Neptune' (IV, pp.128–33). The
base and the entablature correspond, down to the measurements, with those published in the *Quattro Libri*. The
sketches are for a palace or villa – the building is of the Palazzo
Antonini, Montagnana, and Piombino Dese type – and is like a
palace in having its façade articulated with half columns, and
like a villa in its central, columned room (in some of the
alternatives) and its lack of a cortile. Unlike a villa, there are
no ground floor loggie. The solutions range from ones close to
the buildings mentioned above (columned central halls, oval
staircases) to a simple, more traditional solution in the top
right. The site is not quite regular: 56 feet across the front,
67 feet across the back, and 76 feet down the left side.
These dimensions do not correspond to any project published
in the *Quattro Libri*. It is striking that Palladio, thinking on
paper in this way, provides from the start not only for doors,
windows, and fireplaces, but also tries out specific room

sizes. The street reveals his basically pragmatic approach to
proportion: certain shapes of rooms (or, failing that,
approximations to them) are desirable, and one should try to
fit them in, and, if possible, relate them proportionally to one
another. But proportion in a design is not an abstract matter, to
be carefully calculated: it is worked into the design as far as
circumstances permit, as part of a single process of
coordinating different requirements. H.B.

***390 Projects for the villas of Vincenzo Arnaldi at Meledo
Alto and Meledo Basso**
Pen and ink, on rough grey-brown paper: 32 × 42
Lent by the Biblioteca Civica Bertoliana, Vicenza
(Gonz.28.1.4=471)
a) Sketches for 'Meledo alto'
b) Sketch for 'Meledo basso' (on the verso of the above and
here exhibited in a photograph)
c) Photograph of the loggia of the villa

This sheet is bound into a fascicule of notes by Vincenzo
Arnaldi, concerning improvements to his possessions at
Meledo. The identification of the projects for Upper and Lower
Meledo is in Arnaldi's hand. Meledo basso was a more modest
establishment, with stables and vats for wine, though
Palladio sketches a small formal garden.
My attention was drawn to Arnaldi's papers by Lionello
Puppi's important article on Palladio as a constructor of villas

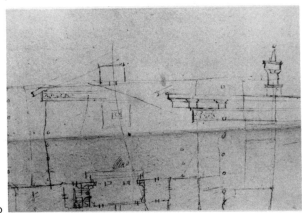

390

(1974), the typescript of which he most generously made available to us. This material, as Puppi points out, is of great interest and includes a whole series of questions (which, I believe, were most probably directed to Palladio himself) dated 1547, as well as records of actual building in 1550. Though the façade of the villa was probably built at this time, it was only in 1565 that Arnaldi consulted Palladio about the vaults of the interior and received a letter and a drawing (preserved in the same volume of the Bertoliana: Zorzi, 1968, figs. 22 and 23) in reply. The two rooms behind the loggia are recognizably the same as those in Palladio's sketches and in the actual building. The work, however, was never done, and the rooms remain with wooden ceilings (Zorzi, 1968, pp.227–8; Puppi, 1973, pp.371–2).

The drawings have not been seriously considered, apart from Puppi's recent contribution, despite the presence of a typescript note attached to the sheet itself, saying 'probable design of Palladio'. Only one writer (Da Schio, see Puppi, 1973, p.371) actually attributes the building to Palladio. Puppi suggests (1974) that the drawings are by Arnaldi himself.

The character of the drawing and the conception is entirely Palladio's, however. The very movements of the pen, the little scribble in front of the loggia with which he tests it, the way of scratching out walls, either with a series of long, slightly curving strokes or a more dense scribble, are all his. So are the conventions for stairs, doors and windows, and fireplaces (cf.389). Walls are drawn not with a single line, but with two overlapping ones. Reference to the two freehand projects for the Villa Mocenigo on the Brenta confirms all these points (393a, b). The profile of an entablature is also characteristic.

Three variants for the plan of the Meledo Alto villa are shown, all identifiable with the present site, and recognisably described in Arnaldi's will, which mentions the chapel. All three provide for porticoed barns which extend towards the front of the forecourt, like the loggie going down to the river in the Villa Thiene project (339). All three are substantially the same in the interior arrangements they show, and most of the walls were probably pre-existing. Only the loggia differs from sketch to sketch. It is shown with four columns in the smallest of the projects and with piers in the others, one of which also has apsidal ends, like the Villa Pisani at Bagnolo.

The sketch for the elevation of the loggia corresponds to that which was executed. The side elements are enlivened, like the piers of the Palazzo Civena façade (45), with rectangular openings and a circular insert in the spandrel. There is also a sketch of the cornice of the villa, where the architrave is clearly indicated as being of wood, and a drawing of a chimneypot, the only surviving drawing of a chimneypot by Palladio.

The sheet is of great importance in that it shows Palladio handling the more homely problems of architectural design, and adds another certain though minor work to his *oeuvre*. H.B.

CRISTOFORO SORTE 1506/10–1594 or later

391 Survey of the site of Leonardo Mocenigo's Villa at Marocco (Treviso)
Photograph from ASV, *Provv. ai Confini*, b.262

In the bulky volume of Sorte's papers in the Venetian archive (315), there is a fascicule of four sheets, which Sorte has entitled 'drawings made for the Cl(arissi)mo messer Lonardo Mocenigo, knight, of things (i.e., his properties) of Padua and of the village of Dolo and of Stra'. Martin Kubelik came upon this material, and, discussing it with him, I noticed that two drawings were not by Sorte himself but were autograph sketches by Palladio for Mocenigo's villa at Marocco. The whole fascicule will be discussed in a later study by Kubelik and myself.

Sorte was either employed privately by Mocenigo or surveyed his properties in connection with proposed alterations to water courses, for which planning permission was necessary (313). Palladio, who was in contact with Sorte over a period of many years (280, 315), possibly sketched his projects on the sheets on which Sorte was recording the site to show him what he intended to do, and to show Mocenigo as well, if he, like Odoardo Thiene (315), was present when the survey was being made.

The present sheet is Sorte's on the spot notes of the site of the villa, which he has labelled 'Palazo'. The plot is shown in greater detail on the same sheet, with the indication 'casa' (house). The survey is typical of Sorte's working notes: a series of compass bearings of rivers and roads are given, together with measurements. These are jotted down as he walked or rode along, his circumferentor (166) in hand, and

not to scale. The scale version would be executed later.
On the basis of Sorte's survey, Martin Kubelik and I were able, without great difficulty, to determine the site of the villa on the main road between Venice and Treviso, a short distance down the road towards Mestre from the bridge over the Dese at Marocco. No trace of it remains, although the ditches round the market garden on the site correspond very closely to the area indicated by Sorte. His survey should probably be dated between 14 November 1561 and 25 October 1562, the two dates on the sheets physically closest to it in the volume.   H.B.

*392 Project for the Villa Mocenigo at Marocco (Treviso)

a) Photograph from ASV, *Confini*, b.262
b) Photograph from *Quattro Libri*, II, p.54

Leonardo Mocenigo was one of Palladio's most important Venetian patrons. Palladio worked on Mocenigo's Paduan house (Puppi, 1973, p.320), designed a villa on the Brenta for him (393), the Church of Santa Lucia in Venice, demolished to make way for the railway station (*ibid.*, p.361), as well as an ebony casket, modelled on the Arch of Constantine (*ibid.*,

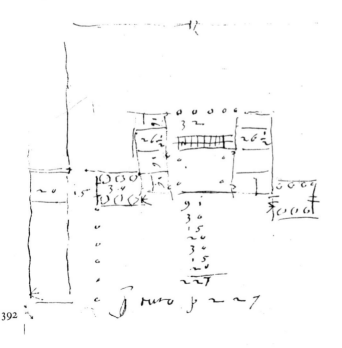

392

p.358). Santa Lucia no longer exists, and the villa which Palladio designed for Mocenigo at Marocco was never finished, and even that was demolished in the early nineteenth century. The date of the project is not clear, but the date 1562 on an inscription, recorded by Magrini (1845, p.xxiv), does not necessarily mean that it was begun much earlier (cf.Puppi, 1973, pp.330–1) and the variations among Palladio's three sketches for the villa preserved among Sorte's papers, indicates that the design was not settled when Sorte made his survey in 1561–2.

The present quick sketch, indubitably autograph, gives the total width of the site, and shows a large forecourt with a centrally placed door, giving access to the villa from the main road. The general layout, with centrally placed stairs and beyond these a four-columned hall like that at Piombino Dese (not so far away), correspond to the *Quattro Libri* plan, as do the outbuildings with their large wine vats.
The River Dese ran just behind the enclosed villa area and doubtless accounts for the fact that there were no basement rooms, which in turn made an upper floor desirable. The greater height, as in the Villa Cornaro (which also has superimposed loggie) would have given prominence to the villa from the main road to Treviso.   H.B.

393 Project for a villa for Leonardo Mocenigo on the Brenta

Lent by the Royal Institute of British Architects (X/1v and X/2)
a) RIBA X/1v. Pen and ink: 30.3 × 42.2
b) RIBA X/2. Pen, ink and wash: 47 × 32.5

Both these typical freehand projects are clearly related to *Quattro Libri*, II, p.66: 'I made at the request of the Clariss(imo) Cavalier il Sig(nore) Leonardo Mocenigo the design which follows for a site of his on the Brenta'. The location of the property itself has not been securely identified, nor has it been definitely established whether Palladio built anything or not. The drawings probably immediately precede the publication of the *Quattro Libri* in 1570 and, with their sweeping porticoes and the unrealistic grandeur of their scale resemble the Villa Trissino at Meledo project (453). They are unusual among Palladio's villa designs in having a large central court, which recalls the layout of the Villa at Poggio Reale, as published by Serlio (1540, III, p.CLI). On X/1v the threshing floor (*Cortile da Batere*) is specifically indicated (Puppi, 1973, pp.358–61).   H.B.

Distribution of rooms and proportion

As has been shown in the sections on villas and on the interior, Palladio distributed functions in domestic interiors vertically. Kitchens, cellars, laundries, etc. were in the basement whenever possible. Otherwise as in the Villa Cornaro or at Marocco, where they had to be on the ground floor, they were pushed out to the sides of the main living block. This separation, above all of the kitchen from the living rooms might seem excessively fastidious, but in fact the heat, smoke and smells of cooking would have made it essential. There then followed either one or two main living floors, and above that an attic, and the granary, which was not only a source of sustenance for the household, but had something of the character of a bank deposit. The living floors in villas always included loggie which sometimes are present in palaces too. The centre of circulation was constituted by the sala, and the other rooms were grouped round this. They usually consist of suites of large (rectangular), middling (square) and small (rectangular) rooms, arranged in a variety of combinations. Stairs are tucked away next to the sala if there is only one living floor, and given a decent space of their own if there are two, though Palladio usually gives the impression that stairs are something to be got out of the way, procedurally and physically, so that one can concentrate on satisfactory room arrangements. The centralised design of the Rotonda, as has been suggested (Prinz, 1969) is in fact the logical conclusion of Palladio's planning predilections.

Proportion in Palladio's building cannot be separated from planning and distribution of rooms, nor from his belief that buildings 'should appear an entire, and well finished body' (I, p.6). Proportions were introduced at an early stage in planning, and came almost as spontaneously to Palladio as did symmetry. Proportion in Palladio's work raises two questions: what it meant to him, and how he achieved it, in terms of operations in the design process. In considering these problems Wittkower's famous analysis of proportion in Palladio is of great assistance (1952, pp.110–24) though it can also mislead. Wittkower's reservations and qualifications to his view of Palladio's villas being bound together by a 'fugal' or 'symphonic' system of related ratios are probably nearer the mark than his interpretation itself.

Palladio is straightforward and anti-esoteric in his cast of mind. He says what he thinks, and why he does what he does. One is forcing the evidence if one says any more than that proportion was studied by Barbaro (Wittkower, 1952, pp.120–1) and by Palladio's friend Belli (394a); that Palladio, like every other educated person of the time knew of the relation between music and linear proportions; that he probably did regard this as having some connection with the underlying structure of Nature; that the architects of his time constantly used proportions (1:2, 2:3, 3:5, 3:4 etc.); and that Palladio fit these ratios into these buildings as far and as often as practically possible, and found these proportions satisfactory both intellectually, and in terms of appearance.

He expresses himself with a stylish modesty on the question 'just as the proportions of voices are harmony to the ears, those of measurements are harmony to the eyes, which according to its habit delights [in them] to a great degree, without being known why, save by those who study to know the reasons for things' (Zorzi, 1966, p.88). Palladio's desire to create a unified assemblage of parts, and his arrangement of rooms in symmetrical bands on either side of the sala meant inevitably that a short side of a larger room would end up as the long side of a smaller one. And, with this as a starting point, his preference for certain basic geometrical forms inevitably generated proportional interrelations throughout the building. But as Battisti has shown (1973) Palladio is not all that systematic in his proportions. In Book II of the *Quattro Libri* the proportion 1:1 appears 87 times; 2:3 (32 times); 1:2 (29), 3:5 (18), 3:4 (17). But other proportions, many of them totally irrational, predominate (*ibid*).

One notable feature of Palladio's architecture is that small rooms are less high than large rooms: room height is adjusted to floor dimensions, and the effect is harmonious and satisfactory. This is an idea which very possibly derives from Francesco di Giorgio (ed. Maltese, 1967, I, p.87 and II, p.345). Palladio gives four rules for calculating height in relation to ground plan (I, pp.53–4). But he concludes his chapter on the topic in a way that serves also to characterise his use of proportions 'there are still other heights for vaults, which do not come under any rule, and the architect will have to make use of these according to his judgment, and according to necessity'.

It should be added that proportional formulae also had structural connotations for Palladio. Piers should not be less than a third of the width of the space between them and in the corners should be two thirds. Thicker piers still should be used when the weight above them is great (I, p.16; Zorzi, 1964, p.100).

Palladio's use of proportion was bound up therefore with the rest of his architectural system, with his desire for structural soundness, and his desire for unified, beautiful effects. Proportion did evoke for Palladio 'this beautiful machine of the world' and he held that churches should be built 'with such proportion . . . that all the parts together bring a suave harmony to the eyes of the beholders' (IV, p.3). But all the same the way in which he introduced proportion into his buildings was pragmatic, and did not involve a total proportional regulation of every part of the building. H.B.

SILVIO BELLI VICENTINO

394 Della Proportione, et Proportionalità Communi Passioni del Quanto. Libri Tre . . .
In Venetia, Appresso Francesco de' Franceshi Sanese, 1573
Photograph

Silvio Belli (394a) was a close friend of Palladio (397). Belli defines a whole series of different types of proportion, and proportionality, including harmonic proportionality (i.e. 6:4:3; 'of these one makes consonance, and melody, when it is in sounds'). The basic principles relating to proportion 'have marvellous usefulness in designing, and executing (in) the most noble arts, like that of the engineer, and that of the architect' (fol.6). 'Proportion is truly the cause of just distribution, of beauty, and of health. Of just distribution it is the cause because it gives to everyone that which is appropriate to them, and not equally to everyone. Of beauty because beauty is the correspondence of all the parts placed in an orderly way'. The closeness of these ideas to Palladio's is striking, above all if one reads the sentence on distribution not in terms of persons, but of rooms. Belli's passage on unequal proportions as a cause of motion (fols.16v–17) is similar to Palladio's rather quaint discussion of the difference between a man and a building, the one mobile, with two legs which are

slighter than what they support, and the other static, with the need for a wall which narrows from bottom to top (Zorzi, 1964, p.166). H.B.

SILVIO BELLI

394a Libro del misurar con la vista
D. de'Nicolini, Venetia, 1565
Photograph

Silvio Belli (c.1510–c.1588) was the son of the brother of Valerio Belli, and a founder member of the *Accademia Olimpica*, where he lectured on mathematics. From 1556 to 1559 he was 'supervisor' at the Basilica. His appointment in 1566 to the important position of *Proto delle acque* in Venice indicates a very wide range of technical knowledge, one aspect of which emerges in this book on surveying. In 1578 Belli was working as 'Ducal Engineer' in Ferrara (Barbieri, 1965, pp.680–2). Palladio shows that he was in close touch with him by the reference he makes to him in Bassi's *Dispareri*, and the compactness of Palladio's world emerges yet again in Belli's dedication of this book to Valerio Chiericati. H.B.

395 Palladio's vault types
Photograph from the *Quattro Libri*, I, p.54

Palladio shows different vaults over different sizes of room: circular, square, 3×4, $1 \times \sqrt{2}$, 2×3, 3×5, 1×2. H.B.

NICOLA VICENTINO

396 L'antica musica ridotta alla moderna prattica
A.Barre: Roma 1555
Photograph

There is no explicit evidence that Palladio was in touch with the well-known Vicentine musical theorist, but this is more than likely, as Nicola describes Cardinal Ippolito d'Este as his patron, and it was to Ippolito d'Este that Barbaro dedicated his Vitruvius in 1556. Probably Palladio met Nicola in Rome in 1554, when he was there with Barbaro. Nicola was in any case *Maestro di Capella* at the Cathedral in Vicenza, 1563–4 (Mantese, 1974, p.934). A medal of Nicola Vicentino is exhibited here (134). H.B.

397 Dispareri in materia d'architettura et perspettiva. Con pareri di eccellenti, et Famosi Architetti, che li risolvano . . . In Bressa. Per Francesco, & Pie.Maria Marchetti Fratelli MDLXXII

Lent by the British Library Board (C.119.c.10)

This little book is partly a by-product of Bassi's attack, supported by the building committee, on Pelegrino Tibaldi's designs for the cathedral in Milan, and partly an exercise in self-advertisement. Bassi wrote to a number of leading Italian architects (Vasari, Vignola, Bertani, and Palladio) putting to them the questions at issue, and published their replies (Puppi, 1973, pp.398–400). Palladio's reply (reprinted, Magrini, 1845; Zorzi, 1966) is favourable to Bassi. He favours an octagonal or round Baptistery for the cathedral (Tibaldi wanted a square one) and says that he had also shown Bassi's projects to 'M.Giuseppe Salviati, a most excellent painter and perspectivist, and to M.Silvio de' Belli, Vicentino, the most excellent geometrician in these parts'. The letter is dated Venice, 3 July 1570. H.B.

398 Oval stairs in the Monastery of the Carità, Venice
Photograph

The oval spiral staircase in the Carità is of a type which Palladio published in the *Quattro Libri* (I, pp.61 and 63) where he writes that stairs of this sort 'are very gracious, and beautiful to see . . . and they are very convenient. I have made one with a space in the middle in the Monastery of the Carità in Venice, which succeeds marvellously'. H.B.

*399 Oval stairs at the Villa Cornaro, Piombino Dese
Photograph

Palladio frequently employs oval stairs, which were both relatively spacious and fairly compact. They could be inserted into any rectangular area in the plan, and were easier to find a place for, and to light, than a normal flight of stairs. H.B.

399

Columns and intercolumniations

Probably the most striking difference between Palladio's architecture, and that of his Central Italian contemporaries (or even that of Sanmicheli and Sansovino, who were trained in Rome, but practiced in the North) was the importance which columns have in his work. They form the porticoes of barns, the loggie of villas and palaces, they support the arches of the Basilica, they are in the vestibules of his palaces and in the central halls of his villas. They form screens in his churches. The Villa Sarego presents nothing but columns to the outside, with the upper floor strung between them. When he could not use free-standing columns, he employs half columns, or pilasters, which are clearly projections of columns on to the wall surface, as they taper like them (371).

In his fondness for columns Palladio shows a closer adherence to one of the two aspects of ancient Roman architecture than any other sixteenth-century architect. He also reveals a continuity with the architectural traditions of the Veneto. The ground floor portico of the Palazzo Chiericati is an updated version of the nearby Palazzo Angaran, and the superimposed loggie of the Villa Cornaro (401) are an antique-cum-modernised version of the traditional Venetian palace façade, opened in the centre with screens of columns (400). Some fifteenth-century Veneto villas have superimposed loggie, with straight entablatures achieved by the use of beams (309). Palladio however gave an entirely classical character to his use of columns, not only in the detail, but by following classical formulae for the diameter: height ratio of the columns, and for the spaces between them, expressing according to Vitruvius' system, in column diameters. Palladio, always visually sensitive, gave his own interpretation to the system, saying that the wider the spaces between the columns, the thicker the columns should be, and the narrower the intercolumniations, the taller and thinner the columns. His awareness of this visual fact, and his absorption of it as a rule, contributes considerably to the effectiveness of both his column and pilaster schemes. Both the portico of the Villa Foscari (353) and the lower loggie of the Villa Cornaro follow the Vitruvian eustyle formula 'the beautiful and elegant manner of intercolumniations' as Palladio calls it (I, p.16), and have $2\frac{1}{4}$ diameters clear between the columns (3 in the middle bay). The use of these visually effective formulae are of great importance in Palladio's designs. They also form a large part of his system, and make it, if not physically, at least conceptually, system built. He tended to compose not merely with rooms of fixed proportions, but of fixed dimensions ($26\frac{1}{2} \times 16$, 16×16, 10×16, etc, I cannot explain the frequency with which $26\frac{1}{2}$ occurs). Rooms of these sizes were conceptual prefabricated units for him, and so too were columns. The Ionic columns of the Rotonda, of the Villa Foscari, of the Villa Cornaro, of the Villa Valmarana at Lisiera are all 18 ft high and 2 ft in diameter. Palladio therefore designed not abstractly in terms of columns of nine diameter height, or of rooms of 3 : 5, but in a very concrete way, knowing what a room of 18 ft ×

30 ft was like or a column of 18 ft × 2 ft. In this again he is faithful to Venetian traditions, as Venetian architecture, with its dependence on stone quarried in Istria, and ordered from masons who were professionally distinct from the builders who would put the cut stone in place, always had a system built quality, in which standard formulae were, for convenience, repeated again and again.   H.B.

*400   The facade of the Ca'Foscari on the Grand Canal, Venice
Photograph

The Ca'Foscari, built for Doge Francesco Foscari in the middle of the fifteenth century was still, despite its Gothic style, one of the first palaces in the city, because of its size, and its commanding position on the turn of the Grand Canal (Sansovino, 1604, fol.266). It was chosen as the residence for Henry III when he visited Venice in 1574 (264).   H.B.

400

401

*401 The rear facade of the Villa Cornaro, Piombino Dese
Photograph

The architraves are formed by beams. In the lower Ionic order
the space between the columns is according to the eustyle
formula of $2\frac{1}{4}$ diameters, except in the middle opening, which
is of three diameters. The columns are 2 ft wide, and 18 feet
high, counting column and base (i.e. a height of 9 diameters).
The underlying elevation scheme is that of the traditional
Venetian palace.   H.B.

*402 The Ionic order
Pen and ink over chalk underdrawing: 43 × 26.9
Lent by the Royal Institute of British Architects (XI/9)

This, and a companion sheet (XI/7) bear witness to Palladio's
early studies of Vitruvius, from which derive his later
formulae for the use of columns. The arrangement here is, as
Palladio writes in his note, systyle, that is with a space of two
column diameters between the columns. The base is the Ionic
base as described by Vitruvius, which Palladio in fact never

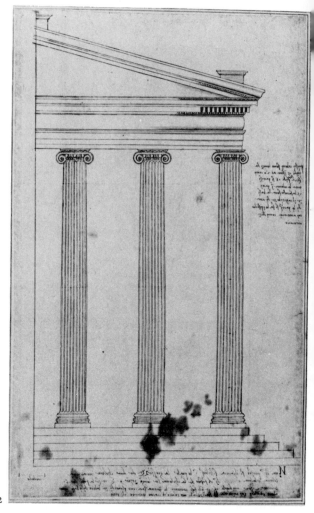

402

used in his own works probably because he had never seen it in
the ancient buildings he studied (IV, p.48). A clue to the date
of the drawing is provided by the handwriting. The note at the
bottom of the sheet is recognisably in Palladio's hand but lacks
the easy flow of his mature writing. The 'e' is normal. Below
it there is added, a note in Palladio's epsilon handwriting.
Palladio's handwriting with an epsilon appears on sheets
dateable between 1541–2 (321) and 1547 (164). This sheet is

therefore not later than 1541–2, and probably falls in the period c.1537–41 when Palladio was conducting a serious investigation of Vitruvius under Trissino's guidance.   H.B.

403 Vitruvian study

Pen, ink, and brown chalk: 42.6 × 28.5
Prov: Lord Burlington
Lent by the Trustees of the Chatsworth Settlement
(Chiswick Box, f.27)

This unpublished and undiscussed early drawing is close in style to other early drawings. The orders resemble those of 402 and R.I.B.A. XI/7; the middle decorative panel that of 367, the Doric order and the figures (which look out of date, even for the 1530s) have points in common with 408.   H.B.

^ Types and formulae: alternatives

Palladio by the early 1550s had built up both a working method which enabled him to analyse design problems easily, and a set of types and formulae which could be adapted to most domestic commissions. These consisted of a series of schemes, each composed, as it were, of different units (the rooms of different sizes, standard column units, etc.) which could be shuffled and recombined according to broad rules to fit many different situations. Palladio's studies of Vitruvius and the antique thus had equipped him with a set of working rules, which was a personal and intellectual achievement, but nevertheless put him in the position of medieval Venetian master builders and master masons, who would have been able, because they worked with set formulae and standard units, to settle the outlines of a new palace with the patron even in the course of only one consultation. Palladio could have designed and probably on occasion did, design a villa in a matter of minutes.

When the commission was particularly demanding, or something new and original was required the conscious, systematic drawing up of alternative designs was part of his working method. He probably observed it in almost all his commissions, as the three alternatives for the Marocco villa indicate (392) as well as the sheet of alternative sketches discussed above (389).

Thus Palladio wrote to the Building Committee for the cathedral at Montagnana on 11 November 1564 'I have not sent the design any sooner because in the midst of many other occupations which have detained me I wanted to make various designs to please myself with one which seemed to me the best and which would be to your greater satisfaction . . .' (Zorzi, 1966, p.82). The different designs for San Petronio (429), the three alternatives for Palazzo Barbaran, the various drawings for the Palazzo da Porto, and for the Villa Pisani at Bagnolo (329, 330, 331) are all reflections of this regular procedure. Palladio of course was following usual contemporary practice: Peruzzi for instance produced a long series of alternative projects for a dam (Toça, 1970). And with Palladio, as with other Renaissance artists one should not be too hasty about putting projects in chronological order, as quite probably they are concurrent alternatives.

Palladio's villa types have been discussed already. His palaces are many fewer in number, and more various. Vicenza provided much more variety of site than its surrounding countryside, ranging from the very shallow on a piazza (Pal. Chiericati), to the very deep, on a street (Pal. da Porto Festa). His commonest palace type is squarish, with a grand vestibule, with four columns supporting a vault (406), above which is the *Sala*. However the organisation of the Palazzo Valmarana, probably because it followed existing foundations (Puppi, 1973, p.371) is quite different, and with its sala over a long rear loggia, conforms basically to a common North Italian Quattrocento type, seen in Vicenza, for instance in the Pal. Colleoni Porto. And whereas villas set many miles from one another now and again could be fairly similar, palace façades, within minutes of each other, could not. In the city there was much greater pressure on both Palladio and his patrons to achieve variety and novelty. Montano Barbaran (or Palladio himself) probably rejected the original design for the façade of Palazzo Barbaran (386) simply because it was too similar to that of Palazzo Valmarana (418). In fact no two of Palladio's executed palace façades are alike.

Apart from their façades, there is even less standardisation in his church and monastery designs, even though formulae were carried over from one to another. They were all very particular, one-off commissions, and would have involved much working out, of which some record remains (254; 358). The

Teatro Olimpico, Palladio's bridges (382, 383), and his designs for public buildings (279, 427) were generally unique commissions, where he could not fall back on a ready-made solution.

It seems likely that Palladio was not ready to be too much limited by his own earlier works, which as has been said were probably the greatest limitation on his artistic freedom. Vasari, in 1568 wrote of Palladio that 'one can hope greater things from him every day' (Vasari, 1881, VII, p.531). Vasari's praise must have been an encouragement to continue on a course of continuous new invention.[8] His later villa projects for instance (Sarego, the Rotonda, Trissino at Meledo, Mocenigo on the Brenta) are all new departures.[9] H.B.

*404 **The vestibule of Palazzo Thiene, Vicenza**
Photograph

The vestibule of Palazzo Thiene is the first appearance in Palladio's work of the 'Room of the Four Columns' (II, p.36) as Palladio calls his version of Vitruvius' tetrastyle atrium. This does not appear to be a motif which he learnt from his studies in Rome. Its direct sources are Vitruvius, VI, cap. iii (which, however, is for an open court with beams over the columns), the vestibule of Giulio Romano's Palazzo del Te (which has a barrel vault), and the fifteenth-century example discussed below (405). It is significant, in relation to the problem of the respective roles of Giulio Romano and Palladio in the design of The Palazzo Thiene, that apart from the roughly blocked out

404

405

columns and the idea of having a vestibule with four columns, the solution is characteristic of Palladio. It combines the serliane of the Casa Civena (45) and the Villa Valmarana (321) with the rectangular cross vault derived from the Baths, which is so common in Palladio's projects from 1541 onwards. It thus more closely resembles R.I.B.A. XVI/16c (325) than anything in Giulio's work.   H.B.

*405   The oratory of San Cristoforo, Vicenza
Photograph of the interior

This elegant and unusual Quattrocentro chapel, with four columns of red Veronese marble which support cross vaults, is of considerable interest in itself, and as a prototype for Palladio's 'Room of the Four Columns'. Palladio certainly knew it and must have pondered its scheme and its structural advantages (the columns carry vaults, and these provide a foundation for an upper room). (The four-columned room at Piombino Dese, whose columns carry beams, is also close to the traditional Venetian scuola type, where columns are used to support an upper room.) This chapel is probably the direct source for one of the key elements in Palladio's system.   H.B.

406   The vestibule of the Palazzo da Porto Festa, Vicenza
Photograph

The four columns here, as Palladio says, 'support the vault and render the place above secure'. They also, by replacing the traditional wooden ceilings with a vault, reduced the fire risk. As in the Palazzo Thiene, the scheme is built up of serliane. Here the room is square and even closer to the oratory of San Cristoforo (or contemporary Venetian churches like San Giovanni Grisostomo). Palladio's four-columned rooms allowed him to reformulate palace and two-storey villa plans completely, while maintaining the traditional functional layout. The sala no longer needed to be long and narrow, its beam floor carried between two parallel walls, but could be square and placed at the back, front, or middle of the building (Prinz, 1969).   H.B.

407   The House of Raphael, Rome
Pen, ink and wash: 27.5 × 37.5
Lent by the Royal Institute of British Architects (XIV/11)

This drawing has usually been attributed to Palladio, but in fact there is no basis for the attribution (*Great Drawings*, 1972, no.3). It shows the corner of Bramante's Palazzo Caprini, usually known as the House of Raphael, as Raphael owned it and lived in it from 1517–20. It no longer exists. It was one of Bramante's most influential works, and introduced a new formula for palace exteriors, which combined elements derived from Florentine fifteenth-century palaces, Francesco di Giorgio's palace designs, the antique door on the side of SS Cosma ed Damiano in Rome, and probably antique tombs which were rusticated below, and had an order above (260; Frommel, 1973, II, pp.80–7).
The scheme was imitated by Sanmicheli in the Palazzo Pompei in Verona, and by Sansovino in the Palazzo Corner (273). Palladio himself adhered to the idea of the rusticated ground floor with an order above in the Palazzo Porto, though as the ground floor in Vicentine palaces was a living floor, it is considerably higher in relation to the upper floor than it is in Bramante's work. Palladio also proposed (II, p.12) the construction of shops to supplement the owner's income on the side of the Palazzo Thiene towards the Corso, probably on the model of Raphael's house, and other Roman palaces where there was generally a small mezzanine window above the shop, and a window under the counter to light the cellars.   H.B.

408   Project for a palace facade
Pen and ink over brown chalk: 34.3 × 28.9
Lent by the Royal Institute of British Architects (XVII/10)

The design contains echoes of Bramante's House of Raphael (407), of Sanmicheli's Palazzo Pompei, and (in the capitals and frieze) of Palladio's early studies after Vitruvius (403). There is no definite reason to identify the project with Palazzo Civena (Cevese, 1964, p.344).   H.B.

409   Elevation of a palace facade
Pen, ink and wash over incised construction lines: 14.4 × 22
Lent by the Royal Institute of British Architects (XVII/26)

This early palace façade shows the influence of Veneto tradition. The loggia with the triple opening on the upper storey above the vestibule, is traditionally Venetian, and the pedimented form given to it appears in Padua. However the façade with its pedimented window tabernacles alternating with niches on the first floor, and the use of the order on the ground floor is related to Raphael's Palazzo dall' Aquila. The central portal recalls that which leads from the cortile of the Palazzo del Te to the garden loggia.   L.F.

410 Project for the façade of the Palazzo Da Monte
Pen, ink and wash over incised construction lines: 22.1 × 26.6
Lent by the Royal Institute of British Architects (XVII/19)

The attribution to Palladio of the design of the Palazzo Da Monte was first made by Pane (1961, p.111), who associated this drawing with the palace. The design is dated by Puppi 1541–5, 1973, pp.248–9). The façade is influenced by Roman palaces (407), and the rustication pattern is very close to the Palazzo Caffarelli Vidoni (Zorzi, 1968, p.31). However the triple opening in the upper storey (here a serliana as in the early villas) is typically Venetian. It was a formula rarely used later by Palladio, though it became almost the trademark of Scamozzi and his father. The elevation of the upper storey like that of XVII/23, echoes the window tabernacles and niches of Raphael's Palazzo dall'Aquila (Puppi, 1973, p.249).   L.F.

411 Elevation of a palace
Pen, ink and wash over incised construction lines: 31.6 × 27.9
Lent by the Royal Institute of British Architects (XVII/11)

This drawing has been associated with the Palazzo Da Monte (Puppi, 1973, p.249). It does however seem much later, and can be grouped stylistically (note the dark yellowish wash) with the drawings for the Palazzo da Porto Festa (415 and 416). The scheme of windows enclosed within flat rusticated arches on the ground floor is also paralleled in the Palazzo da Porto Festa. The serliana in the central bay seems to be a re-elaboration of Palladio's early Sanmichelian project for the Basilica (36). The palace remains unidentified. The drawing had considerable influence. A town house following the design was built by Lord Burlington, who owned the drawing, for General Wade in 1723 (Summerson, 1970, p.333). Burlington's

building was painted by Visentini and Zuccarelli for Consul Smith as one of the series of over doors for his palace on the Grand Canal, representing the chief examples of English architecture (359; and Levey, 1964).   L.F.

412 Palace façade project
Pen, ink and wash over brown chalk: 37.2 × 27.4
Lent by the Royal Institute of British Architects (XVII/16)

This rusticated façade is strongly influenced by Giulio Romano and by Sanmicheli (La Soranza and Palazzo Canossa). The building has not been identified, and the drawing probably belongs to the mid-1540s.   H.B.

*413 The Palazzo da Porto Festa, Vicenza
Model and photographs

The Palazzo da Porto Festa is undocumented but usually dated c.1549 (Puppi, 1973, p.278). About this time Giuseppe Porto married Livia Thiene, the sister of Marc'Antonio Thiene, the builder of what was then (though still under construction), Vicenza's finest modern palace (47). The Portos too were a rich, powerful and ambitious family whose palaces occupy almost the whole of the street in Vicenza named after them (44). They were closely linked with the Thiene already in 1540

413

(16). Vicenza's most important cultural event of the 1530s, the performance of a play in Serlio's theatre had taken place in one of their palaces in the Contra Porti (64). Finding himself architecturally outstripped by the Thiene, it is likely that Giuseppe at the time of his marriage decided to emulate his brothers-in-law, and employ their architect. His later contacts with Palladio were close: in 1561-2 he was building commissioner at the Basilica (30), and in 1572 he was involved in authorising the expenditure for the Loggia del Capitaniato (Zorzi, 1964, p.190).

The site was a rectangular block between two streets. For the façade Palladio adopted what was by that time a standard palace scheme, based on Bramante's house of Raphael (407), with a rusticated basement below and a piano nobile with an order above. The low rusticated basement, in Bramante's palace, housed shops. Here it is much taller with high windows, because the ground floor of Vicentine palaces was used to accommodate living rooms. The palace is regular in plan with the by now standard, four-columned vestibule with a cross vault supporting the sala above (404, 345). The suites of rooms follow a scheme already present in the early villa plans (321, 327): a rectangular room parallel to the atrium and square and rectangular rooms behind it. The stairs are tucked away between the vestibule and the side rooms.

In the Quattro Libri (II, pp.8-10) Palladio exploited to the full the size of the site, and proposed two identical palace blocks with identical façades on each street. Palladio wrote that one block would serve 'for the use of the master and his ladies' and the other would 'provide lodgings for guests so that they will remain free in every respect'. The two blocks were to be united by a cortile which was 'the most beautiful part of the fabric'. It was planned, as the model shows, to have a giant composite order rising to just below the level of the attic and supporting a balcony which gave access to the upper levels. This kind of planning recalls Palladio's house of the ancients which had living blocks separated by courtyards. This scheme was important for him at the time of the preparation of the Quattro Libri plates, and influenced his design of the Villa Sarego (360) and his reappraisals of his executed works, for instance at the Villa Thiene at Quinto (338).

The palace is sited at the end of the Contrà Porti, a fairly narrow street, with the consequence that it is only fully visible in a raking view. The height of the attic, the huge projecting entablature, and the tall ground floor with its window-sills above eye level, suggest not the slightest intention of harmonising with the Gothic Porto palaces in the street. Instead it presents an uncompromising statement of the magnificence of its owner. Underlining Giuseppe's sense of prestige is the interior decoration by India (183) and Brusasorci (184) which imitates that of the Giulio Romano's trend-setting interior decoration for the Gonzagas at the Palazzo del Te. L.F.

414 Elevation of the façade and cortile of the Palazzo da Porto Festa

Pen, ink and wash over incised construction lines: 28.8 × 37.3
Lent by the Royal Institute of British Architects (XVII/3)

This is a preparatory drawing for the Quattro Libri plates (II, pp.9-10) to which it closely corresponds (the cortile with the giant composite columns was never built). There are some differences however. The pulvinated Ionic freize was not represented in the plate or executed on the building, and the voussoirs over the façade windows are shown here as four, in the Quattro Libri there are three, and in the actual building five. L.F.

*415 Alternative façade projects for the Palazzo da Porto Festa

Pen, ink and wash over incised construction lines: 28.2 × 40.6
Lent by the Royal Institute of British Architects (XVII/9r)

The drawing shows two alternative solutions for the façade of the palace. On the right, the attic floor is contained within the tall Corinthian order. On the left, a smaller Ionic order supports a tall attic (as in the executed building). On the right Palladio experiments with the effect of rusticated blocks interrupted by a smooth string course below the window-sills. On the left there is a smooth basement to sill level, which breaks out below the windows. The smooth rustication contrasts with the rough blocks around the portal and at the corner. The roundels above the lower windows on the left, erased by Palladio, are derived from the Porta Aurea in Ravenna. This motif was already quoted by Falconetto on his Porta Savonarola in Padua (Burns, 1973, p.148). L.F.

415

416 Façade project for Palazzo da Porto Festa

Pen, ink and wash over incised construction lines: 28.4 × 41.8
Lent by the Royal Institute of British Architects (XVII/12r)

This drawing is similar to the right half of XVII/9 (415), but
there are no attic windows. The upper level of the façade and
the window frames are close to those of the Palazzo Civena.
On the ground floor level Palladio experiments with a variety
of rustication patterns: smooth and rough rusticated window
frames, contrasting with stucco-covered brickwork, and on the
right of the sheet, overall smooth rustication with a rough
pattern shown on the right of the door. On the left the
columns, trabeation and springing of the arch of the
four-columned vestibule, are drawn, as if the façade wall was
transparent. L.F.

417 Palazzo Antonini, Udine
Photographs

Palladio's collaboration with Daniele Barbaro on the latter's *Vitruvius* led to commissions not only in Venice, but also in other parts of the Veneto. It was probably through Barbaro, who as patriarch-elect of Aquileia had contacts with the nobility of the Friuli, that Palladio met the Friulian representative in Venice, Floriano Antonini (Zorzi, 1965, p.225). From April to October of 1556 Palladio was away from Vicenza, and for some of that time he must have visited Udine, for Fausto da Longiano, in the dedicatory epistle of a book published late in 1556, attests to the recent return of Palladio from that city, bringing with him greetings from Floriano Antonini and other gentlemen (Temanza, 1778, pp.297–8). During his sojourn Palladio would have directed the initial stages of construction for the Palazzo Antonini and apparently furnished the design for the *Arco Bollani* (436; cf.Puppi, 1973, pp.306–8).

Palladio chose the Palazzo Antonini to open the second book of the *Quattro Libri* (II, pp.4–5), a thoughtful selection as the palace shows Palladio's revolutionary principles of design in their most elemental form. In ground plan it demonstrates the strict symmetry of the central block and the arithmetically planned sequence of rooms; in elevation there is the proportioning of storeys and their orders, one to another, as well as the central pediment. The Palazzo Antonini was actually a later version of the solution developed in the Villa Pisani at Montagnana (345), the Villa Cornaro at Piombino Dese (346), and also prepared for the Palazzo Garzadori at Vicenza (II, p.77; Puppi, 1973, p.304). Like the Villa Pisani, the double order of the palace is engaged on the main façade and forms a portico on the rear, but the Palazzo Antonini is distinguished by the rustication of the ground floor Ionic order and of the quoins. The windows of the ground floor are also rusticated although their mouldings are unusual, if indeed they are by Palladio (Cevese, 1973, pp.106–7). The ground floor salone with four columns reflects more particularly the salone of the Villa Cornaro in which an Ionic order with a single canted volute was first employed. The external kitchen unit of the *Quattro Libri* plate confounded the expectations of neoclassicists like Muttoni, who explained its asymmetrical intrusion as an engraver's error (1740, I, pp.6–7). Palladio did, however, favour placing the kitchen outside the body of the owner's residence and advocated it here (II, *loc. cit.*) and elsewhere, notably in the Villa Pisani at Montagnana and in the Villa Cornaro at Piombino (II, pp.52–3); such a solution was contemplated at least in the planning stages of the Villa Pisani at Bagnolo (329) and in the Villa Saraceno at Finale (335).

In the event, the separate kitchen building was never executed, and a make-shift roof took the place of the pedimented structure seen in the *Quattro Libri* and in the foundation medal published by Temanza (*ibid*). Extensive redecoration occurred in the seventeenth century and included the baroque mouldings of the windows of the piano nobile. At some point the windows of the floor beneath the roof were fitted with extraordinary marble frames, wholly alien to the spirit of Palladio's original design.

The Palazzo Antonini has the look of a villa transposed to an urban setting. This is underscored by features of its design as well as by functions like the storage of grain in the floor underneath the roof (which Palladio mentions in passing). The design is indicative of the less than rigid distinction between villas and palaces in Palladio's own mind, and the overlapping of their functions in practice.   B.B.

418 Palazzo Valmarana Braga, Vicenza
Photographs

An inscription on a medal (419) found during the nineteenth-century restoration and published by Magrini (1845, p.XXIV, n.47) dates the palace 1566. The medal shows Isabella Nogarola Valmarana and identifies her as the promoter of the building after the death of her husband (6). This is confirmed by a contract between Isabella and the builder Pietro da Nanto on 14 December 1565 (485; Dalla Pozza, 1943, p.222). Magagnò (1610) however in a poem addressed to Leonardo Valmarana says, probably rightly, that the design was for Giovan' Alvise Valmarana, Leonardo's father, who had supported Palladio's project for the logge of the Basilica (Zorzi, 1964, pp.247–8). In fact it is likely that Palladio prepared a design for Giovan' Alvise *and* revised it substantially for Isabella.

The Valmarana family had owned the property on the site since 1487 when they acquired a house, cortile and garden. In 1493 they bought a large house, cortile and garden next to it

(Puppi, 1973, pp.369–70). They continued to buy property around the central nucleus, evidently to house the very large Valmarana family (6). In 1565–66 the documents speak of improvements to the 'large house', *ibid*, p.370. In fact in plan the palace conforms to traditional Vicentine palaces, with a long rectangular entrance way and a loggia at the rear with a salone above it overlooking the cortile (see H.B., above). Perhaps the pre-existing structure caused Palladio to abandon his usual scheme of placing the salone over the atrium. Similar plans of palaces with a loggia overlooking a garden court with stairs at the side of the property appear in Francesco di Giorgio's palace projects (a similar plan is published by Cataneo, 1554, IV, p.52). In 1593 Leonardo Valmarana bought a house contiguous to the palace, evidently for extra accommodation for the family and guests. He intended to connect these outlying apartments to the modernised block by a system of gates and arches, but there is no evidence that he wanted to complete the palace as it is projected in the *Quattro Libri* (I, p.16) with a loggia, apartments, a narrow garden and stables on the opposite side of the cortile (Puppi, 1973, pp.370–1).

The palace is sited on the fairly narrow Corso Fogazzaro, just on the curve of the street. The only complete long view one gets of it is from the Duomo, and the façade closes the view down the Corso Fogazzaro from behind the Duomo. This is undoubtedly the reason for Palladio's adoption of the giant order which rises to the height of the building next to it. The details, the huge capitals and the puffed out pulvinated frieze are emboldened to heighten their visibility and effect in the distant raking view.   L.F.

419 Medal of Isabella Nogarola Valmarana, 1566
Lead: 4.2
Photograph from the original in the Museo Civico, Vicenza

The medal shows a profile head of the palace's builder at the age of fifty, and on the other side, the Valmarana arms with the date 1566 (*Il Gusto e la Moda*, 1973, p.67).   H.B.

*420 Elevation of the façade and cortile of the Palazzo Valmarana
Pen, ink and wash over incised construction lines: 29 × 31.6
Lent by the Royal Institute of British Architects (XVII/4r)

This is a preparatory drawing for the *Quattro Libri* plate (I, p.17). The pulvinated frieze over the giant order however is not shown on the plate nor was it executed. The elevation of the cortile is shown here but not in the *Quattro Libri* plate. The façade ends with a small order below and a male *all'antica* statue above, which supports the upper entablature. This solution provides an easy transition between the scale of the giant order and that of the nearby buildings. The scheme of the façade is extraordinarily similar to that of the unexecuted project for the cortile of the Palazzo da Porto (413, 414; Gioseffi, 1972).   L.F.

421 Plan and elevation of a villa
Pen, ink and wash: 27.8 × 41.7
Lent by the Royal Institute of British Architects (XVII/17)

This early project for a villa has a high blind attic, a pediment and projecting wings on either side enclosing the steps up to the loggia. The sequence of side rooms is exactly the same as in the Villa Valmarana. The dimensions are 60 × 71 ft, excluding wall thicknesses. The vault patterns shown on the plan are standard in Palladio's early villas; a similar aps:dally ended loggia

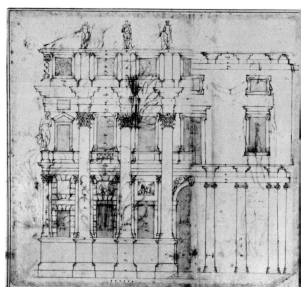

420

appears on XVII/1 (322). Given the similarity in the plan and the dimensions it may well be, that this is a more elaborate project for the Villa Valmarana. This would produce a parallel situation to the Villa Gazzotti, where an elaborate Raphaelesque scheme is presented as an alternative (324). Here too the language of Palladio's version derives from Raphael.   L.F.

422 Elevation of a villa

Pen, ink and wash: 20.7 × 31.2
Lent by the Royal Institute of British Architects (XVII/21)

The central bay projects foreward and the steps give access to the loggia at the side. The grouping of the Doric columns recalls the loggia of the Palazzo Chiericati. The villa follows a standard scheme: a living floor (with an attic above it) raised on a basement. It has not been identified. The dimensions are small (about 69 × 47 ft) and these most closely correspond to the approximate dimensions (50 × 75 ft) of XVI/16c (325), though this drawing is clearly not earlier than about 1549. The decoration on the façade is unusual for Palladio; the foliate panels are based on antique ones (457 and 366).   L.F.

423 Side elevation of a villa

Pen, ink and wash: 20.3 × 23.1
Lent by the Royal Institute of British Architects (XVII/24)

This is the side elevation of XVII/21 (42). It is the only known drawing by Palladio for the side elevation of a villa. Taken with the other drawing it becomes evident that on each side of the loggia there were the standard three rooms. In the note on the left Palladio gives the height of the rooms to the beamed ceiling as 17 ft 3 oncie.   L.F.

*424 Villa Badoer, Fratta Polesine (Rovigo)
Photographs

The Villa Badoer was designed and built for the Venetian noble Francesco Badoer. It is sited on flat land far to the south of Vicenza in the village of Fratta Polesine. Palladio (II, p.48) described the villa as raised on a basement five feet high, which lifts it above its curving Tuscan outbuildings, and expresses the status of its owner, dominating the village and his territorial possessions.

Francesco Badoer inherited the property at Fratta (460 campi) in 1545–48, but evidently made no immediate move to develop the site; a map of 1549 shows only workers' cottages (Puppi, 1973, p.307). In a tax return of 1566 Badoer declared the acquisition (without specifying the date) of 10 fields by the River Scortico, which flows in front of the villa. This purchase must have been related to the decision to build the villa, as it corresponds to the site, and gave Francesco convenient access to his country estate by water from Venice (ibid, p.308). A map dated 1557 (Zorzi, 1968, fig.162) shows the site with the boundary walls of the villa, and on this evidence Puppi in agreement with Pane dates the design 1556 (Pane, 1961, p.276; Puppi, 1973, p.308).

The disposition of the rooms and services follows Palladio's usual scheme for villas: the basement for services, a piano nobile, and a granary under the roof. The plan of the piano nobile is nearly identical to that of the Villa Poiana (341). But the high basement although it has a sound functional basis (to keep the building dry), is here also used to express scenographically in the central block the prestige of the owner. This is underlined in the temple front portico with a pediment which held the arms of Badoer and Loredan families (Francesco was married to a Loredan). Palladio writes 'the cornice like a crown surrounds the whole house'. This is possibly a reference to the history of the site. The villa was on the site of the castle of Ezzelino da Romano (Ackerman, 1967, p.47). The representational and hieratic character of the design of the villa is further emphasised in execution by the total absence of architecturally treated façades on the sides and rear of the building, which were not seen by the world at large. The Villa Badoer is the only one of a group of villa projects with curving porticoes to have been completed. The others are the Villa Mocenigo on the Brenta (393), also for a distinguished Venetian patron, and the Villa Trissino at Meledo (453), for a slightly rising site. The entablatures of the porticoes (with only six intercolumniations as against ten in the Quattro Libri plate) are made of wood and are supported on Tuscan columns, which contrast with the elegant Ionic order of the loggia and underlines the eminence of the central block. The distinction is both symbolic (workers' accommodation and utilities as opposed to the owner's house) and functional; the Tuscan order can be used with much wider spaces between the columns. Palladio wrote (I, p.16): 'if one makes simple

colonnades with this order one can make the spaces (intercolumniations) very wide, because the architraves are made of wood, and it is very convenient for villa use because of carts or other farm instruments'. L.F.

425 The Palazzo, Brescia
Photograph

The lower order towards the Piazza was built between 1494 and 1500, and is an impressive example of early North Italian classicism. Its monumentality, its execution in stone, its massive columns, and the *tondi* in the spandrels (filled, in antique style, with busts) are echoed in Palladio's design for the Logge of the Basilica (30). Both Palladio and the City

Council of Vicenza were probably very conscious of the splendid unfinished building in Brescia. But although Brescia was the richer city, the Vicentines soon outdid it, and the commission of the upper order from Beretta in 1550 was an indication of an attempt to catch up. Beretta was not an architect on the same level as Palladio, and in 1554 Sansovino was called in to design the interior of the upper hall, and in 1562 Alessi and Palladio were consulted (Zamboni, 1778; Zorzi, 1964, pp.90–109; Puppi, 1973, pp.347–8; Burns, 1975). Palladio (jointly with Rusconi) substantially improved the appearance and internal illumination of the building by giving it its large rectangular windows (for what had been built, see 426). These resemble the central element of the Casa Cogollo façade (59). The profile of the crowning entablature is

probably also Palladio's. The photograph indicates how disproportionate the addition of a further storey would have been. H.B.

426 Sketches of palace façades, and of the Palazzo in Brescia
Pen and ink: 43.5 × 28.9
Lent by the Royal Institute of British Architects (X/15)

On 11 April 1549 Palladio's design for the Basilica in Vicenza was approved, and on 31 October of the same year the Brescian City Council decided to choose an architect to make designs for the completion of their own Palazzo, the exact equivalent of Vicenza's Basilica. It had been completed only in the lower storey. It is unlikely that Palladio's sketch reflects a project by

him for the palace, even though he is documented as visiting Brescia in September 1550, shortly before Lodovico Beretta was appointed as architect (4 December 1550; Zorzi, 1964, pp.90–1). Instead Palladio was probably only sketching Beretta's project, whose first floor windows, which were executed, are clearly shown. They were already out of date when designed in 1550, and too small to light the interior adequately. Sansovino wanted to place their columns at the side of the openings, and make an arch above them, thus converting them into replicas of his own Library windows. (He also wanted oval windows in the frieze above.) Palladio simply replaced them with the present large rectangular windows (Zorzi, 1964; Puppi, 1973, p.347). One knows that Beretta included an upper order in his project, and Palladio probably reflects this in his drawing, though its elevation looks like Palladio's own idea. The loggia at the top possibly also reflects, rather than Palladio's fantasy, an idea of Beretta's, as Cavriolo (1585, p.334) actually describes this feature. It never was executed, but perhaps both Palladio and Cavriolo had seen a drawing or model of Beretta in which it appeared. The sections of tower like structures on the left, may well have to do with Brescia too, as they seem to be concerned with the two alternative ways of making a wall less thick on successive storeys. The little sketch at the top probably relates again to Brescia, and possibly in part reflects Sansovino's design for the interior. The palace façades with niches and statues are not typical of Palladio's executed works, and in part reflect Raphael's Palazzo dell'Aquila (note the medallions). The way in which the tabernacles are linked by a continuous cornice resembles the inside of the Choir of S.Giorgio Maggiore, and reflects Palladio's study of the antique (cf.IV, p.43). The left hand, rather clumsily sketched at the bottom of the page, could well be Palladio's own. H.B.

*427 Projects for rebuilding the Palazzo in Brescia, 1575
a) The exterior
Pen and ink over incised construction lines: 82 × 55
b) The interior
Pen and ink over incised construction lines; touches of wash: 89.3 × 55
Lent by the Pinacoteca Tosio-Martinengo, Brescia

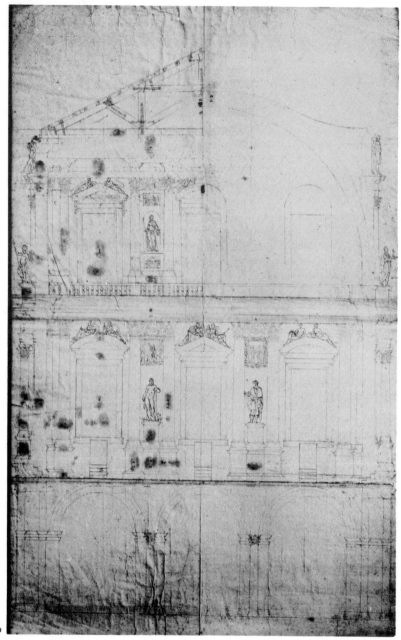

427b

The measurements are in Palladio's hand, and the architectural draughtsmanship is almost certainly his. The figures however are drawn in a darker ink, and are probably by Francesco Zamberlan (Barbieri, 1967) who is described as Palladio's colleague in the presentation of the drawings.

The roofed upper hall of the Palace was gutted by fire on 18 January 1575. The ceiling, with Titian's paintings, was totally destroyed, and 'nothing remained save the ironwork'. Palladio is reported to have wept when he saw the damage (Zorzi, 1964, p.97).

Palladio, though he does not say so, probably decided to give three storeys to his rebuilding project in order to bring the proportions of the upper hall into line with his usual formulae. In fact the height he gives it is close to his rule of the length plus breadth divided by two (I, p.53). The three-storey solution, with the piled up orders, and the statues in front of the columns is close to the other late large scale projects: the Palazzo Ducale (279), S.Petronio (429), the Teatro Olimpico (77). The alternative of a flat wooden roof, or a vaulted one, was offered in the drawings for the interior.

The Brescia authorities called on a local architect, Giulio Todeschini to comment on the projects. Though surprised that he should be asked at such short notice, he conscientiously carried out the task. He points out that the upper cornice, which is appropriate to its position at the top of the building, would become out of scale if another order was built over it. He also, much more conclusively, calls attention to the thinness of the walls in relation to the proposed height. Palladio replied eloquently on this point, citing ancient precedents and the Palazzo Ducale in Venice (Zorzi, 1964, pp.107–8) but Todeschini's doubts were probably justified, and the third order was never added. And although Palladio's design would have made for a splendid interior, it would have looked incongruously tall at the end of the Piazza in Brescia, and would have fallen into just that defect which Francesco Sansovino says his father sought to avoid in making the Library only two orders high, so that the three-bay end elevation should not seem disproportionately tall (Sansovino, 1604, fol.208v). H.B.

BALDASSARE PERUZZI 1481–1536

*428 Project for the façade of San Petronio, Bologna

Pen, ink and wash, on twelve pieces of paper: 92.9 × 53.3
Lent by the Trustees of the British Museum (Inv.1898-3-28-1. Antiquarian)

Peruzzi was paid on 12 July 1522 for 'making a model or drawing of the façade, doors and crossing of the church', and subsequent payments followed on 8 October, and 30 April 1523, to a total of 239 lire. Peruzzi's other known drawings for the façade of the church, and a spectacular, huge drawing, showing a perspective section for adding a crossing and transepts are preserved in the Museum of the church (Zucchini, 1933). This drawing lacks the outermost sections of the façade.

Peruzzi (492) was no admirer of un-antique and out-of-date architectural styles. Another drawing in the British Museum indicates this (Pouncey and Gere, pl.228), as he labels a solution *modernaccia*, nasty modern style, meaning of the last century. All the same he seems to have thrown himself with great energy into the task of drawing up a series of neo-Gothic schemes for S.Petronio, presumably on instructions from the Building Committee, and out of a feeling that the completion of the church should harmonise with what had been built already. The scheme is articulated by a classically proportioned order, which defines a central triumphal arch. But otherwise the details are a Gothic pastiche, with strong echoes of Siena Cathedral. A further Sienese touch (Peruzzi himself was Sienese) is the Coronation of the Virgin in the central pediment. He has lavished attention on details, from the classical central relief, to the gargoyles of the pinnacles.

Although Peruzzi was well enough paid for his efforts, the local architect asked to comment on his projects said 'his designs are most beautiful, and grand, and in truth one cannot deny that he is not a worthy man, and a very great draughtsman' but 'they do not conform to the form of the building'. Peruzzi's projects were never executed, but neither were those of any of the other famous architects, including Palladio, who were called in to make projects for completing the huge church (Gaye, 1840, pp.152–3; Pouncey and Gere, 1962, no.246; Frommel, 1967–8, p.111). H.B.

428

428–31

429 Project for the façade of San Petronio, Bologna
Photograph from the original in the Museum of San Petronio, Bologna (Drawing E.E.)

Palladio's involvement with the problem of completing the façade of San Petronio lasted eight years: from 1572 till his death in 1580. He produced many drawings in these years, of which seven survive which reflect his ideas. The President of the Building Committee, Count Giovanni Pepoli, made contact with Palladio in Venice in May 1572, through his cousin Fabio Pepoli, who was in Venetian service (*Opera nova*, 1570) and was the brother of Odoardo Thiene's wife (152). Fabio Pepoli had lunch with Palladio, found him a 'gentleman and easy to deal with' and showed him the projects for the façade by Terribilia and Tebaldi, both of which, according to Palladio, 'suffered from defects'. Early in July Palladio travelled to Bologna to inspect the church, and received

10 scudi for his travelling expenses, the respectable fee of 25 scudi, and was put up in Giovanni Pepoli's house. In his report (17 July 1572) Palladio praises the projects of Tibaldi and Terribilia: 'both of them please me, nor could I wish for anything better, though it is true that I would remove some carvings and also a certain number of those pyramids (i.e. obelisks) which involve great expense and are very dangerous as regards falling'. He even half-heartedly praises the great Gothic church itself, or at least resigns himself to it saying 'one could say that almost all the cities of Italy and elsewhere are full of this sort of architecture'. But just as in the case of the Ducal Palace (279) his position is only gradually and discreetly revealed, on this occasion in a postscript: 'but if you should wish not to respect either the basement zone [already constructed and Gothic] or anything else, I proffer myself to make the design in as good a fashion as I am capable of' (Zorzi, 1966, pp.105–7). The Bolognese liked Palladio and

his designs ('the truly excellent Palladio', Zorzi, *ibid*, p.107).
He had in fact to deal in this large prosperous university city
with a group of cultured gentlemen (including Ercole Basso,
Zorzi, 1966, p.108) who were very similar in outlook to his
Venetian and Vicentine friends.

An initial project was drawn up by Terribilia, completing the
lower portion in a Gothic style, and from there up combining
Palladio's general scheme with the numerous recessed panels of
Vignola's design. Late in 1572 it was agreed to build according
to a modified version of this project. After a five-year pause,
Giovanni Pepoli passed on to Palladio criticism which had
been made of the project, which is clearly (as the reference to
festoons indicates) still that of 1572. Palladio replied with
unusual violence and lack of cogency. Perhaps he felt the
weight of the accusation that 'it appears discordant to place
Corinthian and Composite orders above the Gothic'
(Zorzi, p.109), and regretted having acceded too easily to a
stylistic compromise. Palladio's letter of 11 January 1578,
clearly stimulated him to revise the project. In November
Camillo Bolognini reported that Giacomo della Porta, the
Papal architect, had seen the new version and 'infinitely
praises the whole design'. He suggested some improvements
and one of these (the tops of the tabernacles to be level with
the tops of doors) is apparently incorporated into E.E.,
whereas it is not to be found in F.F.

This drawing respects the division of the façade into a central
area flanked by divisions which correspond to the side aisles
and side chapels. In its piling up of orders it creates a grid
which easily incorporates the three windows and the three
doors. Stylistically it corresponds to the other late schemes
with superimposed orders (Brescia, 1575; Palazzo Ducale,
1577; Teatro Olimpico, 1580). The alternative version F.F.
also resembles these in the statues placed in front of the lower
columns. It is, as Puppi has observed, much nearer than
Palladio's other church façades to contemporary façade
conventions. Palladio falls back on the Serliana for the
windows; he quotes the bulging pedestals of Raphael's Villa
Madama (491), to which dalla Porta had objected; and he
indicates that he considered preserving the reliefs of Jacopo
della Quercia's famous portal (Timofiewitsch, 1962–II;
Zorzi, 1966, pp.15–117; Puppi, 1973, pp.403–7).   H.B.

430 Project for the façade of S.Petronio, Bologna
Photograph from the drawing in the Museo of S.Petronio
(Drawing G.G.)

This project, for which two alternatives are given, is not
mentioned in surviving documents. It probably, like (429 and
431), should be dated to 1578–9, and it adapts the scheme of
S.Francesco della Vigna (243) to the much wider façade of San
Petronio. As in E.E. the vigorous and unusual bulging pedestal
is used (cf.491). Apart from its visual interest, it would have
seemed appropriate to Palladio, given his tendency to make
naturalistic analogies for architectural details. The pedestal,
which Raphael adapted from the Arco di Portogallo (which
Palladio would also have known) in fact appears to bulge
under the weight of the giant order (cf.369).   H.B.

431 Project for the façade of S.Petronio, Bologna
Pen and ink: 49.8 × 36.8
Lent by the Provost and Fellows of Worcester College,
Oxford

This important and revealing drawing was published and
discussed by John Harris (1971). In it Palladio breaks with all
his earlier attempts to fit a coherent classically inspired scheme
to the openings and divisions of the façade, and instead overrides
all its pre-existing features with a huge free-standing portico,
based directly (as the upper pediment, on the flat wall,
indicates) on that of the Pantheon (433). In his reply of
11 January 1578 to objections to the 1572 scheme Palladio
mentions approvingly the possibility of constructing a portico.
By 10 December 1578 this idea was obviously being seriously
discussed in Bologna: on that day Camillo Bolognini (Zorzi,
p.111) attacked it, on the grounds that a portico would take
up too much of the piazza, above all by visually dominating
it, and making it seem smaller. Ten days later Camillo
Paleotto argued for a portico (*ibid*, pp.112–3). He said it would
be the most beautiful portico in Europe, an ornament to the
church, the piazza, and the city. It would free the inside of the
church 'from profane discussions and every sort of trading
which is carried out there every feast day by the lowest
sections of the city's populace'. Palladio on 12 January 1579
cautiously expressed himself in favour of the idea, and says
'already I have begun making some drawings of it'. On the

indicate the top of the doors into the church.

The debate for and against a portico went on. On 25 April 157
Palladio sent 'the drawing and profiles of the three orders',
which indicates another change in the Building Committee's
ideas, which were now becoming increasingly determined by
the opinions of the Cardinal of S.Sisto and the Pope himself.
The Cardinal's letter of 8 June 1580 was conclusive: 'one
excludes that the portico should be built in any way
whatsoever, so as not to make a receptacle for idlers and refuse'.
On 19 August Palladio died; on 16 November it was decided
to combine elements of the designs of Terribilia and Tibaldi,
and even this back-stepping which cancelled eight years of
discussion, was annulled two days later by the decision to
complete the façade in the Gothic style (Zorzi, 1966,
pp.110–17). Even then nothing was done: the façade today is
as incomplete as it was when Peruzzi went to inspect it in
1522, or Palladio fifty years after him.   H.B.

432 The Tempietto at Maser, Asolo (Treviso)
Model and photographs

The village church of Maser, usually known as the Tempietto,
is among the last works which Palladio supervised before his
death in August 1580. Its frieze bears the names of
Marc'Antonio Barbaro as patron and of Palladio as architect,
in addition to the year 1580, more probably the date of the
building's completion rather than its inception (Cevese, 1973,
p.93).
Lodovico Roncone, in a prefatory letter to Giandomenico
Scamozzi's edition of Serlio (1584), refers to the church as
finished as does Barbaro himself in a document of 1588
(Timofiewitsch, 1968, p.88). Barbaro also mentions the church
in his will of 1594, directing that the villa and the patronage of
its church should descend in his family by the right of
primogeniture (Yriarte, 1874, pp.420–6; see Lewine, 1973).
The Tempietto stands in the piazza of Maser and is in the
tradition of villa churches (as, for example, that of the Villa
Colleoni at Thiene or of the Villa Valmarana at Vigardolo).
It was therefore planned to accommodate the owner's family
and his dependants. For the church Palladio made a design
that was Pantheonic (433) in spirit if not always in detail. The
Tempietto has a central plan with recesses for the presbytery
and lateral altars, thus establishing axes in the manner of a

27th he wrote 'the portico, in truth, will please me very much',
and says that he has taken the intercolumniations of the
Pantheon (spaces equal to two column diameters between the
columns) as his model. In fact this is true of the drawing in the
Phyllis Lambert Collection (Ackerman, 1967–III), which also
agrees with the project described in the letter in having half
columns which frame niches. The Oxford project however
has an intercolumniation of 1½ diameters, and only the sides of
the loggia are closed. The wing, corresponding to the side
chapels, is close to the Lambert Collection project, and to
drawing E.E. (429). The horizontal lines between the columns

Greek cross. Structural support is concentrated in robust piers, out of which are carved the principal altars, the twin sacristies and stairs. The presence of the piers is masked on the interior and is minimized on the exterior by the portico. The stepped, semicircular dome rests directly upon the wall mass and is surmounted by a typically Palladian lantern (194). Thermal windows provide illumination from the walls above the altar recesses (Ackerman, 1966, p.137). The design may, to some extent, reflect a collaboration between Palladio and Marc'Antonio Barbaro (278), whose importance as a student of architecture and as a sponsor of Palladio has been overshadowed by the efforts of his better known brother, Daniele (Puppi, 1973, pp.433–5). A central plan church for Maser would have been in keeping with Barbaro's recorded preference for such a solution in the case of the Redentore (256); moreover, as an amateur worker in stucco (he was reputedly the creator of some of the figures in the nymphaeum at Maser; see Ridolfi, I, 1914, p.303), Barbaro would probably have requested an element of stucco decoration for his church.

Neither of these elements were, however, alien to Palladio's late architectural style. Palladio's arguments for the central plan in church design are well known (1570, IV, p.6; cf. Wittkower, 1962, pp.21–32). His approval was not only theoretical, but also related to his deep admiration for the Pantheon. The Pantheon served as a touchstone for the Tempietto at Maser and for other kindred late church designs (258, 431); it also informed Palladio's reconstruction of the Temple of Romulus, of which only the foundations had in fact survived (194). The articulation of the Tempietto's interior again shows the influence of the Pantheon through the disposition of tabernacles between arched recesses while the framing of those recesses by engaged columns in the manner of a triumphal arch goes back to Alberti (Sant' Andrea in Mantua) and was also employed by Palladio in the Redentore. Neither is the presence of so much stuccoed decoration remote from Palladio's later designs as the drawings for the Palazzo Comunale in Brescia (427) and the eastern façade of the Loggia del Capitaniato (38) show. Both in the Tempietto and in the elevation of the central plan church with cupola and portico (R.I.B.A. XIV, 14), the plastic element of decoration is concentrated in the ground floor without overwhelming the architectural design. Palladio was singularly fortunate with the Tempietto at Maser, for his patron not only shared his

aesthetic principles, but also provided the means to realise them. B.B.

433 Elevation of the façade of the Pantheon
Pen and ink: 30.8 × 37.7
Lent by the Royal Institute of British Architects (VIII/9)

The left half of the portico is shown in section, to expose the roof structure. The drawing is closely related to *Quattro Libri*, IV, pp.76–7. The Pantheon served as a basis for Palladio's Tempietto at Maser (432) and for his project for a portico in front of San Petronio, Bologna (431). His belief, which he held in common with other contemporary architects (Burns, 1966) that the Pantheon was originally built without a portico 'which one understands from the two pediments on the façade' (IV, p.73), probably encouraged him in the adaptation of temple front schemes to a flat wall. Vignola, too, quite explicitly, provides a reconstruction of the Pantheon before the portico was built in his S. Andrea on the Via Flaminia, which Palladio would have seen in 1554. H.B.

434 Reconstruction of the uppermost levels of the theatre at Verona
Pen and ink: 29.2 × 42.4
Lent by the Royal Institute of British Architects (IX/4)

This section of the theatre corresponds to the upper part of Palladio's frontal elevation of it (208). The small temple is a reduced version of the Pantheon, which appears several times in Palladio's reconstructions of ancient buildings (194, 449) before he actually realized it in the Tempietto at Maser (432). H.B.

435 The side door of the Cathedral in Vicenza
Photograph

The entrance to the Cathedral in Vicenza is opposite the chapel of the Sacrament. It was made on the wishes (expressed in 1560) of the canon Paolo Almerico (Mantese, 1964–II, pp.274–6). The design must date from about that time, and Puppi dates the execution 1563–5 (1973, p.351). The design of the portal is classical in spite of its Gothic setting. Paolo Almerico, the patron of the Rotonda (356) clearly favoured unfamiliar classically inspired solutions. The design of the door itself is close to that of the Temple of Fortuna Virilis (IV, p.48), though its narrowing towards the top has other sources (cf.IV, p.94). The scheme of the door enclosed by an order possibly derives from Palladio's orthogonal drawings of temples, for instance the temple of Minerva in the Forum of Nerva (R.I.B.A. XI/15v). Palladio had possibly devised a very similar scheme some years earlier for S.Pietro di Castello, where the lateral doors on the façade are enclosed by an order (Puppi, 1973, pp.321–3). The reason for this very elaborate solution was to give a monumental treatment to the whole wall space between the two pre-existing chapels. L.F.

*435a A window of the Villa Almerico (La Rotonda), Vicenza
Photograph

This is a variant on one of Palladio's standard window types. The frieze is pulvinated, and the cornice is carried on sweeping consoles (compare 13). H.B.

436 The Arch in honour of Domenico Bollani, Udine

During the first half of 1556, the Friulian capital of Udine was beset by plague, famine, and consequent civil unrest. A crisis was largely averted through the actions of the Venetian *luogotenente* or governor, Domenico Bollani, who took steps to succour the starving and the ill while reforming the bureaucratic machinery of the local government. When the plague did pass, the Council of Udine voted to commemorate Bollani's efforts through a mass each Pentecost and by the erection of an arch in his honour (Zorzi, 1965, pp.81–2). The erection of the arch, which carries the date 1556, coincided with Palladio's visit to Udine that year as the architect of the Palazzo Antonini (417). Although no documents exist to prove that Palladio designed it, the slightly later *Chronicles of Udine*, written by a friend of Floriano Antonini, gives the *Arco Bollani* to Palladio (Puppi, 1973, pp.305–6). Moreover, it is conceivable that, as a member of the Council of Udine, Antonini may have nominated Palladio to produce a design. Beyond that, the appearance of the arch, in format and mouldings almost identical with the documented city gate of San Daniele del Friuli (Zorzi, 1965,

435a

pp.87–8; Puppi, 1973, pp.427–8), would endorse an attribution to Palladio. The sober rustication with projecting Doric pilasters had been employed by the architect in the Villa Pisani at Bagnolo (327) and contemplated for the Basilica's logge (35); the Giuliesque combination of rustication and base mouldings for the pilasters also goes back to the Doric order in the vestibule of Palazzo Thiene (404) and to the façade of the Villa Pisani. The arch's frieze terminates with split mutules, a device popularized by Sansovino in the Libreria and used by Palladio in the Basilica. The frieze itself is divided by the commemorative inscription above the arch, a motif later employed by Palladio in the Rotonda (356).

The discreet nature of the Arco Bollani was appropriate to its site at the foot of the flight of stairs leading from the piazza to the castello (the residence of the luogotenente). Originally its view from the piazza was blocked by buildings containing public offices, but in 1563 the Maggior Consiglio of Udine decided to remove the buildings, replacing them with a street that would give direct access from the piazza to the Arco Bollani and the castello above. Palladio was entrusted with the planning of the new street and returned to Udine in June of that year to present his design (Zorzi, 1965, p.88; Puppi, 1973, p.349).

Domenico Bollani, who may already have known Palladio through Daniele Barbaro, was one of the ablest statesmen of the Republic, having risen to prominence in 1547 when on a special mission to Edward VI of England, by whom he was knighted and given the right to place the Tudor rose on his arms. He later served as a member of the Council of Ten and as chief representative of Venice in Udine and Brescia (1558). Like Daniele Barbaro (176), Bollani was 'transferred' from a civil to an ecclesiastical career with an appointment to become the Bishop of Brescia. As a bishop, he took his pastoral cares seriously and embarked upon a series of reforms that aligned him with Carlo Borromeo, whose close friend Bollani later became (Cigogna, 1834, IV, pp.451–5; Pillinini, 1966, pp.291–3). The most ambitious project undertaken by Bollani was the rebuilding of the cathedral of Brescia; although it came to nothing, Palladio was called upon to make amendments to the designs submitted by the local architect (Zorzi, 1966, pp.84–9).   B.B.

Research and development: the function of drawing and drawings

Palladio's practice of devising alternative projects, and his success in avoiding being too much restricted by his own typologies has been mentioned above. Both the elaboration of alternatives, and the invention of new solutions depended on the way he used drawing and drawings, and this formed part of that 'continually attending to studies of the art' of which Vasari wrote (Vasari, 1880, V, p.531). Palladio possessed a large collection of drawings of ancient buildings, some copied after other artists, many based on his own on the spot studies. These were all detailed, and fairly accurate. They served as a basis of further studies, which he could pursue in Vicenza or Venice, and did not need to carry out in Rome. On the basis of his existing drawings he could study architectural details, and could make reconstructions of ancient temples, and the baths. Much of this work he undertook for the *Quattro Libri*, or for the subsequent publications which he planned but never brought out. His reconstructions of ancient buildings were carried out with the commitment and thoroughness of real projects. In producing them Palladio was not under the constraint of cost which a real project imposes, but he was working towards a public presentation (through publication) which demanded a high level of conception and execution in the drawings. This drawing board activity was a continual source of new ideas. It also kept him in touch with large-scale design, and with types of structure which he did not have to deal with from day to day, but which now and again became relevant to his normal work. Thus the studies of the baths were directly relevant to San Giorgio and the Redentore, his studies of the ancient theatres to the Teatro Olimpico, his studies of Palestrina (447) and the Theatre at Verona (208) to the Rotonda, and to the Villa Trissino project, which in effect if not in name is a variant on his Palestrina reconstructions.

Palladio's originality and his advantage over central Italian architects, lay in the fact that he had looked at antiquity with fresh eyes, and with the architectural traditions and needs of the Veneto in mind. For precise information about ancient buildings however he depended on his drawings. These were all orthogonal sections and elevations, like modern architectural drawings, so that recession and depth were not shown, and measurements could be taken with compasses from any point on the drawing (cf.492). Palladio lifted ideas from his drawings both of ancient buildings and his own projects, treating them as schemes which could be interpreted in a variety of ways. Thus an elevation of a temple front could be read as a scheme with pilasters, with half columns or with free-standing columns, and Palladio (who of course knew what the building represented was really like) was ready to interpret a drawing in any of these three ways (438).

This readiness to turn an elevation of a three-dimensional building into a two-dimensional diagram, and then read into the

247

two-dimensional scheme a different spatial arrangement from that which was originally represented lies behind some of Palladio's most interesting compositions (Gioseffi, 1972; Burns, 1973, and 1973–II). It lies behind the Palazzo Chiericati façade, which is an original and imaginative reading of a plate in Serlio (53). It is behind the façade of S.Giorgio, which is probably in part based on Palladio's drawing of the Temple in the Forum of Nerva (439). It lies behind the façade of the Palazzo Valmarana, which derives from Palladio's elevation of the temple at Assisi (438).   H.B.

437   Sketches after the antique
Pen and ink: 41.6 × 29
Lent by the Royal Institute of British Architects (XIV/3v)

It has been stressed (194, 38 and 453) that Palladio's on the spot studies of ancient buildings were only the beginning of a process of research and reflection. Not all of this was recorded in formal drawings, like the reconstructions of the Baths or of Palestrina (447). Palladio frequently went through his drawings after the antique, making quick graphic notes from them. This is one such sheet. At the bottom is a conjectural sketch of the Baths of Agrippa, in the middle an antique vase and an elevation of part of the Baths of Caracalla, and at the top details of the Theatre of Marcellus. The cross-vaulted vestibule, one of two, on either side of the theatre was a source for the vestibule of Palazzo Barbaran (387), and for Palladio's projects for long cross-vaulted halls (389). The conjectural reconstruction (?) of the exterior façade of the vestibule is of considerable interest. It recalls the arcades at Maser (351), the Villa Forni (361), the arcades of the Palazzo Civena (45) or the Villa Arnaldi (390). It is also *precisely* the solution with which the arcades are concluded in Malacarne's drawing of the Villa of Stefano Gualdo at Montecchio Maggiore (Puppi, 1971, fig.112, and p.90, n.103). The whole question of Gualdo's villa needs further investigation (Cevese, 1971, pp.482–3) but if Malacarne's drawing is really a record of the appearance of the villa, and not a project for remodelling it, the possibility of Palladio's involvement in its completion is not to be excluded. Stefano Gualdo was a figure of the first importance, socially and architecturally, in Vicenza in the 1530s (137, 297) and his role would be worth clarifying.   H.B.

438   Elevation of the façade of the Temple at Assisi
Pen and ink: 42.8 × 28.5
Epsilon handwriting
Lent by the Royal Institute of British Architects (XV/9v)

Although Palladio says 'I have not seen any other (temple) which had pedestals' below the columns (IV, 103), this was all the same one of his favourite schemes. He employed it with half columns on S.Giorgio (252), on the Palazzo Porto Breganze (62), and with pilasters on the Palazzo Valmarana (418). The detail in the lower part of the sheet shows only that part of the pedestals which is visible above ground. The rest is a conjectural restoration by Palladio. This fact underlines the extent to which Palladio used his *drawings* of ancient buildings as models, rather than the buildings as they actually stood.   H.B.

439   A plan of the Forum of Nerva and an elevation of the Temple of Minerva
Pen, ink and wash: 29.4 × 40.2
Lent by the Royal Institute of British Architects (XI/19)

This is a study for *Quattro Libri*, IV, pp.24–5. On the left is the plan of the whole Forum; on the right, one half of the temple and the wall of the Forum. There is another version of this reconstruction in Vicenza (Museo Civico, D.21).
The drawing on the left makes it clear how Palladio could justify and arrive at as unclassical a scheme for a church façade as that of S.Giorgio Maggiore (252). He represented ancient buildings in orthogonal elevation and section, and even redrew perspectival drawings which he had copied from other artists so that they conformed to his graphic conventions (481). Thereafter he employed the drawing as a two-dimensional scheme, which could be translated back into three dimensions in a whole variety of ways. There was thus potentially present for Palladio in this drawing not only the Forum of Nerva as it really was, but also a church façade, with half columns, and its side portions articulated with columns which rested on the ground.   H.B.

SEBASTIAN VAN NOYEN 1493(?)–1557
440   Restored section of the Baths of Diocletian, 1558
Engraving: 46 × 325
Lent by the Royal Institute of British Architects

In 1558 Hieronymus Cock published a volume of huge and splendid engravings after Van Noyen's drawings of the Baths of Diocletian (Thieme-Becker, XXV, p.532). These were fitted out with up-to-date architectural details, derived from Michelangelo (above all, the Palazzo Farnese). However van Noyen's drawings are clearly based on the same source as Palladio's early section of the Baths of Diocletian (441), probably a Roman draughtsman of about 1510–15, strongly influenced by Bramante's nymphaeum at Genazzano (Burns, 1973–II, n.14). Van Noyen suppresses the serliane, and replaces them with straight entablatures. Palladio retains them. Both renderings are inaccurate in that loggie are shown on both sides of the cortile on the left, whereas in his plan of the Baths Palladio correctly shows that they occupied only one of the long sides (443).   H.B.

441   Section of the Baths of Diocletian
Pen and ink over brown chalk: 28.2 × 43.1
Epsilon handwriting
Lent by the Royal Institute of British Architects (V/3)

Palladio's drawing, even more than Van Noyen's version, brings out the abstract sculptural aspect of the intersection of wall and vault. The very similar section of the Baths of Diocletian in Vicenza (D.32) probably is copied from the same source. Palladio when he drew his compact series of sections of these baths (R.I.B.A. V/2) must have consulted this earlier drawing, as he repeats its error, which he corrected in his plan, as to the loggie of the side cortili.   H.B.

442   Reconstructed section of the Baths of Diocletian
Pen and ink: 28.8 × 133.7
Lent by the Royal Institute of British Architects (V/4)

Palladio seems to have finalised his elevation of the Baths in large scale drawings of this sort, before making a reduced fair copy, ready for publication. This section is through the central axis, and contains several changes of mind. It is not known whether Palladio produced large scale working drawings of this sort at some stage of elaborating his church projects, but it seems probable.   H.B.

443   Plan of the Baths of Diocletian
Pen, ink and wash: 43.4 × 44.9
Lent by the Royal Institute of British Architects (V/1)

This is Palladio's definitive fair copy of the plan, ready for publication.   H.B.

444   Plan of the Baths of Agrippa
Pen, ink and wash: 40 × 56.5
Epsilon handwriting
Lent by the Royal Institute of British Architects (IX/14v)

This drawing is of considerable interest, in that it shows the starting point of Palladio's subsequent conjectural reconstructions of the Baths. On the right the Pantheon is summarily indicated, and behind it the Basilica of Neptune. This and those other structures which Palladio had located on the ground, are indicated in wash. Everything else is as much Palladio's invention as his projects for new buildings. Palladio identified the central portion of the Baths of Agrippa with a long apsidally ended hall, which recurs in all his reconstructions of them. (In fact the real Baths of Agrippa, which are notably assymetrical, appear to the left.) The reconstructed portion he has drawn in here is somewhat clumsy, in itself and in relation to the central area (Spielmann, 1966).   H.B.

445   Reconstructions of the Baths of Agrippa and of the Maritime theatre at Hadrian's Villa
Pen and ink: 22.4 × 33.1
Lent by the Royal Institute of British Architects (VII/6v)

These sketches are very similar in character to Palladio's freehand sketches for his own projects. Three plan alternatives are drawn, as well as two elevation sketches. Both plans and elevations draw exclusively on motifs which Palladio knew from the better preserved Baths (of Diocletian and Caracalla). Another similar sheet is exhibited here (40).   H.B.

*446   Definitive reconstruction of the Baths of Agrippa
Pen, ink and wash: 42 × 48.7
Lent by the Royal Institute of British Architects (VII/3)

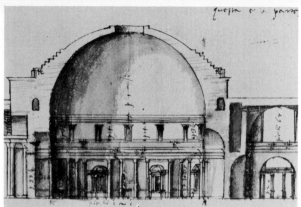

446

Palladio at the top of the sheet draws the frontal elevation of the Baths; below that the section across the complex, parallel to the above; and at the bottom the section along the length of the central hall. Thus, compactly and elegantly these three elevations, taken together with the corresponding plan (Vicenza D.33) record Palladio's concept of the whole complex. As usual the sections and elevations are orthogonal, but the use of wash gives a sense of mass and recession. This reconstruction of the Baths of Agrippa represents Palladio's own ideal of a bath complex, derived above all from the Baths of Caracalla. A close parallel is his 'imagined' version of the Temple complex at Palestrina (451) in which he incorporates his favourite features of several large scale antique complexes.   H.B.

447   Restored plan of the Temple of Fortune, Palestrina
Pen, ink and wash: 42.8 × 52.1
Lent by the Royal Institute of British Architects (IX/1)

This careful restored plan keeps very close to the visible remains of the great late Republican hill side complex, whose main outlines are still clear today.   H.B.

448   Restored elevation of the Temple of Fortune at Palestrina
Pen, ink and wash: 34.3 × 56.3
Lent by the Royal Institute of British Architects (IX/5)

The elevation corresponds fairly closely to the plan and, like it,

shows a round building at the top of the hill, with semicircular loggie below it.   H.B.

449   Reconstruction of the upper part of the Temple of Fortune, Palestrina
Pen and ink: 44.3 × 76
Lent by the Royal Institute of British Architects (IX/9)

This is a variant of RIBA IX/5 (448) and differs from it above all in the temple at the top, which is modelled on the Pantheon and, in scale, somewhat dwarfs the loggie below. The resemblance of the scheme to the Villa Trissino project is obvious (453).   H.B.

450   Reconstructed section of the Temple of Fortune, Palestrina
Pen and ink: 29 × 104.2
Lent by the Royal Institute of British Architects (IX/3)

The crowning temple is here shown as peripteral, and the uppermost court as flanked by loggie. A large court is shown at the lowest level. All these features differ from RIBA IX/1 (447).   H.B.

*451   Ideal reconstruction of the Temple of Fortune at Palestrina
Pen and ink: 39.6 × 24
Lent by the Royal Institute of British Architects (IX/7)

This vivaciously megalomaniac sketch, and the more formal version of it (RIBA IX/6) have puzzled scholars as to its identification. It has been associated with the Temple of Hercules at Tivoli (Zorzi, 1959), with Trajan's Forum (Spielmann, 1966), and both these identifications have been called into doubt (Burns, 1973, p.143). It combines elements from Palestrina, and the Roman theatre at Verona, as well as the two other antique complexes suggested by Zorzi and Spielmann. It is thus Palladio's ideal version of an antique hillside complex, just as his entirely conjectural restoration of the Baths of Agrippa is his ideal version of large antique baths. The most plausible identification has been offered recently by Fancelli (1974), who suggests that it is simply an idealised version of the temple at Palestrina. This interpretation is supported not only by the general layout of the complex, but also by the relationship to certain measurements in Palladio's much more faithful rendering of the area (447). Thus the lower court measures here 338 ft, in RIBA IX/1, 337½ ft. What Palladio has

done is simply to take the existing site of Palestrina, and imagine a scheme for it, even more grandiose than that which he knew to have existed. He treated the Trissino site at Meledo (probably in almost as theoretical a spirit) in much the same way (453). The temple here closely resembles the villa of the Meledo project. The elevation is sketched free-hand straight over the plan. H.B.

452 Ideal reconstruction of the upper part of the Temple of Fortune at Palestrina
Pen and ink: 27.9 × 31.8
Lent by the Royal Institute of British Architects (IX/18)

This plan begins where that of IX/7 leaves off. The crowning temple has four porticoes, and recalls the Rotonda, or the Villa Trissino at Meledo. H.B.

*453 The Villa Trissino, Meledo di Sarego (Vicenza)
Model and photographs

It should be made clear that the spectacular model does not reproduce an existing building. Despite its scale, it derives from only one source, a small schematic and not wholly explicit woodcut in the *Quattro Libri*. Great sensitivity to Palladio's language has been shown in the translation of the woodcut into a three dimensional model, but all the same the model has a conjectural character and is far from being a reproduction of a work of Palladio. In most cases Palladio followed the execution of his buildings closely, and he knew that a detail as small as a single fillet below one of the strips which make up an architrave can alter the whole appearance of a building. The model, therefore, should be accepted as an experiment or a

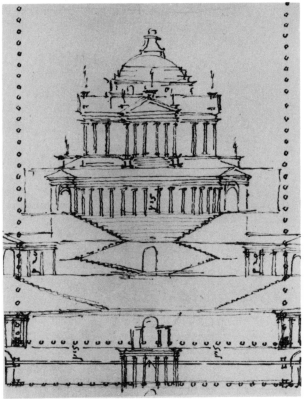

451

453

conjecture, but not as a document.

The Villa Trissino, in any case, is one of the most problematic of Palladio's projects. Writing in 1566 Vasari describes it as 'begun' (1880, V, p.528), and Palladio says the same in 1570 (II, p.60). All that exists on the site is a barn with Tuscan columns and a tower. Palladio mentions 'two dovecotes' but he does not include them on his plan. The existing tower has been incorporated into the model as part of the total scheme, though strictly speaking Palladio's plate does not authorise this.

The work which is documented on the site in 1553 and 1554 was probably very limited in extent, and the value of the whole complex was given in a 1554 tax return as only 150 ducats. The elevation of the tower is so confused and incompetent (although the quality of the detail is high) that Palladio cannot have had anything to do with it (Puppi, 1973, pp.385–8). Further evidence has appeared recently, in the form of bird's eye views of the area (454, 455, Puppi, 1974; Kubelik, 1974), but even this presents problems of interpretation.

My feeling is that the massive and impressive stone foundations on the river, which recall those of Palladio's project for a waterside palace (379), and possibly the Tuscan barns are the 'beginning' of which Vasari and Palladio speak. The project existed by 1566, but the costly stone foundations on the river are the the the only indication that the patron took it seriously. Otherwise, as Puppi (1973, p.389) suggests ,the project is to be connected with Palladio's *theoretical* studies of ancient complexes on hillside sites (see the entries above) and is similar to them in effect if not intention, in being a *theoretical* solution developed for an *actual* site. These investigations and exercises had just one built outcome, the Villa Rotonda (356). The scheme, it should be added, was not totally unrealistic and probably could have been seen through with an expense about double that for the Rotonda (i.e., about 20,000 ducats; cf. Monza, 1888, p.35). It is not known whether the wealth of the Trissinos would have stretched that far. H.B.

POMPEIO CANEPARI and GIACOMO DAL ABACHO
454 Bird's eye view of the Villa Trissino at Meledo
28 January 1569 (m.V.)
Detail from the map in ASV, *Provv. sopra i beni inculti*, Verona, Mazzo 66

The accuracy of this drawing of the Villa Trissino at Meledo is doubtful as the fifteenth century pre-Palladian villa (which still exists) is shown, not in its existing position but turned through 90°. It is, therefore, questionable whether the barchessa and colombara shown are the existing ones attributed to Palladio, or whether they are those shown with them (Kubelik, 1974) on the 1663 map. M.K.

FRANCESCO ALBERTI and ZUANE CIPRIANO
455 Bird's eye view of the Villa Trissino at Meledo,
4 January 1663 (m.V.)
Detail from the map in ASV, *Provv. sopra i beni inculti*, Vincenza, Mazzo 56 B

The executed part of the Villa Trissino at Meledo attributed to Palladio and the fifteenth century building, together with another colombara and barchessa are shown. Palladio's barchessa has six intercolumniations and its proportions differ from those of the other barchessa. The two colombaras also differ, thus excluding the possibility that both were built to Palladio's design. Noteworthy is the inclusion of the boundary wall, not shown in the *Quattro Libri* but executed in the model on the basis of the existing one. M.K.

456 Elevation of an enigmatic structure
Pen and ink over incised construction lines; some metal point underdrawing: 37.6 × 49.6
Prov: Lord Burlington
Lent by the Trustees of the Chatsworth Settlement

This drawing does not appear to have been discussed before. Both handwriting and drawing style, as well as individual motifs, make it certain that it is by Palladio. The scale is considerable, as the central arch is 18 feet wide. There is no visible way up to, or through the building. It does not conform to Palladio's solutions for theatre scenes. The smaller order below a large one is strange. Though there is some possibility that it is a design for festive architecture, it seems much more probable that it is a reconstruction of an ancient building, perhaps from a text, though the lack of a pyramid on top makes it seem unlikely that it is the Mausoleum. Another study exists among Burlington's drawings at Chatsworth for the upper part alone. H.B.

The design of details ·

When Palladio or his patron (the obvious example is the Redentore) had arrived at a final choice between alternatives, Palladio prepared the definitive design which, in the case of an important building, would usually also be expressed in a model (I, p.7; Zorzi, 1966, p.64 on the construction of the model of San Giorgio). Palladio would then turn his attention to the *sagome*, the profiles of details, produced in a scale of 1:1, from which the masons cut their templates (Dalla Pozza, 1943, pp.129–30).

Palladio refers several times to his providing profiles. Thus, in his letter to Montagnana, he writes, 'tell me if you decide to make a beginning on the work because I shall make the profiles of everything that shall be necessary' (Zorzi, 1966, p.82). Similarly, stonemasons regularly undertake to execute details, 'according to the profiles and measurements given to us by Messer Andrea Palladio' (Zorzi, 1966, p.66), and the design of details was a principal part of the architect's work after the overall design was established.

Scamozzi provides the clearest statement of the importance of details on a building. They are, he writes, 'the mark and seal of the work itself, from which come about the perfection or imperfection of the whole (1615, pt.2, p.141). Palladio would certainly have agreed. He also agreed with Vitruvius that one of the three qualities which good architecture should have is beauty. Much of the effect of the building depended upon the form given to its bases, capitals, entablatures, balusters, window and door frames, etc. Not only their form was important, but also their execution: as has been seen, Palladio with his stonemason's training had a keen eye for quality of workmanship. Palladio was influenced in the way he looked at antique architectural detail by Sanmicheli (34) and probably also by Raphael (163, 491) but basically it was through close observation of the antique that he developed his system of architectural detail, noting beauty of workmanship, of proportion, and of profile. He cites a list of successful pedestal solutions in the antique and concludes: 'In Verona, in the Arch of Castel Vecchio (472) which is most beautiful, the pedestal is one-third the height of the columns . . . and these are most beautiful forms of pedestals and have a beautiful proportion to the other parts'

(I, p.51). On the basis of his studies of Vitruvius and of existing monuments, Palladio provided in *Book I* a set of model details for each of the orders (in this he followed Serlio and Vignola), but his basic reference material on the design of details he published in *Book IV*, which deals with ancient temples. Whereas he completed ruined ancient buildings in his drawings, he says he publishes the details exactly as he found them. From these and from a direct knowledge of the light and shade effects of different types of profile, Palladio built up his vocabulary of details. He looked with great attention at the antique. He notes that the great temple on the Quirinal (IV, p.47), whose entablature served as a model for that of Palazzo Barbaran and Palazzo Valmarana (418), 'had a very beautiful design for the upper moulding of its architrave', and this he also reproduces in his own profiles for these buildings. Like Peruzzi (UA 478), he says of the details of the Temple of Castor and Pollux in the Forum, 'I have not seen any work better or more delicately executed' (IV, p.67). He gives a large number of plates to the two temples at Nimes (482; IV, pp.111–23) because of his enthusiasms for their details.

Palladio also concludes from his study of the antique that variety and novelty are not to be avoided in details. Writing of the details of the ancient temple in Naples he says, 'hence, from this, as from many other examples scattered throughout this book, one knows that it is not forbidden to the architect to depart sometimes from common usage, provided that the variation is graceful and partakes of the natural' (IV, p.95)

Palladio himself now and again uses out of the way details (480, 248) or even bizarre ones, like the figures which support the cornice at the ends of the Pal. Valmarana façade. These are probably quoted from Caroto's reconstructions of Veronese antiquities. Through the elaboration of alternatives, variety was built into Palladio's working method. Novelty was desirable and not only in details, provided it was kept within (literally) reasonable limits: 'Variation and novelties should be pleasing to everyone; one should not, however, achieve them in conflict with the precepts of the art and against that which reason teaches. Thus one sees that although the ancients varied, they did not, however, ever depart from the universal and necessary rules of the art' (I, p.52). Palladio's use of blocks under the balconies of the Capitaniato or Palazzo Valmarana is novel.

It is not, however, unreasonable. Nor is it unreasonable for him to have selected from the antique solutions which he recognized were more or less unique. He imitates the Temple at Assisi in different spatial interpretations again and again, even though he says it is the only ancient temple he knows in which there were pedestals under the columns. The arch which closes the ends of the Portico of Octavia (53) is another common motif in Palladio, but he probably knew only this one example of it. And in the cortile of Palazzo Valmarana he imitates the windows of the round temple at Tivoli, even though they 'are different from those which one is accustomed to make' (IV, p.90) or, rather, precisely because of this reason.

It is possible to discern some of the principles, conscious and unconscious, which guided Palladio's design of details. There should be a general overall balance of scale: small columns should not have over heavy cornices (I, p.52). The greater the scale, the more elements Palladio included, as the Capitaniato bases indicate (369), though on the other hand in large-scale buildings whose façades were to be seen from a distance, the detail had to be bold and simple (S.Giorgio and the Redentore). Bases were made very distinct and merely tied to one another by a moulding which continued the upper forms (Palazzo Barbaran). Horizontal bands at eye level across a façade were made visually interesting as in the wave pattern under the loggia of the Palazzo Chiericati or the moulding under the windows of the Palazzo Barbaran. Palladio often uses flat or smooth curved bands of moulding halfway up tall elevations (Palazzo Thiene, S.Giorgio interior, Palazzo Valmarana) while crowning cornices and pediments were usually picked out with brackets, which show as small, lively rectangles of light against the shade of the overhanging cornice. Tall buildings like the Basilica or Palazzo Valmarana present a whole series of light and shade effects in their details, which come forward from the vertical plane to meet the upward gaze of the onlooker. Palazzo Valmarana, as one stands across the street from it, appears designed to be seen exactly from that position, as well as in a long view (418). Palladio's very simple details are as successful as his more complex ones: for instance, the simple impost blocks and keystones of the façade of the Villa Saraceno (335).

Palladio's feeling for unity and harmony in design ('all the parts together should bring a suave harmony to the eyes of the beholders', IV, p.3) is seen too in his details. They seem to flow into one another, with melodious transitions from concave to convex curves, to flat bands, to slightly curving columns, whose bases do not usually terminate sharply with a normal plinth, but instead flow out to meet the cornice of the pedestals. The way in which Palladio contrives different curving profiles, and even more the way in which column and pedestal and sometimes even a further pedestal zone below that (223) are a unified 'organic' creation recalls the Venetian Quattrocento, and even Gothic solutions. The way in which the order is handled in the interior of S.Giorgio shows just the same tendency to unify column and pedestal as in S.Zaccaria in Venice (1458–1500). Palladio's preference for a plinth with curving sides has an antique precedent in the Arco dei Gavi (472) and other Roman monuments in Verona. But all the same it was a traditional Veneto formula (474). H.B.

457 Convex relief panel, 1st–2nd century A.D.
Marble: 37 × 70
Prov: Towneley collection
Lent by the Trustees of the British Museum, London (2619)

Inside a moulding of ivy leaves an arabesque of two acanthus roots curl in opposite directions; birds are perched on the spirals. The relief is convex and presumably decorated a circular or radiussed structure. Palladio shows similar decorative panels in a drawing of a circular structure (366). L.F.

458 Relief with a chariot race
Italian marble: 28 × 117
Prov: Towneley collection, from ruins near Frascati
Lent by the Trustees of the British Museum (2319)

Carved on a concave surface the relief shows four stalls (*carceres*) separated by terminal figures and contained within arches containing metal grills. A winged cupid drives a *biga* drawn by two hounds and part of another chariot is visible in front. The small scale and the recessing of the relief would suggest that it was originally placed low. L.F.

459 A pilaster capital from the upper order of the interior of the Pantheon
Variegated marble with repairs: 45.5 × 52
Lent by the Trustees of the British Museum (cat. no.2594)

The Pantheon was the most complete surviving ancient building in Rome, and was studied and drawn again and again by Renaissance artists (Burns, 1966; Buddenseig, 1968 and 1971; and here, 433 and 489). The capitals of the upper order are unconventional and in fact never imitated by Palladio in his own buildings. He does not even publish them in the *Quattro Libri* chapter on the Pantheon. The upper order of the Pantheon was completely destroyed between 1740–58. A total of six capitals survive in the British Museum, another in the Soane Museum, and one in the Royal Academy, London (Licht, 1968, pp.242–3).   L.F.

460 Ionic base and capital from Daphne
Pentelic marble: capital h. 22.9 diam. 73.7, Base h. 28 Diam. 71
Prov: Elgin collection
Lent by the Trustees of the British Museum (2564)

Removed by Lord Elgin from a wall attached to the church of the monastery at Daphne (the base was cut on each side when the wall was set in). They probably come from a building on the same site commonly identified with the temple of Apollo.   L.F.

461 Composite base
Marble: h.24 diam.57.5
Prov: Elgin Collection
Lent by the British Museum, London

Richly carved bases of this sort were drawn by Palladio (480) and their absence in his buildings is more the result of economy than a dislike of rich ornamentation. (Greek and Roman Antiquities, cat. no.448).   H.B.

462 Venetian Gothic capital
Istrian stone: 42.5 × 42 × 35
Lent by the Victoria and Albert Museum

Towards the middle of the fifteenth century, Gothic capitals of carved foliage became popular in Venice, probably through their use on the balcony capitals of the *Ca d'oro* (Arslan, 1970, pp.159–61, figs.171–81). The present capital is closest to those of the ogival window of a house in Calle Castagna and the capitals of the Gothic window on the Ponte dei Miracoli, both datable to c.1450 (Arslan, 1970, pp.233d, 317–8, 330).   B.B.

463 Venetian capital, c.1520(?)
Istrian stone: 31.8 × 49.5
Lent by the Victoria and Albert Museum

Versions of the Roman composite capital are frequent in the late fifteenth century in Venice, above all in the work of Mauro Codussi (d.1504). This example however differs from Codussi's normal type, and is probably somewhat later, though certainly before Serlio and Sansovino introduced the orthodox forms of the orders into Venice.   H.B.

Workshop of PIETRO LOMBARDO c.1435–1515
464 Balcony screen
Istrian Stone: 91.4 × 91.4
Lent by the Victoria and Albert Museum

The carved screen and eleven others with similar geometrical designs were purchased in 1881 as coming from the recently demolished palace of the Pola family in Treviso (Pope-Hennessy, 1964, pp.521–3). The palace, built about 1490, carried a traditional attribution to Pietro Lombardo (Paoletti, 1893, II, p.229). Pietro's shop was active in Treviso from 1486 and executed a number of sculptural and architectural projects, among them the monument to Bishop Zanetti in the Cathedral and the tomb of Agostino Onigo in San Nicolò (Planiscig, 1937, pp.110–2). The palace balconies have a strong stylistic affinity with these Trevisan works, but the obvious influence on their design was the elaborately carved altar railings of Santa Maria dei Miracoli in Venice, designed by Pietro and constructed between 1481–9. In this context, an attribution of the design of the balconies to the shop of Pietro Lombardo would seem plausible. Carved balconies have more frequently survived in churches at Venice, like the galleries of St Mark's, but one splendid example can still be seen on the Grand Canal in the façade of the Palazzo Contarini-Fasan (Arslan, 1970, p.320, figs.245–8), also datable to the last quarter of the fifteenth century.   B.B.

465 Baluster column from the Palazzo Chiericati
Stone: 92
Lent by the Soprintendenza ai Monumenti, Vicenza.

This slim baluster form appears also on the Palazzo Thiene, and Palazzo da Porto (cf. Wittkower, 1968).   H.B.

466 Baluster column (fragment) from the Basilica
Stone: 54
Lent by the Soprintendenza ai Monumenti, Vicenza

This more robust form was employed by Palladio on the upper order and over the cornice of the Basilica. Its more plastic character, and the strongly modelled ring in the middle is better suited to the context in which it appears than the slimmer balusters of the Palazzo Chiericati. These balusters would not have had their design fixed until 1564–6 (Zorzi, 1964, p.61). H.B.

467 Fragment of the cornice of one of the first floor cortile windows of the Palazzo Valmarana Braga, Vicenza
Stone
Lent by Dr Luigi Braga Rosa

468 Keystone from a demolished house in Thiene, 17th century
Stone
Lent by the Soprintendenza ai Monumenti, Vicenza

Falconetto established a taste in the Veneto for placing heads in keystones, on the basis of his study of Veronese antiquities, above all the arch of Juppiter Ammon. He was followed in this, in a more spectacular and dramatic way by Sanmicheli (Porta Palio, Palazzo Bevilacqua) and Sansovino (Library). Palladio used heads in the keystones of the arches of the Basilica (on the whole male with the Doric and female with the Ionic order) and on the façade of the Palazzo da Porto Festa. This is an attractive later example of the motif. H.B.

469 The Doric and Ionic entablatures of the Theatre of Marcellus
Pen, ink and wash: 44.1 × 29
Lent by the Royal Institute of British Architects (X/20)

Palladio's close study of detail began in his copies of other artists' drawings. These detailed measured profiles must be dated early. The handwriting seems to be transitional between the thorough-going epsilon hand and that which preceded it (i.e., in the late 1530s?). In the notes the original draughtsmen are mentioned by name: 'Ventura' and 'Messer Michiele' (Michele Sanmicheli?; cf. Lotz, 1962). The Theatre of Marcellus probably suggested to Palladio the hollowed upper moulding of the Doric entablature of the Basilica, and the two flat strips in the projecting part of the lower cornice of Palazzo Chiericati. H.B.

470 The Doric order of the Basilica
Photograph

The main cornice is topped by a concave moulding, which makes a strong shadow at the top of the entablature, which is given a razor edge quality by the brightly lit flat strip immediately above it. The main cornice has a large, shadow casting overhang. A small, exotic emphasis is provided in the head in the keystone of the arch. H.B.

471 Study of the Ionic and Composite orders
Pen and ink: 40.5 × 29
Lent by the Royal Institute of British Architects (X/6v)

The Ionic capital and entablature on the left is a study of *Quattro Libri*, I, p.36. The other half carries studies for the plate of the Composite order (I, p.50). Palladio says of the capital 'for this type I have seen one in Rome, from which I have taken the measurements, as it seemed to me very beautiful and well designed' (I, p.49). Palladio's source for the entablature is probably the Temple on the Quirinal (IV, p.47). Although this had Corinthian capitals, Palladio usually (San Giorgio, Palazzo Valmarana, Palazzo Porto-Breganze) combines its cornice with Composite capitals. In the top left of this sheet is a sketch of the Tuscan atrium, probably related to II, p.35. H.B.

472 The pedestals of the Arco de' Gavi, Verona
Photograph

Though the arch is badly worn and sections of it have been replaced in recent times, Palladio's preferred profile of the plinths appears clearly, as it does also in the Arco de' Leoni in the same city. Palladio particularly admired the pedestals of this arch (I, p.51).   H.B.

473   A study of pedestals and bases
Pen and ink: 28.8 × 38.3
Lent by the Royal Institute of British Architects (XIII/19v)

This is a study for *Quattro Libri*, I, p.48. The bases resemble those of the larger order of the façade of the Redentore (479). The treatment of the plinth is Palladio's usual, flowing one. The crosses indicate the overall proportions.   H.B.

*474   Base and pedestal of the façade of S.Rocco, Vicenza
Photograph

The façade of the church of S.Rocco was built in 1530, following a standard Quattrocento Venetian scheme. As in many Venetian works of the later fifteenth and earlier sixteenth century the base is joined to the top of the pedestal with a gentle curve. The desire to give the various elements in the order the apperance of flowing into one another is inherited by Palladio.   H.B.

*475   Base and pedestal of the façade of Palazzo Valmarana, Vicenza
Photograph

The plinth itself, and not just a moulding below it sweeps outwards to the edge of the cornice of the pedestal.   H.B.

476   The impost of the lower arches of the amphitheatre, Verona
Photograph

The architectural antiquities of Verona exercised a strong influence on architectural decoration in the Veneto already in the Quattrocento. The Venetian Quattrocento liking for arches decorated with flutes goes straight back to the Porta de' Borsari. A 'Veronese' quality is also present in Palladio's architectural detail, not only in his plinth/pedestal solution, but

474

in the way in which his impost mouldings spread out in a series of curves to receive the arch placed on them.   H.B.

477   The impost of the first floor of the Monastery of the Carita, Venice
Photograph

The individual mouldings are not dry and isolated, but make up a single pseudo-natural weight receiving form.   H.B.

475

478

479

*478 Capitals and entablature of the interior of the Redentore
Photograph

*479 The bases of the façade of the Redentore
Photograph

Palladio contrasts the scale and profiles of the two bases. He
also unites them, by giving them the same two upper
mouldings, and by making the top of the plinth of the smaller
base concide with the top of the lower torus of the larger.   H.B.

480 Bases at the Lateran, Rome
Pen, ink and wash: 40.7 × 26.8
Lent by the Royal Institute of British Architects (XIV/2)

The lower base stands in the portico of the Lateran Baptistry.
Palladio writes about it (IV, p,61). 'above the base . . . there are
leaves, which support the column shafts. This is worthy of
notice, and the judgement of that architect is to be praised, who
knew so well how to arrange things when he did not have
sufficiently tall column shafts, all without detracting anything

at all from the beauty and majesty of the work. I myself used this idea in the columns which I placed as ornament to the internal portal of S.Giorgio Maggiore in Venice. They did not reach . . . to where it was necessary, and they are of such beautiful marble that they did not deserve to be left out'. Palladio here displays his view that novel and unusual solutions are desirable, provided they are reasonable and do not break any basic rules.   H.B.

JEAN POLDO D'ALBENAS
481 **Discours historial de l'antique et illustre Cite de Nismes . . . Avec les portraitz des plus antiques e insignes bastimens du dit lieu . . . ensemble de l'antique e moderne ville.**
Lyon: 1560
Lent by the British Library Board (183.d.11)

This beautifully illustrated book seems to have been Palladio's source for the plates of the antiquities of Nîmes which he published in the *Quattro Libri* (IV, pp.111–23). He merely redrew the plates.   H.B.

482 **Longitudinal section of 'the other Temple in Nîmes'**
Pen and ink: 30 × 41
Lent by the Royal Institute of British Architects (XI/13v)

The left half of this drawing is preparatory for the *Quattro Libri* IV, p.121. The other half shows the elevation of the side wall. Palladio praises the details of the building: the bases 'have a most beautiful profile' and the unusual capitals of the square columns 'all have such a beautiful and gracious form, and are of such a beautiful invention, that I do not know if I have seen capitals of this sort better, or more giudiciously made'.   H.B.

Execution and supervision

Sometimes Palladio's involvement with a building ended with his submitting a project. This was the case with S.Petronio (429) and the Palace at Brescia (425). Either nothing was done, or done under the direction of another supervisory architect, like Beretta in Brescia in 1562. Some of Palladio's projects for individual patrons were executed, like the Villa Chiericati, by others (349).

In the case of Palladio's major projects, he seems normally to have been employed to supervise the work. This is the case at the Palazzo Chiericati, the Basilica (for thirty years), and at S. Giorgio Maggiore, 'which fabric I govern', as Palladio writes (Zorzi, 1966, p.88). That Palladio was employed in this way was of great importance to him, given that payments for designs were so meagre. It is also important for the extent to which buildings reflect his ideas and sensibility. In many cases Palladio, who always thought of a building as a made thing with its 'stones joined and bound together with the greatest diligence' (IV, p.42) therefore had a very direct role in making it how it is, even though he did not himself, once he became established as an architect, execute any part of a building manually (Zorzi, 1964, p.304). His duties, however, at the Basilica were numerous: he had to go to the quarries to choose stone, measure it when it arrived on the carts, make designs for details, go to Venice to find and negotiate with stonemasons, buy materials (for instance, stones for sharpening the masons' chisels), assess the quality of the work done. On an unidentified project, Palladio himself seems to have kept the accounts (484). Every new stage of a building, and above all the construction of vaults and arches, would probably have involved consultations with him, and usually his presence when the critical moment arrived. Even as apparently simple a matter as plastering the walls of the inside of the Basilica required his opinion (Zorzi, 1964, pp.304; 323ff.). Palladio had a wide range of technical knowledge, which went from the different types of flooring and their respective advantages (373) to the execution of the vaults and dome of S.Giorgio (cf. Zorzi, 1966, pp.88–9). He was constantly being sought after by his employers as his letter to Vincenzo Arnaldi indicates (Puppi, 1973, p.371). Montano Barbaran wrote on 15 July 1570 to another employer of Palladio, Federigo Sarego, that he would send

Palladio over 'just as soon as I shall have put up into place some blocks of my façade which cannot be done without the presence of M(esser) Andrea Palladio (Zorzi, 1964, p.237).

Very many of Palladio's usages were new. He therefore not only had the task of getting his patrons to accept them, but also of getting the workmen to execute them properly. For this his agreeable personality, and his good relations with craftsmen and workers, of which Gualdo speaks (Gualdo, 1959), must have been of great importance. Not only did he have to familiarise the local builders with his unfamiliar vaulting types, but obtain extraordinary accuracy and finish in the construction of brick columns (375). The bricks for the Loggia del Capitaniato columns, for instance, must have been specially made. He also needed to accustom the masons to the new forms – even the standard capital types for the orders would not have been entirely familiar when work began on the Logge of the Basilica. However Palladio's difficulties in this area should not be exaggerated: Vicentine masons and builders were obviously repositories of great skill and experience, as the construction of the Clock Tower, or the elaborate stone details of fifteenth-century altars in the city's churches, indicate.   H.B.

LEANDRO BASSANO 1557–1622
483 The Tower of Babel
Canvas: 139 × 189
Signed
Ollney Bequest
Lent by the National Gallery, London

Leandro dal Ponte was trained in his father Jacopo's shop, where he was involved in producing genre paintings like 302. Although he moved to Venice in 1588 and distinguished himself as a portraitist (Ridolfi, 1924, p.166), Leandro continued to paint numbers of works like *The Tower of Babel*, which is probably datable to about 1595 (Arslan, 1960, I, p.262; Gould, 1975, p.22). As so often in Bassano works the subject is overshadowed by the loving documentation of everyday life: in this case the building process, as Palladio would have known it. In the foreground a labourer (*manovale*) mixes mortar while a stonemason (Palladio's first role on a building site) dresses a stone. Behind him an apprentice prepares to hand him another

chisel. In the middle distance other labourers construct further wooden scaffolding, on which the builders (*muratori*) build up the walls of the ill fated tower. The scene recalls Maganza's poem addressed to Almerico, builder of the Villa Rotonda (356): 'How many poor devils live under you, such as bricklayers, smiths, carpenters and brick makers, and even the suppliers of sand, without counting the sculptors and painters (Zorzi, 1968, p.134).   B.B., H.B.

484 A list of wages paid, drawn up by Palladio
Pen and ink: 29 × 40.7
Lent by the Royal Institute of British Architects (VIII/8v)

The payments appear to be made to a master Marcho and his assistants, and to cover twenty five days' work. The master received 38 soldi a day; Gasparo his *garzon* (assistant), 28 soldi; and 'a journeyman (*lavorante*) of his' 28 soldi; 'Piero, a labourer (*manovale*), 26 soldi; and Marcho's son, 20 soldi. There is also a payment for the hire of a boat, and porters'. Though there is always the possibility that Master Marcho was exceptionally skilled, or the employer exceptionally generous, these rates are high, and on the basis of Pullan's study of the wages of builders at the Scuola di S.Rocco in Venice (1968, pp.156–8) would indicate a date after the plague in Venice, i.e. between 1577 and 1580. This would be consistent with the obviously late study of the Baths on the recto. The text is transcribed by Zorzi (1959, p.26) and documents the way in which Palladio was frequently involved not only in supervising construction, but in the day to day administration of a project.   H.B.

485 The contract for the construction of Palazzo Valmarana, 1565
Photograph from ASVi, Not. Matteo Cerato, 14 December 1565.

The agreement is as follows:
'On the 14 December 1565 in Vicenza.
It is declared in the present document under what terms the Signora Isabella Valmarana gives the building of her palace in Vicenza to Master Pietro da Nanto . . .
That the said Master Pietro should be obliged to be present on the said building and work with his own hands, nor can he go off on any day without the permission of Signora Isabella.

That he should be obliged to find good and competent master builders for the building nor may he employ anyone who should not be satisfactory to Signora Isabella.

That he should be obliged to employ at least four bricklayers (literally, "trowels") all the time, but six or more according to what shall be needed and thus continue in this building until it shall be finished'.

The remaining clauses fix the rate at which Isabella was obliged to pay Pietro da Nanto, and makes clear that he was the sole contractor for the *construction*. It is not clear whether a separate workshop was responsible for stone mason's work. It is in fact normal for the builders to put the cut stones in place, but a separate workshop usually worked the stone on the basis of the profiles supplied by the architect. The 1542 contract for the construction of the Palazzo Thiene (47), is only with the builders (Zorzi, 1964, p.213). Girolamo Chiericati, whose account book for the building of his palace is preserved in the Museo Civico in Vicenza, records separate agreements with a quarrier, who delivered the stone to the site, with a stone mason, to cut it, and with the builder, to do the brick work and set the cut stones in place, as well as payments to Palladio for his designs, and for supervising the work. Palladio's nephew Marc'Antonio (34) was also employed to do the high quality stone work (Zorzi, 1964, pp.203–4). H.B.

Palladio and other Renaissance Architects •

Throughout the catalogue there have been references to Palladio's relation to other architects of the time. Attention has been given to his debt to Sanmicheli (34), his relation to Sansovino (275) and to the way in which he was steeped in the architectural traditions of the Veneto. He has been contrasted with Serlio (202) to whom he owed much, above all in his early years (13). His independence from Central Italian ways of looking at the antique has been mentioned, as well as his debt to Raphael, Antonio da Sangallo, and Giulio Romano (47).

Rather than cover this ground again in photographs of architecture by Palladio's contemporaries, the space has been used to display a selection of drawings by other artists and architects. Some are projects, some are drawings after the antique. Palladio's own personality as expressed in his drawings is directly and abundantly present in the exhibition. Drawings by other artists enable direct comparisons to be made, without the mediation of a photograph.

The Venetian tradition is represented by two drawings (486, 487). The study of the antique before the effects of Bramante's stylistic revolution had been felt, by another, which has, it would seem, never been exhibited before (488). There is a sixteenth-century drawing of Bramante's House of Raphael, two drawings by Raphael, and one unknown drawing from his workshop. There is one of the finest drawings by Peruzzi (492), and a project from Antonio da Sangallo's workshop. Ligorio (498) and Perino del Vaga (495) are also represented.

Of unrepresented artists, Michelangelo is the most important, though some of his finest architectural sheets have been on view in London recently (*Drawings by Michelangelo*, 1975). Palladio mentions him (IV, p.64) as one of the great modern architects. It is however hard to define what influence Michelangelo had on Palladio. The two are close in spirit in their sense of unity in design, of the importance of detail, and of grandeur and drama and feeling in architecture, but they are also often very different in their formal solutions (497). S.Giorgio Maggiore was certainly influenced by St Peter's, and the Cortile of the Carità follows Michelangelo's truly classical sense of design (compare the Coliseum), in closing the upper order of the Palazzo Farnese cortile, and not leaving the upper loggia open, as Sangallo intended to do. Other Michelangelesque touches in Palladio's work, like the giant order of Palazzo Valmarana, or the blocks which support the balconies of the Capitaniato, seem to come straight out of Palladio's own system and sensibility (cf. Lotz, 1973, p.38). And just as a local source can often be found for Palladio's usages, alongside an obvious antique one, so the giant order of the Monte di Pietà in Brescia probably made an earlier and deeper impression on Palladio than Michelangelo's design for the Capitoline Palaces. H.B.

ANONYMOUS VENETIAN C.1480

486 Roman ruins
Pen and ink: 12 × 19.1
Prov: Sebastiano Resta; John, Lord Somers
Lent by the Trustees of the British Museum

These sketches are on the verso of a drawing of the Risen Chris
and two disciples, which was characterised by Popham and
Pouncey (1950, no.329) as 'Bellinesque, strongly influenced by
Carpaccio', and assigned a date around 1500. The character of
the figures however seems closer to the middle works of
Giovanni Bellini. There are even echoes of the Correr
Crucifixion, and the landscape has a strongly Mantegnesque
character. The impression that the drawing is somewhat earlier
and that Carpaccio has little to do with it is reinforced by the
capitals of the building on the right of the verso, which are
clearly Venetian late Gothic in character. A Venetian
draughtsman might still use this formula in 1480, but not in
1490 or 1500.

On the left is the Arch of Constantine, and a chimney pot, in
the centre the Coliseum, and a semi(?) dome decorated with
coffers and rosettes; and on the right a cross vaulted structure,
close to the Basilica of Constantine or the central hall of the
Baths of Diocletian. These sketches are of the sort that painters
made, in order to collect material which could be used in
landscape backgrounds. They testify to an interest in antique
architecture in the Veneto which goes back to Jacopo Bellini
and Mantegna.   H.B.

Attributed to ALVISE VIVARINI C. 1445–1505
*487 The Virgin and Child enthroned
Pen and ink, the architecture over incised lines: 34.7 × 24.9
Lent by Her Majesty The Queen

Popham attributed this design for a large altarpiece to Vivarini
on the strength of its resemblance to his known altarpieces, and
of the impressive and completely Venetian character of the
architectural background. He dated the drawing to the last
decade of the fifteenth century (Popham and Wilde, 1949,
p.178). The drawing demonstrates Palladio's close contacts
with Venetian artistic traditions and methods. The use of
incised construction lines is identical to Palladio's practice.
Palladio's skill and judgment in the design of architectural
details has behind it the close attention to architectural
profiles which one finds not only in the work of Venetian
Quattrocento architects and sculptors, but also in the painted
architectural backgrounds of many of the altarpieces of Cima,
Alvise Vivarini, and Giovanni Bellini.   H.B.

488 Antique buildings
Pen, ink and wash: 24.5 × 25.8
Prov: John Talman
Lent by the Trustees of the Chatsworth Settlement

This is one of four drawings by the same hand in Vol.XXXVI
at Chatsworth (Bookcase table 1, shelf A) entitled *Heathen
Temples Plans and Drawings*. It is no.29; the others are nos.30,
31 and 32. Loukomski (1940) correctly noted the fact that the
drawings are identical to others which appear in the small
sketchbook in the Ambrosiana, usually attributed to

487

Bramantino (published in facsimile by Mongeri, 1880). Although Vasari records that Valerio Belli (120) owned a volume of drawings of ancient Lombard antiquities by Bramantino, which Vasari himself copied in his youth (Vasari, VI, 1881, p.511) there is no reason to attribute the drawings to Bramantino, whose painted architecture is quite different in character. The delicacy of line and the decoration however are typically Milanese, and close for instance to the famous Louvre drawing attributed to Bramante, as well as yet other drawings (Bruschi, 1970, figs.144, 102, 103).

This sheet groups drawings which appear on different pages in the Ambrosiana volume. The elevation of the building on the right, probably S.Urbano alla Caffarella, appears in no.12, the plan in no.5, with a note that it is near S.Sebastian, and that the columns were seven heads high 'which means Corinthian'. Both the would-be Vitruvian analysis, and its total inaccuracy are interesting. The other building appears in no.11 (elevation) and no.6 (plan). The note says it was on the old road to Marino, in the estates of the Cardinal of S.Pietro in Vincoli. H.B.

RAPHAEL 1483–1520

489 Details of the interior of the Pantheon
Pen and ink; red chalk: 23.8 × 18.6
Lent by the Royal Institute of British Architects (XIII/1v)

Of all the ancient monuments of Rome, the Pantheon is the one most closely associated with Raphael. He drew it relatively early in his career (J.S., lecture 1975), he modelled much of the detail of the Chigi Chapel on it, he quoted the tabernacle windows of the Palazzo Pandolfini and the Palazzo dell'Aquila from it, and he converted one of its tabernacles into a tomb for himself, and was buried there, under a statue of the Virgin and Child inspired by an ancient statue (Buddensieg, 1968). Raphael's only surviving drawing of ancient architectural details is appropriately of the Pantheon. The drawing was mentioned by Magrini (1845, p.310) and was first published by Lanciani (1895) with an attribution to Raphael, which on the basis of both handwriting and drawing style, is certain. The recto shows a measured profile of the main entablature of the interior, and the verso a rough sketch of the upper order, with a window and a pilaster, as well as a red chalk drawing of the entablature of the lower order. This is placed on the sheet in

such a way that at first glance it looks as if it belongs with the pilaster drawn below. Whereas the recto gives the detailed measurements of this entablature, this side records it in an equally important way: by indicating with great precision how the mouldings are modelled in light and shade. The rendering is so exact that it may well be that Raphael made the sketch in the Pantheon itself. He quoted the cornice, with its rich shadows, its broad smooth bands, and the flickering effect of its projecting brackets in the upper cornice of the Palazzo dell'Aquila (Frommel, 1973, III, pl.8a). Palladio never made light and shade studies of this sort, but there can be no doubt that the drawing of a profile of a cornice was enough to enable him to visualise exactly how it would look if executed.

The measured drawing on the recto is exactly reproduced in an unpublished sketchbook in the Biblioteca Civica Passionei in Fossombrone (Cod. C. 5. VI; I am indebted to Professor Alessandro Panonchi for calling my attention to the volume). The attribution to Giulio Romano is traditional (the spine of the eighteenth century binding is inscribed DISEG(NI) DE GULIO ROMAN). It is mentioned in the *Touring Club Italiano* guide to the *Marche* and is endorsed by John Shearman (oral communication). It is also supported by the subject matter: the head of the kneeling woman in the Vatican *Transfiguration* (f.85); a sketch of the corridor round the inside of the hemicycle of Trajan's Forum (f.7), the inspiration of the Santa Maria dell' Anima altarpiece; and drawings of the Pantheon corresponding exactly to the RIBA Raphael sheet. The sequence of copying is not entirely certain as Raphael on the recto writes 'lagetta dicto el capitello' which is nonsense; Giulio writes 'la gietto di tutto el chapitello' which is sense. Probably Raphael copied his source hastily, and Giulio corrected the obvious slip, when he copied from Raphael (if he did not have access to the same source). Giulio's version of the verso is less intelligent: he draws the lower entablature as if it were the entablature of the upper order, thus uniting the two sketches made by Raphael at different times and in different media, of different levels of the building. H.B.

RAPHAEL 1483–1520

490 Elevation of a Villa

Pen and brown ink, light bistre wash, over stylus;
250 × 362 mm.
Prov: De Vries, Lawrence, Woodburn
Exh: South Kensington Museum, 1859
Lent by the Visitors of the Ashmolean Museum, Oxford

The drawing was providentially photographed, by Thomas
Thompson, while at South Kensington in 1859; the print shows
that subsequently the sheet, while being purified of foxing, was
remounted and considerably reduced on all sides. The
principal losses are the sloping roof-line on the left and the
perfectly clear indications of the inclined basement-wall in both
bottom corners.

On the *verso* are five much less definitive studies (four plans and
one elevation) for an apparently much smaller villa with a
single, central machicolated tower; this *villino*, perhaps
eventually the one begun c.1518 for Baldassare Turini on the
Janiculum (Villa Lante), seems to be designed for a steeply
sloping site, with its principal loggia and façade overlooking a
fishpond. Dimensional notes are consistent with Raphael's
handwriting.

The traditional attribution, after being out of favour for about
a century, now seems to be generally accepted. The purpose
of the elevation on the *recto*, however, has not been
satisfactorily resolved. Parker was the first to notice a Medici
emblem, the ring-and-diamond, centrally placed on the
balustrade; in addition the six Medici *palle* are laid out on
either side. But it does not follow that the villa was designed
for Raphael's principal Medici patron, Pope Leo X; if the
drawing is correctly dated c.1516–20 the main alternatives
would be Lorenzo, Duke of Urbino (d.1519) and Cardinal
Giulio (later Clement VII). Recent discoveries about the
evolution of Villa Madama, the Cardinal's villa, make it
unlikely that Raphael had that project in mind. It has been
suggested, on the contrary, that Raphael was studying the
adaptation of some Mediaeval structure, from which the
towers were to be retained; to this second hypothesis it may be
objected that the studies on the *verso* show Raphael quite clearly
inventing such a tower as the central core of his *villino*, and in
fact the mixture of strictly classical elevations with such
vernacular crowning elements is a well-established Roman

tradition (the Belvedere of Innocent VIII, Bramante's medal-
design for the Palazzo dei Tribunali).

The whole building of which this is an elevation is not easily
visualised. The shadow cast on the right flank by the triple-
arched loggia suggests that the latter projects considerably from
the main body, and perhaps by as much as an arched bay; the
central balcony projects again, on consoles, and the whole of
this section is set, as a *loggia pensile* like that built much later by
Vignola at Caprarola, above a vertical basement. The small
semicircles drawn between the balusters above the loggia are
probably intended as the ends of the tiles, set orthogonally,
of a section of roof like that visible over the flanks, in which case
the balustrade is entirely decorative. The rest of the building is
set on a basement with inclined walls. The shape of the towers,
and even their number (for there could be four), cannot be
ascertained, and the structure linking them is also not clear – it
may be a *terme* window at the end of an upper *salone*, but it
would be an unusually large window and there seems no space
for a roof over the barrel-vault that would then be implied;
alternatively it may be a column-screen designed to enclose a
court, or hanging-garden, between the towers. The
repetition of the small *serliana* form between towers and loggia,
in the first case in windows and in the second in niches, and of
the small circular forms in gables, pediment and spandrels, is a
device to give unity to the very diverse shapes.

The elevation is drawn – unusually among surviving
drawings of this early date – in strict orthography, save for
minor lapses into perspective, such as Serlio will also have, in
brackets and niches. From the technical point of view the
drawing is interesting in showing evidence of modular
construction; a series of vertical stylus-lines, drawn through
points spaced in the rhythm 1:2:1:4:4:1:2:1, etc., determines
the disposition of the main elements of the loggia;
compass-arcs fix the positions of architrave and arch-centres.
This approach to design is often presumed in the study of
Renaissance architecture; it can rarely be proved, as in this
case. (Parker, 1956, no.579; Shearman, 1967, pp.13ff; Marchini,
1968, p.472.)   J.S.

RAPHAEL workshop

*491 Project for the round courtyard of the Villa Madama, Rome

Pen, ink and grey-green wash, over incised lines: 26.3 × 40
Lent by the Royal Institute of British Architects (XIII/12)

491

This drawing has not, to my knowledge, been published or discussed before. It shows in elevation the greater part of five bays, with the door in the middle. The alternative on the left is so close to the executed half of the round courtyard of the Villa Madama (163) as to leave no doubt as to identification. That this is not a drawing after the executed building, but a project, is indicated by the alternatives shown, and by the differences from the executed building. Thus the pedestal of the window tabernacles is less high than in the building itself, the diameter of the large columns is 1.04 m. as against the actual 0.89 m.; the total height of the small columns is 4.52 m. as against 4.02 m. (The Roman palm is taken here as 0.223 m.; dimensions of the actual structure from Hofmann, 1911, and Pontani, 1845). Other comparisons leave no doubt as to the close relationship of the project to the executed building: diameter of the small columns, 50 cms and 49 cms; width of the window frames, 33 cms and 30 cms; height from the ground to the top of the window sill, in the left-hand alternative, 228 cms and 241 cms (the dimensions of the drawing are first in each case). The hemicycle as it now stands lacks pediments over the windows, capitals to the main order, and entablatures. These features all appear in the earliest view of the villa, in the Sala di Costantino (Marchini, 1968, fig.90). The Villa Madama, which stands on the side of the Monte Mario overlooking the Tiber only a short distance outside Rome, is the principal surviving testimony to Raphael's achievement in the field of architecture. It was begun about

1517, for Pope Leo X's cousin Cardinal Giulio de' Medici, who in 1523 himself became Pope as Clement VII. Trissino (144) served both Medici Popes, and it is not farfetched to imagine him taking Palladio to see the villa. Palladio's drawing of it is exhibited here (163).

Numbers of drawings survive from the planning phase of the villa, though only one, a plan of the gardens, is by Raphael himself. The others are Antonio da Sangallo or his assistants. The central courtyard was originally conceived as a rectangle, and even in its round form UA 179 and UA 314 give different dimensions for it (Frommel, 1969, p.163). A very considerable effort must have gone into the working out of the elevations, of which, as far as the cortile goes, this is the only elevation study to have emerged. The system is a highly effective one, similar to that which Raphael designed for the exterior of the south transept of St Peter's. Columned tabernacles are tightly grouped between larger columns, and this compact vigorous elevation would have enlivened the cortile's overall character as a circular cross roads at the centre of a compact plan, where the two main axes of the villa intersect. The doorway into the main residential area narrows slightly towards the top, probably in obedience to Vitruvius' formulae for doors (cf. 435).

This is not a drawing by Antonio da Sangallo or one of his known assistants. Nor can it be ascribed to Raphael: the numbers and the draughting style do not match up sufficiently closely with his certain architectural drawings (489 and 490). But the drawing style is similar to his. There are the same quick horizontal strokes of shading on the columns that one can find in many of his figure drawings and the elevation is strictly orthogonal, but a little perspective touch is added in the consoles of the door, exactly as in the autograph villa project (490). The drawing can be considered as being produced under Raphael's supervision, by an assistant who modelled his architectural style on Raphael's.

As has already been suggested, the influence of Raphael, and above all of the Villa Madama, on Palladio was immense (163). The features which the two architects have in common are undoubtedly all present in the antique. But it was surely the Villa Madama which focused Palladio's attention on many of these elements. The bulging pedestals of the villa are quoted by Palladio in his San Petronio projects (on the source of the motif, Shearman, 1968, and Burns 1975, p.157). The creation of flat brick arches, with stone key stones inserted into them appears in the Palazzo Valmarana loggia, and in the Carità cortile (251). The placing of a simple profiled stone to fix the course of the freize occurs both in the Villa Madama, and in the Rotonda (356).

There is the slight but intriguing possibility that the provenance of this drawing (and 489) which goes back to Burlington, and probably Talman, is ultimately Palladio. He could have obtained it from Valerio Belli. It is a hypothesis, however, which cannot be demonstrated.   H.B.

BALDASSARE PERUZZI 1481–1536

492 Project for the remodelling of the interior of San Domenico, Siena

Pen, ink and wash, over underdrawing and incised lines:
19 × 43.2
Prov: John Talman
Lent by the Visitors of the Ashmolean Museum, Oxford

The large mediaeval church of San Domenico was gutted by fire in 1532. Peruzzi who was still public architect in Siena produced a whole series of designs for modernising, and spatially enlivening the great T-shaped shell. He displayed in these all his inventiveness, all his skill as a draughtsman, and all his compulsive dedication to the elaboration of innumerable alternatives, which may well have absorbed energies which would have been more profitably spent in selling a rather clearer and more limited choice of alternatives to his patrons. (On Peruzzi's diffidence see Vasari, IV, 1879, p.605).

The Oxford drawing is the only detailed elevation project for S.Domenico which survives, though a quick copy of a similar scheme is in the Biblioteca Comunale, Siena, Cod, S. IV. 7, fol.37v. It corresponds very closely however to UA 340, a plan which is inscribed 'For the church of San Domenico' (Parker, 1956, pp.552ff, Frommel, 1967–8, p.36; G.Chierici, 1923, Toça, 1971). Peruzzi here proposes building triangular piers out from the wall to support a series of shallow domical vaults. He offers the alternative of serliane (compare 429) and thermal windows to light the nave. With this simple device he achieves considerable spatial variety and complication. Typically, as in a the case of his masterpiece, the Palazzo Massimi alle Colonne in Rome, designed about the same time, he avoids setting up a dominant axis, and instead establishes a whole series of axes and centres of attention.

Unlike Palladio, Peruzzi often represents his projects as if they were a model opened up so that one can see the inside. The church is drawn in perspective section, and the three dimensional quality is enhanced by the skillfully graded tones of the wash. Peruzzi was of course aware of, and used the orthogonal section. But he had enormous facility as an architectural draughtsman based on his training and practice as a painter. He was probably the greatest master of the theory and practice of perspective of his time, as the use of his writings on perspective by Serlio (*Book II*; Cellini, 1960, pp.111f) and Vignola (1583) indicates, as well as *tour de force* performances like the illusionistic decoration of the upper room of the Farnesina, his perspective analysis of St Peter's (UA2), or his huge and amazing project for the interior of S.Petronio, Bologna, preserved in the church's museum. His skill in this field probably derived from Leonardo, when the later was in Rome in 1513–6. That the two were in contact is not only in itself likely, but is perhaps demonstrated by the note 'a bladder of Peruzzo's' on a sheet from a Leonardo notebook belonging to this period (Pedretti, 1972, II, p.305).   H.B.

Workshop of ANTONIO DA SANGALLO THE YOUNGER 1485–1546

493 Project for the Cappella Paolina, Vatican Palace, Rome

Pen, ink and wash with metal point construction lines:
54.8 × 42.1
Prov: John Talman
Lent by the Visitors of the Ashmolean Museum, Oxford

This drawing can be dated 1537–8, and represents a late phase in the evolution of the design of the Capella Paolina, whose construction was clearly well advanced in October 1538 (Frommel, 1964, p.6). The scheme is almost identical (apart from the screen which frames the altar) to Antonio's autograph study, UA 1125, with simplified composite capitals, and the top and bottom of the pedestal defined by a simple smooth band (Frommel, 1964, p.30). The drawing, as Frommel noted, does not appear to be by Sangallo himself, who was probably far too busy to prepare a careful study of this sort, whose function would possibly have been to give the Pope a clear idea of Sangallo's project. On the verso there is written, probably in a sixteenth century hand, 'salustio'. Another hand has amplified this summary indication, whose very brevity indicates that it was written by someone in the know, by writing '*figliuolo di baldassare*' (son of Baldassare, i.e. Sallustio Peruzzi). Though Sallustio is not documented as working as a draughtsman for Antonio da Sangallo at this time, it is not unlikely that he had absorbed some of his father's skill in perspective drawing, and is in fact the author of the drawing, and (at most) of the idea of inserting a screen, whose serliana and recessed panels are in fact Peruzzi motifs (492).

Palladio almost certainly saw the chapel in 1541, at which time the vault would have been without stucco, and the walls without Michelangelo's frescoes. The bold vaulting. the simple composite order, and the great thermal windows of the Paolina and the Sala Regia doubtless made a considerable impression on Palladio. Like aspects of the Villa Madama, they probably served to focus his attention on features of antique buildings which he might otherwise have overlooked. The simplified composite capitals which Sangallo often used appear at Bertesina (323), the thermal windows at Bagnolo (327), and the general scheme of the Paolina was possibly recalled by Palladio when he designed the refectory for S.Giorgio (246).   H.B.

CRISTOFORO LOMBARDI (?) First mentioned 1510; d. 1555

494 Design for the façade of S.Maria presso San Celso, Milan
Pen and ink, faint traces of underdrawings: 28.8 × 32.4
Lent by the Victoria and Albert Museum, London (no.646)

This extraordinary project, with two tiers of free standing columns (the right alternative shows pilasters on the upper order) has been attributed to Cristoforo Lombardi by Lotz (1974, p.292). The scheme of the cloister is carried round behind the large columns. The audacity of employing an antique columnar scheme of this sort resembles Palladio, but not the quaintness of handling, the vast angel and candelabrum (with smoking candle) and the use of perspective. If the project is by Lombardi, it must be early in his career at S.Celso, and I feel the drawing might even be earlier still (i.e. in the 1520s); Cristforo in his work was influenced by Bramante and the antique (Cupola of S.Maria della Passione, Milan Lotz, :1974, fig.312). He also submitted a design for San Petronio jointly with Giulio Romano (Hartt, 1958, fig.528) but it is neo–Gothic, and not related to the present design. There is no doubt that this project refers to S.Maria presso S.Celso, as it shows the forecourt, which begun in 1513 after designs by Cesariano.

Lombardi is documented at the church from 1533–55 (Baroni, 1940, pp.215–88).   H.B.

PERINO DEL VAGA (PIETRO BUONACCORSI) 1501–47

495 Study for the stucco decoration of the Massimi Chapel, S.Trinità de' Monti, Rome
Pen, ink, and two colburs of wash: 39.4 × 27.4
Prov: Sir Thomas Lawrence; S.Woodburn
Lent by the Victoria and Albert Museum (no.2270)

This study for the decoration of one of the walls of the Massimi Chapel (Gere, 1960; Pouncey and Gere, 1962, p.101; Oberhuber, 1966, p.173) reveals a contemporary decorative style completely alien to Palladio. It was not restricted to Perino and Salviati but was wholeheartedly adopted by Alessi, who in the cortile of Palazzo Marino and the façade of Santa Maria presso San Celso, both in Milan, converted Perino's bizarre and extravagant stucco motifs into stone. Alessi, who gave his opinion on the Palace at Brescia within days of Palladio (425), in the way in which he introduces perspective touches into his architectural drawings (which Palladio never does) also seems to have modelled himself on Perino (Burns, 1975, p.163, n.84 and fig.322).   H.B.

496 Fragment of a small pilaster capital. 2nd century A.D.
Luna marble: h.6.9 width (intact) 14.9
Lent by the Fitzwilliam Museum, Cambridge

This fragment is part of a miniature acanthus capital from a pilaster which probably belonged to furnishings or an interior wall decoration. In the centre there is a grotesque head whose beard is of acanthus leaves from which volutes spring out at the sides. Satyrs' heads of this sort were a common feature of Roman decorative art in Imperial Roman Italy during the second century A.D., and although the fragment was found in Egypt, it is almost certainly of Italian workmanship. On the top left of the capital there is a thin groove (7mm wide) probably to accommodate a thin facing slab of marble (Budde and Nichols, 1964).

Grotesque heads of this sort were common in late fifteenth century architectural decoration, and are often found in sixteenth century decorative schemes.   L.F.

MICHELANGELO BUONARROTI 1475–1564

497 Pilaster capitals for the Medici Chapel, Florence c.1524
Photograph

Palladio allowed no place (if we exclude the heads in his key
stones) for the bizarre and peculiar motifs to be found in
abundance in ancient art. Michelangelo, however, freely and
frequently adapted them, to provide dramatic touches in his
architecture. Though these capitals appear to be freely invented,
in fact they are closely based on antique examples, like that
exhibited here (496).   H.B.

PIRRO LIGORIO 1513/4–83

498 Design for a lunette, with figures of mathematicians
Pen, ink and wash: 33 × 48.2
Lent by the Trustees of the Chatsworth Settlement

This is a typical drawing by Pirro Ligorio (and already
recognised as such by Philip Pouncey and John Gere, as the
Chatsworth catalogue records). It probably was made for the
decoration of the same room (which has not been identified) as
was a Ligorio drawing of a related subject in the Louvre (Inv.
9686; *Le XVIe siècle*, 1965, no.123; cf. Louvre Inv. 9688) and
possibly a drawing sold in Vienna in 1918, which
interestingly was in Ferrara in 1856 (Kerner Sale, Kende,
Vienna).
Though Ligorio worked as an architect and painter, his
energies went above all into his voluminous illustrated
manuscripts on all aspects of ancient art, topography, and
mythology. He was praised by Barbaro in his *Vitruvius* (178)
which was dedicated to Ligorio's own patron, Cardinal
Ippolito d'Este, for whom Ligorio designed the Villa d'Este at
Tivoli (Coffin, 1960; Lamb, 1966). This and the beautiful
Casino of Pius IV in the Vatican gardens are the most
important record of Ligorio's imitation of the antique, which
differed greatly from Palladio's. Ligorio concentrated not on
extracting a set of basic principles from surviving monuments,
but on the creation of what he thought of as the atmosphere of
ancient art, which he identified with complex decorative and
architectural schemes, often bordering on the bizarre and
fantastic. Just as one of the starting points for Palladio's view of
the antique was the exterior of the Villa Madama, so Ligorio's
was another aspect of Raphael's attempt to recreate the

splendours of ancient architecture and architectural decoration
the Palazzo dell'Aquila. Ligorio and Palladio were certainly in
touch with one another in 1554, and probably in 1545–7
(Burns, 1973, and 1973–II). Palladio copied Ligorio's drawing
of the Tempietto di Clitumno, and the Roman villa at
Anguillara, and Ligorio copied Palladio's section of the
amphitheatre at Verona, and his studies of the Porta Aurea at
Ravenna (Museo Civico, D.31) in his encyclopedia of classical
antiquities (AST, Ligorio mss, Vol.18, VERONA, and
Vol.15, fol.23f). The so-called Fra Giocondo albums in
Leningrad (Mikhailova, 1970; Goukowski, 1963) in fact contain
many drawings by or after Pirro Ligorio, so that the note on
on Album B, fol.130 verso 'this book was Andrea Palladio's' is
significant (Fabriczy, 1893, p.108; Lotz, 1962, p.64, Puppi,
1973, p.23, n.23).   H.B.

BIBLIOGRAPHY

COMPILED BY BRUCE BOUCHER

Archival sources:
Florence, Archivio di Stato Cosimo Bartoli, despatches from Venice, Mediceo del Principato, buste 2979, 2980, 2981.
Venice, Archivio di Stato, Capi del Consiglio dei Dieci, Lettere dei Rettori, b.223, b.224.
Senato, Relazioni (Vicenza), b.51.
Senato, Relazioni Miste, b.32, b.33.
Provveditori ai Beni Inculti.
Provveditori sopraintendenti alla Camera dei Confini, b.262 (notes and sketches of Cristoforo Sorte).
Vicenza, Archivio di Stato.
Archivio Torre, in the Biblioteca Bertoliana.

Manuscripts:
Cambridge, Fitzwilliam Museum, Commissione of the Podestà of Vicenza Pietro Tagliapietra, 1535 (Morlay Cutting I, 43).
Eton, Eton College, Venetorum Nobilium Liber, 16th cent. (MS 193).
Fossombrone, Biblioteca Civica Passionei, Giulio Romano, sketchbook (Cod.C, 5, VI).
London, British Library (BM Add. MS 39633).
Breviary, late 15th cent.
Mariegola of the Confraternity of Boatmen at Mestre, 1508 (BM Add. MS 42125).
Promissione of Doge Antonio Grimani, 1521 (BM Add. MS 18000).
Commissione of the Capitanio of Vicenza, Nicolò Morosini, 1531 (BM Add. MS 15518).
Jacopo Veronese, Dialogo che trata de l'arte di bombardier, 1562 (BM Add. MS 10897).
Commissione of Nicolò q. Giovanni Donà as Podestà of Vicenza, 1574 (BM Add. MS 18066).
Miscellany of Venetian history (BM Add. MS 10815).
Letters of Doges to the Rettori of Vicenza (BM Add. MS 15141).
Antonio Visentini, Reconstructions of Palladio's works for the entry of Henry III into Venice, 1756 (BM Add. MS 18066).
Milan, Biblioteca Braidense (Berra), Trissino MSS. (MSSS. Castiglioni, 8/1, 8/2, 8/3).
Siena, Biblioteca Comunale. After B.Peruzzi, Sketchbook (Cod. S.IV.7).
Venice, Biblioteca Correr, Marcantonio Michiel, Diarii (Cod. Cicogna, 2848).
Biblioteca Marciana, Ponte di Rialto e Prigioni (MSS Italiani, Classe VII, no.295 = 10047).
Francesco da Molino, Compendio (MSS Italiani, Classe VII, no.533 = 8812).
Vicenza, Biblioteca Bertoliana. Andrea Palladio and Vincenzo Arnaldi, materials relating to

the Arnaldi properties at Meledo (Gonz. 22.6.15 = 181).
Bartolommeo Ziggiotti, Memorie dell'Accademia Olimpica (Gonz. 21.11.2 = 2916).

Books:
1495
Crescentio, P., De Agricultura, Venice.
1511
Jucundus, J., M.Vitruvius, Venice.
1521
Cesariano, C., Di Lucio Vitruvio Pollione de Architectura libri dece, traducti de Latina in Vulgare, Como.
1524
Trissino, G.G., La Sofonisba, Rome.
1525
Dragonzino, G.B., Nobiltà di Vicenza, Venice.
1529
Trissino, G.G., Dialogw intitulatw Castellanw nel quale si tratta de la lingua italiana, Vicenza.
Trissino, G.G., A.B.C. a.b.c., Vicenza.
1537
Serlio, S., Regole generali di Architettura, Libro IV, Venice.
1538
Rutulius Taurus Aemilianus Palladius, tr. P.Marino, Venice.
1539
Beccanuvoli, L., Tutte le donne vicentine maritate, vedove e dongelle, Vicenza.
1540
Piccolomini, A., L'Amor Costante, Venice.
Saraynus, T., De origine et amplitudine urbis Veronae, Verona.
Serlio, S., Regole generali di Architettura, Libro III, Venice.
1541
Caravia, A., Il sogno dil Caravia, Venice.
1544
Serlio, S., Regole generali d'Archtettura, Libro V, Venice.
1545
Serlio, S., Il primo libro d'Architettura [with Book II], Paris.
1547
Serlio, S., Quinto Libro d'Architettura, Paris.
Trissino, G.G., La Italia liberata da Gotthi, Venice.
Tolomei, C., Delle lettere . . . libri sette, Venice.
1550
Doni, A.F., La Libraria, Venice.
1551
Serlio, S., Quinto Libro dell'Architettura . . . [with Book IV], Venice.
1552
Dialogo di duoi villani padoani . . ., Venice.
Eliano: Del modo di mettere in ordinanza, tr. per

Fr. Ferrosi, Venice.
Salviati, G., Regola di far perfettamente col compasso la voluta et del capitolo ionico, Venice.
1554
Cataneo, P., I Quattro primi libri di architettura . . ., Venice.
Lamento di un Bergamasco venuto in poverta per la carestia . . ., no place of publication.
Palladio, A., Lantichita di Roma, Rome.
Palladio, A., Descrittione de le chiese . . . brevemente raccolta, Rome.
1555
Doni, A.F., Seconda Libraria, Venezia.
Vicentino, Nicola, L'antica musica ridotta alla moderna prattica, Venice.
1556
Vitruvius, M.P., I dieci libri dell'architettura, tr. Daniele Barbaro, Venice.
1557
Barbaro, D., Della eloquenza, Venice.
Labacco, A., Libro appartenente a l'architettura, Rome.
1559
Willaert, A., Musica nova, Venice.
1560
Caroto, G., De la Antiqutate di Verona, Verona.
Poldo D'Albenas, J., Discours historial de l'antique et illustre Cité de Nismes . . . Avec les portraitz des plus antiques e insignes batiments du dit lieu . . . ensemble de l'antique et moderne ville, Lyon.
1561
Pietro Crescentio, tr. F.Sansovino, Venice.
[Sansovino, F.] Delle cose notabili che sono in Venetia . . ., Venice.
1564
Bartoli, C., Del modo di misurare . . ., Venice.
1565
Alberti, L., L'architettura, tr. C.Bartoli, Venice.
Belli, S., Libro del misurar con la vista, Venice.
Caravia, A., Naspo Bizaro, Venice.
1566
Ruscelli, G., Le imprese illustri, Venice.
1567
Barbaro, D., I dieci libri dell'Architettura tradotti et commentati, Venice.
Bartoli, C., Raggionamenti sopra alcuni luoghi difficili di Dante, Venice.
Ceredi, G., Tre discorsi sopra il modo di alzar acque da' luoghi bassi, Parma.
Jus municipale vicentinum cum additione partium illustrissimi Dominii, Venice.
L'Orme, P. de, Le premier tome de l'Architecture, Paris.
1568
Barbaro, D., La pratica della perspettiva . . ., Venice.
Vasari, G., Le vite de' più eccellenti pittori, scultori, 1569 e architettori, Florence, III vols.
Maganza, G.B., Rava, A., and Rustichello, B.,

*La prima-quarta parte de le rime di Magagnò,
Menon, e Begotto*, Venice.
1570
*Opera nova sopra l'allegrezza de' buoni
Christiani . . .*, Venice (?).
Palladio, A., *I Quattro Libri dell'Architettura*,
Venice.
Scappi, B., *Opera . . .*, Venice.
1572
[Bassi, M.] *Dispareri in materia di architettura et
prospettiva . . .*, Brescia.
1573
Belli, S., *Trattato della proportione*, Venice.
1574
Benedetti, R., *Le feste et trionfi fatti dalla
Serenissima Signoria di Venetia nella felice venuta di
Enrico III*, Venice.
Della Croce, M., *L'historia della publica et famosa
entrata in Venegia del Serenissimo Henrico III*,
Venice.
Montecchio, S., *De Inventario haeredis*, Venice.
Porcacchi, T., *Le attioni d'Arrigo terzo re di
Francia et quarto di Polonia*, Venice.
Porcacchi, T., *Funerali antichi di diversi popoli*,
Venice.
1575
Palladio, A., *I Commentari di C.Giulio Cesare*,
Venice.
1576
Gratiolo, A., *Discorso di peste*, Venice.
1579
Paruta, P., *Della perfettione della vita politica*,
Venice.
1580
Sorte, C., *Osservazioni nella Pittura*, Venice.
1581
Caroso, F., *Il Ballarino*, Venice.
Palladio, A., *I Quattro Libri dell'Architettura*,
Venice.
Sansovino, F., *Venetia città nobilissima et singolare*,
Venice.
1583
Magagnò [Maganza, G.B.] . . ., *Quarta parte delle
Rime rustiche*, Vicenza.
Scamozzi, V., *Discorsi sopra le antichità di Roma*,
Venezia.
1584
Ingegneri, A., *La danza di Venere. Pastorale*,
Vicenza.
Rossetti, G.B., *Dello scalco del Duchessa d'Urbino*,
Ferrara.
Serlio, S., *Tutte le opere d'architettura . . . et un
indice copiosissimo raccolto da M.Gio.Domenico
Scamozzi*, Venice.
1585
Cavrioli (Capreolus), E., *Delle historie Bresciane*,
Brescia.
1587
Bardi, G., *Dichiaratione di tutte istorie che si

contengono ne i quadri posti novamente nelle Sale
dello Scrutinio, et del Gran Consiglio . . .*, Venice.
1589
Vecellio, C., *Habiti antichi e moderni di tutto il
mondo*, Venice.
1591
Marzari, G., *La Historia di Vicenza*, Vicenza.
Porcacchi, T., *Funerali antichi . . .*, Venice.
1594
Maggio, B., *Trattato delle ferite delli arcobugi*, tr.
B.Polli, Verona.
1598
Franco, G., *Habiti d'Huomeni et Donne Venetiane*,
Venice.
Ingegneri, A., *Della Poesia Rappresentativa e del
modo di rappresentare le favole sceniche*, Ferrara.
1604
Sansovino, F., *Venetia città nobilissima et
singolare*, ed. G.Stringa, Venice.
1610
Franco, G., *Habiti d'Huomeni et Donne Venetiane*,
Venice.
Maganza, G.B., et al., *Rime rustiche . . .*, Venice.
1615
Scamozzi, V., *L'Idea dell'Architettura Universale*,
Venice.
1619
Serlio, S., *Tutte l'opere d'architettura et prospetiva
di Sebastiano Serlio Bolognese*, Venice.
1624
Wotton, H., *The Elements of Architecture*,
London
1648
Ridolfi, C., *Le Maraviglie dell'Arte*, Venice,
II vols.
1663
Sansovino, F., *Venetia città nobilissima et
singolare*, ed. G.Martinioni, Venice.
1670
Zabarella, G., *Il Pileo, overo Nobilità heroica et
Origine gloriosissima dell'eccellentissima Famiglia
Capello*, Padua.
1715-25
Campbell, C., *Vitruvius Britannicus or the British
Architect*, London.
1721
Leoni, G., *The Architecture of A.Palladio in four
Books . . .*, London.
1740
Bandello, M., *Le Novelle*, London, IV vols.
1740-8
Muttoni, F., *Architettura di Andrea Palladio*,
Venice.
1749
Cornaro, F., *Ecclesiae Venetae Antiquis
Monumentis . . .*, Venice, vol.VIII.
1758
Grevenbroeck, J. van, *Raccolta di bataori a
Venezia*, ed. G.Brusa, Venice.

1760
Muttoni, F., *Architettura di Andrea Palladio*,
Venice.
1762
Temanza, T., *Vita di Andrea Palladio*, Venice.
1769
Arnaldi, E., *Delle Basiliche antiche . . .*, Vicenza.
1776
Bertotti Scamozzi, O., *Le fabbriche e i disegni di
Andrea Palladio*, Vicenza, vol.I.
Rodella, G.B., *Memorie sucose intorno al Palazzo
Pubblico di Brescia*, Venice.
1778
Bertotti Scamozzi, O., *Le fabbriche e i disegni di
Andrea Palladio*, Vicenza, vol.II.
Temanza, T., *Vite dei più celebri architetti . . .*,
Venice.
Zamboni, B., *Memorie intorno alle fabbriche
pubbliche più insigni della Città di Brescia*, Brescia.
1781
Bertotti Scamozzi, O., *Le fabbriche e i disegni di
Andrea Palladio*, Vicenza, vol.III.
1783
Bertotti Scamozzi, O., *Le fabbriche e i disegni di
A.Palladio*, Vicenza, vol.IV.
1788
Chambers, E., *Cyclopaedia, or an Universal
Dictionary of Arts and Sciences*, London, II vols.
1803
Blundell, H., *An Account of the Statues . . . and
Paintings at Ince*, Liverpool.
1814
Selva, G.A., *Delle differenti maniere di descriverla
voluta ionica*, Padua.
1815
Moschini, G.A., *Guida per la Città di Venezia*,
Venice.
1824
Cigogna, E.A., *Delle Inscrizioni veneziane*,
Venice, vol.I.
1830
Quatremère de Quincy, A.C., *Histoire de la vie et
des ouvrages des plus celebres architects*, Paris, vol.II.
1834
Cigogna, E.A., *Delle Inscrizioni veneziane*,
Venice, vol.IV.
1837
Rondelet, A., *Essai historique sur le Pont de Rialto*,
Paris.
1840
Gaye, G., *Carteggio inedito di artisit dei secoli XIV,
XV, XVI*, Florence, vol.II.
1843-4
Malipiero, D., 'Annali veneti dall' anno *1457* al
1500', ed. A.Sagredo, in *Archivio Storico
Italiano*, VII.
1845
Magrini, A., *Memorie intorno alla vita e le opere di
Andrea Palladio*, Padua.

Pontani, C., *Opere architettoniche di Raffaello Sanzio incise e dichiarate*, Rome.

1854
Waagen, G.F., *Treasures of Art in Great Britain*, London, vol.III.

1866
Bartsch, A., *Le Peintre Graveur*, Leipzig, vol.XII.

1868
Lorenzi, G., *Monumenti per servire alla storia del Palazzo Ducale di Venezia*, Venice.

1874
Yriarte, C., *La vie d'un patricien de Venise au seizième siècle*, Paris, vol.2.

1876
Fortnum, C., *A Descriptive Catalogue of the Bronzes of European Origin in the South Kensington Museum*, London.

1877
Bressan, B., *Serie dei podestà . . . con lo statuto e la matricola de' dottori collegiali vicentini*, Vicenza.

1878
Morsolin, B., ed., *Lettere del Cardinale Nicolò Ridolfi, Vescovo di Vicenza a Giangiorgio Trissino* (Nozze Lampertico-Piovene), Vicenza.

1878-85
Vasari, G., *Le vite . . .*, ed. G.Milanese, Florence, IX vols.

1880
Mongeri, G., 'Le rovine di Roma al principio del Secolo XVI', Studi del Bramantino . . ., Milan.

1883
Armand, A., *Les Mèdailleurs Italiens*, Paris, III vols.

1885
Bortolan, D., *Saggio di un dizionario biografico di artisti vicentini. Lettera A*, Vicenza.

1886
Molinier, E., *Les Bronzes de la Renaissance : Les Plaquettes*, Paris.

1887
Molmenti, P., *La dogaressa di Venezia*, Turin and Naples.
Bortolan, D., *Locuste a Vicenza*, Vicenza.

1888
Monza, F., *Cronaca*, ed. D.Bortolan, Vicenza.

1889
Bortolan, D., ed., *Cronicha che comenza dall' anno 1400 . . .*, Vicenza.

1890
De Nolhac, P., Solerti, A., *Il viaggio in Italia di Enrico III re di Francia*, Turin.

1893
Fabriczy, C. de, 'Il libro di schizzi d'un pittore olandese nel museo di Stuttgart', *Archivio Storico dell'Arte*, VI, pp.106–26.
Paoletti, P., *L'architettura e la scultura del Rinascimento in Venezia : Ricerche storico–artistiche*, Venice, II vols.

1894
Lanciani, R., 'Di un frammento inedito della pianta di Roma antica riferibile alla regione VII', *Bollettino della Commissione Archeologico Comunale di Roma*.
Morsolin, B., *G.G. Trissino. Monografia di un gentiluomo letterato nel secolo XVI*, Florence.

1895
James, M.R., *A descriptive catalogue of the manuscripts in the library at Eton College*, Cambridge.
Lanciani, R., 'La Pianta di Roma antica e i disegni archeologici di Raffaello Sanzio', *Rendiconti dell'Accademia dei Lincei*, 25 November.

1899
Rumor, S., *Il blasone vicentino descritto e illustrato*, Venice.

1900-11
Hofmann, T., *Raffael in seiner Bedeutung als Architekt*, Dresden, Zittau, Leipzig, IV vols.

1904
Ruskin, J., *The Stones of Venice*, ed. E.T.Cook and A.Wedderburn, London, vol.III.

1905
Molmenti, P., *La storia di Venezia nella vita privata dalle origini alla caduta della Repubblica*, Bergamo, vol.I.

1907
Berenson, B., *North Italian Painters of the Renaissance*, New York and London.
Papadopoli, N., *Le monete di Venezia*, Venice, vol.II.
Smith, L., *The Life and Letters of Sir Henry Wotton*, Oxford.
Venturi, A., 'Bronzi nel Museo Comunale di Trento', in *L'Arte*, vol.X.

1908
Predelli, R., ed., *Le Carte e le memorie di Alessandro Vittoria*, Trent.

1909
Caliari, B., *Paolo Veronese*, Rome.

1910
Bode, W., *Collection of J.Pierpont Morgan : bronzes of the Renaissance and subsequent periods*, Paris.

1911
Egger, H., *Roemische Veduten: Handzeichnungen aus dem XV. bis XVIII. Jahrhundert zur Topographie der Stadt Rom*, Vienna, vol.I.

1912
Hill, G.F., *Portrait Medals of Italian Artists of the Renaissance*, Oxford.

1913
Bode, W., *Catalogue of the Otto Beit Collection*, London.
Cust, L., 'Notes on Pictures in the Royal Collection', *The Burlington Magazine*, XXIII, pp.150–62, 267–76.
Strong, Mrs S.A., 'Six Drawings of the Column of Trajan with the Date 1467 . . .', *Papers of the British School at Rome*, VI, pp.174–83.

1914
Ridolfi, C., *Le maraviglie dell'Arte*, ed. D.v. Hadeln, Berlin, vol.I.

1915
Zorzi, G.G., 'Come lo studio di Valerio Belli trasmigrò a Trento', *L'Arte*, XVIII, pp.253–7.

1916
Huelsen, C., and Egger, H., *Die Roemischen Skizzenbuecher von Marten van Heemskerck*, Berlin, II vols.
Zorzi, G.G., 'Il matrimonio di Andrea Palladio', *Nuovo Archivio Veneto*, N.S., XXXII.

1919
Planiscig, L., *Die Estensische Kunstsammlung*, Vienna.

1920
Dodgson, C., 'Marcus Curtius: A Woodcut after Pordenone', *The Burlington Magazine*, XXXVII, p.61.
Zorzi, G.G., 'Alcuni rilievi sulla vita e le opere di Valerio Belli detto Vicentino', *L'Arte*, XXIII, pp.181–94.

1921
Planiscig, L., *Venezianische Bildhauer der Renaissance*, Vienna.

1923
Chierici, G., 'Baldassare Peruzzi e la Chiesa di S.Domenico a Siena', *Rassegna d'Arte senese*, XVI.

1924
Hadeln, D.V., 'A Drawing after an Important Lost Work by Pordenone', *The Burlington Magazine*, XXXXIV, p.149.
Maclagen, E., *Victoria and Albert Museum, Department of Architecture and Sculpture : Catalogue of Italian Plaquettes*, London.
Ridolfi, C., *Le maraviglie dell'Arte*, ed. D.v.Hadeln, Berlin, vol.II.

1924-5
Gerola, G., 'Nuovi documenti veneziani su Alessandro Vittoria', *Atti del Real Istituto Veneto di Scienze, Lettere, ed Arti*, LXXXIV, pp.339–59.

1927
Babelon, J., *La Médaille et les Médailleurs*, Paris.
Huelsen, C., *Le chiese di Roma nel medioevo*, Florence.
Read, C.H., *The Waddesdon Bequest*, 2nd ed., London.

1928
Fiocco, G., *Paolo Veronese*, Bologna.
Rovelli, L., *Paolo Giovio : Il Museo dei Ritratti*, Como.

1929
Kris, E., *Meister und Meisterwerke der Steinschneidekunst*, Vienna, II vols.

1930
Frey, K., ed., *Der literarische Nachlass Giorgio*

Vasaris: Briefwechsel . . . CDXII – ML, Munich, vol.II.

Parker, K.T., 'Allegory on the Victory of Lepanto', *Old Master Drawings*, IV, pp.66–7.

Suida, W., 'Lombardische Bildnisse', *Pantheon*, V, pp.250–62.

1931

Egger, H., *Roemische Veduten: Handzeichnungen aus dem XV. bis XVIII. Jahrhundert zur Topographie der Stadt Rom*, Vienna, vol.II.

Westphal, D., *Bonifazio Veronese*, Munich.

Witt, M.H., 'A collaboration by Visentini and Zuccarelli', *The Burlington Magazine*, LVIII, pp.294–9.

1932

Planiscig, L., 'Gasparo, fonditore Veneziano', *Bollettino d'Arte*, XXVI, pp.345–51.

1933

British Museum, *Catalogue of Additions to the Manuscripts 1916–20*, London.

Fratti, L., 'Bibliografia dei manoscritti, Pier de' Crescenzio', *Studi e Documenti, Societa Agraria di Bologna*.

Sorbelli, A., 'Bibliografia dei manoscritti, Pier de' Crescenzio', *Studi e Documenti, Societa agraria di Bologna*.

Tassini, G., *Curiosità veneziane*, ed. E.Zorzi, Venice.

Zucchini, G., *Disegni antichi e moderni per la facciata di S.Petronio di Bologna*, Bologna.

1934

Cessi, R., and Alberti, A., *Rialto: L'isola, Il ponte, Il mercato*, Bologna.

Gerola, G., *Il Castello del Buonconsiglio e il Museo Nazionale di Trento*, Rome.

1936

Borenius, T., *Catalogue of the Pictures and Drawings at Harewood House*, Oxford.

Foscari, L., *Affreschi esterni a Venezia*, Milan.

1937

Planiscig, L., 'Pietro, Tullio, und Antonio Lombardo', *Jahrbuch der Kunsthistorichen Sammlungen in Wien*, N.S. XI, pp.87–115.

Zorzi, G.G., *Contributo alla Storia dell'arte vicentina dei secoli XV e XVI. Il preclassicismo e i prepalladiani*, Venice.

1937–8

Kurz, O., 'Giorgio Vasari's "Libro de' Disegni",' *Old Master Drawings*, XII, pp.32–44.

1938

Fasolo, G., *Notizie di arte e di storia vicentina*, in 'Archivio Veneto', pp.261–301.

The Walpole Society: Vertue Notebooks V, XXVI, Oxford.

1939

Fiocco, G., *Giovanni Antonio Pordenone*, Udine.

Tietze-Conrat, E., 'Pordenone and not Parmigianino', *The Burlington Magazine*,

LXXIV, p.91.

1940

Baroni, C., *Documenti per la storia dell'architettura a Milano nel Rinascimento e nel Barocco*, Florence.

Rackham, B., *Catalogue of Italian Maiolica in the Victoria and Albert Museum*, London, II vols.

1942

Dinsmoor, W.B., 'The Literary Remains of Sebastiano Serlio', *The Art Bulletin*, XXIV, pp.55–91, 119–54.

Puyvelde, L. van, *The Flemish Drawings in the Collection of his Majesty the King at Windsor Castle*, London.

1943

Dalla Pozza, A.M., *Andrea Palladio*, Vicenza.

1943–63

Dalla Pozza, A.M., *Palladiana. VIII–IX, Odeo Olimpico*, pp.99–131.

1944

Tietze, H., and Tietze, Conrat, E., *The Drawings of the Venetian Painters in the 15th and 16th Centuries*, New York.

1947

Berenson, B., 'Ristudiando Tintoretto e Tiziano', *Arte Veneta*, I, pp.22–36.

1948

Trincanato, E.R., *Venezia minore*, Milan.

1949

Popham, A.E., and Wilde, J., *The Italian Drawings of the XV and XVI Centuries in the Collection of His Majesty the King at Windsor Castle*, London.

Zorzi, G.G., *Ancora della vera origine e della giovinezza di Andrea Palladio secondo nuovi documenti*, in 'Arte Veneta', III, pp.140–2.

1950

Pallucchini, R., *La giovinezza del Tintoretto*, Milan.

Pastor, L., *Storia dei papi*, Rome, vol.VII.

Peltzer, A., 'Chi è il pittore "Alberto de Ollanda"?', *Art Veneta*, IV, pp.118–22.

Popham, A.E., and Pouncey, P., *Italian Drawings in the Department of Prints and Drawings in the British Museum: The Fourteenth and Fifteenth Centuries*, London, II vols.

1952

Barbieri, F., *Vincenzo Scamozzi*, Vicenza.

Cevese, R., *I Palazzi dei Thiene*, Vicenza.

Wittkower, R., *Architectural Principles in the Age of Humanism*, London.

1953

Rodolico, F., *Le pietre delle città d'Italia*, Florence.

1953–6

Lotz, W., 'Das Raumbild in der italienischen Architekturzeichnung der Renaissance', *Mitteilungen des Kunsthistorichen Institutes in Florenz*, XVII, pp.193–226.

1954

Ives, H., *The Venetian Gold Ducat and its Imitations* (American Numismatic Society), New York.

Robertson, G., *Vincenzo Catena*, Edinburgh.

Santangelo, A., *Museo di Palazzo Venezia, Catalogo delle sculture*, Rome

1955

Fleming, J., 'The Hugfords of Florence (Part II), *The Connoisseur*, CXXXV, pp.197–206.

1956

Barbieri, F., Cevese, R., and Magagnato, L., *Guida di Vicenza*, Vicenza.

Cevese, R.; see Barbieri, F.

Benisovich, M.N., 'The drawings of Stradanus (Jan van der Straet) in the Cooper Union Museum for the Arts of Decoration', *The Art Bulletin*, XXXVIII, pp.249–51.

Damerini, G., *L'Isola e il Cenobio di S.Giorgio Maggiore*, Venezia.

Parker, K.T., *Catalogue of the Collection of Drawings in the Ashmolean Museum: Italian Schools*, Oxford.

1957

Berenson, B., *Italian Pictures of the Renaissance: Venetian School*, London, II vols.

Gallo, R., 'Contributi su Jacopo Sansovino', *Saggi e memorie della storia dell'arte*, I, pp.83–105.

Mariacher, G., *Il Museo Correr di Venezia: Dipinti dal XIV al XVI Secolo*, Venice.

Portogruaro, P.D., da, *Storia dei Cappuccini veneti*, Mestre.

1958

Lieb, N., *Die Fugger und die Kunst*, Munich, 1958.

Magnuson, T., *Institute of Art History, University of Uppsala: Studies in Roman Quattrocento Architecture*, Stockholm.

Mantese, G., *Memorie storiche della chiesa vicentina: Il Trecento*, Vicenza.

Parker, K.T., *Disegni veneti di Oxford* (Fondazione G.Cini), Venice.

Sacchetti-Sassetti, A., 'Antonio Sangallo e i lavori delle Marmore', *Archivi d'Italia e Rassegna internazionale degli Archivi*, Quaderno, n.d., Rome.

1959

Crema, L., *L'architettura romana*, Turin.

Gualdo, G., 'Vita di Andrea Palladio', ed. G.G. Zorzi, *Saggi e memorie di storia dell'arte*, II, pp.91–104.

Zorzi, G.G., *I disegni delle antichità di Andrea Palladio*, Venice.

1960

Arslan, E., *I Bassano*, Milan, II vols.

Catalogue of Paintings: Rijksmuseum, Amsterdam.

Cellini, B., 'Della architettura', in *Opere di Baldassare Castiglione, Giovanni della Casa, Benvenuto Cellini*, ed. C.Cordié, Milan and Naples.

Cessi, F., *Alessandro Vittoria Medaglista*, Trent.
Coffin, D.R., *The Villa d'Este at Tivoli*, Princeton.
Corsi, G., 'La villa prepalladiana di Cusignana', *Architettura*, LIII.
Dickinson, G., *Du Bellay in Rome*, Leiden.
van der Doort, A., 'Abraham van der Doort's Catalogue of the Collections of Charles I', ed. O.Millar, *The Walpole Society*, XXXVII.
Gallo, R., 'Michele Sanmicheli a Venezia', *Micheli Sanmicheli: Studi raccolti . . .*, Verona, pp.95–160.
Gazzola, P., *Palladio a Verona*, in 'Bollettino del C.I.S.A.', II, pp.34–9.
Gere, J.A., 'Two Late Fresco Cycles by Perino del Vaga: The Massimi Chapel and the Sala Paolina', *The Burlington Magazine*, CII, pp.9–19.
Kahnemann, M., *Michele Sanmicheli* (Palazzo Canossa), Verona.
Sorte, C., 'Osservazioni nella Pittura', *Trattati d'Arte del Cinquecento*, ed. P.Barocchi, Bari, vol.I.

1961
Beltrami, B., *La penetrazione economica dei veneziani in terraferma. Forze di lavoro e proprietà fondiaria nelle campagne venete dei secoli XVII e XVIII*, Venice and Rome.
Cessi, F., *Alessandro Vittoria Scultore, I Parte*, Trent.
Mazzotti, G., 'Relazione sul restauro di alcune ville venete e dei relativi affreschi', *Arte Veneta*, XV, pp.298–311.
Pane, R., *Andrea Palladio*, Turin.
Pope-Hennessy, J., *Rijksmuseum, Meesters van het brons*, Amsterdam.
Schulz, J., *Vasari at Venice*, in 'The Burlington Magazine', CIII, pp.500–11.

1961-3
Schulz, J., *Cristoforo Sorte and the Ducal Palace of Venice*, in 'Mitteilungen des Kunsthistorischen Institutes in Florenze', pp.193–208.

1962
Ballarin, A., 'Profilo di Lamberto d'Amsterdam', *Arte Veneta*, XVI, pp.61–81.
Barbieri, F., *Il Palazzo Chiericati sede del Museo Civico di Vicenza*, in 'Il Museo Civico di Vicenza', vol.I, pp.9–62.
Boymans-van Beuningen Museum, *Catalogus schilderijen tot 1800*, Rotterdam.
Cessi, F., *Alessandro Vittoria Scultore, II Parte*, Trent.
Constable, W.G., *Canaletto*, Oxford, II vols.
Forssman, E., *Palladio e Vitruvio*, in 'Bollettino C.I.S.A.', IV, pp.31–42.
Gould, C., 'Sebastiano Serlio and Venetian Painting', *Journal of the Warburg and Courtauld Institutes*, XXV, pp.56–64.
Lotz, W., *Osservazioni intorno ai disegni palladiani*, in 'Bollettino C.I.S.A.', IV, pp.61–8.

Moschini-Marconi, S., *Gallerie dell'Accademia di Venezia: Opere d'Arte del Secolo XVI*, Rome.
Pedretti, C., *A chronology of Leonardo' da Vinci's architectural studies after 1500*, Geneva, 1962
Popham, A.E., *Smithsonian Institution; Old Master Drawings from Chatsworth*, Washington, D.C.
Pouncey, P., and Gere, J.A., *Italian Drawings in the Department of Prints and Drawings in the British Museum: Raphael and His Circle*, London, II vols.
Timofiewitsch, W., *Eine Zeichnung Andrea Palladios für die Klosteranlage S.Giorgio Maggiore*, in 'Arte Veneta', XVI, pp.160 sgg.
Timofiewitsch, W., *La chiesetta della Rotonda*, in 'Bollettino C.I.S.A.', IV, pp.262–70 (II).
Timofiewitsch, W., *Fassadenentwurfe Andrea Palladios für S.Petronio, Bologna*, in 'Arte Veneta', XVI, p.82 sgg. (III).
Wittkower, R., *Architectural Principles in the Age of Humanism*, London.
Zorzi, G.G., *La famiglia di A.Palladio secondo nuovi documenti*, in 'Archivio Veneto', pp.15–54.

1963
Barioli, G., *Restauro di una fabbrica palladiana*, in 'Prospettive', 26, pp.16–24.
Goukowski, M.A., *Ritrovamento dei tre volumi di disegni attribuiti a Fra' Giocondo*, in 'Italia Medioevale e Umanistica', pp.263–70.
Jaderosa-Molino, G., 'Riconoscibili decorazioni ad affresco di Giuseppe Porta detto Salviati', *Arte Veneta*, XVII, pp.164–8.
Menegazzi, L., *Il Museo Civico di Treviso: Dipinti e sculture dal XII al XIX Secolo*, Venice.
Storia di Brescia: II La Dominazione Veneta (1426–1575), Brescia.
Timofiewitsch, W., 'Ein neuer Beitrag zu der Baugeschichte von S.Giorgio Maggiore', *Bollettino C.I.S.A.*, V, pp.330–9.
C.I.S.A., V, pp.330–9.
Zorzi, G.G., 'Quattro Monumenti sepocrali disegnati da Andrea Palladio', *Arte Veneta*, XVII, pp.96–105.

1964
Alberigo, G., 'Daniele Barbaro', *Dizionario biografico degli Italiani*, Rome, vol.VI, pp.89–95.
biografico degli Italiani, vol.VI, pp.89–95.
Budde, L., and Nicholls, R., *The Catalogue of Greek and Roman Sculpture in the Fitzwilliam Museum, Cambridge*, Cambridge.
Cantagalli, R., and Blasi, N. de, 'Cosimo Bartoli', *Dizionario biografico degli Italiani*, vol.VI, pp.561–3.
Cevese, R., 'Le opere pubbliche e le fabbriche private di Andrea Palladio di G.G.Zorzi', *Bollettino C.I.S.A.*, VI, pp.334–59.
Frommel, C.L., 'Antonio da Sangallos Cappella Paolina . . .', *Zeitschfift fuer Kunstgeschichte*, XXVII, pp.1–42.

Levey, M., *Later Italian Pictures in the Royal Collection*, London.
Levi D'Ancona, M., 'Postile a Girolamo da Crèmona', in *Studi di bibliografia e di storia in onore di T. De Marinis*, Vatican City, vol.III, pp.45–104.
Mantese, G., *Memorie storiche della Chiesa Vicentina: 1404–1563*, Vicenza, vol.III.
Mantese, G., 'Tristi vicende del Can. Paolo Almerico munifico costruttore della Villa 'Rotonda',' in *Studi in onore di A.Bardella*, Vicenza, pp.162–86 (II).
Mantese, G., 'Contributo a una storia artistica della Cattedrale', in *Studi in onore di A.Bardella*, Vicenza, pp.255–76 (III).
Pope-Hennessy, J., *Catalogue of Italian Sculpture in the Victoria and Albert Museum*, London, III vols.
Pullan, B.; see Pullan, 1968.
Zorzi, G.G., *Le opere pubbliche e i palazzi privati di Andrea Palladio*, Venice.

1964-5
Mantese, G., *L'attuazione dei decreti tridentini a Vicenza*, in 'Odeo Olimpico', V, pp.75–95.
Dalla Pozza, A.M., *Palladiana. X.XI.XII*, in 'Odeo Olimpico', V, pp.203–238.
Zanazzo, G.B., 'Bravi e signorotti in Vicenza e nel Vicentino nei secoli XVI eXVII', *Odeo Olimpico*, V, pp.97–138.

1965
Barbieri, F., 'Silvio Belli', *Dizionario biografico degli Italiani*, Rome, vol.VII, pp.680–2.
Barbieri, F., 'Valerio Belli', *Dizionario biografico degli Italiani*, Rome, vol.VII, pp.682–4.
Cevese, R., *Appunti palladiani*, in 'Bollettino C.I.S.A.', VII, pp.305–15.
Collection d'un grand amateur, Paris (Palais Gallièra), 29 Nov.–3 Dec.
Fiocco, G., *Alvise Cornaro: Il suo tempo e le sue opere*, Vicenza.
Forssman, E., *Palladios Lehrgebaude*, Uppsala.
Mantese, G., *Nuovi documenti relativi all'attuazione dei Decreti Tridentini a Vicenza*, in 'Archivio Veneto', pp.27–44.
Pope-Hennessy, J., *Renaissance Bronzes from the Samuel H.Kress Collection*, London.
Spencer, J., *Filarete's Treatise on Architecture . . .*, New Haven and London, II vols.
Zorzi, G.G., *Le opera pubbliche e i palazzi privati di Andrea Palladio*, Venice.
Zorzi, G.G., 'Le prospettive del Teatro Olimpico di Vicenza nei disegni degli Uffizi di Firenze e nei documenti dell'Ambrosiana di Milano', *Arte Lombarda*, II, pp.70–9 (II).

1966
Ackerman, J.S., *Palladio*, Harmondsworth.
Builders and humanists, Houston (University of St.Thomas).
Burns, H., 'A Peruzzi Drawing in Ferrara',

Mitteilungen des Kunsthistorischen Institutes in Florenz, XII, pp.245–70.

Gere, J., *Gabinetto di disegni e stampe degli Uffizi: Mostra degli Zuccari*, Florence.

Lamb, C., *Die Villa d'Este in Tivoli . . .*, Munich.

Murray, P., *Palladio's Churches*, in 'Arte in Europa'.

Oberhuber, K., 'Observations on Perino del Vaga as a Draughtsman', *Master Drawings*, IV, pp.170–82.

Padoan-Urban, L., 'Teatri e "teatri del mondo" nella Venezia del cinquecento', *Arte Veneta*, XX, pp.137–46.

Pillinini, G., 'Domenico Bollani', *Dizionario biografico degli Italiani*, Rome, vol.XI, pp.291–3.

Prinz, W., 'Vasaris Sammlung von Kuenstler-bildnissen', *Mitteilungen des Kunsthistorischen Institutes in Florenz*, XII, Beiheft V.

Rosci, M., *Il Trattato di architettura di Sebastiano Serlio*, Milan.

Spielmann, H., *Andrea Palladio und die Antike*, Munich and Berlin.

Sweeny, B., *John G.Johnson Collection: Catalogue of the Italian Paintings*, Philadelphia.

Wolters, W., *Der Programmentwurf zur Dekoration des Dogenpalastes nach dem Brand vom 20. Dezember 1577*, in 'Mitteilungen des Kunthistorischen Institutes in Florenz', XII, pp.271–318.

Zorzi, G.G., *Le chiese e i ponti di Andrea Palladio*, Venice.

Zorzi, G.G., *Un nuovo soggiorno di Alessandro Vittoria nel Vicentino. II*, in 'Arte Veneta', pp.157–176 (II).

Zorzi, G.G., *Porti, ponti e fortificazioni di Andrea Palladio*, in 'Bollettino del C.I.S.A.', VIII, pp.151–63 (III).

1966–7

Mantese, G., *Tre cappelle gentilizie nelle Chiese di S.Lorenzo, S.Michele e S.Corona di Vicenza*, in 'Odeo Olimpico', pp.227–58.

1967

Ackerman, J., *Palladio's Villas*, Locust Valley (New York, U.S.A.).

Ackerman, J.S., *Palladio's Vicenza: a Bird's eye Plan of c.1571*, in 'Studies in Renaissance and Baroque Art presented to Anthony Blunt', London, pp.53–61 (II).

Ackerman, J.S., *Palladio's lost Portico Project for San Petronio in Bologna*, in 'Essays in the History of Architecture presented to Rudolf Wittkower', London, pp.119–51 (III).

Barbieri, F., *Francesco Zamberlan architetto de 'La Rotonda'*, in *La Rotonda di Rovigo*, Venice, pp.37–72.

Barocchi, P., and Ristori, R., eds., *Il Carteggio di Michelangelo*, Florence, vol.II.

Bascapè, M., 'I disegni di Martino Bassi nella Raccolta Ferrari', *Arte Lombarda*, II, pp.33–64.

Cessi, F., *Vincenzo e Gian Gerolamo Grandi scultori*, Trent.

Gombrich, E., 'Celebrations in Venice of the Victory of Lepanto', in *Studies in Renaissance and Baroque Art Presented to Anthony Blunt*, London, pp.62–8.

Hill, G.F., and Pollard, G., *Renaissance Medals from the Samuel H.Kress Col'ection*, London.

Kleinbauer, W.E., 'Some Renaissance Views of Early Christian and Romanesque San Lorenzo in Milan', *Arte Lombarda*, II, pp.1–10.

Laven, P.J., 'The "*Causa Grimani*" and its political overtones', *Journal of Religious History*, IV, pp.182–205.

The Loyd Collection of Paintings and Drawings, London.

Maltese, C., ed., *Francesco di Giorgio Martini: Trattato di architettura . . .*, Milan, II vols.

Mantese, G., *Ancora sul Palazzo da Monte a Santa Corona*, in 'Bollettino del C.I.S.A.', IX, pp.425–8.

Olivieri, A., *Alessandro Trissino e il movimento calvinista vicentino nel Cinquecento*, in 'Rivista di Storia della Chiesa in Italia', pp.54–117.

Puppi, L., *Per la Storia del Teatro Olimpico di Vicenza . . .*, in 'Arte Lombarda', 2, pp.144–5 (II).

Shearman, J., *Mannerism*, Harmondsworth.

Shearman, J., 'Raphael . . . "Fa il Bramante,"' *Studies in Renaissance and Baroque Art presented to Anthony Blunt*, London, pp.12–17.

Weihrauch, H.R., *Europaeische Bronzestatuetten*, Brunswick.

1967–8

Frommel, C.L., 'Baldassare Peruzzi als Mahler und Zeichner', *Roemische Jahrbuch fuer Kunstgeschichte*, XI, Beiheft.

1968

Barbieri, F., *La Basilica Palladiana*, Vicenza.

Buddensieg, T., 'Raffaels Grab', in *Minuscula Discipulorum* (Festschrift Kauffmann), Berlin, pp.45–70.

Canova Mariani, G., 'La decorazione dei documenti ufficiali in Venezia dal 1460–1530', *Atti del Instituto Veneto di Scienze, Lettere ed Arti*, CXXVI, p.319ff.

Clark, K., and Pedretti, C., *The drawings of Leonardo da Vinci in the Collection of the Queen at Windsor Castle*, London, III vols.

Licht, K., *The Rotunda in Rome: A study of Hadrian's Pantheon*, Copenhagen.

Marchini, G., 'Le architetture', in *Raffaello: L'Opera, le fonti, la fortuna*, ed. M.Salmi, Novara, vol.II, pp.431ff.

Mantese, G., *I mille libri . . .*, Vicenza.

Pullan, B., 'Wage Earners and the Venetian Economy, 1550–1630', *Crisis and Change in the Venetian Economy in the 16th and 17th Centuries*, London.

Rearick, W.R., 'Jacopo Bassano's later genre paintings', *The Burlington Magazine*, CX, pp.241–9.

Rinaldi, S.Mason, 'Un Nuovo ciclo di Paolo Fiammingo', *Arte Veneta*, XXII, pp.72–9.

Rosci, M., 'Forme e funzione delle ville venete prepalladiane', *L'Arte*, N.S. I, pp.26–54.

Rossi, P., *Girolamo Campagna*, Verona.

Semenzato, C., *La Rotunda di Vicenza*, Vicenza.

Schulz, J., *Venetian painted Ceilings*, Berkeley ar Los Angeles.

Schweikardt, G., *Studien zum Werke des Giovanni Maria Falconetto*, in 'Bollettino del Museo Civico di Padova', pp.17–67.

Shearman, J., 'Raphael as Architect', *Journal of the Royal Society of Arts*, CXVI, pp.388–409.

Timofiewitsch, W., *Die Sakrale Architektur Palladios*, Munich.

Wilinski, S., *La serliana di Villa Poiana Maggiore*, in 'Bollettino C.I.S.A.', X, pp.79–84.

Wittkower, R., 'Il balaustro rinascimentale e il Palladio', *Bollettino C.I.S.A.*, X, pp.332–46.

Woolf, S.J., 'Venice and the Terraferma: Problems of the Changes from Commercial to Landed Activities', in *Crisis and Change in the Venetian Economy in the Sixteenth and Seventeenth Centuries*, ed. B.Pullan, London, pp.175–203.

Zorzi, G.G., *Le ville e i teatri di Andrea Palladio*, Venice.

Zorzi, G.G., *La interpretazione dei disegni palladiani*, in 'Bollettino del C.I.S.A.', X, pp.97–111.

1968–9

Cevese, R., *Licenze nell'arte di Andrea Palladio*, in 'Odeo Olimpico', VII, pp.69–79.

Mantese, G., *Tre cappelle gentilizie nelle Chiese di S.Lorenzo e S.Corona*, in 'Odeo Olimpico', VII, pp.225–58.

1969

Alexander, J.G., 'The Provenance of the Brooke Antiphonal', *The Antiquaries Journal*, XLIX–2, pp.386–7.

Ballarin, A., 'Quadri veneziani inediti nei musei di Varsavia e di Praga', *Paragone*, XX, pp.52–68.

Bruschi, A., *Bramante architetto*, Bari.

Carpeggiani, P., *Un documento dell'architettura di Giulio Romano: la Villa Zani di Villimpenta*, in *Ville e dimore del contado mantovano*, Florence, pp.49–64.

Edinburgh Festival: Italian Sixteenth Century Drawings from British Private Collections, Edinburgh.

Fiocco, G., *Giovanni Antonio Pordenone*, Pordenone, II vols.

Forssman, E., 'Del sito da eleggersi per le fabbriche di villa', *Bollettino C.I.S.A.*, XI, pp.149–62.

Frommel, C.L., 'Villa Madama e la tipologia

della Villa Romana', *Bollettino C.I.S.A.*, XI, pp.47–64.

Hofer, P., *Palladios Erstling. Die Villa Godi Valmarana in Lonedo bei Vicenza*, Basel and Stuttgart.

Lenz, C., *Veroneser Bildarchitektur*, Bremen.

Mantese, G., *Per una storia dell'arte medica in Vicenza alla fine del Secolo XVI*, Vicenza.

Marchetti, G., *Antichi ferri e bronzi d'arte nelle porte degli edifici di Bologna*, Bologna, 1969.

Neiiendam, K., 'Le théatre de la renaissance à Rome', *Analecta Romana Instituti Danici*, V, p.157ff.

Padoan-Urban, L., 'Apparati scenografici nelle feste veneziane cinquecentesche', *Arte Veneta*, XXIII, pp.145–55.

Prinz, W., 'La 'sala di quattro colonne" nell' opera di Palladio', *Bollettino C.I.S.A.*, XI, pp.370–86.

Tafuri, M., *Jacopo Sansovino e l'architettura del Cinquecento a Venezia*, Padua (I).

Tafuri, M., *L'architettura dell' Umanesimo*, Bari (II).

Tafuri, M., 'Committenza e tipologia delle ville palladiane', *Bollettino C.I.S.A.*, pp.120–36.

Timofiewitsch, W., *La Chiesa del Redentore*, Vicenza.

Wethey, H., *The Paintings of Titian: I. The Religious Paintings*, London.

Wilinski, S., 'La finestra termale nelle ville di Andrea Palladio', *Bollettino C.I.S.A.*, XI, pp.207–21.

Zampetti, P., *Lorenzo Lotto: Il libro di spese diverse*, Venice and Rome.

Zorzi, G.G., *Le ville e i teatri di Andrea Palladio*, Venice.

1969–70

Bandini, F., 'Lingua e cultura nella poesia di Magagnò, Menon, e Begotto', *Odeo Olimpico*, VIII, pp.42–64.

Mantese, G., 'La famiglia Thiene e la riforma protestante a Vicenza nella seconda metà del secolo XVI', *Odeo Olimpico*, VIII, pp.81–6.

Puppi, L., 'Giambattista Albanese Architetto', *Odeo Olimpico*, VIII, pp.15–31.

1970

Arslan, E., *Venezia gottica*, Venice.

Barbieri, F., 'Palladio in Villa negli anni quaranta: Da Lonedo a Bagnolo', *Arte Veneta*, XXIV, pp.63–79.

Blair, C., 'A Royal Swordsmith and Damascener: Diego de Çaias', *Metropolitan Museum Journal*, III, pp.149–98.

Bordignon Favero, G.P., *La Villa Emo di Fanzolo*, Vicenza.

Chambers, D.S., *The Imperial Age of Venice*, London.

Cohn, N., *The Pursuit of the Millenium*, London.

Inigo Jones on Palladio, ed. B.Allsop, Newcastle upon Tyne, II vols.

Lugli, G., *Itinerario di Roma antica*, Milan.

Mikhailova, M., 'Bridges of Ancient Rome: Drawings in the Hermitage Ascribed to Fra Giocondo', *The Art Bulletin*, LII, pp.250–64.

Richter, J.P., *The Literary Works of Leonardo da Vinci*, London, II vols.

Rigoni, E., *L'arte rinascimentale in Padova. Studi e documenti*, Padua.

Schulz, J., *The printed plans and panoramic views of Venice*, in 'Saggi e Memorie di Storia dell'Arte', Venice.

Summerson, J., *Architecture in Britain: 1530–1830*, Harmondsworth.

Tait, A.A., *Inigo Jones – Architectural Historian*, in 'The Burlington Magazine', CXII, p.235.

Toça, M., 'Un progetto peruzziano per una diga di sbarramento nella Maremma', *Annali della scuola normale superiore di Pisa: Lettere, Storia, e Filosofia*, Ser.II, XXXIX, pp.107–17.

Vitzthum, W., *A Selection of Italian Drawings from North American Collections*, Montreal, 1970.

Yale, *Catalogue of European Drawings at Yale*, New Haven.

1971

Ackerman; see Ackerman, 1967 (II).

Ballarin, A., 'Considerazione su una Mostra di Disegni veronesi del Cinquecento', *Arte Veneta*, XXV, p.92ff.

Bassi, E., *Il Convento della Carità*, Vicenza.

Buddensieg, T., 'Criticism and Praise of the Pantheon in the Middle Ages and the Renaissance', in *Classical Influences on European Culture A.D. 500–1500*, ed. R.R.Bolgar, Cambridge, pp.259–67.

Burns, H., 'Quattrocento Architecture and the Antique: Some Problems', *Classical Influences on European Culture, A.D. 500–1500*, ed. R.R. Bolgar, Cambridge, pp.268–86.

Cevese, R., *Le ville della provincia di Vicenza*, Milan, II vols.

Falk, T., 'Studien zur Topographie und Geschichte der Villa Giulia', *Roemisches Jahrbuch fuer Kunstgeschichte*, XIII, pp.101–78.

Forster, K.W., and Tuttle, R.J., 'The Palazzo del Te', *Journal of the Society of Architectural Historians*, XXX, pp.267–93.

Harris, J., 'Three Unrecorded Palladio Designs from Inigo Jones' Collection', *The Burlington Magazine*, CXIII, pp.34–7.

Mantese, G., 'Nel Quarto centenario di Lepanto', *Archivio Storico Veneto*.

Mariacher, G., *Bronzi Veneti del rinascimento*, Venice.

Motterle, E., *Una pianta del Peronio del Peronio di Vicenza del 1480 c.* in 'Bollettino del C.I.S.A.', XIII, pp.332–48.

Mullaly, T., *Disegni veronesi del Cinquecento*

(Fondazione G.Cini), Venice.

Olivato, L., 'Per il Serlio a Venezia: Documenti nuovi e documenti rivisitati', *Arte Veneta*, XXV, pp.284–91.

Parronchi, A., 'Sulla composizione dei trattati attribuiti a Francesco di Giorgio Martini', *Atti e Memorie dell'Accademia Toscana di Scienze e Lettere, 'La Colombara'*, XXXVI, pp.166–230.

Pinelli, A., and Rossi, O., *Genga architetto: Aspetti della cultura urbinate del primo Cinquecento*, Rome.

Pope-Hennessy, J., *Italian Renaissance Sculpture*, London, 1971.

Popham, A.E., *Catalogue of the Drawings of Parmigianino*, New Haven and London, III vols.

Pullan, B., *Rich and Poor in Renaissance Venice*, Oxford.

Puppi, L., *Michele Sanmicheli architetto di Verona*, Padua.

Puppi, L., 'Un letterato in villa: Giangiorgio Trissino a Crico', *Arte Veneta*, pp.72–91 (II).

Puppi, L., 'Gli spettacoli all'Olimpico di Vicenza dal 1585 all'inizio del'600', in *Studi sul teatro veneto fra Rinascimento ed Età barocca*, Florence, pp.73–96 (III).

Toça, M., 'Sui disegni di Baldassare Peruzzi per la Chiesa di San Domenico a Siena', *Bollettino degli Ingegneri*, no.7.

Wethey, H., *The Paintings of Titian: II. The Portraits*, London.

Zuccolo Padrono, G.M., 'Il maestro "T° V" e la sua bottega: miniature veneziane del XVI secolo', *Arte Veneta*, XXV, pp.53–71.

1971–3

Mantese, G., *Lo storico vicentino p. Francesco da Barbarano O.F.M. Cap. (1596–1656) e la sua nobile famiglia*, in 'Odeo Olimpico', pp.27–137.

1972

Braudel, F., *The Mediterranean and the Mediterranean World in the Age of Philip II*, London, vol.I.

Finoli, A.M., and Grassi, L., *Antonio Averlino detto il Filarete: Trattato di Architettura*, Milan, 1972, II vols.

Gioseffi, D., 'Il disegno come fase progettuale dell'attivita palladiana', *Bollettino C.I.S.A.*, XIV, pp.45–62.

Harris, J., *Catalogue of the Drawings Collection of the Royal Institute of British Architects: Inigo Jones and John Webb*, Farnborough.

Lewis, D., 'La datazione della Villa Corner a Piombino Dese', *Bollettino C.I.S.A.*, XIV, pp.381–93.

Pedretti, C., *Leonardo da Vinci: The Royal Palace at Romorantin*, Cambridge, Mass.

Puppi, L., *La Villa Badoer di Fratta Polesine*, Vicenza.

Puppi, L., ed., *1650: Giardino di Chà Gualdo*,

Florence.

Puppi, L., 'Palladio e l'ambiente naturale e storico', *Bollettino C.I.S.A.*, XIV, pp.226–34.

Royal Institute of British Architects, Drawings Collection, *Great Drawings from the Collection*, London.

Vertova, L., 'La visita del medico: Osservazioni su alcuni dipinti di Bonifazio de' Pitati', *Mitteilungen des Kunsthistorischen Institutes in Florenz*, XVI, pp.175–86, 336.

1973

Barbieri; see Motterle, E.

Battisti, E., 'Un tentativo di analisi strutturale del Palladio tramite le teorie musicali del Cinquecento e l'impiego di figure retoriche', *Bollettino C.I.S.A.*, XV (to appear in 1975).

Burns, H., 'I disegni', *Palladio: Catologo della Mostra* (Basilica Palladiana), Vicenza, pp.131–54.

Burns, H., 'I disegni del Palladio', *Bollettino C.I.S.A.*, XV (to appear in 1975).

Byam-Shaw, J., *Victoria and Albert Museum: Old Master Drawings from Chatsworth*, London.

Cevese, R., 'L'opera del Palladio', *Palladio: Catologo della Mostra* (Basilica Palladiana), Vicenza, pp.43–130.

Forster, K.W., 'Il Palazzo Thiene', *Bollettino C.I.S.A.*, X (toappear in 1975).

Frommel, C.L., *Der Roemischen Palastbau der Hochrenaissance*, Tubingen, III vols.

Gioseffi, D., 'Appunti sui disegni del Palladio', *Bollettino C.I.S.A.*, XV (to appear in 1975).

Goldthwaite, R.A., 'The Building of the Strozzi Palace: The Construction Industry in Renaissance Florence', *Studies in Medieval and Renaissance History*, X, pp.99–194.

Il Gusto e La Moda nel Cinquecento vicentino e veneto (Museo Civico), Vicenza.

Harris, J., Orgel, S., and Strong, R., *The King's Arcadia: Inigo Jones and the Stuart Court* (Arts Council of Great Britain), London.

Howard, D., 'Sebastiano Serlio's Venetian Copyrights', *The Burlington Magazine*, CXV, pp.512–16.

Lane, F., *Venice: A Maritime Republic*, Baltimore and London.

Lewine, M., 'S.Andrea in Via Flaminia del Vignola e la chiesa a Maser di Palladio', *Bollettino C.I.S.A.*, XV (to appear in 1975).

Lotz, W., 'Palladio e l'architettura del suo tempo', *Palladio: Catologo della Mostra* (Basilica Palladiana), Vicenza, pp.27–42.

Low, J., *The Knowledge and Influence of Classical Sculpture in Venice and Padua, c.1460–1530*. M.A. report, Courtauld Institute of Art, London.

Mostra dell'Arredamento del Cinquecento Veneto (Palazzo Barbaran da Porto), Vicenza.

Motterle, E., *Il 'Peronio' di Vicenza nel 1481*, ed. F.Barbieri, Vicenza.

Pallucchini, R., 'I dipinti', *Palladio: Catalogo della Mostra* (Basilica Palladiana), Vicenza, pp.191–203.

Puppi, L., *Andrea Palladio*, Milan, II vols.

Puppi, L., *Scrittori vicentini d'architettura nel Secolo XVI*, Vicenza (II).

Puppi, L., 'Bibliografia e letteratura palladiana', *Palladio: Catalogo della Mostra* (Basilica Palladiana), Vicenza, pp.171–90 (III).

Salza Prina Ricotti, E., 'Villa Adriana di Pirro Ligorio e Francesco Contini', *Atti della Accademia Nazionale dei Lincei*, S.8, XVII, pp.1–46.

Sotheby's Sale Catalogue (13 December), London.

Tafuri, M., 'Palladio verso Sansovino', *Bollettino C.I.S.A.*, XV (to appear in 1975).

1974

de Bellaigue, G., *The James A.Rotheschild Collection at Waddesdon Manor: Furniture, Clocks, and Gilt Bronzes*, Office du livre.

Fancelli, P., *Palladio e Praeneste: Archeologia, modelli, progettazione*, Rome.

Forster, K.W., 'Back to the Farm', *Architettura*, IV, pp.1–13.

Heydenreich, L.H., and Lotz, W., *Architecture in Italy: 1400–1600*, Harmondsworth.

Huse, N., 'Palladio und die Villa Barbaro in Maser: Bemerkung zum Problem der Autorenschaft', *Arte Veneta*, XXVIII (forth-coming).

Kubelik, M., 'Gli edifici palladiani nei disegni del Magistrato Veneto dei Beni Inculti', *Bollettino C.I.S.A.*, XVI (to appear in 1975).

Lotz, W., see Heydenreich, L.

Magagnato, L., *Cinquant' anni di pittura veronese, 1580–1630*, Verona.

Mantese, G., *Memorie storiche della Chiesa Vicentina: Parte I, 1563–1700*, Vicenza, vol.IV.

Mckillop, S., *Franciabigio*, Berkeley.

Stefani-Perrone, S., *I Misteri architettonici di Galeazzo Alessi al Sacro Monte di Varallo*, Bologna.

Puppi, L., 'Dubbi e certezze per Palladio costruttore in villa', *Arte Veneta*, XXVIII (to appear in 1975)

Reclams Kunstfueherr Italien: Venedig, ed. E.Hubala, Stuttgart.

Rossi, P., *Jacopo Tintoretto: I ritratti*, Venice.

Sinding-Larsen, S., 'Christ in the Council Hall: Studies in the Religious Iconography of the Venetian Republic', *Acta ad Archaeologiam et Artium Historiam Pertinentia*, V.

Sutton, D., 'Sunlight and Movement', *Apollo*, C, pp.274–81.

1975

Berger, U., *Palladios Fruehwerk: Bauten und Zeichnungen*, Munich (forthcoming).

Boucher, B., 'Jacopo Sansovino and the Choir of St Mark's', *The Burlington Magazine*, CXVII (forthcoming).

Burns, H., 'Le idee di Galeazzo Alessi sull' architettura e sugli ordini', *Galeazzo Alessi e l'architettura del Cinquecento . . .*, Genoa, pp.147–66.

Burns, H., 'Progetti di Francesco di Giorgio per i conventi di San Bernardino e Santa Chiara di Urbino', *Atti del Congresso Bramantesco*, Rome (II).

Cevese, R., *I modelli lignei nella Mostra del Palladio*, Vicenza.

Drawings by Michelangelo (British Museum: Department of Prints and Drawings), London.

Gould, C., *The National Gallery: The Sixteenth-Century Italian Schools*, London.

Howard, D., *Jacopo Sansovino: Architecture and Patronage in Renaissance Venice*, New Haven and London.

Kubelik, M., ed., *Andrea Palladio: Katalog der Ausstellung* (Akademie der bildenden Kuenste), Vienna.

Kubelik, M., *Zur typologischen Entwicklung der Quattrocento-Villa im Veneto*, Aachen (forthcoming).

Stefani-Perrone, S., 'L'urbanistica del Sacro Monte e l'Alessi', *Galeazzo Alessi e l'architettura del Cinquecento . . .*, Genoa, pp.501–16.

de Rothschild, K., *Exhibition of Old Master Drawings: June 30–July 11* (William Darby's Gallery), London.

Shearman, J., 'The Collections of the Younger Branch of the Medici', *The Burlington Magazine*, CXVII, pp.12–27.

Prinz, W., *Anfaenge des oberitalienischen Villenbaues*, no date or place of publication.